CREATION OF THE GODS

Volume I

Translated by GU ZHIZHONG

NEW WORLD PRESS · BEIJING · CHINA

Cover design by Wu Shousong
Cover drawing and illustrations by Dai Dunbang
and Dai Hongjie

First Edition 1992

Second Printing 1996

ISBN 7-80005-134-X
CREATION OF THE GODS (Vol. I)

Published by
New World Press
24 Baiwanzhuang Road, Beijing 100037, China

Printed by
Foreign Languages Printing House
19 Chegongzhuang Xilu, Beijing 100044, China

Distributed by
China International Book Trading Corporation
35 Chegongzhuang Xilu, Beijing 100044, China
P.O. Box 399, Beijing, China

Printed in the People's Republic of China

TRANSLATOR'S NOTE

The first two recorded dynasties in China's long history are the Xia Dynasty (26th-16th century B.C.) and the Shang Dynasty (16th-11th century B.C.). This novel tells the story of King Zhou, the fated last ruler of the Shang Dynasty and one of the most notorious tyrants in Chinese history. Zhou was cruel and lascivious and worst of all, deluded by his beautiful concubine Daji (who was, according to this novel, a fox sprite). He was finally defeated by King Wu of the Zhou Dynasty who, with Jiang Ziya's help, rebelled and sent an army to punish the tyrant for his cruelty to the people. King Zhou lost his throne and burned himself to death.

Like many Chinese novels handed down from antiquity, *Creation of the Gods* developed over the centuries as a folk tale among the people. According to historical documents, it first appeared in book form in the Ming Dynasty (1368-1644) and though copies from this time have not been traced, several block-print editions from the early Qing Dynasty (1644-1911) still exist. The unknown author (or more probably, authors) wove the tale of King Zhou's downfall with popular folklore images of fairies, gods and immortal beings, thus creating a novel entertaining to both the common folk and their feudal rulers. This slightly abridged English edition now makes it possible for readers at home and abroad to enjoy this Chinese classic.

CONTENTS

KING ZHOU AND GODDESS NU WA

The Shang Dynasty replaced the Xia Dynasty and ruled China for nearly 650 years. The Shang court produced twenty-eight kings of whom King Zhou was the last.

Before King Zhou ascended the throne, he and his father, King Di Yi, and many civil and military officials were walking in the royal garden one day, viewing the blooming peonies, when suddenly the Flying Cloud Pavilion collapsed and a beam flew towards them. Rushing forward, King Zhou or then Prince Shou, caught the beam and replaced it in a display of miraculous strength. Deeply impressed, Prime Minister Shang Rong and Supreme Minister Mei Bo advised King Di Yi to name him Crown Prince.

When King Di Yi passed away after thirty years on the throne, Crown Prince Shou was immediately crowned king to rule the country in his father's place. King Zhou established his capital at Zhaoge, a metropolis on the Yellow River. The king appointed Grand Tutor Wen Zhong to be in charge of civil affairs and Huang Feihu, Prince for National Pacification and of Military Prowess, to supervise military affairs. In this way, the king hoped the nation would live in peace under a civil administration backed up by the military. The king placed Queen Jiang in the Central Palace; Concubine Huang in the West Palace and Concubine Yang in the Fragrant Palace. They were all virtuous and chaste in their behavior and mild and gentle in manner.

King Zhou ruled his country in peace, and was respected by the neighboring states. His people worked happily in their different professions, and his peasants were especially blessed

第四回 紂王女媧宮進香

by favorable winds and rains. There were 800 marquises in the country who offered their allegiance to four dukes, each of whom ruled over 200 of these marquises on behalf of King Zhou. The four dukes were: the East Grand Duke Jiang Huanchu, the South Grand Duke E Chongyu, the West Grand Duke Ji Chang and the North Grand Duke Chong Houhu.

In the second month of the seventh year of the reign of King Zhou, a report reached Zhaoge of a rebellion of seventy-two marquises in the North Sea district, and Grand Tutor Wen Zhong was immediately ordered to lead a strong army to suppress the rebels. One day when King Zhou was holding court, Shang Rong stepped out from the right row, knelt and said, "Your humble Prime Minister Shang Rong begs to report something urgent to Your Majesty. Tomorrow is the 15th day of the third month, the birthday of Goddess Nu Wa, and Your Majesty should honor her and hold a ceremony at her temple."

"What has Goddess Nu Wa done that a great king such as myself is obliged to go to her temple and worship her?" King Zhou asked.

"Goddess Nu Wa's been a great goddess since ancient times and possesses saintly virtues. When the enraged demon Gong Gong knocked his head against Buzhou Mountain, the northwest section of Heaven collapsed and the earth sunk down in the southeast. At this critical moment, Nu Wa came to the rescue and mended Heaven with multi-colored stones she had obtained and refined from a mountain," Shang Rong explained. "She's performed this great service for the people, who've built temples to honor her in gratitude. Zhaoge is fortunate to have the chance to worship this kind goddess. She'll ensure peace and health to the people and prosperity to the country; she'll bring us timely wind and rain and keep us free from famine and war. She's the proper guardian angel for both the people and the nation. So I make bold to suggest that Your Majesty honor her tomorrow."

"You're right, Prime Minister. I'll do as you advise."

Returning to his residential palace, King Zhou ordered a notice be issued that His Majesty, together with his civil and military officials, were to make a pilgrimage to worship Goddess Nu Wa at her temple the next day.

It would have been better if he hadn't gone at all, for it was this very pilgrimage that caused the fall of the Shang Dynasty, making it impossible for the people to live in peace. It was as if the king had tossed a fishing line into a big river and unexpectedly caught numerous disasters leading to the loss of both his throne and his life.

The king and his entourage left the palace and made their way through the south gate of the capital. Every house they passed was decorated with bright silk, and the streets were scented for the king by burning incense. The king was accompanied by 3,000 cavalrymen and 800 royal guards under the command of General Huang Feihu, Prince for National Pacification and of Military Prowess and followed by all the officials of the royal court.

Reaching the Temple of Goddess Nu Wa, King Zhou left his royal carriage and went to the main hall, where he burned incense sticks, bowed low with his ministers and offered prayers. King Zhou then wandered about the hall, finding it splendidly decorated in gold and other colors. Before the statue of the goddess stood golden lads holding pennants, and jade lasses holding S-shaped jade ornaments which symbolized peace and happiness. The jade hooks on the curtain hung obliquely, like new crescent moons suspended in the air, and hundreds of fine phoenixes embroidered on the curtain appeared to be flying towards the North Pole. Beside the altar of the goddess, made of fragrant wood, cranes and dragons were dancing in the scented smoke rising from the gold incense burners and the sparkling flames of the silvery candles.

As King Zhou was admiring the splendors of the hall, a whirlwind suddenly blew up, rolling back the curtain and exposing the image of the goddess to all. She was extremely beautiful, much more than flowers, more than the fairy in the moon palace, and certainly more than any woman in the world. She looked quite alive, smiling sweetly at the king and staring at him with joy in her eyes.

Her utter beauty bewitched King Zhou, setting him on fire

with lust. He desired to possess her, and thought to himself in frustration, "Though I'm wealthy and powerful and have concubines and maidservants filling my palace, there's none as beautiful and charming as this goddess."

He ordered his attendants to bring brush and ink and wrote a poem on the wall near the image of the goddess to express his admiration and deep love for her. The poem ran like this:

> The scene is gay with phoenixes and dragons,
> But they are only clay and golden colors.
> Brows like winding hills in jade green,
> Sleeves like graceful clouds, you're
> As pear blossoms soaked with raindrops,
> Charming as peonies enveloped in mist.
> I pray that you come alive,
> With sweet voice and gentle movements,
> And I'll bring you along to my palace.

When he finished writing, Prime Minister Shang Rong approached him. "Nu Wa's been a proper goddess and the guardian angel for Zhaoge, I only suggested that you worship her so that she would continue to bless the people with timely rains and favorable winds and ensure that they'll continue to live in peace. But with this poem, you've not only shown your lack of sincerity on this trip but have insulted her as well." He demanded, "This isn't the way a king should behave. I pray you wash this blasphemous poem off the wall, lest you be condemned by the people for your immorality."

"I found Goddess Nu Wa so beautiful that I wrote a poem in praise of her, and that's all. Hold your tongue. Don't forget that I am the king. People will be only too glad to read the poem I wrote in my own handwriting, for it enables them to identify the true beauty of the goddess."

King Zhou dismissed him lightly. The other civil and military officials remained silent, none daring to utter a word. They then returned to the capital. The king went directly to the Dragon Virtue Court, where he met his queen and concubines in a happy reunion.

On her birthday, Goddess Nu Wa had left her palace and paid her respects to the three emperors, Fu Xi, Shen Nong and Xuan Yuan. She then returned to her temple, seated herself in the main hall, and received greetings from the golden lads and jade lasses.

Looking up, she saw the poem on the wall. "That wicked king!" She flew into a rage. "He doesn't think how to protect his country with virtue and morality. On the contrary, he shows no fear of Heaven and insults me with this dirty poem. How vile he is! The Shang Dynasty's already ruled for over 600 years and is coming to an end. I must take my revenge on him if I'm to assuage my own conscience."

She took action at once. She mounted a phoenix and headed for Zhaoge.

King Zhou had two sons. One was Yin Jiao, who later became the "Star God Presiding over the Year," and the other Yin Hong, who later became the "God of Grain." As the two gods paid their respects to their father, two red divine beams rose from the tops of their heads and soared high in the sky, blocking the way of the goddess. Looking down through the clouds, Nu Wa at once realized King Zhou had still twenty-eight years to go before his downfall. She also realized that she could do nothing about it at this moment, since that would go against the will of Heaven.

The goddess returned to her temple, highly displeased. Back in her palace, Goddess Nu Wa ordered a young maidservant to fetch a golden gourd and put it on the Cinnabar Terrace outside her court. When its stopper was removed, Nu Wa pointed at the gourd with one finger and suddenly a thick beam of brilliant white light rose from the mouth of the gourd and shot up fifty feet into the air. Hanging from the beam was a multi-colored flag called the Demon Summoning Pennant. As soon as this pennant made its appearance, glittering high up in the sky, all demons and evil sprites, no matter where they were, would gather round.

Moments later, dark winds began to howl, eerie fogs enveloped the earth, and vicious-looking clouds gathered in the sky.

All the demons in the world had arrived to receive her command. Nu Wa gave orders that all the demons return home except the three sprites that dwelt in the grave of Emperor Xuan Yuan.

Who were these three sprites? The first was a thousand-year-old female fox sprite; the second was a female pheasant sprite with nine heads; and the third was a jade lute sprite.

"May you live eternally, dear goddess!" the three sprites greeted Nu Wa, kowtowing on the Cinnabar Terrace.

"Listen carefully to my secret orders. The Shang Dynasty's destined to end soon. The singing of the phoenix at Mount Qi augurs the birth of a new ruler in West Qi. This has all been determined by the will of Heaven, and no one has the power to change what must happen. You may transform yourselves into beauties, enter the palace, and distract King Zhou from state affairs. You'll be richly rewarded for giving the new dynasty an auspicious start and helping the old one to its downfall. However, you mustn't bring harm to the people."

At the end of her order, the three sprites kowtowed, turned themselves into winds, and flew away.

Since his visit to the Temple of Goddess Nu Wa, King Zhou had sunk into a deep depression. He ardently admired the beauty of the goddess and, yearning for her day and night, lost all desire to eat and drink. He had no passion for his queen, his concubines, or the numerous maids in his palace. They now all appeared to him like lumps of clay. He would not be bothered with state affairs.

One day, he remembered Fei Zhong and You Hun, two minion courtiers who would flatter and slander as he pleased. King Zhou sent for Fei Zhong, and the latter appeared in no time.

"I went to worship Goddess Nu Wa recently," King Zhou began. "She's so beautiful I believe she has no rival in the world, and none of my concubines is to be compared with her. I'm head over heels in love, and feel very sad as I cannot get her. Have you any ideas with which to comfort me?"

"Your Majesty! With all your honor and dignity, you're

the most powerful and the richest man in the world. You possess all the wealth within the four seas, and are virtuous as the sage emperors Yao and Shun. You may have anything you wish for, and you should have no difficulty in satisfying your desires. You can issue an order tomorrow demanding 100 beauties from the grand dukes. You'll then have no trouble finding one as beautiful as Goddess Nu Wa," Fei Zhong suggested.

King Zhou was delighted. He said, "Your suggestion appeals to me greatly. I'll issue the order tomorrow. You may return home for the time being."

He then left the throne hall and returned to his royal chambers to rest.

If you wish to know what happened thereafter, please read the following chapter.

THE REBELLION OF SU HU

The next morning, after he had received the respects from his ministers, King Zhou addressed his messengers, "Transmit my orders to the four grand dukes that they must each present me with 100 beautiful virgins to serve in the palace. Their family background, in terms of rank and wealth, may be ignored, but they must be gentle, virtuous, and above all beautiful."

But before the king had finished this announcement, a great minister stepped out from the ranks, and knelt down before him, "Your old minister Shang Rong begs to advise Your Majesty that if you rule the country properly the people will continue to take pleasure in their work and obey your wishes without having to be ordered." Shang reminded him, "Your Majesty has already 1,000 beautiful women at least, who serve you in your chamber palace. If you now order the conscription of so many beautiful virgins, the people will be dissatisfied and oppose you. Remember the saying, 'When a ruler rejoices with his people, they also rejoice with him; when he grieves at the sorrow of his people, they also grieve at his.' Your people are now suffering seriously from floods and droughts. How can Your Majesty seek pleasure in women at a time like this? You must recall how emperors Yao and Shun rejoiced with the people and ruled the country with kindness and virtue, without resorting to violence and without bloodshed or war. During their reigns, lucky stars shone brightly over the sky and sweet dew drenched the earth. Phoenixes danced in the palace courtyard and herbs of immortality grew in the fields. The people were rich and everything was in abundance. Rain fell at night and every day was sunny. Two ears would grow on each rice stalk. If Your Majesty seeks only short-lived pleasures: fixing your eyes on obscene events, filling your ears with lewd music, drinking until you become intoxicated, and hunting in the mountains and forests, this is a poor way to rule and will bring about the downfall of the dynasty. As prime minister in your government, and one who's served under three kings, I'm obliged to present Your Majesty with the truth and hope that you won't conscript the virgins and indulge in lascivious pleasure."

King Zhou remained silent for a long time. Finally he said, "You're right. I'll repeal my edict at once."

Annoyed by what had happened, he had little patience to remain in the hall discussing state affairs with his ministers and quickly retired to his chamber palace.

The following summer, all 800 marquises came to Zhaoge to pledge their allegiance to the Shang Dynasty. As Grand Tutor Wen Zhong had been sent to the front to subdue the rebels of the North Sea, Fei Zhong and You Hun had become extremely influential at court and demanded of the dukes and marquises bribes and presents. But Su Hu, Marquis of Jizhou, refused to comply. Su Hu had an indomitable spirit and a fiery temper, but was a righteous man. He refused to ingratiate himself by dishonest means and would explode at the slightest injustice or wrongdoing. He did everything according to law, and refused to confer gifts upon Fei Zhong and You Hun, who as a result were very much annoyed.

At court that morning, after King Zhou had received the respects from his ministers, the gate guard came forward and reported, "To mark this year of celebration, all the dukes and marquises of the nation have arrived in the capital to make obeisance to Your Majesty. At present, they are waiting for your orders outside the palace gate."

When King Zhou discussed the matter with Shang Rong, the latter replied, "I suggest that Your Majesty grant an audience only to the four grand dukes, whom you can question about the livelihood of their people and about peace and security in their districts, and that the marquises make their obeisance outside the palace gate."

"You're right, Prime Minister," King Zhou said in delight.

The four grand dukes, all splendidly dressed, entered the Meridian Gate and walked over the Nine Dragon Bridge to the Cinnarbar Terrace, where they knelt and prostrated themselves before King Zhou. The king, in turn, thanked them for their services.

"You labor diligently for me, spending your energy and time educating the people and protecting them from starvation and war. You've achieved great things for the nation," the king said in encouragement. "I'm greatly pleased you've come."

Jiang Huanchu, the East Grand Duke, replied, "It's by grace of Your Majesty that we were created dukes. We're obliged to be diligent and watchful at our posts, so that Your Majesty's mind will always remain at ease. Any service we've rendered comes within the limits of our duty and isn't worthy of praise. However, we greatly appreciate the kind concern shown us by Your Majesty."

The king was delighted with this reply and ordered Shang Rong and Vice Prime Minister Bi Gan to entertain the four grand dukes, while he himself retired to his private court with his favorites Fei Zhong and You Hun.

"Though you advised me to ask the four grand dukes for beautiful virgins, I was stopped by Shang Rong. Now that we've got the dukes here, I'll issue the order to them directly tomorrow morning. That way I can save the trouble of sending messengers to them later. What do you think about that?"

"It was virtuous of Your Majesty to suspend the conscription of beautiful virgins on the Prime Minister's advice." Fei Zhong said but then admonished the king, "Your Majesty's decision is known to everyone, and you mustn't change your mind or you'll lose their trust. I learned recently that Su Hu has a daughter as beautiful and charming as an angel. She's fully qualified to serve you in the palace. Furthermore, by having her brought to the palace, Your Majesty won't upset the whole nation."

King Zhou was overjoyed when he heard this and immediately sent an order for Su Hu to see him at the Dragon Virtue Court to discuss urgent state affairs.

When he came, Su Hu kowtowed and then waited on his knees for the king to speak.

"I'm told that your daughter's mild, virtuous, and modest. I would like to have her serve me in the rear palace. As her father, you'll become related to the royal family and enjoy wealth and rank, known and admired throughout the country. How do you feel about it, Marquis?" asked King Zhou.

"Your Majesty's got a queen consort and thousands of concubines. They're all charming and beautiful and possess talents to please all of your senses. How is it that you're so unwise as to be deluded by your lying courtiers?" Su Hu protested. "My daughter, moreover, is crude and ignorant of the rites and has a very homely face. I beg Your Majesty to take my humble advice and take immediate action to behead your malicious courtiers so that you may rule with virtue. The future generations will know that you're a good and proper ruler and not a womanizer."

King Zhou burst out laughing. "You're both ignorant and lacking in common sense. Since ancient times, none has been so foolish as to refuse royal connection. Once a daughter is lucky enough to be chosen queen or royal concubine, she's honored as highly as the king. You would enjoy untold glory as my relative if you let your daughter serve in my palace. Don't be muddle-headed. Think it over."

At this, Su Hu flew into a rage. He shouted sternly, "The rule can only last when the king reigns with virtue and diligence and the people remain satisfied. You're now careless of state affairs, distracted from your duties by an unbridled passion for women. Behaving this way, I'm afraid you'll end up the downfall of your 600-year-old dynasty."

King Zhou was enraged. "You must obey the king, even if it means giving up your life. How dare you oppose my order! And how dare you offend me with your rubbish and insult me for a wicked king! This is the gravest of offences. You should be arrested and put to death according to law!" he threatened.

When the palace guards placed Su Hu under arrest, Fei

Zhong and You Hun entered the court, knelt down and kowtowed to the king. "Su Hu should be punished for his
disobedience. However, you would be looked upon as a bad ruler, and people would say that you had insulted a good man
and imposed limitations on freedom of speech just because you
were unable to get his daughter. It would be better to set him
free and let him return to his post. This way he'll be grateful
for your generosity and be willing to give you his daughter. By
so doing, the people will admire you as a good ruler, generous
and kind, permitting all to enjoy the freedom of speech and al-
lowing dutiful ministers to live in peace. You'll be killing two
birds with one stone."

Now calming down a little, King Zhou said, "I'll do as
you advise. Set him free and let him return to his post. But he
may no longer remain here in the capital."

Su Hu was expelled from the court and ordered to leave
the city at once. When he reached his residence, he was met by
his generals, who asked him, "What important problem did
His Majesty discuss with you?"

Su Hu was still in a rage and cursed the king soundly. "If
I don't send my daughter to him, the bloody bastard is sure to
send an army. But if I do, he'll neglect state affairs, and people'll curse and ridicule me. What shall I do, Generals?"

"It's said that when the ruler is immoral, ministers may
abandon him and seek their future abroad. Our king ignores
his good and faithful ministers and devotes himself solely to sexual pleasure. Chaos is bound to overrun the country soon.
Let's leave this place and declare independence to save our
own homes and lives and the land inherited from our ancestors," they advised him.

Su Hu was greatly excited. "A hero must act in public.
Hand me a brush and ink, and I'll write a poem on the Meridian Gate to express my strong resolve never again to serve the
Shang Dynasty." Eventually, he wrote the following on the
wall:

> *You ignore the rites between king and ministers,*
> *You corrupt the five cardinal virtues of mankind.*

Thus, Su Hu, the Marquis of Jizhou, has decided
To offer no further obeisance to the Shang Dynasty.

King Zhou pondered deeply after Su Hu was removed
from the palace, "Though I've set him free, I still don't know
whether he'll give his daughter to me or not."

But his meditation was interrupted by a gate officer, who
knelt before him and said, "While on duty at the palace
gate, I discovered a quatrain written by Su Hu, in which he an-
nounces a rebellion. Not daring to keep it to myself, I'm reporting this to Your Majesty."

Reading over the explosive poem, King Zhou once more became infuriated. "How dare that bloody bastard act like this.
As Heaven prefers not to kill, I didn't cut his damned head off
but set him free instead. This is the way he shows his gratitude! This time he must be punished," he cursed, and gave
the order, "Generals Yin, Chao and Lu are hereby ordered to
lead six armies under my command to attack Jizhou. Our goal
is the utter decimation of the city."

Hearing this order and cheering the king before his throne,
General Lu Xiong thought, "Su Hu is a good and faithful minister, but how did he offend the king so much that His Majesty himself is going to Jizhou. Woe to the city!" Feeling a
pang of compassion for Su Hu, he knelt down and reported,
"Though Su Hu was offensive in Your Majesty's presence, it's
unnecessary for you to venture personally to the front. Since
the grand dukes are still in the capital, Your Majesty may appoint one or two of them to command the attack. You
shouldn't place yourself in danger on the front."

"Who would be the best qualified to act on my behalf?"

"Since Jizhou's in the north, under the administration of
the North Grand Duke, Your Majesty may logically appoint
Chong Houhu," Fei Zhong said.

This was quickly approved by the king.

"Chong Houhu's avaricious and cruel. Wherever his army
goes, people suffer terribly," General Lu Xiong thought. "But
the West Grand Duke Ji Chang is virtuous, loved and well-
trusted by the people. Better I recommend him to prevent

things from getting worse." The king was ordering to publish the appointment when he objected. "Though Chong Houhu is the North Grand Duke, he's not fully trusted by the people, and it may be difficult for him to accomplish his mission. However, Ji Chang has long been known for his virtue. I recommend that you appoint him to take your place. This way, Su Hu'll be punished according to law without your having to confront the danger of arrows and spears."

After a long hesitation, King Zhou approved both recommendations, and appointed Chong Houhu and Ji Chang as joint command of the army. When the announcement reached him, Ji Chang remarked to the two prime ministers and the three other dukes at the banquet, "Though Su Hu came to offer his allegiance, he wasn't admitted to the palace, nor was he received by His Majesty. How could he possibly have offended the king? He's known to all for his loyalty and good conduct, and for his many outstanding military successes. There must have been a good reason for him to write the poem. His Majesty'll lose sympathy from the marquises if he believes the malicious accusations by his minions and attacks Su Hu. Would you two prime ministers try to find out at court tomorrow morning what crime it is that Su Hu's committed. Should he be guilty, Su Hu must be punished. If not, we must do something about it."

"You're right, Grand Duke," Deputy Prime Minister Bi Gan agreed.

But Chong Houhu held a different view. "The king's words, if unspoken, are like silk threads, but turn into satin once he begins to speak. Who would dare to oppose an order he had already issued! Besides, Su Hu did indeed write an abusive poem, and His Majesty hasn't made his decision groundlessly. Should the 800 marquises all begin to disobey the king, how can His Majesty maintain order?"

"Your point seems quite reasonable, yet it's only one-sided. No one doubts that Su Hu's a faithful minister. He serves the country with loyalty, educates the people methodically and commands his army brilliantly. He's acted faultlessly for years now." Ji Chang refuted him. "I'm at a loss as to

who's tricked His Majesty into punishing the innocent. This
isn't an auspicious omen for the country. I pray that His Majesty won't choose to use violence. War is a serious disaster. It
wastes money, slaughters the people and destroys the peace of
the nation."

"You may be right, Grand Duke, but how can we disobey
His Majesty's orders? We're compelled to follow them, lest
we commit the crime of opposing the king," replied Chong
Houhu.

"If it be so, lead your army to the front first, and I'll follow you there soon," said Ji Chang.

The banquet ended, and the party went their separate
ways. Before his departure, the West Grand Duke said to the
prime ministers, "Chong Houhu'll be there first. I have to
return to West Qi for the time being, and will join him
shortly."

Arriving back at Jizhou, Su Hu was met in the suburbs by
his eldest son Su Quanzhong at the head of his generals. When
he entered the city, he held a meeting and told his generals all
that had happened to him in the capital. "We must train men
and horses and make preparations to defend the city walls with
catapults and rolling logs against the king's army," he warned
them.

All of his generals and soldiers took extra care while on
guard and prepared themselves for the anticipated attack.

Without the least delay, Chong Houhu gathered a
50,000-strong army and left the capital for Jizhou. He was well-
equipped with cannons powerful enough to shake the earth,
and his troops with their spears and swords were imposing as
huge mountains. After marching through countless cities and
towns, a report came from the vanguard, "The army's arrived
at Jizhou and requests orders from the commander." He ordered the army to halt, and encamp within stockades and
strongholds.

When he learned of the arrival of the invaders, Su Hu
asked an intelligence officer, "Who's the commander of the
army?"

"It's Chong Houhu, the North Grand Duke."

Su Hu was infuriated. "I'd settle this matter with a compromise if it were any other grand duke but Chong Houhu," he declared. "Chong's an evil fellow, and it's absolutely hopeless to try to settle in peace with him. I'll take him by surprise, and ensure that people won't suffer any harm."

Amid the firing of cannons, Su Hu led his generals and soldiers out of the city roaring like thunder. He lined up his men and shouted, "Let me talk with your commander now!"

Chong Houhu led his men out of the strongholds to meet the challenge. He rode on a tall stallion, wore golden chain mail, a red robe and a jade belt, and held a cutlass across his saddle. Behind him came his eldest son, his generals and two great banners, one embroidered with a dragon and the other with a phoenix.

Seeing Chong Houhu in front of him, Su Hu bowed. "How are you, Grand Duke. I'm terribly sorry that I cannot offer you a complete salutation, as I'm in helmet and armor," he greeted and then came to the point, "King Zhou has of late become corrupt and immoral as a ruler. He shows no respect for his ministers, cares little for the state and listens only to the minion courtiers. He compelled me to give him my daughter as a concubine. Addicted to sex and wine, he now leads a life of dissipation. The kingdom'll soon suffer from great disturbances and is bound to fall before long. But I've always stayed within my own marquisate, and am surprised to see you here with your army."

In anger, Chong Houhu said, "You disobeyed the orders of His Majesty and wrote a treasonable poem on the wall of the Meridian Gate. You're a rebel and ought to be punished by death. By order of His Majesty, I'm here to carry out his sentence. You should have knelt down before my army in unconditional surrender, but you stand there in armor brandishing your weapons and mouth glib rubbish!" Turning towards his men he demanded, "Who'll take that filthy bandit for me?"

A general, wearing a phoenix-feather helmet, a scarlet robe and golden armor, urged forward his black stallion crying, "I'll take that bloody bastard."

Galloping swiftly to the front, he was met by General Su Quanzhong, Su Hu's eldest son, who, brandishing a halberd, shouted, "What's the big hurry? Come on, let's fight." He recognized his opponent as General Mei Wu.

"Su Quanzhong, you and your father are rebelling against His Majesty. Lay down your arms and surrender, or else your whole clan will die."

Su Quanzhong remained silent. Urging his horse forward, he stabbed at Mei Wu's chest with his halberd. Mei Wu resisted bravely and struck at him with his battle-axe. Their combat proceeded vigorously. After twenty rounds, Mei Wu received a fatal wound and fell dead to the ground.

Now that his son had won the first encounter, Su Hu ordered his men to beat the drums, signaling an all-round engagement. At this Zhao Bing, Chen Jizhen and the Jizhou soldiers launched into the enemy line. After a fierce battle, the field was soon piled high with the dead and wounded, and blood flowed freely over the wilderness under a gloomy sky. Chong Houhu and his generals Jin Kui, Huang Yuanji and Chong Yingbiao were utterly defeated and retreated to a distance of ten miles.

Returning, Su Hu held a meeting to discuss the future with his generals. "Though we've defeated Chong Houhu today, he'll come here again with a stronger force," Su Hu said. "Jizhou's still in great danger. What shall we do now?"

Zhao Bing stepped forward and said, "In my humble opinion, since we've taken the first step, we must take the second. Chong's suffered defeat this time and retreated, though not too far from us. We might launch a surprise attack tonight and smash his stockades in the darkness. When we've routed him completely Chong'll come to realize that we're not to be trifled with. Only then can we hope to come to terms with a duke other than Chong and save the city from destruction. What do you think, Marquis?"

Su Hu was overjoyed at this suggestion. "You're quite right. I agree with you completely," he said, then issued orders, "Su Quanzhong with 3,000 men are to lay an ambush at Wugang, about ten miles beyond the west gate; General Chen

Jizhen's to lead his army on the left and Zhao Bing on the right,
while I'll be in the middle."

After dusk, Su Hu's armies were ordered to march to their
positions, flags rolled up, drums quiet and horses moving in silence. Soon they would take the enemy by surprise.

Chong Houhu had not expected such a defeat and the loss
of his generals and soldiers. With nowhere to turn to, he gathered his troops and encamped anew. He addressed his men,
"Though I've fought countless battles in my day, never have I
suffered such a defeat as today! The death of Mei Wu in partic-
ular is a great loss to us. What shall we do?"

General Huang Yuanji consoled him, "Don't you know,
Grand Duke, that victories and defeats are routine business in
the army. The West Grand Duke'll soon be with us, and we'll
be able to smash Jizhou as easily as snapping our fingers. You
shouldn't worry too much."

At this Chong Houhu brightened up and drank with his
generals in their new camp. Meanwhile Su Hu led his army quietly out of the city and waited patiently for the moment to
come. By the time of the first watch, the army had marched
ten miles, and the enemy camp was in sight. At a prearranged
signal, Su Hu's cavalry and infantry bravely launched their attack, taking Chong completely by surprise. They rushed in like
tigers and wolves, slaughtering and maiming on all sides. Su
Hu was riding alone, lance in hand, in search of Chong Houhu.

Chong was startled from his dreams by the battle cries. He
dressed quickly, mounted his horse, grabbed his cutlass and
stormed away from his tent into the combat. Soon he came
upon Su Hu, in a golden helmet and armor, mounted on a
black horse and wielding a long fire dragon lance. Su Hu saw
him. "Chong Houhu! How dare you flee so shamelessly. Get
down from your horse and be my captive," he shouted.

Chong was greatly frightened, and had little choice but to
match his cutlass against Su Hu's lance. At this moment, his
son Chong Yingbiao, Jin Kui and Huang Yuanji came to his
aid. But Zhao Bing and Chen Jizhen appeared moments later
to right the temporary imbalance. The men on both sides battled furiously in the dark of night. Su Hu's troops were well-

prepared for the attack, while Chong Houhu's men were taken by surprise. Thus, the soldiers of Jizhou fought with extraordinary bravery, and Chong Houhu's men were totally overwhelmed.

In the midst of the fight, Jin Kui was felled from his horse by Zhao Bing and died instantly. Realizing that the situation was not to be saved, Chong Houhu was forced to beat a fighting retreat with Chong Yingbiao. They ran like homeless dogs, while the soldiers of Jizhou fought as bravely as tigers and fiercely as wolves. The ground was strewn with corpses, and blood flowed in streams. After pursuing the fleeing troops for twenty miles, Su Hu gave the order that his men return to Jizhou.

Fleeing, Chong Houhu and Chong Yingbiao met Huang Yuanji, Sun Ziyu and their soldiers. Chong Houhu groaned. "Since I first became a soldier, I've never suffered such a big defeat as this. I never expected those treacherous bandits would attack our stockades in the middle of night, and cost us officers and many soldiers. We must take our revenge. I'm also displeased that Ji Chang should rest peacefully in his dukedom, and ignore His Majesty's orders. He doesn't send us a single soldier but sits back and watches me suffer a defeat. I won't tolerate this."

"We've lost our fighting spirit," Chong Yingbiao said. "I suggest that we take a defensive position and take no further action for the present. Let's send a messenger to Ji Chang to request reinforcements."

"You're right, my son. Let's discuss this again at dawn," replied Chong Houhu.

He was not aware that an ambush was prepared for them. As they rode, the sudden thunder of cannons rent the air and they heard the Jizhou soldiers roaring "Chong Houhu dismount from your horse and die!"

Looking up, Chong Houhu saw a brave young general in a golden helmet and armor, with a face round as the full moon and lips red as vermillion. "On my father's orders I've waited for you for a long time. Throw down your cutlass, get off your horse and meet your death," cried Su Quanzhong. "What are you waiting for?"

"You bloody bastard! Both you and your father are wicked rebels, killing generals and soldiers sent here by His Majesty. Your crimes are weighty as mountains, and you deserve to be sliced into a thousand pieces. It's too early for you to brag about victory, though I've suffered from your surprise raid. As soon as the reinforcements from His Majesty arrive, you and your father shall meet instant deaths," Chong Houhu reviled in return. "Who'll take this rascal for me?"

General Huang Yuanji spurred his horse forward and swung his cutlass at Su Quanzhong, who met the charge with his halberd. They fought an intense battle, with neither side taking the immediate upper hand. Then, Sun Ziyu galloped out with his forked spear to join the fight against Su. With a mighty roar, Su Quanzhong pierced Sun Ziyu's helmet with his weapon, bringing him crashing to the ground.

Though the combat was joined by Chong Houhu and his son, Su Quanzhong fought on single-handedly against the three generals, displaying the courage of a tiger in the mountains or a dragon in the sea. Su Quanzhong's halberd slashed Chong Houhu's armor, knocking off a piece covering his thigh. Much alarmed, Chong spurred his horse and with a rapid leap fled the scene of combat. Seeing his father flee, Chong Yingbiao became discouraged and distracted. A thrust of Su's halberd at his heart caught him unawares, but hastily avoiding it, he took a heavy blow in the left arm. Blood soaked his robes and armor. He would have fallen from his horse had not his generals rushed forward to support him. Once again, Chong Houhu's army suffered a terrible defeat.

Su Quanzhong dared not pursue any further in the darkness, and went back to the city.

At dawn, Su Hu held a conference at court. He asked Su Quanzhong, "Have you captured that rogue?"

"By your order, I had my men lay an ambush at Wugang, and the defeated enemy troops fell into the trap at midnight. I fought bravely and managed to stab Sun Ziyu to death, knock off Chong Houhu's armor and pierce Chong Yingbiao's left arm. They were thoroughly defeated, but I dared not chase them farther in the dark. I had no choice but to return," Su

Quangzhong reported.

"Chong Houhu was lucky. You may rest now, my son." Su Hu was very pleased with this outcome.

If you wish to know what happened after that, please read the next chapter.

DAJI ENTERS THE PALACE

Chong Houhu and his wounded son fled for their lives the whole night through. Gathering the remnants of his troops, Chong was deeply grieved to find that only one-tenth of his men were left, most of them severely wounded.

General Huang Yuanji came forward to offer him comfort. "Why are you so full of worries again, Grand Duke? I still hold that victory and defeat are commonplace events in a general's life. Though we were defeated last night, we can still gather new forces." He urged Chong, "Why not send an urgent dispatch to the West Grand Duke and request reinforcements as soon as possible, so that we may continue our combat and seek our revenge? What do you think?"

Chong Houhu pondered a while. "Since the West Grand Duke takes no action while we've suffered defeat and seems indifferent as to whether we win or lose, I'm reluctant to ask him for help," he said, "lest he be acquitted of the crime of disobeying His Majesty's orders."

As the discussion went on, a report was delivered, "A huge army is marching towards us at great speed." Not knowing where the army was coming from, or whether it was friendly or hostile, Chong Houhu became scared. He hurriedly mounted his horse, and looking ahead wildly, saw a general with a face black as the bottom of a cauldron, a red beard and round golden eyes. He was wearing a coronet embroidered with clouds, flames, and flying birds, a suit of mail and a bright red robe. He was riding a fiery-eyed monster, and held two golden axes in his hands. Chong Houhu soon realized that this was none other than his own younger brother Chong Heihu, the

Black Tiger, the Marquis of Caozhou.

This new arrival set Chong Houhu's heart at ease. After exchanging greetings, Black Tiger said, "When I learned that you had suffered defeat on the front, I rushed here with my army to help you. How good it is to be with you once again."

Chong Yingbiao saluted his uncle from his saddle. "You must be tired after marching so far," he asked his uncle with concern.

But Black Tiger Chong Heihu only replied, "My army will join yours under one command. Let's go back to Jizhou and see what we can do there."

Chong Heihu had brought 3,000 Flying Tiger Soldiers with him, and there were another 20,000 following later on. The two armies marched to Jizhou, encamped and prepared themselves for battle. Meanwhile, in Jizhou, Su Hu had heard about the arrival of Chong Heihu. He lowered his head and remained silent for a long time.

"Black Tiger's highly skilled in combat and learned in the art of war. There's no rival for him among the generals in this city!" he finally said, and asked his generals, "What shall we do?"

"Generals are accustomed to fighting against invading armies, just as earth is commonly used to cover water. We mustn't be timid before Black Tiger," Su Quanzhong commented.

"You're too young and inexperienced. Don't you know that Black Tiger Chong Heihu was tutored by a magician? He can chop off the head of a great general as easily as pulling something out of a bag," Su Hu warned. "You mustn't underestimate him."

"Father! By praising the enemy, you're only compromising yourself!" Su Quanzhong replied. "I'll meet the challenge at once and not return until I capture Black Tiger."

"You'll suffer from your mistakes and soon regret what you've done," Su Hu warned again.

Despite these warnings, Su Quanzhong leaped upon his horse and galloped out of the city, shouting, "Tell Black Tiger to come out and fight at once."

Hearing the report, Black Tiger was secretly glad. "I'm here first to avenge my brother's defeat and second to try to save Su Hu," he thought. "I must help him for friendship's sake."

Before the camp, Black Tiger watched Su Quanzhong display his martial skills and called to him, "Dear nephew! Go back and tell your father to come and see me. I've something important to tell him."

But Su Quanzhong was young and uncultured and longed to engage in combat with Black Tiger, because his father had praised him as a brave fighter. He did not take the cue.

"We're enemies, though my father was friends with you. You had better leave this place at once, lest you lose your life," he shouted back.

"How dare you speak so rudely to me, you little beast," Black Tiger cursed him furiously and lunged forward with his gold axes at Su's face.

Su met the blows with his halberd. Thus began a fierce combat between the two heroic generals. Su Quanzhong did not know that since his childhood Black Tiger had been the disciple of a mystical sage, who had given him a magic gourd, which he always carried on his back and enabled him to perform miracles. But Su Quanzhong had only his bravery to rely on and looked with contempt upon anyone who chose to fight with short-handled axes. He exerted every effort to fulfill his ambition of taking Black Tiger alive.

Their violent combat caused Black Tiger to perspire all over. He said to himself, "I admire Su Hu for having such a good son. A brave general's son must certainly be a brave general."

He made a feint with his axes, pulled his horse around and fled. Su Quanzhong laughed at his cowardice, and urged his horse after him. Seeing that his enemy was unwilling to give up, Black Tiger stealthily removed the lid from his gourd and began to mutter incantations under his breath. Suddenly a stream of black smoke rushed out of the gourd, filling the sky, and a flock of Heavenly Eagles could be heard calling loudly as they flew back and forth. The eagles opened their iron beaks and swooped down to peck at Su Quanzhong. He tried to defend himself with his halberd, but he could not protect his horse at the same time. When one of his horse's eyes was pecked out, the horse fell. Su was thrown onto the ground and taken captive by Black Tiger.

When Su Quanzhong was brought before Chong Houhu, he did not beg for mercy, but continued cursing and swearing. Chong Houhu lost patience with him and ordered the executioners to behead him at once. But Black Tiger saved him, suggesting that he be escorted to the capital and dealt with personally by the king.

Hearing the bad news, Su Hu groaned to himself. "What can I say now? My son didn't listen to my warning, and as a result was taken captive today. I've been a hero all my life, but now my son's been taken captive, and with such a strong enemy, Jizhou's bound to be taken before long. Why have I ended up in such a miserable situation?" he wondered to himself. "Is it because I've given birth to a daughter? The bloody king's been deluded by the minions, and demands her as a concubine. Because of my refusal, my family and the innocent citizens of this city shall meet their ends. The disaster's due solely to her, my daughter.

"It will be my greatest humiliation if the city's taken and my wife and daughter are sent to Zhaoge as prisoners. They would be tried and put to death and their corpses would be displayed in the market. I would certainly be ridiculed and despised by all the marquises in the kingdom. I'll be a greater hero if I kill them first and then put myself to the sword."

Thus thinking, he took his sword and rushed to the rear palace. When Daji saw him, she ran up and greeted him with a sweet smile. "Dear papa! Why do you come here with your sword in hand?"

How could Su Hu possibly raise his sword against Daji? She was his beloved daughter, not an enemy in battle. He broke into tears. "My darling daughter! Because of you, your elder brother has been taken captive. Because of you, this city is surrounded at this very moment. Because of you, your parents shall lose their lives. Because of you, our entire family will perish...."

But before he could finish, a challenge from Black Tiger was reported, and he immediately returned to the court. He held a conference with his staff. "Since Black Tiger's skilled in witchcraft, we mustn't answer his challenge," he remarked. "We had better defend the city wall with arrows, stones and rolling logs."

At the foot of the city wall, Black Tiger was also confused. "Brother, if only you would only consult with me, I could withdraw my troops. Why do you fear and refuse to see me? I don't understand!" He had to return to the camp. Chong Houhu suggested that they attack the city with tall ladders, but Black Tiger had a better idea. "There's no need to launch an attack. Let's rather surround the city and block their supply lines. They'll be left inside without anything to eat, and we can take the city without an effort. Besides, we can rest now while waiting for the arrival of the West Grand Duke."

Su Hu was thus hopelessly besieged. One day, it was reported to him that General Zheng Lun had brought in provisions, and was waiting outside for further orders. "Though we've got rice now, what use is it!" he sighed, then said, "Tell him to come in." When Zheng Lun came in, Su Hu described the whole situation to him. "No one can beat Black Tiger since he's both brave and skilled in magic," he concluded. "There's no one that I can turn to for help in the whole kingdom. There are four in my family, but my son's already been taken captive. I've decided to kill my wife and my daughter first, and then myself; otherwise, we'll be ridiculed by the future generations. You generals may as well pack up and find yourselves a new master!"

"Marquis! Are you drunk? Are you mad? Or are you possessed? Even if the other three dukes and all the 800 marquises joined forces, I wouldn't even glance at them. How can you be so cowardly?" Zheng said in anger. "I've been in your service since my youth and owe my present position to you. I'll always do my best for you."

"I see that General Zheng's been possessed by an evil

sprite, and that's why he's speaking nothing but non-sense," Su Hu declared to his other generals. "Let's forget about the 800 marquises for now. But this Black Tiger alone is a headache. Tutored by a sage in magic arts he's a source of alarm to both gods and demons. He's also a great strategist and can stand up to 10,000 men without fear. You mustn't underestimate him."

"Let me go and fight him. If I can't take Black Tiger, I'll have my head cut off and presented to all the generals assembled here." Zheng shouted and drew. Without waiting for further orders, he jumped onto his fiery-eyed monster, grasped his two Demon Subduing Clubs and left the city at the head of his army. His 3,000 Crow Soldiers, dressed in black, resembled a huge black cloud rolling swiftly over the plains. "Come out here, Black Tiger," he shouted at the top of his voice when he got to the enemy camp.

Black Tiger rushed out with his Flying Tiger Soldiers, and found himself in front of a general with a date-purple face and a shining beard. He was wearing a scarlet robe, gold chain mail and a jade belt, mounted as Black Tiger himself was on a fiery-eyed monster.

"State your name before combat," Black Tiger called out, as he did not know Zheng Lun.

"I'm General Zheng Lun of Jizhou. You must be Black Tiger. You think you're very brave, seizing my young master. Set him free at once, dismount and surrender! If you dare say no, I'll turn you into dust."

"You dolt! Su Hu's committed a capital crime, and you're his accomplice. How dare you speak such arrogant nonsense."

Black Tiger urged his mount forward and slashed at Zheng Lun with his axes. Zheng Lun met the charge with his clubs. They fought twenty-four rounds vigorously, neither giving way.

As they struck back and forth Zheng Lun caught sight of a red gourd on Black Tiger's back. "My commander told me that Black Tiger was taught by a sage in magic powers. This must be his secret weapon. As the saying goes, 'In a fight always make the first move.' I must use mine first," he thought to himself.

Zheng Lun himself was a disciple of the Woe Evading Sage of the West Mount Kunlun. Predicting that Zheng Lun would someday be created a god, the immortal taught him a magic skill whereby he might exhale a magic vapor and snatch the souls of his enemies. After a period of apprenticeship, Zheng Lun left the mountain and came to Jizhou.

And now in the midst of combat, Zheng Lun waved his club in the air, and immediately his Crow Soldiers lined up like a long snake. They shouted battle cries and, carrying hooks and chains, raced up like a piece of dark cloud. Before Black Tiger knew what was happening, two strong beams of light gushed forth from Zheng Lun's nostrils with a noise like the clanging of a huge bell. Black Tiger suddenly became dizzy, his vision blurred. Tumbling from his monster, he passed out and was seized and tied up by the Crow Soldiers. When he regained consciousness he realized that he was trussed up as a prisoner of war. He was furious. "That scoundrel really has some crafty tricks. How did he manage to capture me?"

Hearing the drums rolling outside the city, Su Hu groaned. "Poor Zheng Lun! He must be done for." But his doubts and worries were suddenly interrupted by a report that General Zheng Lun had won the battle and had taken Black Tiger alive.

Zheng Lun arrived and reported how he had captured Black Tiger Chong Heihu. Even as he spoke, his soldiers brought in the captive to the stone steps at the front of the court. Su Hu hastily left his seat, curtly dismissed the guards, untied Black Tiger and knelt before him. "I've offended His Majesty and committed a grave crime. Zheng Lun's rude and should be dealt with severely."

"I've never forgotten that we're sworn brothers. I'm ashamed to be a captive and greatly appreciate your courtesy," Black Tiger said in response.

Su Hu invited Black Tiger to take the place of honor, and ordered Zheng Lun and other generals to come and pay him their respects.

"General Zheng's skilled in the most ingenious arts. His capturing me today's filled me with the utmost respect for him," Black Tiger remarked.

At the feast that followed, Su Hu told Black Tiger the whole story of how King Zhou had demanded him for his daughter as a concubine. Black Tiger said, "The main reasons for my coming here are to discuss my brother's defeats and your way out of trouble. But I never expected that your son would be so naive, and so stubborn that he refused to understand me and take my message back to you. I was forced to take him. I'm actually trying my best to help you."

"I'll never forget your friendship, Brother," Su Hu said earnestly.

Hearing the report of how his brother had been taken, Chong Houhu was taken aback. "Who would have thought that such a miracle could take place?" He began dispatching his men for further news when the report came that a messenger had arrived from the West Grand Duke. Though Chong Houhu was upset, he ordered his men to let the messenger in. This messenger was none other than San Yisheng, supreme minister and a well-known scholar from the West Grand Dukedom. After San Yisheng had offered his respects, Chong Houhu began to reproach him. "Minister! Why does your master ignore His Majesty's orders and remain in the comfort of his palace indulging in pleasure?" he said in anger. "Your master's guilty of disloyalty to both His Majesty and the country. What have you got to say to me today?"

"My master always says 'War's a calamity,' and should be resorted to only in desperate need. You're involved in a war on account of a trivial incident. It'll result in a great waste of manpower and money. People are panic-stricken; all the houses and farms are left empty and unattended. How terribly the people and the soldiers have suffered! For this reason, my master's sent me here with a letter, exhorting Su Hu to cease resistance, and give up his daughter on condition that he retains his title as the Marquis of Jizhou. If he remains stubborn, then we'll use a stronger force which he'll be unable to resist," San Yisheng explained.

Chong Houhu burst into a great roar of laughter. "Ji Chang's making excuses, since he realizes that he's guilty of dis-

obeying His Majesty's orders," he mocked. "I've already fought
Su Hu a few times, but suffered heavy losses. How can that bri-
gand be persuaded to send his daughter to the king by just reading a letter? Go and see Su Hu, and let's just see what happens."

San Yisheng left the camp and advanced to the foot of the
city wall. "Here's a messenger from the West Grand Duke,
bringing a letter to you," he shouted to the soldiers above,
and minutes later the city gates were opened, admitting him.
He was brought before Su Hu, who was dining with Black
Tiger.

"What instructions do you bring me in this humble city,
Officer?" Su Hu asked him.

"I've come here by order of the West Grand Duke. As
you offended His Majesty by writing that poem, my master
was ordered to punish you. But he knows that you're loyal,
and refuses to cooperate with Chong Houhu. He sent me with a
letter to you, and hopes you'll read it carefully," San Yisheng
said as he took out the letter.

Su Hu took the letter and began to read:

Knowing that you are virtuous and loyal I cannot rest
unconcerned in my palace and allow you to continue in
your misfortune. But I know that you may turn your misfortune into future if you place your trust in me and accept
the advice that I offer you in this letter.

There will be three advantages if you send your daughter to the royal palace: (1) As long as she enjoys the favor
of the king, her father will be honored as a royal relative
with a high stipend; (2) Jizhou will remain untroubled by
war, and Su Hu's whole family will enjoy peace and the respect of the court forever; and, (3) The people will no
longer suffer, nor will soldiers in the army be slaughtered.
Yet, if you choose to remain obstinate, three terrible things
will happen: (1) Jizhou will be taken and occupied, and neither your home nor the temple of your ancestors will be
spared; (2) Every member of your family will be extermi-
nated; and, (3) The innocent people and soldiers will suffer
disaster. A hero should concern himself with matters of great

importance and ignore everything which smacks of the trivial. You should not destroy yourself like a common fool.

We are both ministers of the Shang Dynasty. Thus, I must speak the truth and offer my advice so that you may make a quick decision....

After reading the letter over, Su Hu remained silent, only nodding his head. San Yisheng noticed this. "You needn't hesitate any more, sir! The war'll be over if you agree, but continue if you don't. Why do you remain silent?" he urged.

Su Hu turned to Black Tiger, "Brother, please read it. It's full of reason and truth and in the best interests of the nation and the people. How could I dare to oppose his wishes!" He then invited San Yisheng to join the feast and put him in his own mansion for the night. The next day, He asked San Yisheng to deliver his reply to the West Grand Duke along with gifts of gold and satin.

When San Yisheng left, Su Hu said that he would personally escort his daughter to the palace and make amends for his errors. The power of a single letter was much greater than that of 100,000 soldiers! At this, Black Tiger said to Su Hu, "The West Grand Duke's a reasonable man. You should pack your bags and make ready to send your daughter to His Majesty as soon as possible. For this is a noble act of obeisance to the Shang Dynasty."

Both Su Hu and Black Tiger were greatly pleased with themselves.

4

THE FOX SPRITE MURDERS DAJI

Taking his leave, Black Tiger said to Su Hu, "We've settled everything now, Brother. Make haste to escort your daughter to the capital. Any delay might mean a possible change for the worse. As soon as I return, I'll set your son free. Both my brother and I will return with our armies. We'll present our reports to the king to smooth the path for you. If you attempt to do things in any other way, disaster may befall you once again."

"In gratitude for your affection and the kindness of the West Grand Duke, I won't sacrifice my life on account of my adoration for my daughter. Please set your heart at rest. I'll certainly set off as soon as possible," Su Hu reassured him. "But my only son's in your camp. Would you set him free, lest my old wife worry herself to death. Once again I greatly appreciate your kindness."

"You need't worry, Brother. He'll leave as soon as I reach the camp," Black Tiger said earnestly. They then thanked each other once again and parted reluctantly.

Black Tiger returned to the camp and sat down in his brother's tent. "What a vile wretch the West Grand Duke is. He keeps his army idle, awaiting the outcome of the battle without lifting a finger. He sent San Yisheng to see me yesterday with a letter to Su Hu, trying to persuade him to send his daughter to the palace. I let San Yisheng see Su Hu yesterday, but he still hasn't come back," Chong Houhu complained. "Ever since you were taken captive, I've been worried and constantly sent my men to make inquiries. You must know how pleased I am that you're free now. I don't know whether Su

33

Hu will admit his faults or not, but you must know all about it since you've just come from Jizhou. Please tell me the details, Brother."

"Though we share the same ancestors and father, yet as an old proverb says, 'one tree may bear both sweet and sour fruit, and sons born of the same mother may be either bad and foolish or good and wise. Listen, Brother!" Black Tiger snapped. "When Su Hu rose up against King Zhou, you recklessly attacked him, suffering heavy losses. You're also a grand duke of the Shang Dynasty, but you've never performed any good deeds for the government. You've egged on the king to accept the minions and caused hatred the country over. That's why your 50,000 men have less power than a letter from the West Grand Duke. Su Hu's already promised to send his daughter to the king, and to beg His Majesty's pardon at the same time. Doesn't this make you feel embarrassed? You're a disgrace to the family. I'm going to leave you now, and I never want to see you again," Black Tiger swore, and then ordered that Su Quanzhong be set free. When the boy appeared in his tent and expressed his gratitude, Black Tiger warned again. "My dear nephew! You must tell your father to begin his journey immediately. I'll send a petition to the king and report what your father intends to do, so as to make it easier for him."

Su Quangzhong then bade him farewell and left the camp for Jizhou. Burning with fury, Black Tiger also mounted his monster and led his 3,000 men back to Caozhou. Chong Houhu, embarrassed and ashamed, filed a report to the king and withdrew to his own dukedom. Meanwhile father and son met again in Jizhou.

"We cannot forget the virtue and grace of Ji Chang. It is he that has saved us from destruction. As I cannot let the family perish on account of Daji, I've got no choice but to send her to the palace and apologize to His Majesty. While I'm away, you must look after Jizhou and take care not to disturb the people. I'll return as soon as possible," Su Hu told his son.

He then entered the inner palace to see his wife Madame

Yang and tell her of Ji Chang's advisory letter. Knowing that her husband was going to take her daughter away, she burst into tears. When Su Hu tried to comfort her, she said, "She's so delicate that I'm afraid she'll be unable to serve the king properly. My worst fear is that she may bring annoyance to His Majesty."

"Unfortunately, there's very little we can do about that now," Su Hu said. The old couple spent the whole night in despair and sorrow. The next morning, Su Hu mobilized 3,000 soldiers and 500 officers, made ready his carriages, and told Daji to prepare for the long journey. When she heard this, Daji broke down in a flood of tears and bade a sorrowful farewell to her mother and brother. She was beautiful, radiating as much sweetness and charm as peony blossoms dripping with dew. Though unwilling to be separated from each other, they were compelled to say their goodbyes at last. Madame Yang returned weeping to her bed chamber, while Daji stepped into her carriage in tears. Su Quanzhong escorted his father and sister for five miles before he returned home.

Flags and pennants led the long train, and Su Hu rode behind his daughter's carriage in order to offer her protection in case of emergency. Many days passed as they traveled over rivers and mountains until they came to Enzhou. Arriving at the courier station, Su Hu met the station officer. He asked the officer to prepare a room for his daughter.

"I should tell you the truth, sir!" the officer replied. "About three years ago, an evil sprite appeared here, and ever since then, not a single honorable guest passing through this area has taken up residence here. For the sake of security, you're advised to reside at the hostel in the military camp."

"Do you really think that a royal relative could be terrified by a mere sprite?" Su Hu demanded. "We're not going anywhere else. Clean up the place at once."

Once the bedrooms were cleaned up, Su Hu placed Daji in a room in the rear hall in the company of fifty maidservants. The station was in addition surrounded by the 3,000 soldiers and the gates were tightly guarded by the 500 officers.

Sitting in the candle-lit hall, Su Hu was in deep thought.

"Though the station officer warned me about an evil sprite, I don't believe it, situated as it is in the middle of a busy market, with people coming and going," he said to himself. "Nevertheless, I must heighten my vigilance, lest something unexpected should take place."

So thinking, he first placed a leopard-tail staff beside his desk before picking up a book about war strategy. As the first watch struck in the city, Su Hu still could not set his heart at rest. With the iron staff in hand, he walked silently towards the rear hall where his daughter was staying. When he discovered that Daji and her maidservants were all sleeping soundly, he returned to the front hall and started reading his book on war strategy again. Soon the second watch was sounded and then the third. Suddenly, there was a great whirlwind, an unusual coldness bit into his flesh and bones, and the candles flickered off and on again. It seemed as if a wild beast had bounced into the room and was about to snatch someone away.

This wild wind gave Su Hu goose-bumps all over his body. As he puzzled over it, he suddenly heard voices from the rear hall, "A ghost! It's a ghost!" He picked up the iron staff and a lamp and rushed into the rear hall. The lamp, however, was blown out before he arrived. As he could do nothing in the darkness, he rapidly returned to his own room and urgently ordered for another lamp.

When he rushed to the rear hall a second time, he saw the maidservants running about in a panic. Entering Daji's room, he pulled open the bed curtains. "How are you, my child? Did you see the ghost come in?" he asked.

"I was dreaming when I heard the cries, but when I looked up and round, I saw only you coming in with the lamp in hand. I haven't seen any ghost."

"Thank heaven and earth that you were not terrified. Rest easy, my child."

Saying goodnight, Su Hu returned to his own room and remained on watch through the rest of the night, not daring to sleep for even an instant.

What Su Hu did not know was that the woman whom he talked to was none other than the thousand-year-old female fox

sprite. During the few minutes it took him to return to his
room for a second lamp, the fox sprite had sucked out Daji's
soul and then occupied her body. Her purpose was to seduce
King Zhou and overthrow the Shang Dynasty, as Goddess Nu
Wa had ordered.

Su Hu could not sleep that night, yet he was satisfied.
"It's lucky that the future concubine of the king wasn't
alarmed at all," he thought to himself. "This must be a blessing from Heaven, earth and my ancestors. Otherwise, I would
be accused again of offending the king and would never be able
to explain myself."

At dawn they set out from Enzhou, traveling by the day
and resting by night. Several days later, they forded the Yellow
River and arrived at the capital, camping outside the city. Su
Hu sent a messenger to the royal court to announce his arrival.
Hearing the report, Prince Huang Feihu realized that Su Hu
had changed his mind about his daughter. He sent a messenger
of his own to tell Su Hu to station his troops outside the city
but bring Daji in and put her up at the Golden Reception
House.

But Fei Zhong and You Hun were displeased, as Su Hu
had brought them no gifts. "That treacherous thief Su
Hu!" they commented. "He hopes to atone for his crimes, but
the royal wrath or joy are subject to our influence, and it is we
that decide whether he should live or die, be rich or poor. Yet
he seems to have no regard for us at all!"

In the Dragon Virtue Court the next day, Fei Zhong
stepped forward and knelt before King Zhou, "Su Hu's here
to offer his daughter. He's awaiting your orders outside the palace."

At this the king exploded in a great rage. "That common
oaf! When he offended me that day, I decided to put him to
death at once, but then I took your advice and sent him back
to his territory," he cried out. "However, he showed no appreciation for my generosity, and wrote that poem! He insulted
me so shamelessly that I must put him to death tomorrow.
Such is the law of this land."

"The laws pronounced by Your Majesty are applicable to

every soul in the country. It would be anarchy if rebellious and treacherous acts were not dealt with seriously. A nation without law will be forsaken and soon fall into ruin," Fei Zhong at once took the cue.

"You're right, Fei Zhong. See what I do tomorrow," King Zhou said.

As drums were beaten and bells struck, King Zhou made his solemn appearance at the morning court session. All his civil and military ministers were lined up in order beside him. After greetings and cheers, the gate officer rushed up and reported to the king, "Su Hu of Jizhou's waiting outside the palace to offer you his daughter and redeem his faults."

"Let him in."

Su Hu, not daring to wear the coronet and red robes of his rank, was dressed in the garb of a convict. He knelt down and kowtowed. "This criminal Su Hu has committed a capital crime in opposing you. I deserve to die!" he said.

"Su Hu of Jizhou! You wrote that poem stating that you would never again offer allegiance to this dynasty. You dared to resist the royal army and slaughtered my generals and soldiers. How can you justify yourself coming to my court again today? For these crimes you must die at once!" King Zhou ordered his guards to take Su Hu away and decapitate him outside the palace gate.

But at this moment, Prime Minister Shang Rong left the ranks and fell on his knees before the king. "Su Hu should have his head cut off for rebelling against the Shang Dynasty. However, Ji Chang has sent a petition here and reports that Su Hu is willing to offer you his daughter and atone for his crimes. For this, Su Hu may be pardoned. He committed a crime, but how can you treat him so severely after he has changed his mind. I beg you to have mercy on him."

King Zhou was still thinking this over when Fei Zhong stepped out. "I suggest that Your Majesty accept the Prime Minister's proposal and bring Daji in right now. If she's indeed beautiful, virtuous, familiar with the rites, eloquent in speech and ready to serve you, you may take her and forgive Su Hu at once. If, on the contrary, she's not and doesn't appeal to you at all, Your Majesty may cut off both their heads in the market and show the people that you deal with important matters in a solemn and strict fashion."

"You're right, Fei Zhong. Bring Daji here to see me at once," the king ordered.

Daji moved gracefully towards the palace gate, crossed over the Nine Dragon Bridge, and when she reached the entrance to the court, raised the ivory tablet in her hands, knelt down and saluted the king, "Long live the King! Long live the King!"

King Zhou fixed his eyes on her, She had soft black hair, cheeks as pretty as peach blossoms, a body slender as a tender willow branch, and was dressed as elegantly as floating clouds. She gave one the impression of a begonia drunk with sunshine, or a pear blossom drenched in rain. She was as ethereal as a fairy from either the Ninth Heaven, or the moon palace. When she parted her cherry lips, she gave off a breath of perfumed fragrance. Her eyes were like autumn ripples, radiating coquettish charm.

When she said in her sweet voice "The daughter of your criminal servant prays that Your Majesty be blessed with 10,000 years," King Zhou was entirely bewitched and seemed to be flying towards the sky. His body went limp, his ears grew hot and his vision blurred. He could hardly control himself. He stood up and ordered, "Rise, my beauty! You may stand." Turning towards his palace maidservants he said, "Lead Lady Su to the Fairy Longevity Palace and await my arrival," and then pronounced, "Su Hu's whole family is now pardoned. Su Hu is restored to his original rank, and as a royal relative he's granted an extra monthly allowance of 2,000 piculs of rice. He's to be entertained for three days at the Celebration Court, and escorted back to Jizhou by two civil and three military ministers."

Su Hu knelt down and thanked King Zhou, but the ministers, seeing the king's blind passion for women, were extremely displeased. The king rose and returned to his palace, leaving no chance for them to give advice. They had no choice but to go to the Celebration Court and entertain Su Hu.

King Zhou returned to the Fairy Longevity Palace, where he banqueted with Daji and then spent a passionate, blissful night in her company. Their love developed swiftly and King Zhou began to spend all of his energy and time taking pleasure in her. He lost his patience for state affairs and his civil and military officials, and mountains of reports, petitions and other documents piled up awaiting his decision. None of the 800 marquises had a chance to discuss urgent matters with him, and orders ceased to be issued from the palace. The kingdom rapidly sank into chaos.

If you wish to know what happened after that, please read the next chapter.

5

A Vain Attempt
By Master of the Clouds

On Mount Zhongnan dwelt a Taoist immortal named Master of the Clouds, who had made his home on the mountain for several thousand years. One day, having nothing to do, he took a flower basket and went to pick medicinal herbs near Tiger Cliff.

As he rode off on a floating cloud, he suddenly noticed the emanation of an evil sprite shooting high into the sky in the southeast. Looking down from the cloud, Master of the Clouds sighed.

"It's only a thousand-year-old female fox that's occupied the body of Daji to bewitch the king. She'll bring great calamities to the people unless she's exorcised. This is my duty, since my mission's to deliver mercy." He called over his disciple, Golden Haze, and instructed, "Bring me a withered pine branch. I'll make a sword out of it and take care of that lewd sprite."

"Why don't you use your steel sword, Master?"

Master of the Clouds smiled. "A pine sword's entirely sufficient for the task. There's no need for me to use my steel sword to knock off a fox sprite."

Golden Haze fetched a pine branch for his master, who whittled it into a wooden sword in a few minutes, and told the lad, "Look after my cave while I'm gone. I'll be back quite soon."

He then left Mount Zhongnan, riding upon an auspicious cloud, and sped directly to Zhaoge. A poem recorded the event:

> *No steed has he mounted, no boat does he ply,*
> *Yet he flies over the world in a wink.*

Thousands of ages pass by in a day,
In only a moment pines rot, stones decay.

Meanwhile King Zhou had become so dissipated by wine
and women that he did not make a single appearance in court
for more than ten months. The king's behavior both puzzled
the ministers and caused much anxiety. Supreme Minister Mei
Bo went to see Prime Minister Shang Rong and Vice Prime
Minister Bi Gan.

"His Majesty's so involved with wine and women that he
totally neglects state affairs. This is a bad omen and the kingdom's sure to suffer as a result. We're his most powerful ministers and obliged to serve the country and people with loyalty.
The king should have ministers to remonstrate with him, just
as a father should have a son to point out his mistakes, and
scholars, friends to correct them when they go astray. We must
take action today. Let's call together all the civil and military
officials and ask the king to appear on the throne. Otherwise,
we'll be failing in our duty," he suggested, and the two prime
ministers were in full agreement.

King Zhou was drinking with Daji at the Star Picking
Mansion when he heard the clamor of drums and bells. An attendant reported, "Your Majesty's requested at the Grand
Court." He had no choice but to go. "My dear lady! Rest for
a while. I'll return soon," he comforted Daji, who knelt down
as he left.

The king mounted his chariot and drove off to the Grand
Court. Seated on his throne, he received cheers from his ministers and officials. He now felt great disgust at the sight of his
two prime ministers, eight supreme ministers and Prince
Huang Feihu, each holding files of reports for him to read.
The king had indulged so long in wine and sex with Daji that
he was of no mind to read so many reports. Knowing well that
he couldn't read them all in a short time, he felt inclined to retire and go back to Daji.

Before King Zhou said anything, however, Shang Rong
and Bi Gan stepped forward and knelt down. "All the nobles
are eagerly awaiting your decisions about their reports. Why

has Your Majesty been absent from the court for so long, and why have you not shown any regard for state affairs? We can only assume that there's someone misguiding you. We pray earnestly that Your Majesty will pay more attention to state affairs, and less to your concubines. This goes against the will of your people and ministers, and we fear that Heaven will be so dissatisfied that famines, floods and drought will be visited on us. We sincerely hope that Your Majesty will stay away from women, avoid the minions, and be diligent in your duty. We hope, too, that you'll please Heaven, make the nation prosperous and the people rich, and allow the country to enjoy peace and the four seas to be blessed with boundless happiness."

"I know that the people of our kingdom are living in contentment and rejoice in their work. The only exception is the North Sea district, where Grand Tutor Wen Zhong's been suppressing a rebellion. It's a mere skin disease, and we needn't worry about it at all. I fully accept your suggestions. However, all important state affairs have been taken care of by you as my prime ministers, and how can there be any backlog of work? Even if I hold regular court, I'll just let things alone, and it's not my way to talk so much," the king argued.

They were thus debating when a messenger arrived from the Meridian Gate and reported, "An immortal has arrived from Mount Zhongnan, wishing to see Your Majesty about an urgent and confidential matter. Will you see him, Your Majesty?"

"How can I be expected to have enough patience to read over so many reports from so many ministers? It would be better for me to have an idle chat with that Taoist, since that's bound to be more interesting than these garrulous ministers," King Zhou thought to himself, and ordered that the Taoist be ushered in.

Master of the Clouds entered the gate of the palace, walked over the Nine Dragon Bridge and strolled down the broad royal way. He was dressed in a long robe with wide sleeves and held a dust whisk in his right hand and a flower basket in his left. When he walked on his cloud, stars and planets trembled and shook. When he passed through the moun-

tains tigers kowtowed before him, and when he traveled
through the seas, dragons bowed and scraped before him.
When he reached the entrance to the court, he said, "Your Majesty, this humble Taoist greets you."

Seeing that the Taoist did not kneel down and kowtow before him, King Zhou was displeased. "I'm king, master of the
four seas. Though he's a Taoist immortal, he also lives within
my territory. How dare he act so rudely! He should be punished for this, though my officials would criticize me for being
intolerant. Let me ask him some questions and see whether he
can answer me properly," he decided. "Where do you come
from, Sir?"

"I come from the clouds and rivers," the Taoist replied.

"What do you mean by the 'clouds and rivers'?"

"My heart's as free as the white clouds, and my mind
flows like water."

King Zhou was a witty ruler, and he asked a philosophical
question, "Where will you go when the clouds disperse and the
rivers dry up?"

"When the clouds disperse, a bright moon hangs in the
sky and when the rivers dry up, a brilliant pearl appears before
me."

King Zhou's rage turned to happiness, and he exclaimed
with joy, "At first I was rather displeased with the way you
greeted me, but from your answers, I realize that you're a
great and wise saint."

King Zhou told his attendants to show Master of the
Clouds to a seat, and without further ado the Taoist sat down
at the king's side.

Master of the Clouds lowered his head respectfully and addressed the monarch, "Your Majesty knows only that a king
must be accorded the highest honor, but has no idea that of
the three religions— Taoism, Buddhism and Confucianism,
Taoism is the most honored."

"How is that?"

"Let me tell you. Among the three religions, Taoism is
the most highly esteemed. A Taoist neither makes obeisance to
a king nor calls on dukes and high ministers. He resides in his

hermitage and avoids the entrapments of political powers. He thoroughly rejects the vulgar world, regarding it as a net, and endeavors throughout his life to seek truth. He distances himself from fame and riches, he finds joy in forests and streams, he abandons all concepts of honor and dishonor, and he takes refuge in caves. He's got a blanket of stars above by night, and of sunshine by day. He wears cotton gowns, weaves hats of fresh flowers and plucks wild grass for mattresses. He drinks from sweet springs, eats pine and cypress seeds to ensure his longevity, claps his hands when he sings and sleeps in the clouds when the dancing's over. He discusses the Way, and essays and poems over wine with his friends. He disdains wealth and rejoices in purity and poverty. He lives a carefree life, spending his time discussing the rise and fall of dynasties.

"Though the four seasons follow in an endless cycle, he can turn his white hair black and rejuvenate his old body. He helps people with medicinal herbs and saves them from death. He exorcises spectres and demons by means of charms and spells. He gathers refined emanations from both Heaven and earth and collects the essences of the sun and moon. He cultivates himself with the *yin* and *yang* and achieves rebirth by means of fire and water. Collecting the ingredients in the appropriate season, he refines the elixirs of life. He rides upon green phoenixes or white cranes and calls upon the Purple Jade Palace of the Supreme Emperor.

"Unlike the Confucians who seek positions as high ministers, Taoists see riches and political power as floating clouds. Unlike the Jieists who practise sorcery and witchcraft, the Taoists care only for the Way. Thus, of the three religions, Taoism is the most respectable."

King Zhou was delighted by what he heard, and said, "What you've said refreshes my spirit as if I had moved beyond the vulgar world, and really looked upon riches and power as floating clouds that would soon pass away. Where's the cave that you live in? And why do you come here to see me?"

"I reside in the Jade Pillar Cave on Mount Zhongnan, and my name's Master of the Clouds. When I went out to gather medicinal herbs the other day, I noticed the aura of an evil sprite soaring up into the sky above your palace. Since I've always had feelings of good will towards Your Majesty and the people, I came here to rid the kingdom of this danger."

King Zhou just laughed. "The palace walls are tall and strong and the palace is closely guarded all the time. As it's situated in the city rather than in the forests and mountains, how could a spectre possibly get in? Perhaps you've made a mistake, sir."

Master of the Clouds smiled and said, "If you could recognize the sprite, it would never have dared to run such risks. It's only because Your Majesty cannot recognize it that it dares sneak into the palace and bewitch you. A great disaster will take place if you allow it to remain here. Here's a short poem I've composed about this:

> *She's bewitching and fresh,*
> *But she saps your spirit, devors your flesh.*
> *If you detect her before it's too late,*
> *You'll save countless souls from a miserable fate.*

"What can we do if indeed there's a spectre hidden in the palace?" King Zhou asked.

Master of the Clouds opened his flower basket, removed his pine sword and held it up to show the king. "This pine sword has magic properties. Though it emits no strong light that penetrates to the depth of the sky, it can turn any spectre to ashes within a period of three days."

Taking the pine sword in his hands, King Zhou asked, "In which part of this palace will this sword be most effective?"

"Hang it before the Central Palace Tower and observe the results in three days."

King Zhou ordered that his attendants do as the Taoist had directed, then turned to him, "You're marvelous, telling about spirits and devils. Are you willing to give up your hermitage and come here to protect me? I'll give you a high rank and let your name be known to all future generations.

Wouldn't this be better than living in poverty, unknown to the world?"

Master of the Clouds thanked King Zhou but declined his invitation. "I greatly appreciate your kindness, but I'm a mere idler and know nothing about ruling a nation. I sleep until the sun rises high over the bamboos and wander barefooted in the mountains."

"What good is that for you! It would be better if you could dress in purple robes and serve in the palace, for this would glorify your life and enable your sons to receive a good inheritance. You may live in luxury for the rest of your life."

"I've got my own pleasures, Your Majesty. My body's light and my heart's free. I fight with nobody and know no tricks. I ignore politics, preferring to spend my days cultivating leeks. I never wear satin robes or jade-studded belts, and have no intention of serving at the palace as a minister. I'll never stroke the beard of the prime minister nor kneel down before the throne of the king. I've no desire for rich emolument or glory for my descendants. I prefer to reside in a small cave and wear old, worn-out clothes. I never enquire about the emperors of Heaven, earth or man. I dream only of being invited to the Feast of Immortal Peaches held in paradise or taking a mid-afternoon nap in the mountains. I don't care about the sun setting in the west or the bright moon rising in the east."

King Zhou sighed. "Sir, you're truly a man devoted to purity and quietitude."

The king ordered his attendants to fetch two big plates, one full of silver and the other of gold, and gave them to Master of the Clouds to use on his return journey. But the Taoist only smiled. "Your silver and gold are useless to me. Though I thank you very much, I cannot accept them. Here's another poem I've composed:

> I forsake the dusty world, leave my lot to destiny,
> Like rivers and clouds my heart e're roams free.
> A sword, a walking stick, a lute and sutras,
> To pass the hours, these are all I need.
> With herbs the old and sick I treat,

New poems in my mind I chant to those I meet.
My elixir adds to your years,
More precious than all the gold in this poor world.

His long sleeves swinging, Master of the Clouds bowed and strolled out.

The ministers had been forced to wait with their petitions, but the visit of the Taoist had left the king thoroughly exhausted. Rising from his throne, he returned to his residential quarters, dismissing the court at the same time.

When King Zhou reached the Fairy Longevity Palace, and Daji failed to come and meet him, he became very uneasy. He asked his attendants, "Why doesn't Lady Su come out to meet me?"

When he was told that Daji had suddenly fallen ill and taken to bed, King Zhou rushed into the bed chamber, pulled aside the golden dragon curtains and looked down at his lover. Daji's face was yellow as gold, her lips white as paper, and she seemed to be having trouble breathing. "Oh! Daji! You were so healthy when I left here this morning. How is it you suddenly became ill? What shall I do now?"

The fox sprite occupying Daji's body was actually suffering from the effects of the pine sword. It was evident that she had little time to live.

Daji opened her eyes a little and spoke with a sigh, "Your Majesty! I escorted you to the Grand Court this morning and went to meet you at noon. When I reached the Central Palace Tower I chanced to look up and saw a sword hanging high up there. I was shocked and began sweating all over, I'm now so ill that I may be unable to enjoy sexual pleasure with you anymore. For this I'm terribly sorry, Your Majesty." Tears poured down her cheeks.

King Zhou was terrified and remained silent for a long while. "I was deceived outright by a sorcerer. Master of the Clouds presented me that sword. He told me that there was the aura of an evil sprite in the palace, and advised me to exorcise the menace by hanging up that sword. How could I have guessed that the Taoist was actually plotting to harm you!" He ordered, "Take down that wooden sword and burn it immediately, lest Lady Su be disturbed again."

King Zhou comforted Daji the whole night through, never letting his attention wander from her.

The Shang Dynasty grew weaker and weaker as a result of Master of the Clouds' failure to exorcise the spectre from the palace.

If you want to know what happened after the sword was destroyed, please read the next chapter.

THE BURNING PILLAR TORTURE

Terribly upset by Daji's illness, King Zhou ordered that the wooden sword be burned at once. Daji recovered rapidly and continued to lure the king into feasting and merry-making with her day and night.

Master of the Clouds did not return directly to Mount Zhongnan, but remained at Zhaoge to observe the situation. He soon caught sight of the spectral light soaring up again into the sky from the king's palace. "I tried to save the Shang Dynasty, but it's by fate that the sword was turned into ashes without fulfilling its purpose," he thought. "The causes are rather complex: First, the Shang Dynasty must come to an end; second, the Zhou Dynasty's rising to replace it; third, immortals will meet with disaster; fourth, Jiang Ziya will enjoy worldly glory and, fifth, gods are to be created. What can I do about it? I might as well leave a poem to tell the people what'll happen in the near future."

He took a brush, dipped it in ink and wrote on the wall of the observatory in the busy marketplace:

A lascivious spectre holds sway in the palace,
While sacred virtue flourishes in the West Land.
E're many years will pass,
Zhaoge will be stained with the blood of war.

When finished, Master of the Clouds returned straight to Mount Zhongnan. People at once gathered round the wall, but no one could understand what it meant. They were still debating and deciphering when Grand Tutor Du Yuanxian

第六回　紂王無道造炮烙

came over on his way home and read over the poem from his saddle. He knew immediately that the poem must have been written by the Taoist, and though he did not understand every word of it, he agreed that a lascivious spectre was occupying the palace. "I've spent nights recently observing the heavenly bodies, and noticed that an ever more powerful spectral aura has been enveloping the palace. This is a bad omen, a warning of the disaster to come. The king pays scant attention to politics, and his unseemly behavior causes Heaven to worry and people to grumble. We were so kindly treated by the late king that we cannot sit back and simply watch the situation develop. I must write to the king, and make it on behalf of the people and nation as I've got nothing personal to gain," he decided.

He spent the night writing this report. He showed it to Prime Minister Shang Rong the next morning, asking him to present it to the king in person.

"I cannot disregard your report, but the king's failed to appear in court for many days already. It'll certainly be difficult for your report to be transmitted to him, but I'll try to see him in his residence," Shang Rong reassured him, and immediately made his way through the Grand Hall, the Celebration Court, the Hall of Ceremonies, the Hall of Clemency and the Central Palace Tower to the Fairy Longevity Palace, where he was stopped by the royal guards.

"Prime Minister! This is the forbidden court where His Majesty lives. No intrusion's permitted."

"I know that well. Would you kindly tell His Majesty that I desire to see him?"

A royal guard entered the Fairy Longevity Palace, knelt down before King Zhou and reported, "Prime Minister Shang Rong asks to see you."

"What could he possibly want? Admit him, since he's an old minister and has served three emperors in succession."

Shang Rong came forward, knelt down on the steps and said, "Your Majesty!"

"What urgent business brings you to my inner palace?"

"The Chief Official of the Observatory Du Yuanxian dis-

covered last night that your palace is enveloped in a spectral
aura, and is afraid that the state will suffer from some
unexpected disaster. He's served the Shang Dynasty loyally
since your grandfather's time and wouldn't be put off. Besides,
the ministers have been fretting over your sustained absence
from court. Offending your dignity today, I risk committing a
capital crime and having my head cut off by either axe or
sword, but I'm not seeking personal gain. I pray that you attend to our faithful advice," Shang Rong said boldly, and
submitted the report.

King Zhou placed it on his desk and began to read. It ran:

> The Chief Official of the Observatory, Du Yuanxian,
> ventures to report to Your Majesty with the end to ridding
> the palace of spectres and demons, and to secure peace and
> blessings for the nation and the people. As we know, good
> omens appear when the nation is enjoying progress and
> prosperity, and spectres and demons appear when the na-
> tion is about to collapse. While making my observations at
> night, I was astonished to discover that the royal palace is
> covered by an aura of spectres and demons which pervades
> every court as well as the royal residence. When you made
> your appearance at the Grand Hall several days ago, a
> Taoist presented you with a wooden sword to help you
> exorcise the spectre, but you had it burnt, which only
> served to intensify the aura. You disregarded the Taoist's
> warning, and the spectral aura has grown stronger and
> stronger, until it can now even be observed in the Ninth
> Heaven, suggesting that woe and calamity will soon plague
> the nation. I have given this matter careful consideration.
> Facts show that ever since Su Hu sent his daughter to the
> palace, you have ceased paying attention to your admini-
> stration, and your desk has become covered with dust. The
> steps before the Grand Court are overgrown with weeds,
> grass and slippery moss. While the ministers await an audi-
> ence with Your Majesty in vain, you are taking pleasure in
> a woman. This has created a gap between Your Majesty
> and the ministers like the sun being covered up by floating

clouds. I venture to present this admonition, irrespective of punishment by axe or sword, as my obligation to Your Majesty....

"Though he speaks the truth, my Lady Su nearly lost her life the day before yesterday, and she was saved when I had that wooden sword destroyed," the king pondered. "But here again, this fuss over the spectral aura!" He turned to Daji. "Du Yuanxian's sent me a written report about the palace being haunted by a demon. Do you know what this is all about?"

At this, Daji fell at once on her knees, "That Taoist is a sorcerer. He spreads rumors about a spectre and throws the nation into confusion. Du Yuanxian cooperates with him, and must be one of his accomplices. People are innocent; they're gullible and easily disturbed. I ask that such rumors be suppressed, and anyone spreading them have their heads cut off," Daji begged the king.

"You're right, my beauty. Give my order to stop this rumor at once, and Du Yuanxian be executed in public."

"You can't act like this, Your Majesty. Du's a loyal minister and would willingly sacrifice his life for the benefit of the people and nation. His heart's in the right place. As an observer of heavenly phenomena, it's his duty to tell you the truth," Shang argued, warning, "But if you repay his loyalty with death, your officials are bound to uphold his innocence, and you'll be criticized for your cruelty. I implore you to pardon him."

"You don't know, Prime Minister, that if I don't cut his head off, more people will invent stories and disturb the people's lives without an end. I must weed out such threats." King Zhou then ordered his attendants to escort Shang Rong away from the palace.

Back at his own office, Shang Rong met Du Yuanxian, waiting eagerly to learn of His Majesty's response to his petition. Before long, the king's guards also arrived with the following order, "Du Yuanxian has committed the serious crime of deceiving the people by spreading rumors about spectres.

For this, he shall be punished with death and beheaded at once according to law." Without further delay, the royal guards removed Du's coronet and red robe, bound him with thick ropes and iron chains and dragged him off to the palace gate.

On the way, however, they met an official dressed in a scarlet robe. This was Supreme Minister Mei Bo. When he saw Du Yuanxian bound in chains, Mei Bo was bemused. "Why are you being treated in this fashion, Grand Tutor?" he asked, and when Du told him what had happened, he said, "Don't worry, Grand Tutor! I'll try to speak with the king about this."

Rushing into the palace, Mei Bo met Shang Rong at the Nine-Dragon Bridge. "What did Du Yuanxian do to have offended His Majesty?"

"Du Yuanxian delivered a written report to the king about the palace being haunted by the spectral aura, but since Lady Su is His Majesty's favorite, he accepted her advice and sentenced Du Yuanxian to death. I pleaded with His Majesty to spare Du, but to no avail. What shall we do now?"

"You're prime minister and it's your responsibility to administer the nation in harmony and peace, to put the wicked to death, and to recommend loyal subjects to high posts. You may keep your mouth shut as long as the king acts in an upright fashion, but you ought to admonish him when he acts improperly. Now that he's about to slaughter the innocent, how can you keep your mouth shut, making excuses that you feel sorry and can do nothing! You care only for your own honor and position, and disregard the fate of your colleagues. You cherish your life and fear death. For the good of the country, no prime minister should fear spilling his blood or losing his life," Mei Bo cried out, very angry. "Executioners! Take no action at present, and await our return," he shouted, and led Shang Rong by the arm through the Grand Hall to the inner palace.

They knelt down when they arrived at the Fairy Longevity Palace and awaited the king's permission to enter.

"Since Shang Rong's already served three Shang Dynasty emperors, his intrusion into the inner palace may be excused, but how dare Mei Bo ignore the law!" King Zhou was displeased when he heard the report of their arrival, but nevertheless, he ordered that both Shang Rong and Mei Bo be admitted.

Shang Rong led the way into the Fairy Longevity Palace and both knelt down before the king.

"What do you have to report to me?"

"Your Majesty! May I learn what crime Du Yuanxian has committed that you should have ordered his death?" Mei Bo asked.

"He conspired with a sorcerer and spread rumors about a spectral aura in the palace, to deceive the people and disrupt the peace. An official of the top rank that commits such evil acts should be put to death. I'm merely attempting to eliminate a traitor from the kingdom."

"I've heard that Emperor Yao ruled according to the will of Heaven. He accepted political advice from his civil officials and strategies of war from his military ministers. He held daily discussions on how to rule the country and serve the people, and was pious and upright in his comportment. He avoided minions, and distanced himself from beautiful concubines. But Your Majesty's been absent from court for more than half a year. You drink and feast by day and lust by night. You've long ceased to show any concern for the people and state, and for the faithful advice of your loyal ministers." Mei Bo worked himself up. "Du Yuanxian's a loyal minister. If you put him to death on account of your concubine, you'll be cursed for butchering your father's old minister, and denounced as the destroyer of the nation, for your act tantamount to wrecking a house by removing its pillars and beams. I exhort you to let Du Yuanxian live, for if you do, people will honor you as a saintly ruler."

King Zhou was displeased. "Mei Bo must be an accomplice of Du Yuanxian, and must be likewise punished, for he's committed the crime of trespassing the forbidden inner palace. Yet I'll pardon him since he's served me so well in the past. However, he should be dismissed from his post in the royal government forever," he announced.

"You licentious tyrant! You place your trust in your concubine Daji, but have only disdain for your ministers," Mei Bo
protested sternly. "If you execute Du Yuanxian, you're
actually decapitating thousands of the citizens of Zhaoge. Dismissing me from my post will cause me no regret; I'm glad to
shake this dust from my body. Yet, I'm indeed sorry to see the
Shang Dynasty, which has lasted for hundreds of years, about
to collapse in the hands of a licentious tyrant! State affairs
have taken a bad turn ever since the Grand Tutor Wen Zhong
left for the front. You listen daily to the fawning courtiers and
spend your nights in dissipation with Daji. The kingdom will
suffer disaster soon, and I fear that I won't have the face to
confront our deceased kings in the nether world."

King Zhou became enraged and ordered his guards to seize
Mei Bo and smash his skull at once. As the guards were about
to lay hands on Mei Bo, Daji stepped in and said, "Wait!
I've got a suggestion, Your Majesty."

"How do you intend to deal with him, my love?" King
Zhou asked.

"I must say that any minister who dares to stand before
Your Majesty, eyebrows raised, eyes bulging and insult Your
Majesty shouldn't be treated as an ordinary criminal and
shouldn't be put to death in the ordinary way. Put Mei Bo in
gaol temporarily. I'll deal with him in a new form of torture
and give a warning to the cunning and the wicked."

"What's this torture?" asked King Zhou.

"It uses a hollow pillar of brass, twenty feet in height and
eight in circumference. It has three fire doors in its upper, middle and lower part through which charcoal is placed inside.
Strip the criminals, chain and wrap them around the red-hot pillar. In a second, bones, flesh and blood will turn to a fetid
smoke and disappear. This new torture's called the Burning Pillar, and we may use it to subdue the wicked ministers that
dare to break the law."

"This is indeed a perfect idea, my dear lady!" King Zhou
said. "Decapitate Du Yuanxian for spreading rumors about the
palace spectral aura, and send Mei Bo to gaol," he ordered,
and then told his engineers to make burning pillars according

to Daji's design.

Observing the king's atrocities, and his blind faith in Daji, Shang Rong was filled with despair. "I must report to you, Your Majesty. As all urgent matters are now settled, and as everything in the kingdom is thriving, my old age and poor health make it difficult for me to bear the heavy burden of office. I'm afraid I may make errors in my confusion and offend Your Majesty. I pray that you'll have mercy on me and permit me to retire and live out my life in peace."

But King Zhou tried to comfort him, saying, "Though you're in the evening of life, you're still healthy. Nevertheless, I must approve your resignation since you've approached me with due sincerity. You've labored faithfully for so many years and I'm very reluctant to let you go."

He ordered that two ministers escort Shang Rong to his native home and that he be given rewards. He also issued an order that Shang Rong should be well taken care of by the local magistrate.

When the ministers learned that Shang Rong had retired and was returning to his native place, they gathered at the Changting Pavilion beyond the capital to see him off. Among them were Prince Huang Feihu, Bi Gan, Wei Zi, Ji Zi, Wei Ziqi, and Wei Ziyan, all close relatives of King Zhou. When Shang Rong arrived, he dismounted from his horse and went up to greet his colleagues.

A spokesman for them all said, "Prime Minister! You're retiring in honor. But as an elder statesman, how can you cast the dynasty aside and gallop away home. Will you be able to remain there with your heart at ease?"

Shang Rong was visibly moved. "Colleagues! I'm sorry that I cannot give my body and soul in return for the grace bestowed on me by the nation; yet it's also against my will to spend the rest of my days in retirement. You're all well aware that His Majesty blindly trusts Daji. She's now suggested the idea of the burning pillar to deal with the loyal. My petitions all go unheeded, and I'm afraid that before long new disorders will erupt in the kingdom. As I no longer had the competence to serve His Majesty, I decided to retire and give someone

more qualified than myself a chance. I'm saying farewell to
His Majesty out of selfish concern for my own personal safety
and happiness. Let's toast to our brief separation, for we'll
soon meet again," he said and, cup in hand, chanted a poem:

> *For seeing me off this far,*
> *I raise my glass, tears falling.*
> *Away from the king, as if in another world,*
> *I'll pray for peace from my native place.*
> *I would sooner shed blood, like martyrs of old,*
> *Than aid a tyrant, the history's worst.*
> *Sorrows linger among us this day,*
> *When shall we meet again, and recall this parting?*

When Shang Rong finished, his colleagues tearfully took
their leave. Shang Rong mounted his horse and rode away, and
they returned to Zhaoge.

King Zhou continued to indulge with Daji day and night,
ignoring all state affairs. Several days later, it was reported to
the tyrant that the burning pillars were ready. Greatly pleased,
King Zhou asked Daji, "Now that the burning pillars are
ready, what shall we do?"

Daji ordered that the pillars be brought in for her inspection. When they were, she looked them over carefully. She
noted with satisfaction that they were made precisely according
to her design, and each was fitted with two wheels so that they
might move around.

King Zhou pointed his finger at Daji and laughed. "My
beauty! You're so clever to have invented such a marvelous torture. Let's try it out on Mei Bo at the Grand Hall tomorrow." Early the next morning, King Zhou ascended his
throne. After the official greetings were over, Huang Feihu saw
twenty shining brass pillars standing at the eastern end of the
court. He was wondering what they were for when the king ordered that Mei Bo be brought in and a brass pillar moved to
the center of the court. The fire was lit and fanned until the
heat turned the pillar molten red. Then Mei Bo entered. He
knelt down before King Zhou, his hair dishevelled, his face

unwashed and his thin cotton garments in dirt.

"You damned fool! Do you know what this is for?" the king asked.

Mei Bo raised his head, and looked at the burning brass pillar. "No, I've no idea what it is for, Your Majesty."

The king laughed. "You damned fool! All you know is how to insult your own king with your sharp tongue, but it seems you're ignorant of the fact that I've invented the burning pillars specifically to deal with you. I'll now use it to roast your flesh and bones. Let those who would blaspheme me with rumors and slanders take this as a warning."

"You licentious tyrant!" Mei Bo shouted. "I'm not afraid of death. I've already served three emperors of this dynasty. What crime have I committed that you'll put me to such a cruel death? I only regret that the Shang Dynasty will end tragically in your hands. Won't you be ashamed to meet your ancestors in the nether world?"

King Zhou was infuriated and immediately had Mei Bo stripped, shackled and placed upon the red-hot brass pillar. Mei Bo let out a single piercing scream, and his body turned to ashes, leaving a nauseating stink pervading the court. What a pity that Mei Bo should meet a tragic end simply because he served his people, his nation, and his king with loyalty!

King Zhou thought that the burning pillar was a wonderful invention, but he did not know that all of his ministers were in full sympathy with Mei Bo and that there was not one of them who didn't want to leave the palace and give up his official life. It was clear that by now the unity of the kingdom was broken and that the dynasty's days were numbered.

As they left the Grand Hall, Wei Zi, Ji Zi and Bi Gan met Huang Feihu. "The state is now unstable. Uprisings broke out in the North Sea district, and Grand Tutor Wen rushed there to suppress them. How could we ever imagine that the king would devote himself wholeheartedly to Daji, and treat us so mercilessly. Now he's invented that cruel torture in order to slaughter his loyal ministers. If word of it reached the nobles, our troubles would multiply endlessly," they said, greatly troubled.

Huang Feihu stroked his long beard. "Princes! As I see it, the worst victim of the burning pillar isn't Mei Bo, but the Shang Dynasty. It'll be reduced to ashes and vanish from the face of the earth. An ancient proverb says, 'If a king regards his officials as his hands and feet, they will regard him as the heart and stomach; but if he looks upon them as dust, they will hate him as a thief.' The king's ruthless killing of Mei Bo is a bad omen, and great disasters will soon follow. How can we sit calmly and watch the downfall of this Dynasty!"

When he arrived at his residence, King Zhou was met by Daji. "It's your wonderful idea. Mei Bo's death will serve as a warning to anyone who won't keep his mouth shut! The pillar's truly an efficient tool," he told her and took her in his arms.

He then ordered a feast in honor of Daji. They ate and drank to the accompaniment of music until midnight, when a sudden gust of wind flew the sweet strains to Queen Jiang's bedroom. Hearing it, she asked her attendants, "Where does that alluring music come from at this hour of night?"

"Your Majesty! It comes from the Fairy Longevity Palace, where His Majesty and Lady Su are still drinking together."

Queen Jiang sighed deeply. "I was informed that His Majesty took Daji's advice, built the burning pillars and has put Mei Bo to death. That cheap wench is luring him into evil deeds. Prepare my coach. I'll go to the Fairy Longevity Palace and see His Majesty at once," she ordered.

This visit was undoubtedly prompted in part by jealousy, and would lead to greater calamities.

If you want to know what happened next, you must read the next chapter.

7

FEI ZHONG
PLOTS TO DEPOSE THE QUEEN

Accompanied by her maids holding lanterns, Queen Jiang got into her coach and headed for the Fairy Longevity Palace. When the guards announced her arrival, King Zhou glanced at Daji with half-closed eyes. "Lady Su! Would you please meet Her Majesty for me?" he asked.

Daji walked out, bowed courteously, and escorted the queen into the court. After exchanging greetings, the queen sat down on the right side of the king, while Daji, as a mere concubine, had to remain standing. King Zhou offered a cup of wine to the queen. "I'm very glad to see you here tonight, my dear wife!" he said, then ordered Gun Juan, a palace maid, to play upon a hard-wood clapper and Daji to sing and dance to entertain the queen.

Daji danced beautifully and sang with a sweet voice. When she danced her long sleeves waved up and down like graceful butterflies. It seemed as if her feet did not touch the ground. Her performance was applauded by everyone except Queen Jiang, who never even glanced at her. She sat there staring down her nose and breathing into her breast. When King Zhou noticed her expression, he smiled.

"Don't you know that the years pass away in a wink, like flowing water, and that we have very little time to enjoy the pleasures of life? Daji sings and dances, and she sings as marvelously as the fairies in Heaven. Talents like hers are certainly rare in this vulgar world. Why can't you enjoy yourself?" he asked her.

At this Queen Jiang stood up, left her seat, and knelt down before the king. "There's nothing wonderful or precious

63

about Daji's singing and dancing," she replied.

"What, then, is wonderful and precious, if not this?"

"As I've learned, a good ruler is pleased by virtue and contemptuous of material things. He distances himself from minions and lewd concubines. A king's self-awareness is the most precious treasure of the country. The treasures of Heaven are the sun, moon and stars; those of the earth are grains and fruits; those of a country, loyal ministers and fine generals, while those of a family, filial sons and grandsons. However, Your Majesty prefers lewdness and wine, slaughters the loyal, forsakes the elders, connives with the wicked, and trusts only your favorite concubine. There's actually nothing to be prized here, for they only spell the end of the dynasty. I pray that you will repent your errors, hold fast to law and discipline, and be diligent about state affairs, so that Heaven will bless us, the people will be happy and the state will enjoy peace. I'm a mere woman, and I apologize if I've said something wrong," she stated bravely and then excused herself.

Annoyed with her words, King Zhou turned to Daji. "What's the matter with that woman! She really doesn't know how to appreciate favors. To please her, I asked you to dance and sing, but all she did was say things to annoy me. If she weren't the queen, I would have had her beaten to death with the gold-clawed cudgel." At the third watch, King Zhou was totally drunk. "My beauty! I'm still upset by what happened earlier this evening. Would you please dance for me again to drive my depression away?" he asked.

Daji knelt down before him. "I dare not dance again, Your Majesty."

"What's that? What do you mean?"

"Her Majesty reproached me very severely, saying that dancing and singing are the downfall of both the family and the state. I'm sure she's right, and I'm now quite worried. To return your favor, I must serve you to the best of my ability. But what can I do if Her Majesty holds that I've seduced you so that you enjoy only sexual pleasure and become a tyrant? For this I would be condemned by all the nobles and ministers, who would have all my hair pulled out before they put me to death. But even this would be insufficient punishment for the crimes I've committed," she said, tears rolling down her cheeks like rain.

"You only have to concern yourself with me," the king said, and added angrily, "I will depose her let you take her place. Don't worry, my beauty, I know how to deal with this matter."

Daji thanked King Zhou and they continued to indulge in drinking, dancing, sweet music, and love-making day and night.

On the first day of the month, as was the custom, Queen Jiang received congratulations from the royal concubines. She was talking with Concubine Huang and Concubine Yang when Daji's arrival was announced. When she was admitted, she knelt down to greet Queen Jiang, and the latter returned the salutation, asking her to get up and stand beside her.

"This must be Lady Su that we've heard so much about," the two other concubines said.

"Yes, this is indeed," Queen Jiang replied then turned to Daji. "His Majesty spends all his time with you, disregarding state affairs. Why don't you talk to him about it? You've seduced and incited him to all manner of evil," she rebuked. "You're the instigator and must repent at once. If you continue to wreak havoc upon this dynasty, I will deal with you according to the law! You may leave now."

Daji suppressed her temper, thanked the queen, and returned to her own court feeling humiliated.

"You've been sighing and moaning ever since you returned from the queen's palace. What's wrong?" Gun Juan asked.

"I'm the favorite of His Majesty, but I was rudely insulted by the queen in front of Concubine Huang and Concubine Yang. For this I must seek my revenge," Daji said bitterly, gnashing her teeth.

"Oh! You needn't worry about that. His Majesty's already promised that you would become the queen."

"Even though he's promised me, it's impossible with Queen Jiang still alive. Only with her gone can I have the chance to take her place. Otherwise, the ministers will make it difficult for me to live in peace. Have you any good ideas?

You will be richly rewarded if I succeed."

"I'm a mere maidservant. How could I have any ideas like that? Let's consult a minister outside the palace and see what we can do."

Daji pondered for a long while. "How can we get in touch with a minister outside the palace? There are so many eyes and ears here, and there's no one we can trust."

"When His Majesty goes to the royal garden tomorrow, you may ask Fei Zhong privately to come and think up a way for you. All you have to do is promise him that he will be promoted if the plan succeeds. He is well known for his skill in such matters. We can trust him to help us."

"Though your plan's a good one, what shall we do if he refuses to cooperate?"

"Fei Zhong is one of His Majesty's favorites at court. Moreover, he was the one who recommended you to His Majesty. I assure you that he would be glad to be of service to you," Gun Juan spoke with such confidence that Daji was overjoyed.

The next day, when King Zhou went to the royal garden with Daji to enjoy the scenery, Gun Juan secretly summoned Fei Zhong to the Fairy Longevity Palace. She told Fei Zhong, "Your Honor! Here's a private letter to you from Lady Su. Please read it over carefully at home, and keep its contents a secret. Lady Su will be sure to remember any help you can render her. But please hurry!"

Fei Zhong returned home at once, entered his study and read the letter. Daji requested him to contribute a plot against Queen Jiang. "The way I see it, Queen Jiang's the official wife of King Zhou. Her father, East Grand Duke Jiang Huanchu, commands hundreds of thousands of soldiers and generals, and Jiang Wenhuan, her brother, can defeat 10,000 men by himself. How dare I stir up trouble with the queen," Fei Zhong thought to himself. "But if I refuse Daji's orders or even delay in the slightest, she can easily speak ill of me before His Majesty, either in bed when they're enjoying themselves or at the table when His Majesty's half drunk, and I will surely lose my life."

Fei Zhong could not set his mind at rest. He felt as if there were thorns pricking his back. He thought about Daji's proposal all day long but was unable to decide how to deal with the problem. He paced to and fro, numb as a drunken man. Just as he was racking his brains, he caught sight of a stranger walking in front of him. The man was broad-shouldered, about fifteen feet tall, and looked tough and brave.

"Who are you?" Fei Zhong asked.

The stranger knelt down. "My name's Jiang Huan," he replied.

"How long have you served in my place?"

"It's already been five years since I left East Lu and came here. I'm very grateful to you for the way you've treated me. I don't know how to repay you. Seeing you look so worried, I meant to stay out of your way; I hope you will pardon me for interrupting you."

When he heard that Jiang Huan was from East Lu and shared the queen's surname, a plot suddenly leaped into Fei Zhong's mind. "You may get up, Jiang Huan. I would like you to do something for me. If you accomplish this mission, I will reward you generously with wealth and honor."

"I will do everything within my power to carry out your orders. I would even dare to rush into fire or leap into boiling water on your behalf."

"I had no idea how to solve the problem at hand, but seeing you has given me the perfect solution. If you succeed, you will be promoted and wear a golden belt around your waist," Fei Zhong promised.

"That is the most I could hope for. I will do just as you order," Jiang Huan replied with great sincerity.

Fei Zhong leaned over and whispered the entire plot into Jiang Huan's ear. "If our plot succeeds, both of us will be rewarded with boundless wealth and power. But you must keep this absolutely secret, or else will only meet disasters," he warned.

Jiang Huan nodded in silent agreement and left the place. Fei Zhong hastily sent a note to Gun Juan telling Daji what he was planning to do. Several days later King Zhou was relaxing

at the Fairy Longevity Palace when Daji said, "Your love for
me has caused you to be absent from the Grand Hall for nearly ten months now. I pray that you hold court tomorrow morning so as not to lose the respect of your ministers."

"You're right. Your words are as virtuous as those of the
great empresses of old. I will appear tomorrow in the Grand
Hall and deal with state affairs, for this is your wish, my
lady."

The next morning, he left the Fairy Longevity Palace in
his coach, with generals and soldiers, carrying red lanterns and
fragrant incense, guarding him closely. The magnificent train
had passed through the Dragon Virtue Hall and come to the
Central Palace Tower when a man, fourteen feet tall, and
wearing a red scarf, leaped out from behind a corner. He held
a sword in hand, and was fierce as tiger.

"You wicked and lascivious tyrant! You've drowned your
reason in wine and sex. I've come by order of my mistress to
put you to death so that the Shang Dynasty won't come to an
end. The power to rule over the kingdom shall pass into the
hands of my mistress' father," he cried, swinging his mighty
sword at King Zhou, but the king was immediately surrounded
by a cordon of generals and guards. The assassin was forced
back, seized and tightly bound up. When he was thrown on the
ground, he knelt before the king.

King Zhou was both shocked and enraged, yet he continued on his way, entered the Grand Hall, and ascended the
throne. After the greeting ceremonies were over, the king ordered Huang Feihu and Bi Gan to approach the throne.
"Ministers! Something quite extraordinary happened this morning. A man attacked me near the Central Palace Tower with a
sword. I've no idea who is behind this plot."

Huang Feihu was stunned. "Who was the general on duty
last night?" he demanded sharply.

Lu Xiong stepped out and knelt down before the king. "I
was on duty, but neither my guards nor myself found anyone
suspicious in the palace. The assassin may have entered the palace at the fifth watch among the ministers who came here to
see Your Majesty on state affairs," he explained.

Huang Feihu ordered that the assassin be brought to the court and when he was pushed in, King Zhou asked, "Who will interrogate him."

Fei Zhong stepped forward and knelt down before King Zhou. "Though your servant is lacking in talent, I will handle the case and report it to you as quickly as possible," he said. Though he was not a judicial official, he sought this task so as to complete the trap to ensnare Queen Jiang and prevent other officials from uncovering the truth. He held the trial outside the palace gate, and without having to apply any torture, the assassin willingly pleaded guilty. Having obtained a full confession, Fei Zhong returned and reported the case. All the court officials listened carefully, not knowing that it was a preconceived plot.

"I dare not submit my report about the trial, Your Majesty, unless you exempt me from guilt for making such a report," Fei Zhong pleaded.

"You certainly won't be judged guilty for reporting the results of the case."

"The assassin is Jiang Huan, a general under Jiang Huanchu, the East Grand Duke. He was ordered by Queen Jiang to put you to death as part of a conspiracy to usurp the throne and replace you with her father. Thanks to the blessings of your ancestors, the kindness of Heaven and earth, and to the good fortune of Your Majesty, their plot has been exposed and the assassin arrested. I pray that Your Majesty discuss this case with your ministers and come up with a verdict," Fei Zhong said.

King Zhou banged his fist down on his desk. "Madame Jiang is my wife and Queen. How can she be so reckless, despite the relationship between us, as to commit treason!" he cried out in anger. "Conspiracies are difficult to uncover, and rebellious cliques aren't easy to guard against. I will appoint Concubine Huang of the West Palace as Chief Justice of the trial for this case."

When he had returned, violent as thunder, to the Fairy Longevity Palace, a heated discussion raged among the ministers in the Grand Hall, but no one could determine whether the alleged facts of the case were true or not.

"Queen Jiang is virtuous and kind and runs palace affairs strictly according to the regulations. This case is rather complicated, and it's likely that there are hidden conspirators involved," Supreme Minister Yang Ren said to Huang Feihu. "We must remain here and wait for Concubine Huang's report before we determine the truth."

Meanwhile, Queen Jiang was kneeling on the ground as the court herald read the king's decree:

> The queen is enthroned in the Central Palace. As the highest ranking female in the kingdom, she is equal in status to the king. Nonetheless, she has failed to heighten her vigilance, refine her virtues, observe the good conduct befitting her sex, or help the king rule the nation properly. Now she has committed the crime of treason, dispatching her underling, Jiang Huan, to the Central Palace Tower to assassinate the king, but he has already been arrested. The assassin has confessed his guilt and has submitted a statement to the effect that the queen and her father conspired against the king in violation of the rites governing the relations between husband and wife and between the king and his ministers. The queen is now under arrest and will be sent to the West Palace for trial. The case will be dealt with severely.

When the herald finished reading, Queen Jiang burst into tears. "Who has so shamelessly condemned this innocent woman?" she cried out. "I've served the king with diligence and frugality for years, daring not commit the slightest error, just as my mother taught me. How can he place me under arrest and send me to trial without even checking the facts? My life now hangs in a balance."

When she arrived at the West Palace, Queen Jiang knelt before Lady Huang. "Heaven and earth know that I am loyal and chaste. I implore you to have pity on me. There are devils that have designs upon me. I earnestly hope that you will base your verdict on my daily behavior and clear me of this unjust charge," she begged.

"The royal decree states that you dispatched Jiang Huan to kill the king in order to place your father on the throne. Should these facts be substantiated, you would be guilty of violating the ethics governing the relationship between husband and wife, and your father, mother, and their close relatives would all be put to death," Lady Huang warned.

"Please hear me out, Lady! My father is in charge of 200 marquises in East Lu. He holds one of the highest posts in the government, and as father-in-law of His Majesty, is also a royal relative. Since his daughter is the queen and he himself the highest ranking duke, he has no motive to usurp the throne. Moreover, my son Yin Jiao is the Crown Prince. When His Majesty passes away, I shall become the queen dowager, with the privilege of being worshiped at the royal temple. Yet I would lose that privilege if my father took the throne. Though I am a woman, I would not act so foolishly as to risk losing all of this. Furthermore, there are so many nobles in this country that if we did perpetrate such a crime, they would immediately attack us with their armies, and the state would soon collapse. I beg you to report these facts to His Majesty."

But before she could finish, a herald was sent from the king, urging Lady Huang to complete the trial, and Lady Huang rushed to the Fairy Longevity Palace.

"Has she confessed yet?" the king asked.

Concubine Huang repeated the queen's statement with great accuracy. "I urge Your Majesty to treat the queen with sympathy; she is obviously the victim of injustice. Don't allow your wife to be wronged by a conspiracy framed by unseen hands. Have mercy on her, for she's the mother of the Crown Prince," she implored.

King Zhou listened carefully to the queen's statement and Huang's opinions. "The report from Concubine Huang is quite clear. If the queen is being framed, there must be a complex reason behind it," he pondered, and while he was thus torn by doubt, he noticed Daji smiling coldly beside him. "What are you smiling about without saying anything, my beauty?"

"I think that Concubine Huang must have been deceived. The guilty always brag and praise themselves as virtuous while pushing the blame onto others. Treason against Your Majesty is a very grave crime. We cannot expect her to confess easily. Jiang Huan was in the employ of her father; this is one fact she cannot deny. With so many concubines and maids in this palace, why is Queen Jiang the only woman mentioned in his confession? The reason is clear. She won't never tell the truth until she is severely tortured. Doesn't that make sense, Your Majesty?" Daji suggested.

"Yes, you're absolutely right, my beauty," King Zhou agreed.

Concubine Huang lost her patience. "Please don't talk like that, Su Daji. The queen is the wife of the king and the first lady of the country. Ever since ancient times, a queen may be deposed but never beheaded, even if she has committed a great error. That is the law," she refuted.

"The law is applicable to every person in the country. Even the king, who rules and educates the people on the model from Heaven, isn't permitted to deal with the law in a selfish or unjust way. Everyone, rich or poor, common or noble, is equal before the law. Your Majesty, you may decide. If Queen Jiang refuses to confess, one of her eyes must be removed. As the eyes are the external manifestation of the soul, she will certainly tell the truth, for she would be unwilling to lose an eye. Let the ministers understand that this is the way the law must be enforced," Daji argued.

"You're quite right, Daji," King Zhou supported her.

Concubine Huang started with fright but had no choice but to return to the West Palace. Entering her chamber, she wept in despair. "Your Majesty! Daji must be your deadly enemy from a previous incarnation. She's proposed to the king that one of your eyes be taken out if you fail to make the confession she wants. To save yourself from suffering, you'd better make a false statement. No king in history has ever put his queen to death; the worst that could happen is to be deposed and confined," Lady Huang begged tearfully.

Queen Jiang was also in tears. "Sister! Though you speak out of concern for me, I've been educated in the ethics ever since childhood; how can I confess to such a humiliating crime as treason? That would be the greatest insult to my father and my ancestors. Dispatching an assassin to kill one's husband is a crime so serious that to admit guilt would make my father a treacherous minister and me an unprincipled woman, cursed by later generations. How can I make a false confession? My eyes are expendable. I won't confess even if I'm thrown into a caldron full of boiling oil, or minced to bits and pieces, or beaten to a pulp. I would rather have my flesh and bones smashed than compromise my chastity, purity, and loyalty."

She was still speaking when an order arrived from King Zhou to remove her eyes if she still held out.

"Hurry! Hurry! Confess, Your Majesty!" Concubine Huang urged.

"How can I! I would rather die...!" the queen cried pitifully.

The royal guards, impatient by nature, grabbed her and gouged out one eye with a dagger. Blood streamed down her face, staining her clothing. She fell on the floor unconscious. Weeping at the sight, Concubine Huang ordered her attendants to help the queen up and offer first aid, but it took a long time before she came to. The royal guards placed the queen's eye on a tray and returned to the Fairy Longevity Palace with Concubine Huang.

"Has that worthless woman confessed to her crime?" King Zhou asked Concubine Huang.

"No, as she never committed it. She would rather die than admit to disloyalty. We thus removed one of her eyes as Your Majesty ordered," Concubine Huang said, presenting the tray to him.

Looking at the bleeding eye, King Zhou lowered his head and remained silent. There was deep regret in his heart, but it was already too late. He turned to Daji. "I took your advice and had her eye gouged out. What shall we do if this cruel act of mine becomes known and she still refuses to plead guilty?"

"We must now force her to confess to treason, or else all

the ministers will criticize us. Her father may even raise an army and launch an attack on us for making his daughter suffer cruelly without reason," Daji replied.

King Zhou remained silent, for he knew not how to deal with the matter. Finally, he asked Daji, "What's the proper course of action for us now?"

"Since we've already taken the first step, we're compelled to follow through with the second. We will be able to live in peace if she admits to her guilt, but we will have a great deal of trouble if she doesn't. We must use violence now. Concubine Huang must prepare a brass dipper and fill it with burning charcoal. If Queen Jiang still refuses to admit to her crime, her hands should be burned in it. The fingers are connected directly to the heart, and the pain will be so unbearable that she will readily admit her guilt."

"According to Concubine Huang's report, Queen Jiang has committed no such crime. If we force her to suffer another cruel torture, the ministers are bound to protest. We've already erred in having her eye taken out; how can we do something like that again?" King Zhou rebuked her.

"You're wrong, Your Majesty! The situation before us is similar to riding on the back of a fierce tiger. We will be devoured instantly if we get off. We mustn't give the nobles and ministers any good reason to oppose us!"

King Zhou said nothing to refute her. "If she still refuses to confess, burn her fingers and hands without mercy!" he ordered.

Concubine Huang was terrified when she heard this and immediately returned to her apartments, where she found Queen Jiang lying in a pool of blood. She burst into tears.

"My virtuous queen! What sin did you commit against Heaven and earth in your previous incarnations that should lead to your suffering like this today!" she cried, helping the queen up. "Worthy Lady! It would be better for you to admit that you're guilty! That empty-headed tyrant believes everything that base woman says. If you still refuse to do as they wish, they will burn your hands with a brass dipper. I couldn't bear to see such brutal torture!"

With blood streaming down her face, Queen Jiang cried, "I've no fear of death. But if you will be witness to my innocence I will be able to die in peace!"

The royal attendants had already fired the charcoal in the brass dipper to a fiery red. As Queen Jiang staunchly refused to yield to the unjust accusation, her hands were pushed into the dipper, and in a moment, skin, flesh, bones, and blood were burned and turned to ashes, giving off a horrible odor which filled the room. The poor queen fainted and collapsed to the ground.

Watching this tragic scene, Concubine Huang felt as if her heart was being pierced by knives. She wept bitterly. But after she regained her strength, she got into her coach and went to see King Zhou.

"Though she's been cruelly and mercilessly tortured, the queen still denies that she's committed the crime she's accused of. Don't you think that someone might have conspired to hurt her? This could become a great calamity in the near future if it were proven true," she told the king.

King Zhou was greatly alarmed. "I followed the advice of Lady Su in this matter. What should I do now?" he said worriedly.

"Don't worry, Your Majesty! As we already have Jiang Huan in our custody, Your Majesty may order that he be brought in and tried together with the queen. She will be unable to make any further denial, and we will obtain a full confession," Daji said, kneeling down.

"That's a very good idea," King Zhou said, feeling much relieved.

Concubine Huang returned to the West Palace and Chao Tian and Chao Lei soon followed in with Jiang Huan. If you want to learn how the queen fared, please read the next chapter.

第八回 方弼方相反朝歌

PRINCES TAKE FLIGHT

When Generals Chao Tian and Chao Lei brought Jiang Huan into the West Palace, Concubine Huang said, "Queen Jiang! Your enemy's arrived."

Queen Jiang opened her eye. "You wretch! Who is it that pays you to make false accusations against me? Heaven will punish you for this!"

"I dared not refuse the orders you gave me. How can you deny that, Your Majesty?"

Concubine Huang became enraged. "Jiang Huan, you vile clod! Queen Jiang's been cruelly tortured, even though she's entirely innocent. For this act, Heaven won't spare you."

In the East Palace, Crown Prince Yin Jiao and his brother Prince Yin Hong were playing chess when the eunuch Yang Rong hurried in.

"Your Highness, a great calamity's about to befall you!"

Yin Jiao was only fourteen years old and Yin Hong two years his junior. Neither of them paid any attention to Yang Rong's report.

"Your Highness! Stop your game. A true disaster's taken place, and will bring both your family and the entire kingdom to ruin," Yang Rong said again.

The two looked up from their game and asked, "What great calamity you say's taking place right here in the palace?"

Yang Rong was all tears. "Someone's dared to slander the queen with a false accusation, and His Majesty's deceived. Her Majesty was tried in the West Palace. When she denied the accusation, one of her eyes was gouged out, and then her hands were burnt to ashes. I urge you to hurry to her rescue."

Yin Jiao let out a roar and ran with his brother to the

West Palace. When they got there and saw the pathetic condition the queen was in, they knelt down beside her and sobbed.

"Why have you been so cruelly tortured, Mother? Even if you had committed a crime, as queen you're not to be subjected to torture."

Hearing their voices, Queen Jiang opened her eye. "My sons! Look at your mother. I've lost my eye and my hands. Jiang Huan's made a false accusation of me, and Daji convinced the king to torture me. You must clear your mother of this injustice and seek revenge," she cried out bitterly, and soon died.

The brothers saw a man still kneeling at one side. "Who's Jiang Huan, and where is he now?" Yin Jiao asked.

Lady Huang pointed to Jiang Huan and said, "That man kneeling there, your mother's deadly enemy."

The crown prince was so enraged that he grabbed a sword hanging on the gate of the West Palace and slashed Jiang Huan in two. In seconds, the ground was covered with blood. But slaying Jiang Huan served only to fire his rage. "I'll cut off Daji's head in revenge for my mother!" Yin Jiao cried, and sword in hand, he flew out of the palace.

Chao Tian and Chao Lei, fearing that the crown prince would kill them next, fled before him to the Fairy Longevity Palace. Concubine Huang was shocked. "The boy's too young to understand what's happening," she said, and called to Yin Hong, "Hurry and tell your brother to come back here at once. I've something to say."

Yin Hong rushed after Yin Jiao. "Brother! Lady Huang wants you to go back at once. She has something urgent to tell you!" he cried.

Yin Jiao heard this and returned to the West Palace.

"Dear prince! You've acted too rashly. Now that you've killed Jiang Huan, how can we ever learn the truth! If he were still alive, I could have tortured him with the burning dipper and found out who was behind him. Now that he's dead, what can I do? I'm afraid Chao Tian and Chao Lei have already reported everything to the king and you'll have trouble soon!" Concubine Huang reprimanded Yin Jiao.

The boys expressed their regrets, but it was too late. Chao Tian and Chao Lei had rushed into the Fairy Longevity Palace. ''The princes are rushing over here with their swords drawn,'' they reported.

"Those treacherous young curs! Their mother sent an assassin to murder me, for which I've yet to put her to death. How dare they try to kill their father! They must die at once. I hereby order Chao Tian and Chao Lei to decapitate those unfilial brats with my Dragon Phoenix sword," the king, infuriated, cried out the order.

Back at the West Palace, Concubine Huang had heard the report that "Chao Tian and Chao Lei are coming with the king's sword to decapitate the two princes." She rushed out to the palace gate, met the two generals, and demanded to know what they were about.

"By order of His Majesty, we've come to cut off the heads of the two princes as punishment for attempting to kill their father."

"You stupid fools! The two princes chased you out of here just now. Why don't you go and look for them in the East Palace? Why do you come looking for them here? You're just utilizing His Majesty's orders as an excuse to wander around the inner palace and insult His Majesty's concubines and maidservants. You two wretches are out to cheat and offend His Majesty. I'd chop your donkey heads off right now, if you didn't have the king's sword. Get out of here immediately!"

Frightened, Chao Tian and Chao Lei immediately made their way to the East Palace.

Concubine Huang went back inside. "That tyrant's killed his wife and now he wants to kill his sons. I can't protect you here, so you'd better seek shelter in the Fragrant Palace with Concubine Yang for a few days. You'll be safe once a powerful minister speaks to His Majesty on your behalf," she told the two princes.

The two princes knelt down and expressed their gratitude. "Dear Lady! How can we thank you for your kindness? Mother's still lying here exposed to the elements. If you could provide her with a coffin, we'll never forget you for the rest of our lives."

"You had better leave here as soon as possible. I'll try to do as you say," the concubine reassured them.

The two princes left the palace and made their way to Fragrant Palace. They found Concubine Yang leaning on the gate, anxious to hear about the fate of Queen Jiang. The two princes ran forward, knelt down before her and started to cry. This surprised Concubine Yang. "How's your mother, my good princes?" she asked them.

Yin Jiao was all tears again. "My father's been taken in by Daji and does whatever she says. He's tortured mother to death. And now he listens to Daji again and wants to kill us. I beg you to save our lives."

Concubine Yang wept aloud. "My good princes, come in quickly," she told them. She thought to herself, "When the generals find that the princes are not in the East Palace, they're bound to come here looking for them. I'll get rid of them first and then decide on the next step." She went out again and stood at the gate of the palace. She soon saw the generals bounding up like wolves. "Guards! Arrest these men. This is the inner palace, where intrusion is forbidden under penalty of death," she ordered.

Chao Tian and Chao Lei stepped forward respectfully. "Honorable lady! We're Chao Tian and Chao Lei. On His Majesty's order, we're here to search for the two princes," they said.

"The princes are in the East Palace. How dare you be so rude as to come to my Fragrant Palace! I would have you arrested if you weren't sent by the king. Get out of here now!" Concubine Yang shouted at the top of her voice.

Chao Tian and Chao Lei dared not say anything and left. When they were outside, Chao Lei said to his brother, "We've been to three palaces already, but we still can't find the princes. We're strangers here and don't know our way around. We should return to the Fairy Longevity Palace and report this to His Majesty."

After the generals left, Concubine Yang returned to her apartments. "This isn't a safe place for you, dear princes.

There are too many ears and eyes about, and it's difficult to predict what the king'll do next. I suggest that you go to the Grand Hall and speak with Wei Zi, Ji Zi, Wei Ziyan and Huang Feihu. Even if your father makes trouble for you, they'll protect you," she told the princes.

The two princes kowtowed to her in gratitude and bade her farewell in tears. When they left, Concubine Yang sat alone on a silk cushion in her own room. "Queen Jiang was the queen, but she died tragically, a victim of torture and injustice. What can I expect as a mere concubine! Daji makes use of her position to deceive the king. If someone reports to her that the two princes were here, I'll be found guilty and suffer terrible tortures. Though I've served the king for many years, I haven't borne him any children. The crown prince is his own child, yet he feels no fatherly affection for him. Now that he's killed his wife, and ordered his sons' death, the sacred relationships between husband and wife, father and son, and king and ministers have been defiled. My future's dark; very little hope remains," she pondered, and mourned over her fate.

She then shut herself in her inner room and hanged herself. When King Zhou learned of her death, he was puzzled as to why she had taken such a step, and ordered that her coffin be placed in the White Tiger Hall, according to the customary funeral rites.

When Chao Tian and Chao Lei arrived at the Fairy Longevity Palace, they saw Concubine Huang entering to make her report.

"Is Queen Jiang dead?" King Zhou asked her.

"Yes, she is. But before she took her last breath, she cried out, 'I've served His Majesty for sixteen years and borne him two sons, one of them the crown prince. I've always behaved myself carefully, performing my duties faithfully. I still don't know who it is that dispatched Jiang Huan to assassinate His Majesty and to accuse me of treason. Though I've been queen, this is of no more significance than fleeting clouds, now that the king's love has flowed away like a river. I'm dying more wretchedly than the birds and beasts. I cannot right the injustice done me and can only trust that future generations will judge me fairly.' Now her corpse is still lying in the West Palace. I pray that Your Majesty might take it into consideration that she's the mother of the crown prince, and grant her a coffin and the right to be placed in the White Tiger Hall in accordance with the burial rites. That way your officials will be satisfied, and you'll preserve your sovereignly virtue."

King Zhou approved her request, and when she had left, turned to Chao Tian and Chao Lei. "Where are the princes?"

"We looked in the East Palace, but couldn't find them. They aren't in the West Palace or the Fragrant Palace either."

"If they weren't there, then they must have fled to the Grand Hall. Go arrest them and put them to death," King Zhou ordered.

The Grand Hall was still crowded with ministers and officials waiting for news from the palace. Suddenly Huang Feihu heard the sound of flurried footsteps, and saw the panic-stricken princes rushing into the hall. Going forward to meet them, he asked, "What are you so upset about, my good princes?"

"Please save our lives, General Huang!" Yin Jiao cried out, and all tears, he clung tightly to Huang Feihu's robes. "My father's performed every sort of terrible deed ever since he placed his trust in Daji. When I saw my mother die from the cruel torture he ordered, I cut Jiang Huan in two and wanted to kill Daji. Chao Tian brought this to my father, and now he's ordered our deaths. I beg you to take pity on my dead mother and save our lives so as to prolong the rule of the Shang Dynasty."

All the ministers approached the princes in tears. "How can we possibly disregard the unjust death of Her Majesty? We'll strike the bells and beat the drums, and ask to see His Majesty so that we can discover the identity of the real criminal and right the injustice done to Her Majesty," they said in one voice.

"The king's failed to play his proper role in the kingdom; he's slaughtered his queen and attempted to kill his sons; he's tortured the loyal to death with burning pillars," a voice exploded like thunder at the west end of the hall. "If we're true heroes, we should right the injustice done to the queen and seek revenge for the princes! Yet all we do now is stand around crying like women! As the old saying goes, 'A good bird chooses a solid tree to roost in; a good minister chooses a good master to serve.' The king's recent behavior attests to the fact that he's no longer fit to act as the ruler of this nation, and we should be ashamed to serve him. It would be better for all of us to leave Zhaoge in revolt and select a new ruler to protect our country."

Everyone turned to see who dared to speak so recklessly. It was Fang Bi and Fang Xiang, Chiefs of Guards in the Grand Hall.

Huang Feihu was angry. "How dare you speak like this? There are senior statesmen and supreme ministers here to discuss this matter; there's certainly no need for the likes of you to take part. You should be arrested! Get out of here at once!" he swore at them.

Fang Bi and Fang Xiang dared not argue with Huang Feihu. They lowered their heads and remained silent. But Huang Feihu had also realized that the dynasty was in trouble. He remained quiet, watching Wei Zi, Ji Zi, Bi Gan and the others sigh and fret and gnash their teeth. None knew what to do.

"What happened today is just as the Taoist predicted. An ancient saying goes, 'An improper ruler will have corrupt ministers!' The king's unjustly cut off the head of Grand Tutor Du Yuanxian, cruelly killed Supreme Minister Mei Bo with the burning pillar, tortured his queen to death, and ordered the execution of his two sons. This is bound to bring smiles on the faces of the wicked among us. It is a pity that the Shang Dynasty will fall to ruin and we'll all be prisoners before long," Supreme Minister Yang Ren said.

"You're right, Supreme Minister," Huang Feihu agreed.

The rest of the officials kept silent while the two princes wept bitterly. Fang Bi and Fang Xiang forced their way through the crowd. "King Zhou's a wicked tyrant. In ordering his sons' execution, he's trying to sever his own ancestral line, and in killing his wife, he's violated the ethical code. We'll escort the two princes to East Lu and raise an army to uproot him. This is a rebellion," they cried out.

Fang Bi picked up Yin Jiao and Fang Xiang Yin Hong, and with the princes on their backs, they left the capital through the south gate. Fortunately they were both strong, for they had to fight their way through numerous officials who tried to stop them.

All the ministers were astonished at what was taking place, except Huang Feihu, who remained entirely unmoved. Vice Prime Minister Bi Gan approached him. "Why do you remain in complete silence while this rebellion is taking place?" he asked Huang Feihu.

"It is truly a pity that among so many ministers, none are as loyal as they. They may be vulgar and uncivilized, but they cannot bear to have seen the queen die unjustly and to see the princes die for no reason. They must have realized that they were so low in rank that they couldn't possibly deliver admonitions directly to the king, so they chose to carry away the two princes. They risk their lives doing this, for they know that they'll probably die if the king sends men after them on horseback. They were acting exclusively out of conscience and loyalty," Huang Feihu explained with a sigh.

At this moment, hurried footsteps were heard at the back of the court, and Chao Tian and Chao Lei entered carrying the king's sword. "Ministers!" they cried out, "have any of you seen the princes here?"

Huang Feihu told the Chao brothers what had happened and urged them to chase after the four of them. But this was a terrifying thought to the Chao brothers, for they knew that Fang Bi was thirty-six feet tall and Fang Xiang thirty-four and that they were not to be trifled with. They also knew that Huang Feihu was deliberately putting them in a difficult position. They returned to the Fairy Longevity Palace and reported what they had learned to King Zhou.

The king was greatly enraged. "Go and arrest the Fang brothers and the two princes and put them all to death without further delay!" he bellowed.

"Fang Bi is very strong and brave. I'm afraid that we can

never capture him. Only Prince Huang Feihu can carry out your request," Chao Tian suggested.

When the order was issued, Huang Feihu smiled. "I'm well aware that it is Chao Tian who's placed this burden on my shoulders." He took the king's sword and left the palace. Generals Huang Ming, Zhou Ji, Long Huan and Wu Yan came forward and offered to go with him, but he replied, "You needn't come with me. I can manage on my own."

He mounted his divine Rainbow Ox, which could cover 800 *li* in one day, and rode off at high speed.

Carrying the young princes on their backs, Fang Bi and Fang Xiang could only walk thirty *li* a day. While they were discussing what route to take, they noticed Huang Feihu rushing towards them on his Rainbow Ox. Trembling in fright, they cried to the two princes, "We've acted much too impulsively. Now that death is staring us in the face, what shall we do?"

"How can you say things like that? You've saved our lives," the two princes replied in wonder.

"Look! Marshal Huang's come to take us back. We're sure to be executed," Fang Bi said.

When Huang Feihu arrived before them, the two young princes knelt down on the road. "Marshal Huang! Do you come to bring us back?"

Huang Feihu immediately threw himself down on the ground. "I should die for what I've done. Your Highnesses, please stand up," he begged.

"What are you going to do with us, Marshal?" Yin Jiao asked.

"By His Majesty's order, I came here with the royal sword for you two princes to take your lives at once. I myself daren't commit such a crime, but I've got no choice but to obey the king! I beg you to do it swiftly."

Yin Jiao was on his knees again. "You know we have been grievously wronged. My mother was killed after being cruelly tortured, and if we die, there'll be no one left in our family. Please have pity on us and give us a chance to live. Your generosity will never be forgotten," he implored.

Huang Feihu remained on his knees. "I know quite well that you both are the victims of injustice. But the king's order gives me no choice. If I set you free, I'll have committed the crime of deceiving him, and should I not set you free, I'll commit the sin of going against my conscience."

Yin Jiao realized that he and his brother had little chance of escaping doom. "Marshal Huang! You're certainly right to follow the king's order, but I beg your leniency and help us in another way."

He decided to appeal to Huang Feihu's kind heart.

"What's that? Please tell me, Your Highness."

"You may cut off my head and take it to the king, but take pity on my younger brother. Set him free and allow him to flee elsewhere. When he grows up, he'll lead a big army and seek revenge for the injustice perpetrated on our innocent mother."

At this, Yin Hong came forward and interrupted his brother. "Marshal Huang! This is all wrong! He is the crown prince. And I'm young and have no talents. You should cut off my head and take it to the king. If you let him go to East Lu or West Qi and seek revenge for the death of my innocent mother and myself, I won't regret dying now," he begged.

Yin Jiao put his arms around his brother and cried bitterly. "How could I bear to see my younger brother meet such a cruel death!"

The two brothers each argued that the other should live. Observing the scene, Fang Bi and Fang Xiang found tears rolling down their cheeks. "How sad it all is!" they exclaimed.

Huang Feihu was moved by the princes, and by the devotion the Fang brothers showed to the princes. Tears welled up in his eyes. "Fang Bi! Fang Xiang! Stop your weeping. Princes, worry no more! I've got an idea," he told them, "but it must remain a secret among the five of us, for the slightest leak will spell death for every member of my family. Fang Bi, you escort the princes to East Lu, to their grandfather Jiang Huanchu. Fang Xiang, you go and see E Chongyu, and tell him that I've released the princes and that he should join with Jiang Huanchu in an attack on Zhaoge from two different directions. We must remove traitors from the palace and right the wrong done to Queen Jiang."

"Since we left the palace this morning in a great hurry, we brought no funds with us. How shall we make the journey?" Fang Bi asked.

After thinking it over, Huang Feihu said, "Though I've got no money in my pocket, I'll give you my jade pendant inlaid with gold. You may easily exchange it for 100 taels of silver to cover the expenses of your journey. Take good care of yourselves."

Huang Feihu returned to Zhaoge at dusk and saw that all the ministers had gathered before the palace gate. He dismounted from his Rainbow Ox, and met Bi Gan.

"How did it go, Marshal Huang?" Bi Gan asked.

"I couldn't overtake them and had to return," Huang Feihu told him.

All the officials were delighted. He then entered the court to see King Zhou.

"On your order, I pursued the princes and the Fang brothers for seventy *li*, all the way to the triple crossroads, but failed to catch up with them. I made enquiries along the way, but no one had seen them. I had to return," he reported.

"My unfilial sons and those two rebellious officials have been lucky this time. You may retire now. We'll discuss this further tomorrow," the king replied.

"If you let them get away, they'll be sure to flee to Jiang Huanchu, and he'll raise a powerful army against us," Daji reminded him, after Huang Feihu had left. "Since Grand Tutor Wen Zhong's far away at the front, let's dispatch Yin Pobai and Lei Kai with 3,000 cavalrymen to pursue them through the night. We must kill the plant by uprooting it, so as to prevent any calamity."

"You're right. This is just as I wish," King Zhou said, and gave the order, "Yin Pobai and Lei Kai lead 3,000 flying horsemen to seize the two princes without delay."

Huang Feihu was alone in his rear hall. "The king's acted improperly. People are grumbling and Heaven's dissatisfied. The state will collapse into chaos and no one will be able to live in peace," he thought to himself. "What shall I do now?" His meditation was interrupted when the arrival of Generals Yin and Lei was announced.

"I've just come back from the court. What is it that you want?" Huang Feihu asked when the two entered and greeted him.

"By order of His Majesty, we must take 3,000 flying horsemen to pursue the princes and the Fang brothers, and put them to death," they reported. "We've come for men and equipment."

"If they capture the princes, then all my efforts will have been in vain," Huang Feihu thought to himself, and said, "It's late now. How can I possibly supply you with the men and horses straight away. Come back here at the fifth watch tomorrow morning, and I'll have everything ready then."

Since Huang Feihu was commander and Yin and Lei were under his command, they dared not utter a word, and so they left. Then Huang Feihu summoned his general Zhou Ji. "Yin Pobai was here with the king's official tally and asked me to supply him with 3,000 flying horsemen to pursue the princes. Select only the old, the weak and the infirm. General Yin Pobai may take them along with him at the fifth watch," he ordered.

The next morning, Yin Pobai and Lei Kai arrived and found that their men were both old and weak and nearly unable to march. This army of stumbling and floundering men was certainly something to laugh at.

By now the Fang brothers had already traveled for two days with the young princes.

"Now that we've come this far, I'm afraid we need to spend some money. Though the Marshal gave us his precious jade piece, selling it may get us into trouble if someone realizes whom it belongs to," Fang Bi said to Fang Xiang. "We've come to a fork in the road. One road leads to the east and the other to the south. Let's send the princes on their way, while we head off in an entirely different direction. This way all the four of us won't be captured."

"You're right, Brother," Fang Xiang agreed.

Fang Bi then turned to the two princes. "There's something we have to tell you, Your Highnesses. Though we're loyal and brave, we're crude and uncultivated. When we saw you wrongly treated, we became infuriated and fled with you from Zhaoge. In so doing we declared our rebellion against the king. However, we didn't bring enough money to defray the expenses for our journey. What shall we do? Though Marshal Huang's given us his jade piece, we can't sell it for fear that the secret will be discovered." he said, and suggested, "After thinking it over, we've decided that it'll be safer if we go our own ways. We apologize for not accompanying you all the way."

"You're right, Generals, but we're too young to find our own way. What shall we do?" asked Yin Jiao.

"This road leads to East Lu and that to the South Grand Dukedom. Both are busy highways full of travelers, and you needn't worry about losing your way," Fang Bi reassured them.

"Where will you two generals go? When shall we meet again?" Yin Jiao asked.

"We'll take refuge in any dukedom that'll take us in, and join your vanguard when your army starts advancing towards Zhaoge," Fang Xiang replied.

The four of them bade farewell to each other in tears.

"Which way will you take, Brother?" Yin Jiao asked.

"As you please, Brother," Yin Hong replied.

"I'll head for East Lu, and you can make your way to the south. When I speak with grandfather, I'll tell him about mother's sufferings, and he'll certainly mobilize his troops. I'll inform you of our route, and you may join us in the attack on Zhaoge. We'll take Daji alive to get our revenge. Don't forget this, Brother."

Yin Hong nodded and wept. He said, "Brother! When shall we meet again?"

They burst into tears and set off on their separate ways.

Yin Hong's tears did not dry as he walked alone on his way. He was young, and brought up with every possible comfort in the palace, had never experienced the hardships of travel. He walked in fits and starts, and before long became both hungry and tired. When he was living in the palace he wore nothing but satin and ate only the finest delicacies, and certainly never had to beg anyone for anything. When he arrived in a small village, his hunger led him to a home where he saw the family eating dinner. He walked in.

"Bring over food. Let the prince eat!" he ordered.

When the family looked up and saw him in red satin, both smart and gallant, they hurriedly stood up. "Take a seat, please, and we'll bring you food," they said with respect and put more rice and dishes on the table for their unexpected guest.

Yin Hong sat down to his meal. He soon finished and stood up. "I'm sorry to trouble you for this meal, and hope that I'll be able to repay your kindness some day," he said gratefully.

"Where are you going? Where do you come from? What's your honorable surname?" the cottagers asked him.

"I'm the younger son of King Zhou. My name's Yin Hong. I am now heading south to see E Chongyu, the South Grand Duke," he told them.

When they learned that the boy was a prince, they immediately knelt down on the ground and kowtowed. "Your Highness! Please pardon us for not offering you a warm welcome, as we were ignorant of your honorable arrival in our village."

"Does this highway lead to the South Grand Dukedom?" Yin Hong asked.

"Yes, it does, Your Highness," they replied.

Ying Hong set out again on his way. He could only manage to cover twenty or thirty *li* that day. Accustomed to all the comforts of the palace, he was naturally unable to walk very far.

That night he came to a place where there were neither houses nor inns, and could find nowhere to spend the night. He was just beginning to get agitated when he spotted an ancient temple that stood in a dense forest of pine trees, two or three *li* ahead of him. He raced towards it and discovered a board set horizontally over the gate. From the characters carved on it, Yin Hong learned that this was the Temple of

Emperor Xuanyuan.

He entered and knelt down before the image of the ancient emperor. "You were a virtuous and saintly emperor. You taught the people how to make clothing, to observe the rites and laws and to conduct themselves in the marketplace. You were honored and respected by all the people. I belong to the thirty-first generation of the Shang Dynasty and am the son of King Zhou. My father has behaved improperly, killing his wife and then trying to kill his sons. I have chosen to flee from these woes and must spend the night in your temple. I shall leave here first thing in the morning. If you are kind enough to protect me for the night, I shall rebuild your temple and recast your image in gold," he prayed.

He was so tired from the day's walking that he collapsed in front of the image and fell fast asleep.

Meanwhile Yin Jiao made his way towards East Lu, but had traveled only forty or fifty *li* before dusk fell. He found himself in front of a Grand Tutor's mansion, as he could tell from the board hanging on the gate.

"As this is the home of a high official, I can rest for the night here and resume my journey early tomorrow morning," Yin Jiao thought and called out, "Is anybody home?"

But no one answered. He entered the compound and heard someone sighing deeply over a poem:

> As prime minister for years,
> Loyalty still wells up in my heart.
> For the benefit of the state,
> Never once did I act for personal gain.
> A sudden spectre appears in the palace,
> The innocent turn into ghosts!
> Retired, I care still for the kingdom.
> Sadly I watch the downfall of this reign!

Yin Jiao listened, and then asked once again, "Is anybody home?"

"Who is that?" called a voice from inside.

It was dark out by then, and neither of them could see

clearly. "I'm just passing through on my way to visit a relative. As it's late now, I'm wondering if you would kindly permit me to stay here for the night. I'll be leaving very early tomorrow morning," Yin Jiao explained politely.

"Are you from Zhaoge? From your voice, I can tell you're a native of the capital."

"Yes, I am."

"Where do you live there, inside the city walls or beyond?"

"In the city, sir."

"Come on in, please. I've some questions for you."

When Yin Jiao walked in, he found much to his surprise that the old man speaking to him was none other than Shang Rong who, equally surprised, instantly knelt down before the crown prince.

"Why do you come here, Your Highness? Excuse me for not going out to welcome you, as I had absolutely no idea that you were here. As crown prince, why is it that you're traveling alone? Something unfortunate must have happened in the capital. Please sit down and tell me all the details."

Yin Jiao broke into tears and told Shang Rong all about King Zhou's cruelties.

Shang Rong stamped his foot. "That damned tyrant is inhuman!" he cried. "He's already severed the sacred ties between husband and wife, father and son, and between himself and the ministers. Though I've retired from political life, I haven't stopped worrying about what takes place in the palace. Like a storm blowing up from nowhere, the palace has been thrown into chaos, the likes of which have never been seen before. Why did all the ministers keep their mouths shut when the king began to act in this fashion? Rest easy, Your Highness! I'll return to Zhaoge with you and directly petition His Majesty to abandon his course of misconduct and save the kingdom from doom."

Shang Rong then ordered his attendants to prepare wine and fine dishes for the prince, while he himself started on his petition to the king. He would deliver it as soon as he reached Zhaoge.

On King Zhou's order, Generals Yin Pobai and Lei Kai took 3,000 mounted soldiers in pursuit of the princes, but because every one of them was either old or infirm, they were incapable of riding quickly and could only cover some thirty *li* per day. When they finally reached the triple fork in the road, Lei Kai said, "Brother! Let's select 100 stronger men from among this lot and divide them into two platoons. You take fifty of them in the direction of East Lu and I'll head south with the other half. The rest can all wait here. What do you think?"

"This is certainly a very good idea. Otherwise, we can only expect to cover twenty or thirty *li* a day with this bunch of worn-out warriors."

"If you catch up with them, bring them back here and wait for me. Likewise, I'll wait for you here if I succeed on my mission."

"I'll do as you say," Yin Pobai said.

If you want to learn what happened to the two princes, please read the next chapter.

THE PRIME MINISTER'S DEATH

General Lei Kai took his fifty soldiers southwards. At dusk Lei Kai gave the order, "Let's eat our fill, and then continue through the night. The princes cannot have gotten very far ahead of us."

The soldiers did as he said and they were soon back on the road. Near the second watch, his soldiers, wearied of the fast pace of advance, began napping on the saddles, many of them nearly falling off. "Traveling at this speed in the dark, efforts will have been in vain. It would be better to rest now and go after them again early in the morning when our strength's renewed," Lei Kai thought, then ordered his men, "See if there's a village nearby where we can rest for the night."

His order greatly pleased the soldiers, who raised their torches and saw in the distance a village in the dense pine trees. When they got there, however, they found that it was nothing more than a temple. One of the soldiers reported to the general, "There's an ancient temple ahead. We can spend the night there."

"That is an excellent idea," Lei Kai replied.

When he arrived at the gate, Lei Kai learned from the horizontal board that it was the Temple of Emperor Xuanyuan. He saw that there were no monks there to take care of it. When the soldiers pushed the door open and entered, their torch light fell upon a youth sleeping soundly before the emperor's image. Looking closely, Lei Kai saw that it was Prince Yin Hong.

"If we had continued further, we certainly would have missed him. Fate has delivered us here." Lei Kai sighed, and cried to Yin Hong, "Your Highness! Your Highness!"

Yin Hong woke up and was astonished to find so many people crowded into the temple. As soon as he caught sight of Lei Kai, he called out, "General Lei!"

"Your Highness! By His Majesty's order, I've come here to ask you to return to the palace. Hundreds of officials have been speaking on your behalf, and you needn't worry."

"Say no more, General. I know very well that it is utterly impossible to escape from this great calamity. I'm not afraid of death, but I'm so tired from my journey that I can no longer walk. Would you be kind enough as to let me ride on your horse?"

"You may ride on my horse, and I'll follow on foot, Your Highness."

And thus they made their way directly to the fork in the road as previously arranged.

After he had traveled east for two days, General Yin Pobai came to Fengyun, a small village, and ten *li* beyond he noticed a big mansion with high walls and a horizontal board with "The House of the Grand Tutor" inscribed in gold. This, he soon discovered, was the residence of the retired Prime Minister Shang Rong. He jumped off his horse and entered the mansion to pay a visit to his patron. When he saw that Shang Rong was dining and drinking with Yin Jiao, he stepped forward.

"Your Highness! Prime Minister!" he announced himself. "By order of His Majesty, I've come here to ask Your Highness to return to the palace at once."

"Welcome, General Yin!" Shang Rong replied. "I often wonder how it is that there are 400 civil and military officials at Zhaoge, yet not one of them dares to admonish the king. In their vain pursuit of rank and fame, they hold their positions but fail to serve the nation dutifully!"

The old prime minister's fury scared Yin Jiao. "Prime Minister! Please control your temper. Now that General Yin's come to arrest and take me back to the palace, I've little hope that I'll live much longer," Yin Jiao said, his voice trembling. Tears fell like rain.

"Don't fear, Your Highness! Though I haven't yet completed my written report, I'll go to the king and speak to him in person," Shang Rong comforted him.

Yin Pobai began to worry that the king might accuse him of conspiring with Shang Rong. "Pime Minister! Since I have an order to bring His Highness back to the palace at once, we can depart first. You may set off somewhat later, so as to demonstrate that there have been no private dealings between us."

"General Yin! I see what you mean, and you're quite right. Prince, you may leave at once with General Yin and I'll follow later," Shang Rong said with a smile.

Before their departure, Shang Rong warned Yin Pobai, "Now that I've permitted the crown prince to go with you, just don't be too anxious about a promotion, nor should you disregard the relationship between yourself and the crown prince, lest you commit a serious error and risk capital punishment."

"Your disciple will certainly do as you've ordered," General Yin said, kneeling down and kowtowing.

"Though I'll meet my death, my younger brother will survive and take revenge for the injustice done to our beloved mother." Yin Jiao comforted himself.

After a couple of days' journey they came to the fork in the road. When Lei Kai saw the crown prince alongside Yin Pobai, he said joyfully, "I should offer you my congratulations, Your Highness."

When the two brothers met again as captives they embraced and wept bitterly. "What sins did we commit to Heaven and earth in our past lives that we have to end up like this! It's unfair that we'll fail to avenge our poor mother's death!"

The heart-rending laments of the two doomed princes moved the 3,000 soldiers to tears, but the two fierce generals could do nothing but drive their men back to Zhaoge in all haste. When they arrived, Generals Yin and Lei were secretly delighted at their success. They encamped their 3,000 soldiers and escorted the two princes to the city to see King Zhou. Huang Feihu exploded in a rage when he learned that they had returned with the princes.

"You damned wretches! You seek only to please that tyrant, but show no regard for the future of the Shang Dynasty. I promise you that you'll taste my sword before you get any promotion! Blood will stain your garments before you obtain any honor," he swore, and gave an urgent order to his generals Huang Ming, Zhou Ji, Long Huan and Wu Yan, "Have all the ministers and all the princes assemble at the palace gate."

He rode his Rainbow Ox to the palace gate, and soon Bi Gan, Jizi, Wei Ziqi, Wei Ziyan and the other ministers also arrived.

"Your Highnesses! Ministers!" Huang Feihu began. "The fate of the state rests in your hands. I'm merely a military officer and know little about such affairs. I hope that you'll all consider these matters carefully."

They were discussing what to do when the two princes arrived at the palace gate under armed escort. They all moved forward to greet them.

"Members of the royal clan! Ministers!" Yin Jiao addressed them in tears. "You know as well as we what a disaster it would be if we're to be slaughtered! My brother and I have never behaved improperly. Even if we had committed an error, we should only be demoted but not punished by decapitation! I pray that all of you show your concern for the state and rescue us from death!"

"Your Highnesses! Don't worry so much! A large number of officials here are ready to speak out on your behalf," Wei Ziqi said sympathetically.

Meanwhile Generals Yin Pobai and Lei Kai had arrived at the Fairy Longevity Palace and made their reports.

"Now that you've got them, there's no need for them to come and see me. Simply behead them at the palace gate, bury their corpses, and then come back to report to me," the king ordered.

"How can we execute them without your written order?" Yin Pobai asked.

King Zhou wrote, "Supervise the execution," and gave the order to Yin Pobai. The two generals came out only to run into the princes and ministers waiting at the gate. When he saw them, Huang Feihu felt a burning rage rising in his heart. He stepped in their way. "Yin Pobai! Lei Kai! I congratulate you both on achieving this marvelous feat! I trust that you'll be given well-deserved promotions for cutting their heads off. I only want to warn you that high positions are fraught with danger."

Before the two generals could say a word to Huang Feihu, Supreme Minister Zhao Qi came up, grabbed the king's order, and tore it to pieces. "The cursed king's committed every possible offence, and you stupid wretches have encouraged him in his wantonness! I dare you to slay the crown prince! I dare you to behead them with the king's sword! How can we ignore this violation of the ethical code? How can we overlook the corruption of sacred virtues?" he roared. "Princes and ministers, the palace gate isn't the proper place to discuss state affairs. Let's go to the Grand Hall and invite His Majesty to attend. We must admonish him whether he likes it or not. We must save the state from destruction."

Generals Yin and Lei were greatly taken aback to see them so agitated. They stood dumbfounded, not knowing what to do. Huang Feihu ordered Generals Huang Ming, Zhou Ji, Long Huan and Wu Yan to protect the princes from any possible harm that might befall them. The eight executioners, who had bound up the princes and were waiting for the execution order, could do nothing but stand around and wait.

The ministers streamed into the Grand Hall. They struck the bells and beat the drums to announce their intentions of speaking to King Zhou.

The king was with Daji in the Fairy Longevity Palace. He heard the clanging and banging, and was about to send someone to see what was going on when a report was delivered by one of his attendants, "Your Majesty is requested to ascend the throne in the Grand Hall and meet with your ministers."

King Zhou turned to Daji. "It must be the ministers that attempt to plead on behalf of my two unfilial sons. What shall I do?"

"Issue an order that the princes must be executed today, and if there's anything to discuss, it can wait until tomorrow morning. You must urge Yin Pobai to carry out your order as soon as possible," she suggested.

King Zhou agreed with her and wrote a decree to be read before the ministers:

The king's order must be carried out at once. All royal death warrants are irrevocable; this has been the law since ancient times. No one may ignore it, not even the king himself. My unfilial son Yin Jiao and his accomplice Yin Hong have trespassed the boundaries of filial piety. After murdering Jiang Huan in an effort to eradicate all traces of their crimes, they pursued royal officers with swords drawn in an attempt to end their father's life. This is the most wicked form of unfilial behavior, for which they must be executed at the palace gate in accordance with the law inherited from our ancestors. Gentlemen, you shall obey my instructions and lend no further support to my wicked sons. If any state affairs need discussing, let them wait until tomorrow morning. Consider yourselves officially informed of these matters.

While the ministers argued among themselves about the king's pronouncement, the executioners had already gone stealthily out of the palace gate, and were making ready to decapitate the two princes.

Actually, the two princes were not destined by fate to die at this time, as their names were both on the List of Creations. There were two immortals, one called Pure Essence, who lived in the Exalted Cloud Cave on Mount Taihua, and the other Grand Completion, who lived in the Peach Spring Cave on Nine Immortal Mountain. Because immortals were fated to break the commandment against killing, Heavenly Primogenitor, Grand Master of Chan Daoism, had stopped giving lectures on the Way. This left the two immortals with very little to do except travel about the sacred mountains.

One day, they were passing over Zhaoge when two red beams of light rose from the skulls of the princes and blocked their way. The two immortals poked a hole in the clouds they were riding, looked down, and saw vapors of death hanging around the palace gate. They instantly understood what was taking place.

"Brother! The Shang Dynasty's coming to an end, and the new ruler's already living in West Qi. Look at the two boys down there in the crowd. They're bound up, but exude beams of light. It's wrong for them to die now, for they're destined to serve West Qi," Grand Completion said. "Why not do them a favor and rescue them from death? You take one and I the other. We may bring them back to our caves, and when the time comes enjoin them to help Jiang Ziya on his expedition to the five passes. We will be killing two birds with one stone."

"You're right, Brother, but we must act quickly."

Grand Completion issued an order to his yellow-scarved genii, "Bring the two princes back to our mountains without delay."

The genii did as they were ordered. They stirred up a great gust of divine wind, raising dust and rocks in the air, blocking the sun and turning day into night. Cracks of thunder rolled in the sky, threatening to split the mountains in two. This unnatural storm frightened the executioners and General Yin Pobai so badly that they ran about wildly, covering their faces with their sleeves and protecting their heads with their arms. When the wind subsided and the thunder died down, the princes had vanished without trace. This scared Yin Pobai out of his wits, and all the soldiers guarding the palace gate began crying in wonder at what had just taken place. Huang Feihu and the other officials were listening to King Zhou's order when they heard a clamor of voices outside.

As Bi Gan hurried out to enquire what had happened, Zhou Ji came in. "A few moments ago, a blast of wind with a strange fragrance blew in from the palace gate with a terrifying noise. It was so strong that the air was filled with sand and rocks, so that no one could see what was going on right under their own noses. It seems as if this wind has blown the two princes away! This is an extremely strange phenomenon!" he exclaimed.

Most of the officials were greatly relieved by this strange occurrence. "Heaven's kind to the innocent, and earth won't cut off the lifeblood of the Shang Dynasty," they sighed.

Chief Executioner Yin Pobai rushed off to the Fairy Longevity Palace to see King Zhou. "I was overseeing the execution of the two princes when a strong gust of wind blew them away. I've come to report this most odd happening."

King Zhou did not speak, silently pondering, "How strange it all is."

On his way to Zhaoge, Shang Rong heard people everywhere talking about the miraculous wind that had blown the two princes away. When he arrived at the palace gate, he noticed that it was crowded with people and horses and that soldiers and guards were busily rushing about. Entering the palace and crossing the Nine Dragon Bridge, Shang Rong was met by Bi Gan and a number of other ministers, who greeted him warmly.

"Princes and ministers! How wrong I was to retire from my post and take up a life of ease in the forest!" he began. "I never expected that the king would behave so foully, killing his wife and attempting to kill his innocent sons while indulging in his favorite concubine. What a shame that you prime ministers and supreme ministers receive high salaries from the government and are of no service to the state! Why do you all keep your mouths shut?"

"Prime Minister! Don't you realize that His Majesty hides himself away in the inner palace and rarely makes an appearance at the Grand Hall? His orders are transmitted by his messengers, and we rarely have a chance to see him," Huang Feihu explained. "Today, when Generals Yin and Lei caught the two princes and brought them back to the palace, Zhao Qi grabbed and tore to pieces the royal order for execution. The ministers rang the bells and beat the drums to call His Majesty before us, yet he insisted that the princes be beheaded today and put off the audience until tomorrow. It was a great surprise to all of us when Heaven mercifully sent a strong gust of wind and blew the two poor princes away. Yin Pobai's now with the king. When he returns, you'll learn the whole story."

Minutes later, General Yin entered the hall.

"Congratulations, General!" Shang Rong greeted him. "Though the princes are lost, you've set a fine example by your meritorious acts. No doubt, you'll soon be granted vast territory and honorable titles!"

Yin Pobai knew quite well what Shang Rong meant. He bowed. "Prime Minister, I'm terribly sorry, but I couldn't possibly have refused His Majesty's orders. You're blaming me most unfairly."

Shang Rong turned to the ministers. "I've come here to remonstrate with the king, though I will surely die. I'll tell him the whole truth; for only in this way can I bear to confront the emperors of yore after my death." He ordered the guards on duty to strike the bells and beat the drums.

When he heard the loud ringing in the Grand Hall, King Zhou became very angry, yet he had little choice but to proceed to his throne. He received the cheers from his ministers. "What memorials are to be presented?" he asked.

Shang Rong knelt down at the foot of the Cinnabar Steps without speaking. The king saw only a man dressed in mourning kneeling before him.

"Who's that man?" he asked again.

"The former Prime Minister Shang Rong dares to risk his life and appear before Your Majesty."

"Since you've retired to the forest, how can you return to this palace again without my orders? Explain this reckless behavior!"

Shang Rong crawled forward on his knees until he was beneath the eaves and wept.

"Though I served as prime minister, I'm ashamed that I failed in my duties. Recently, I've heard of many improprieties committed by Your Majesty, and of your gross dereliction of duty. I don't fear your axe and sword, and earnestly beg you to accept what I've written in my report. If indeed you follow this course, it would be like the brilliant light of the sun shining through a sky full of dark clouds. The entire country will admire and praise you for your boundless virtue," said Shang Rong and handed his report to Bi Gan, who spread it out on the king's desk.

King Zhou began to read it carefully:

> I am submitting this report in response to a marked worsening in the affairs of state. With your neglect of the law and rites, the state is facing danger of destruction. When Your Majesty first ascended the throne you acted virtuously and diligently, and untiringly served the country and the people. You honored the dukes, treated your ministers generously, were economical in terms of labor and money, and won over the barbarian tribes and foreign countries with your wisdom. In this way, you were blessed by Heaven with timely wind and rain, and people went about their work happily. At that time, you could easily be compared to the ancient emperors Yao and Shun. Yet, recently you have placed your trust in traitors and dealt with state affairs in a cruel and ruthless way. You avoid good people but are intimate with the wicked; you indulge in wine and women, and have been led by the fawning courtiers to murdering your queen. You trust blindly in Daji and have ordered the death of your own sons, seeking to cut short your family line and abandon a father's love. You have destroyed the relationship between ruler and subject by putting the loyal to death. You are a tyrant and no longer qualified to sit on the throne.
>
> At whatever risk, I beg Your Majesty to have Daji end her own life as a means of righting the gross injustice done to the queen and the princes. I urge you to behead all those who conspired with her to requite the innocent death of the loyal ministers. Only in this way can you regain the respect of the people and gladden the hearts of the officials, restore the nation to order and bring peace to the palace. Only in this way will you continue to live happily and in good health for 10,000 years.
>
> Though I deserve death for what I say, my deeds shall live on forever. I earnestly urge you to consider this and act upon it promptly.

King Zhou became so infuriated by Shang Rong's memorial that he tore it up into shreds and ordered his guards, "Take this useless fool out to the palace gate and beat him to death with the gold hammer."

As the royal guards approached Shang Rong, the old prime minister stood up. "Who dares to take me away? I've been the right-hand man of three Shang rulers, caring for the dynasty as if it were a motherless child!" he cried out, pointing a finger at King Zhou. "You damned tyrant! Your mind's so muddled with wine and sex that you've neglected state affairs. You've completely forgotten that your ancestors were blessed with this kingdom because of their diligence and virtuous conduct. In ceasing to show proper respect to Heaven and your ancestors, you'll only bring humiliation on them when the dynasty falls and you die in the near future. You've murdered your wife on the false accusations by your concubine. You've attempted to put your own sons to death. And you've put the loyal to death on the burning pillar. It's obvious that disaster will soon befall this dynasty and that it will soon be replaced by a successor. Since you're the master criminal behind all this treachery, will you have the conscience to confront your ancestors upon your demise?"

King Zhou banged on his desk with his fist and roared, "Grab that old wretch and beat him to death at once!"

"I'm not afraid to die. I'm only sorry that I've failed to transform this tyrant into a good ruler. You scourge! You won't last long on that throne of yours, that's for sure! The kingdom will be done for in a matter of years," Shang Rong shouted back, and turning around, he threw himself at a stone pillar. His skull was crushed and his brains and blood began to drip down over the collar of his robe.

The ministers exchanged horrified glances at Shang Rong's tragic death, but King Zhou was still very angry. He ordered that the corpse be tossed into an empty field beyond the capital.

If you want to know what happened after that, please read the next chapter.

10

THE DISCOVERY OF THUNDERBOLT

Seeing this tragedy, Zhao Qi was enraged and could not contain himself any longer. He stepped out of the ranks.

"As I've never forgotten the benevolence bestowed upon me by your predecessors, I'm willing to sacrifice my life for the country today and accompany the old prime minister on his way to the underworld," he cried and then pointed at King Zhou, swearing, "You wretched tyrant! You've killed your prime minister, forsaken the loyal, and gravely disappointed your dukes. You trust in Daji, listen to the minions and propel the state towards ruin. It's not necessary to enumerate all the vicious crimes you've committed. Your state's like a tree without roots, and bound to topple in a short time! You're unworthy of the throne, for you've brought untold shame upon the Shang Dynasty, shame that even your death won't wipe out."

King Zhou was furious and pounded his desk. "You damned wretch! How dare you insult me! Dispose of this treacherous villian with the burning pillar!"

"Death's nothing to me, for I'll leave my loyalty behind in this world. But you, you tyrant, shall lose your throne, and be condemned for 10,000 years!"

The guards had already heated the burning pillar until it glowed bright red. They took and stripped Zhao Qi of his official robes and hat, bound him to it, and in a matter of seconds his body was reduced to ashes, emitting a noxious odor that filled the Grand Hall. As the officials remained in sorrowful silence, the king felt greatly satisfied with himself for having ordered such a barbarous torture. He ordered his attendants to

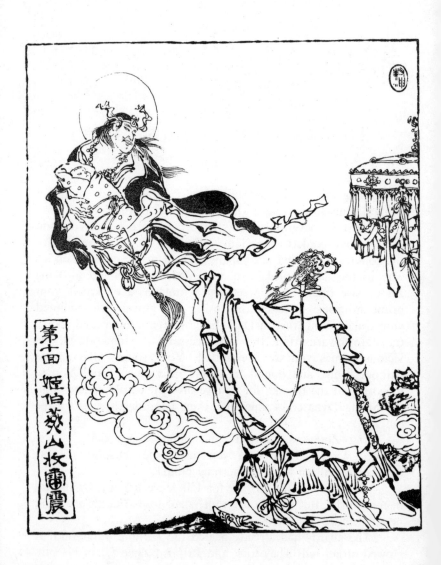

第十四　姬伯燊山收雷震

prepare his coach, and he returned to the Fairy Longevity Palace. When he arrived, Daji came out to meet him. He embraced her and sat down beside her on a silk cushion embroidered with dragons.

"Today Shang Rong committed suicide by smashing his head on a pillar, and then I put Zhao Qi to death on the burning pillar. Those stupid wretches heaped no end of insult on me. The problem is that they don't seem to be intimidated by any of the existing methods of torture. Have you any better means to deal with these stubborn jackasses?" he asked Daji.

"Let me think it over," Daji replied.

"Your position as queen is assured, my beauty, as none of the ministers would dare to oppose it. My only worry is Jiang Huanchu. Once he learns about his daughter's death, he's bound to rise in rebellion and entice other nobles to join him. Grand Tutor Wen Zhong hasn't yet returned from the North Sea district. What shall we do?"

"I'm a woman and lack good political sense. I suggest that you summon Fei Zhong. He's sure to think of an ingenious plan to pacify the country."

Before long, Fei Zhong was summoned at the Fairy Longevity Palace to see King Zhou.

"As Queen Jiang's dead, I fear that Jiang Huanchu will rise in rebellion against us, and people in the area may not be able to live in peace. Have you any advice for me?" King Zhou asked him.

Fei Zhong knelt down. "As Queen Jiang's dead, the princes are missing, Shang Rong's killed himself and Zhao Qi's burned to death, the ministers are beginning to express dissatisfaction with Your Majesty. Were they to conspire with Jiang Huanchu, we would face the danger of being trapped by our enemies from within and without. I advise you to summon the four dukes secretly to Zhaoge, then take immediate action to behead all of them. This way, the 800 marquises will be able to do nothing to oppose you. They would be like a dragon without the head, or a tiger without teeth and claws. Only then will the state be in peace," he suggested.

King Zhou was greatly pleased. "Your gifted strategy will

enable all under Heaven to live in peace. Queen Daji recommended you, and you certainly haven't let me down."

After Fei Zhong had left the Fairy Longevity Palace, King
Zhou issued four secret orders to summon Jiang Huanchu, E
Chongyu, Ji Chang and Chong Houhu to Zhaoge.

The royal messenger to the West Grand Dukedom traveled
through dust and wind and desolate grasslands. Several days
later, he crossed Mount Qi and covered the last seventy *li* to
the capital of the dukedom. Entering the city, he found that
people appeared well-to-do and the markets were full of things
for sale. People behaved courteously to each other and a general sense of peace and security prevailed. "The West Grand
Duke's well known for his kindness and virtue. Now I can see
with my own eyes that he rules his dukedom so that his people
are as happy as in the days of the ancient emperors Yao and
Shun," he sighed.

When he arrived at the local guesthouse, he dismounted
from his horse and was invited in to be entertained. The next
morning, when Ji Chang held court, the gate officer reported
his arrival. Ji Chang led his civil and military officials out to
welcome him. They then went back inside, where Ji Chang and
his officials knelt respectfully while the royal messenger read
the decree:

> The North Sea district is undergoing a great disturb-
> ance, causing the people to suffer severely. The ministers
> are at a loss what to do. I summon the four dukes to
> Zhaoge to discuss this matter and seek better ways of sup-
> pressing the rebellions. By this decree I request the West
> Grand Duke to start on his journey at once. There must
> be no delay. Upon the successful completion of the mis-
> sion, each grand duke shall be rewarded with land and ti-
> tles....

After acknowledging the decree, Ji Chang entertained the
royal messenger, and before he returned to Zhaoge, Ji Chang
presented him with gold and silver. "I'll be on my way at
once," he assured the messenger. Back in the Proper Bright-

ness Court, he said to San Yisheng, "After my departure, you'll be in charge of all internal affairs while Nangong Kuo and Xin Jia will take care of external affairs." He then sent for his eldest son Bo Yikao. "I've been summoned to Zhaoge for an important meeting. I've divined and found that the trip is ominous. Though I may not lose my life, I'll suffer for seven years," he told his son when the latter arrived. "Thus I would like you to take my place. You must rule according to law and custom, and ensure peace among your brothers and among the ministers. You mustn't act in your own interest, and should frequently ask your elders for advice. Provide gold and silver to those who are too poor to marry, and distribute a monthly grain allowance to orphans, widows and widowers. I'll return after seven years, during which time you shall never send anyone to see me."

Bo Yikao knelt down before his father and said, "Dear Father! Let me go in your stead."

"A wise man should keep out of harm's way, but when something's destined by the will of Heaven, he can do nothing to escape from it. You'll be behaving as a filial son if you obey me," Ji Chang said, then went to the inner palace to bid farewell to his mother Tai Jiang.

"My son," she said, "the oracle predicts that you'll suffer for seven years!"

Ji Chang knelt down. "After I received the royal decree, I also divined and learned that I should suffer misfortunes for seven years, though I won't lose my life. I've asked my officials and my son to perform various duties during my absence. I'll set out for Zhaoge tomorrow. I've come especially to bid you farewell," he told her.

"Please be cautious in everything you do, my son," Tai Jiang urged.

"I'll do just as you say, Mother."

He left his mother's to see his wife Tai Ji. He had twenty-four concubines and ninety-nine sons. Bo Yikao was his eldest son, while Ji Fa, his second son, later became the first king of the Zhou Dynasty. There were three saintly women in the kingdom of Zhou— his mother Tai Jiang; his wife Tai Ji; and Ji

Fa's wife, Tai Ren.

The next morning, he set out for Zhaoge with fifty attendants. San Yisheng, Nangong Kuo, Xin Jia, Bo Yikao and many other civil and military officials gathered at Changting Pavilion and a farewell banquet was held.

"Though we're parting today, we'll meet again in seven years," said Ji Chang to his ministers. Pointing at Bo Yikao, he went on, "I'll have no worries if you and your brothers can live in peace."

The ministers and Bo Yikao toasted him in farewell, and Ji Chang mounted, starting on his way. He and his attendants traveled seventy *li* the first day and got as far as Mount Qi. One day they were approaching Mount Yan when Ji Chang announced to his men, "Try to find some cottage nearby and take shelter from the coming rainstorm."

"The sky's clear and blue and the sun's shining brightly. How could it possibly rain now?" his attendants murmured among themselves perplexedly.

Nevertheless, within a few minutes, the sky was filled with clouds and mist. Ji Chang ordered his men to hurry into a nearby forest to take cover. In no time the storm began, and in a matter of minutes, giant waves were rolling down from the mountain tops, and the paths in the valleys were transformed into broad rivers. It was as if the ocean were falling from the sky.

"Be careful! Here comes the thunder!" Ji Chang shouted.

A moment later a great thunderclap exploded, shaking the sky and earth. The party was frightened and ashen-faced, they huddled together in one place. But before long, the clouds disappeared, the rain stopped and the sun reappeared in the sky.

As they started to leave the forest, Ji Chang, soaked through, said from his saddle, "The appearance of a glowing light in the sky after the clap of thunder means that the star of a great warrior has come into existence. I would like you men to find it for me now."

All the soldiers grinned at this strange request. "What's this warrior star? Where shall we begin looking for it?"

However, none of them dared to disobey his orders, and

so they started roaming about in search of the star. Nearing an old tomb, they heard a baby crying. And when they got closer, they discovered a little boy.

"What a strange thing! Could this be what he means by 'the star of a warrior'?"

They brought him to Ji Chang, who examined the baby carefully and discovered that he was a handsome child indeed, with a face like a peach blossom and eyes sparking like stars.

"I really should have 100 sons, but now I've got only ninety-nine. If I make this child my son, I'll have 100," he thought and told his men to find a local family who would take and raise the boy for seven years until he claimed him.

Ji Chang got back on his horse and set off again. After crossing many steep mountains, they came to Mount Yan. They traveled another twenty *li* and came upon a Taoist coming from the opposite direction. The Taoist had an air of refinement about him, and in his large robe with broad sleeves, he looked more like an immortal than a human being. Approaching Ji Chang, the Taoist bowed low.

"Grand Duke! I offer you my respects," he began.

Ji Chang dismounted and returned the salutation. "Forgive my lack of courtesy, but where do you live, Your Holiness? Why do you come to me?"

"I'm Master of the Clouds. I reside on Mount Zhongnan. A few minutes ago, the star of a warrior appeared in the sky in a thunderclap, and I've traveled a long way to look for it."

Hearing this, Ji Chang ordered his men to give the boy to Master of the Clouds.

"You're the star of a warrior! Why did you make your appearance so late?" the Taoist addressed the child, then turning to Ji Chang, he said, "Grand Duke! Let me take this baby with me to Mount Zhongnan. He can be one of my disciples. I'll give him back to you when you return from Zhaoge."

"As you like, sir. But what's his name, and what shall I call him when I meet him again in the future?"

"His name'll be 'Thunderbolt,' since he made his appearance in a great thunderclap," Master of the Clouds suggested.

"That's a very good idea," Ji Chang replied politely.

And without further ceremony, they parted and went their own ways.

Continuing on his journey, Ji Chang traversed the five passes, crossed the Yellow River and finally entered Zhaoge. At the Golden Reception House, Ji Chang was entertained in the company of Jiang Huanchu, E Chongyu and Chong Houhu.

"Dukes! What urgent matter could have so upset His Majesty that he had to summon us all at once? General Huang Feihu and Bi Gan are here to aid him with state affairs. What help can we be?" Ji Chang asked, after a few rounds of wine.

Deep in his cups, E Chongyu's tongue was loosened. "We're the leaders of the nobles, but you do nothing but indulge in vice," he began to express his disapproval of Chong Houhu. "You exploit the people for your own benefit and curry favor with the likes of Fei Zhong and You Hun. You work people to death building lavish mansions and exempt from labor all who are willing to bribe you. Your heart's as greedy as a wolf's and as fierce as a tiger's. It's likely that you're hated by every person in the capital. There's an old proverb, saying, 'Calamity arises from accumulated vices; blessings arise from acts of benevolence.' You'd better repent at once and change your ways."

"E Chongyu! How dare you insult me like this," Chong Houhu was enraged. "We're all ministers of the nation, but why do you slander me before our colleagues?"

He rose to strike at E Chongyu.

"Duke E's only trying to help you mend your ways. You really shouldn't become so annoyed," Ji Chang stopped him.

At this, Chong Houhu could not very well raise his fists, but E Chongyu had picked up a wine pot and struck Chong Houhu in the face. Chong leaped again out of his seat to strike back, but he was stopped by Jiang Huanchu.

"How disgraceful it is for us dukes to be fighting like this. Duke Chong! It's already quite late. You'd better retire for the night."

Chong Houhu suppressed his anger and returned to his room, while the other three continued with their drinks. At the second watch, an attendant who had been watching them sighed and muttered to himself, "You're drinking so joyfully tonight, but little do you know that your blood will stain the marketplace tomorrow."

In the silence of the night, Ji Chang heard him.

"Whoever said that must come forward!" he demanded.

All the attendants knelt down before the dukes.

"Who just said that our blood will stain the market tomorrow?" Ji Chang asked again.

"We didn't hear anyone say that, Grand Duke," they answered in chorus.

"We didn't hear it either," said the two other dukes.

"I heard every word clearly, but how can you say that no one said it?" Ji Chang demanded, then he ordered the guards, "Take them all out of here and cut their heads off!"

None of the attendants was willing to give up his own life to protect the man. They pushed him out of the line. "Grand Dukes! It has nothing to do with us. Yao Fu's the culprit you're looking for."

"You may all return to your places," Ji Chang ordered, and then he questioned Yao Fu. "Why did you speak like that? If you tell us the truth, you'll be well rewarded; but if you don't, you'll be severely punished."

"An open mouth's the worst source of trouble," Yao Fu sighed, and continued. "What I was talking about is a matter of the greatest secrecy, but I learned about it because I serve in the family of a royal messenger. After the death of Queen Jiang and the disappearance of the princes, His Majesty took Daji's advice and summoned you here with the end of putting you all to death. When His Majesty holds court tomorrow morning, you'll all have your heads cut off. I couldn't bear imagining such a tragedy. I spoke what I felt as I watched you drinking happily."

"Tell me, how did Queen Jiang die?" Jiang Huanchu asked anxiously.

Yao Fu had already divulged the secret, so he decided to tell Jiang Huanchu the whole story from beginning to end. "The wicked king tortured Queen Jiang to death and then was about to murder his own sons when a great wind blew them away from the palace. Now he's even set Daji on the throne as his queen!"

Jiang Huanchu was heartbroken when he heard the story of his daughter's death and collapsed to the floor in a faint.

Ji Chang's men helped Jiang Huanchu up, and when he regained consciousness, he wept bitterly. "Oh! My dear daughter! How horribly you must have suffered when your eye was gouged out and your hands burnt to ashes. Never before has such cruel torture been applied."

"Since the queen's already dead, and the princes are missing, all we can do is present a petition to His Majesty tomorrow morning, claiming that a great injustice was done. Let's work on the petition tonight," Ji Chang comforted him.

"The Jiang family's ill-fated. Why should I trouble you to petition the king on my behalf? I'll go alone to see him and clear up this injustice with him directly," Jiang Huanchu said, still in tears.

"You may petition as you wish. We three will submit our own reports in any case," Ji Chang replied.

Tears continued to roll down Jiang Huanchu's cheeks as they returned to their own rooms.

Fei Zhong was quick to announce the arrival of the four dukes to King Zhou, who was delighted at the news.

"When you ascend your throne tomorrow morning, the dukes will inevitably present their reports, but you needn't read any of them. Just order the royal guards to tie them up, take them out and cut their heads off at the palace gate," Fei Zhong suggested.

The night passed quietly. The next morning, King Zhou arrived in the Grand Hall. After the officials had lined up before him, the gate officer reported, "The four grand dukes are awaiting your orders at the palace gate."

"Send them in to see me."

Minutes later, the dukes walked in and knelt down before him.

When Jiang Huanchu handed in his written report, King Zhou shouted at him, "Are you aware of the crimes you've committed against the royal government?"

"I protect East Lu with my strong army and deal with everything according to the law. I've always been loyal to the state and have never committed a single error," Jiang Huanchu promptly replied. "You, on the other hand, wallow in flattery and have no shame for your evil deeds. You've killed the queen and attempted to slay the princes to sever your own family line. You listen only to your concubine and minions and put the loyal to death. I fear neither axe nor sword, for I speak only for truth and justice."

King Zhou exploded in a great rage. "You treacherous old wretch! You and your daughter planned to murder me in an attempt to usurp the crown. This is a crime as great as a mountain. How dare you argue such nonsense in hope of slipping through the net of the law," he swore, and ordered his guards, "Take him out and cut him into 1,000 tiny pieces!"

As the royal guards began to remove Jiang Huanchu's robes and hat to take him out to the palace gate, the three other dukes rushed in, protesting Jiang's innocence. Determined to kill all four of them, King Zhou took their petitions and placed them on the desk before him.

If you want to learn the fate of the dukes, you must read the next chapter.

11

THE ILL-FORTUNES OF
THE GRAND DUKES

Seeing how King Zhou put Jiang Huanchu's report aside without reading it and how he harshly ordered his death, Ji Chang and two other dukes were shocked. They immediately knelt down before him.

"The king's honored as the head while the ministers are his limbs. To order so rashly the death of a duke without even reading his memorial is cruelty towards a subject, and no one in this court would approve of it. Such an act would disrupt the proper relationship between the king and his ministers. We beg Your Majesty to reconsider your decision," they pleaded.

As they spoke, Bi Gan spread their petition open on the king's desk, and he had no choice but to read it:

Your Grand Dukes E Chongyu, Ji Chang and Chong Houhu present this petition for the purpose of restoring the country to order by law, eliminating flatterers, rectifying injustices, reestablishing the proper relationships and ridding the palace of hidden conspirators.

We understand that the ancient sagely emperors ruled with diligence and good administration and took no interest in building gorgeous palaces or large gardens. They worked closely with the able and virtuous but distanced themselves from flatterers. They did not preoccupy themselves with the pleasure of hunting, nor did they indulge in wine and women. They respected only the will of Heaven and effortlessly maintained order throughout the nation. All the people enjoyed their work and were content in their daily life. But in contrast, Your Majesty has achieved nothing praiseworthy since coming onto the throne. You neglect state affairs, trust flatterers, distance yourself from the loyal, and indulge yourself in wine and women. Queen Jiang was virtuous and observed the rites, yet she was cruelly tortured and met a tragic death, while Daji, obscene and lewd, has been favored with the position of queen. The Grand Tutor was unjustly beheaded and loyal ministers were silenced with the burning pillar. You even ordered the death of your own sons, indicating that no fatherly love remains in your heart. We earnestly beseech that you take immediate action to demote Fei Zhong and You Hun and behead Daji, so that the whole palace may be cleansed and the whole nation returned to peace and order. Not evading death, your subjects venture to speak frankly, expecting your generous acceptance and swift action....

As King Zhou read, he exploded with fury. He tore up the petition, and pounded his desk. "Take those traitors away and cut their heads off at once," he shouted.

As the guards bound up the three dukes and pushed them out of the palace, Fei Zhong and You Hun left the ranks of ministers and knelt before King Zhou. "At the risk of offending Your Majesty we would like to reveal the true situation: The four dukes have committed an unpardonable crime by gravely offending Your Majesty and should be punished by death. Nevertheless, they're guilty in different degrees. Jiang Huanchu's committed the capital crime of attempting to murder his king; E Chongyu's guilty of harshly rebuking his liege; Ji Chang's used his skilful tongue to insult you, while Chong Houhu's committed the error of foolishly following the others. As we see it, Chong Houhu's loyal at heart. He spent all his energy and time in constructing the Star Picking Mansion and spared no effort in building the Fairy Longevity Palace. He's faultless and innocent. To fail to differentiate between worthy men and criminals is like burning jade with stone or confusing black with white. This is unjust and nobody will approve of it. For these reasons, we beg that Your Majesty spare Chong

Houhu so that he can make amends for today's error with outstanding service in the future!"

As Fei Zhong and You Hun were both favorites of the king, he granted their request, saying, "I haven't forgotten Chong Houhu's outstanding service in the past. He's granted a special pardon."

Fei Zhong and You Hun thanked the king and returned to their positions. But the fact that only Chong Houhu would be pardoned greatly annoyed Huang Feihu and the other princes. They all left their positions and knelt before the king.

"We're of the opinion that the dukes and ministers are like the limbs of Your Majesty," Bi Gan spoke on their behalf. "Jiang Huanchu enjoys great prestige, and is highly respected in East Lu, where he's fought many victorious battles. There's no evidence to prove that he plotted to murder Your Majesty. How can he be given the death sentence! Ji Chang's loyal, working solely for the nation and people. His virtues please Heaven and earth and his benevolence unites all the dukes. He treats his civil and military officials with righteousness, and rules his people in accordance with the rites. Rebels are won over by his wisdom and he enjoys the trust of both the army and people. His administration's strict and orderly. In his domains the ruler is kind and officials are loyal; sons are filial and fathers full of paternal love; brothers are affectionate and respectful. There are neither quarrels nor wars in the dukedom. People are courteous and honest, and no door need be closed at night. He's praised by all as the West Sage. E Chongyu guards against the invasions that occur from time to time and serves the country tirelessly. They're all mainstays of the state. We beg that Your Majesty show pity and forgive them. For this your ministers would be deeply grateful!"

"Jiang Huanchu has committed treason, while E Chongyu and Ji Chang insulted me with a lot of nonsense. They're all unpardonable. How can you speak so rashly and seek to protect them?" King Zhou rejected the plea completely.

"Both Jiang Huanchu and E Chongyu are renowned dukes and have committed no errors. Ji Chang's a kind gentleman, skilled at divining. They're all cornerstones of the state. If you execute these three innocent men in one day, how can the people and officials approve of your action?" Huang Feihu protested. "Moreover, they each have strong armies and brave generals. War would be on if the dukes are slaughtered for crimes of which they're innocent. Civil war would bring disasters to the people and endanger the dynasty. In addition, Grand Tutor Wen Zhong's still tied down in the North Sea district, and there would be no peace for the nation. We beg that you pardon them for the nation's sake."

Observing the vehemence of the princes, King Zhou was obliged to yield a little. "I know well that Ji Chang's loyal to me; nevertheless, he shouldn't have echoed the insults. He should be dealt with severely, but in response to your plea I'll pardon him. Should he stage an uprising against me after returning to his dukedom, however, you'll be held responsible. Notwithstanding, I can't extend the pardon to Jiang Huanchu and E Chongyu. They must be executed at once."

At this, the seven supreme ministers headed by Yang Ren and Jiao Ge stepped out from the left line and knelt before the king. "Your Majesty, for the sake of national peace we wish to offer our advice."

"What is it?"

"On the petition of the seven princes you've generously forgiven Ji Chang. But as leaders of marquises, both Jiang Huanchu and E Chongyu bear heavy responsibilities and have rendered outstanding services. Their frank advice only shows that they're loyal, seeking to save the nation from disaster. We beg that you take pity on these gentlemen, and with a magnanimity that'll be eulogized by all, set them free and allow them to return to their dukedoms," Yang Ren said.

"They're traitors and have ganged together and spread vicious lies about me. Even cutting Jiang Huanchu to pieces isn't punishment enough for his attempted murder! It's only proper that E Chongyu be decapitated for slandering me. Your petition shows your sympathy with them and is an insult to the king and a violation of law. You shall be dealt the same punishment if you insist on helping them," King Zhou roared furiously and ordered, "Execute them at once!"

When the order arrived, one executioner beheaded E Chongyu while several others nailed Jiang Huanchu's hands and feet to a big board and sliced his flesh off in a thousand pieces. When news came that the execution was over, King Zhou returned to the Fairy Longevity Palace.

Ji Chang thanked the seven princes who had saved his life. "Though innocent, Jiang Huanchu met a tragic death, while E Chongyu paid with his life for his admonitions. Henceforth, there can be no peace in the south and east of the kingdom," he said, with tears in his eyes.

Everyone wept. They ordered the palace guards to bury the two corpses in shallow earth, so that they could be exhumed for full funeral rites sometime in the future. The attendants of the two dukes fled home under the cover of night, and reported the misfortunes to the dukes' sons.

When King Zhou appeared at the Celebration Court the next morning, Bi Gan requested that the corpses be buried and Ji Chang be sent back to his dukedom. The king promptly approved all that Bi Gan proposed. But as soon as Bi Gan left the court, Fei Zhong, who was standing beside the king, came forward.

"Ji Chang appears loyal and honest, but he's really treacherous, and confuses the ministers with his eloquent tongue. He says one thing and thinks another, and is unreliable. If you let him return to his dukedom he's bound to join forces with Jiang Wenhuan in the east and E Shun in the south. They would throw the whole country into chaos, and we would have to send our soldiers and generals to war. The result would be that the people couldn't live in peace and the capital would be endangered. If we send the dragon back to the sea and the tiger back to the mountain, we're bound to regret it."

"The pardon's already been issued, and everybody knows about it. How can I go back on my word now?" King Zhou hesitated.

"I've got a plan to get rid of Ji Chang."

"What is it?"

"He's bound to attend a farewell feast before returning to his dukedom. I'll be there to find out where he truly stands. If he's really loyal, you may forgive him and let him go; otherwise, you may have him executed to nip any future disaster in the bud," Fei Zhong replied.

"Your idea's excellent."

Bi Gan left the palace and made his way directly to the guesthouse where Ji Chang was staying. Ji Chang welcomed him at the gate, and when greetings were over each took a seat inside. "This morning I petitioned His Majesty to bury the corpses of the dukes and allow you to return to your dukedom. Both requests were granted," Bi Gan told him.

Ji Chang bowed and thanked him. "Your virtue's profound. I hope I may have the opportunity some day to repay you for saving my life," Ji Chang said gratefully.

Bi Gan moved forward, took Ji Chang's hand and spoke in a low voice, "We've neither law nor discipline in the country at present. It isn't a good omen that the dukes were put to death unjustly. My worthy duke, you ought to leave here with all speed. You should bid farewell at the palace and quit the place early tomorrow morning. Any delay might mean a change for the worse, as the minions hate you very much. Bear this in mind."

"I'm deeply grateful for your invaluable advice, Prime Minister, and will never forget your abundant virtue," Ji Chang answered with emotion.

Early the next morning, Ji Chang presented himself at the palace gate, knelt down and kowtowed in farewell to the king. Then he left the city by the west gate and rode to the Changting Pavilion, about ten *li* beyond the capital. Huang Feihu, Bi Gan, Wei Zi, Ji Zi and the other ministers had been waiting there for him. As soon as Ji Chang dismounted, Huang Feihu and Wei Zi moved up to greet him. "As you're going home today, we've prepared wine to bid you farewell. However, we've got to make an appeal and hope you'll give it kind consideration."

"I'll only be delighted to listen," Ji Chang answered politely.

"Though His Majesty's so ungrateful, you should recall the virtues of the deceased emperors and continue to serve him as a good minister. Take no harsh action that would throw the country into a turmoil," Wei Zi advised solemnly.

"I cannot forget the grace His Majesty showed in pardoning me, and I'm deeply grateful for your kindness in saving my life. I've got no ambition to do anything to upset the country," he said and bowed.

All the ministers raised their glasses to wish Ji Chang good luck on his journey. Ji Chang could drink an extraordinary quantity of wine, and the party went on for a long while, as they were unwilling to part. They were thus enjoying themselves when Fei Zhong and You Hun rode over with food and wine to bid farewell to Ji Chang. At the sight of them, the ministers became displeased and instantly dispersed.

"Your Honors, I really don't deserve the favor of your coming far," Ji Chang said.

"As you're returning to your dukedom today, we've come here to wish you a pleasant journey. Please forgive us for being a little late," Fei Zhong said.

Ji Chang was a virtuous and honest man and treated people sincerely. He felt pleased to meet them, as Fei Zhong and You Hun were very solicitous. As the other ministers had already left, the three of them drank alone.

"Let's use larger cups," Fei Zhong suggested, after they'd been drinking for some time.

He then filled a large wine cup and handed it to Ji Chang, who emptied it in a single draught.

"I must thank you for your hospitality. I hope that I might return it some day," Ji Chang thanked him.

He had a prodigious capacity for wine and drank several more cups in succession.

"Duke, you're well-known for your divination, but is it really reliable?" Fei Zhong asked.

"The theory of *yin* and *yang* is completely logical, so the divination's naturally reliable," Ji Chang said with confidence.

"As His Majesty handles state affairs in a most haphazard way, can you predict the fate of this dynasty?" Fei Zhong asked on purpose.

Ji Chang, already half drunk, forgot to guard against them.

"The future's so dark that his rule won't last long. King Zhou will be the last monarch of the dynasty. The way he rules only serves to speed up his own downfall. It's unbearable even to mention it."

"When do you think the end will come?" Fei Zhong asked further.

"In a few decades, no more," Ji Chang replied.

Fei Zhong and You Hun sighed deeply and plied Ji Chang with more wine.

"Would you be kind enough to predict our fate, Duke?"

Ji Chang was a virtuous and honest man. Not realizing their real intentions, he made a divination, but then fell silent for a long time before saying somberly, "Your fates are most strange."

"What's so strange about them?"

Ji Chang hesitated. "Though life and death are destined by fate, the manner of death varies widely. Some lives are taken by disease such as tuberculosis, heart attack, ascites or the plague, while others by fire, flood, torture or suicide. But yours are exceptions to all these. It puzzles me that you two should die in such a bizarre manner."

"How are we going to die? And where?" Fei Zhong and You Hun asked, laughing uproariously.

"For some unknown reason you'll be caught in snow and frozen to death in the ice!"

Fei Zhong and You Hun smiled. "The time of birth and place of death are preordained. Let things be as they are destined."

As they continued drinking, Fei Zhong and You Hun asked cunningly, "Duke, have ever divined your own fate?"

"Yes, I have. I found that I'll have a natural death in a good place."

Fei Zhong and You Hun congratulated him falsely, saying, "Duke, you're sure to be blessed with both happiness and longevity."

Ji Chang thanked the two flatterers sincerely, and the three men drank several more cups together. Then Fei Zhong and You Hun got up and said, "Please excuse us. We have business to attend to in the palace and must take our leave. Take care on your journey." But on their way back, they began swearing. "That old beast! He's facing immediate death, yet he spouts nonsense about dying naturally! He claims that we'll be frozen in ice. He was obviously cursing us."

When they reached the Fairy Longevity Palace, Fei Zhong and You Hun dismounted and entered to see King Zhou.

"What did he say about me?" the king asked hurriedly.

"Ji Chang's bitter and resentful. He insulted you with a lot of unruly talk and is guilty of gross disrespect towards Your Majesty."

"That old bastard! I forgave him and set him free, but he isn't at all grateful. On the contrary, he insulted me! What wickedness! Tell me what he said."

"He predicted that the dynasty would end in this generation. Only a few decades remain. Besides that, he said that you wouldn't be blessed with a good and proper death."

King Zhou roared with anger. "Did you ask the old bastard how he would die?"

"We did ask such a question, and he said that he would be sure to enjoy a good death. He wags his tongue and deceives people with nonsense. His life or death is controlled absolutely by Your Majesty, but he fails to realize it and still says that he'll have a good death. He's simply deceiving himself! When we asked him to divine our future, he said that we would be frozen to death in ice. No one, not even a plebeian has ever been frozen to death in ice. He's absurd. We suggest that you have him executed without delay!"

"Let Chao Tian bring him back. Chop his head off and hang it on the city wall as a warning to sorcerers," King Zhou ordered.

When Ji Chang got on his horse, he realized that he had spoken rashly while under the influence of wine. He ordered his party to set out with all haste, lest any incident should occur.

As they hurried along, Ji Chang was busy thinking. "The divination I made showed that I would suffer for seven years. How can I return home now so peacefully? Those thoughtless words I spoke before Fei Zhong and You Hun are bound to cause trouble!"

He pondered and noticed a horse galloping towards him. As it drew nearer, he recognized General Chao Tian.

"Grand Duke, by order of His Majesty, you're requested to return to Zhaoge at once," Chao Tian shouted to him.

"I knew, General Chao," Ji Chang answered calmly. He then addressed his men, "It's difficult to escape the present calamity. Return home with all speed, and I'll be back safely in seven years. Tell Bo Yikao to be obedient to his mother, to live in harmony with his brothers, and to not change the laws and customs of the land. I've nothing more to say. You may go."

As his attendants continued their westward journey in tears, Ji Chang followed Chao Tian back to Zhaoge.

Huang Feihu was shocked to hear the unexpected news that Ji Chang was returning to Zhaoge. He silently pondered, "Why is he coming back again? Could Fei Zhong and You Hun be conspiring to hurt him?" He immediately ordered General Zhou Ji, "Ask all the old princes, ministers and high officials to hurry to the palace gate."

Galloping with urgent haste to the palace gate, Huang Feihu saw Ji Chang waiting there and quickly asked him, "Why did you come back again?"

"His Majesty's ordered my return. I don't know the reason."

When Chao Tian reported Ji Chang's return, King Zhou ordered furiously, "Bring him in here right now."

Ji Chang knelt down on the cinnabar terrace steps before the king and reported, "By your bountiful grace, you set me free and allowed me to return to my dukedom. For what reason did Your Majesty order my return?"

King Zhou swore in a loud voice, "You damned wretch! I forgave you and let you return to your grand dukedom, but you didn't think how to return my kindness. On the contrary, you wantonly insulted me."

Ji Chang answered, "Though I'm extremely stupid, I know that there's Heaven above, earth below and the king between them. I know I was brought up by my parents and educated by my teachers. I have respected Heaven, earth, the king, parents, and teachers all my life. How could I dare commit the capital crime of insulting you?"

King Zhou's anger was unabated, "You still dare to use your enticing tongue to defend yourself with sophistry! You must be put to death for insulting me with your divinations."

"Divination by the eight diagrams was invented by the ancient sage emperors Shen Nong and Fu Xi. It's used to predict the success or failure of events and wasn't falsely forged by me. I simply read what's predicted. I wouldn't have dared to make rash predictions on my own."

"Try making a divination to see how my dynasty will fare," King Zhou demanded.

"I made one for you with inauspicious results. I told Fei Zhong and You Hun about it, but merely said the results weren't auspicious and nothing more. I wouldn't have dared to give my own presumptuous opinions."

King Zhou sprang up from his throne. "You cursed me, saying I wouldn't be blessed with a good death, and bragged that you would live a long life and die in a proper place. What's that if not an insult to your king! You confuse the masses with your sorcery and are sure to bring chaos to the nation. I'll show you right now that your prediction about your own good death isn't true," he mocked Ji Chang, then ordered, "Take him out and behead him."

As the royal guards came forward for Ji Chang, King Zhou heard voices outside the court, "Your Majesty! You mustn't put him to death. We've got written reports." He looked up and saw Huang Feihu, Wei Zi and five other princes hasten into the court. They knelt down before him.

"Both the people and your ministers appreciated your great virtue in setting Ji Chang free and letting him return to his dukedom. Divination was invented by the sage emperor Fu Xi, not by Ji Chang. He just made his divination according to the theory, whether it's true or not. He's really an honest gentleman, not a cunning bootlicker. We beg you to forgive him this minor error, Your Majesty."

"How can I when he uses his sorcery to insult me?" King

Zhou retorted.

"We don't speak for Ji Chang but for the future of the nation," Bi Gan replied. "His execution is of minor importance compared with the safety and consolidation of the Shang Dynasty. Ji Chang is known to all and is loved by all. His divinations are made according to fixed theories and aren't his own fabrication. If you don't believe them, Your Majesty, you may order him to divine the immediate future. You may pardon him if he proves accurate and charge him with sorcery if he doesn't."

King Zhou yielded to their plea and ordered Ji Chang to predict the development of current events.

Ji Chang divined with gold coins and gave a cry of alarm. "Your Majesty! The divination indicates that the Ancestral Temple will catch fire tomorrow. You must quickly remove all the images and spirit tablets of your ancestors, lest they be destroyed."

"According to your divination, at what time tomorrow will the fire break out?"

"It will happen at noon," Ji Chang answered with confidence.

"In that case, put him in gaol temporarily, and we'll see what happens tomorrow," the king decided.

All the ministers left the court, and at the palace gate, Ji Chang expressed his gratitude.

"Duke, you will be facing a crisis tomorrow. You must take great care!" Huang Feihu warned him.

"I can only abide by the will of Heaven."

"Ji Chang predicts that the Ancestral Temple will catch fire tomorrow. What shall we do if it comes true?" King Zhou asked Fei Zhong, when all the ministers were gone.

"Your Majesty, order the temple guards to watch the Ancestral Temple very carefully. Don't let anybody burn candles or incense sticks for worship. That way there's no way a fire can start," Fei Zhong replied.

"You're quite right," King Zhou nodded.

On the following day, Huang Feihu invited the seven princes to his home to wait for the fire. At noon everyone became alarmed as no fire had occurred in the Ancestral Temple. But then a sudden thunderbolt cracked through the sky, shaking the mountains and rivers.

Attendants rushed in. "The Ancestral Temple's on fire," they reported.

"This strange fire is an omen that the dynasty won't last long!" Bi Gan sighed.

Everyone left the mansion to watch the big fire. Dark smoke from the temple covered the sky, turning day into night. Flames flashed like lightning, and the roar of the fire could be heard all over the capital. A strong wind blew and fanned the flames and in a short time the gold and pearl doors, carved pillars and glazed roof tiles were completely destroyed. The Ancestral Temple of the Shang was reduced to ashes. By this, Heaven decreed the downfall of the dynasty. It was no longer in the power of man to prevent it.

King Zhou was holding a discussion with some of his officials in the Dragon Virtue Court when a royal guard rushed in. "The Ancestral Temple caught fire at noon, just as predicted." The king almost fainted with terror, and the two minions were also very frightened. They had to admit that the West Grand Duke really was a sage!

"Ministers! Ji Chang's prediction has come true. What can we do with him now?" King Zhou asked disappointedly.

"Though his prediction has come true, it's only accidental. How can we set him free? It would be better to keep him here so that the kingdom will remain in peace," Fei Zhong and You Hun suggested.

"You're right," King Zhou agreed.

Just then, Huang Feihu, Bi Gan, Wei Zi and the others arrived.

"The fire has proved Ji Chang's divination. I hope Your Majesty will keep your word and pardon him," Bi Gan said.

"Yes, his prediction has come true, and I'll repeal the death sentence. Nevertheless, I can't set him free. He must live at Youli until the state is restored to peace and order. Only then may he return home."

They thanked the king for his kindness and left the court.

At the palace gate, Bi Gan told Ji Chang what the king had decided. Ji Chang immediately knelt down and kowtowed towards the palace in gratitude.

When Ji Chang arrived under escort at Youli, people surged into the streets, knelt and welcomed him with wine and mutton. Ji Chang lived there peacefully, his mind at ease, bearing not the slightest grudge against the king.

One day, Huang Feihu received the report that Jiang Wenhuan had rebelled and was attacking Youhun Pass with 400,000 men; E Shun was attacking Sanshan Pass with 200,000 men. This meant that 400 marquises had already risen against King Zhou. Sighing deeply over the fate of the kingdom and its people, Huang Feihu issued orders to his generals to tightly guard the strategic passes.

But now let's turn to Fairy Primordial in the Golden Light Cave on Qianyuan Mountain. One day he was sitting idly in his cave when White Crane Lad arrived from the Jade Emptiness Palace with a letter. Taking the letter, Fairy Primordial turned to face Mount Kunlun and kowtowed respectfully. "Jiang Ziya will soon leave Mount Kunlun, and you're requested to send the Pearl Spirit to the world straightway," White Crane Lad told him.

"I know that already."

When the White Crane Lad had left, Fairy Primordial sent the Pearl Spirit down to the world of men.

If you want to know how events developed, you must read the next chapter.

第十二回 陳塘關哪吒出世

12

THE BIRTH OF NEZHA

The commander at Chentang Pass was Li Jing, who had devoted himself to Taoism since childhood. His master was Immortal Woe Evading Sage on the West Kunlun Mountain, from whom he had learned some magic arts. He could ride on metal, wood, water, fire or dust, but as he was not destined to be an immortal, he was instructed to enjoy riches and power in the human world.

His wife Madame Yin had given him two sons. The elder was called Jinzha and the younger Muzha. Now she was pregnant for the third time, but was still not in labor though three years and six months had already passed. The prolonged pregnancy made the husband and wife extremely worried.

"This pregnancy's been so long that the child must be either a demon or a monster," Li Jing said one day, pointing at her belly.

"It's indeed inauspicious. I've worried about it day and night," Madame Yin agreed.

His wife's words made him even more worried than before. Late that night Madame Yin fell asleep, and had a strange dream in which a Taoist rushed directly into their bedroom:

"How dare you intrude so rudely into our bed chamber! How destestible you are!" she scolded him.

"Hurry, Madame, and receive this excellent baby," the Taoist called to her.

Before she could say anything, the Taoist threw something at her belly. Greatly startled, she woke up in a cold sweat and quickly woke her husband. As she told him about the dream, she began to feel pains in her belly. Li Jing immediately left the room and waited in the front hall.

"Three and a half years of pregnancy, and the moment's here at last! Whether it's fortuitous or not still remains to be seen," he mused.

But just then two maidservants rushed up to him. "Sir, Madame's just given birth to a demon!" they cried out.

Sword in hand, Li Jing rushed into the bed chamber. There he found the chamber full of red light and fragrance and saw a fleshy ball rolling to and fro near the bed. Shocked at the sight, he moved forward and struck the fleshy ball with his sharp sword. As it split in two, a baby boy jumped out amidst the red light. He had a white, beautiful face, wore a gold bracelet on his right wrist, and his belly was covered with a piece of red damask silk that shone with golden light.

He was the reincarnation of the Pearl Spirit, disciple of Fairy Primordial. The gold bracelet was a magic weapon called the Universal Ring and the red silk was the magic Sky Muddling Damask. They were both treasures from the Golden Light Cave.

Li Jing was astonished to see this baby boy running about the room. He caught him and held him in his arms. He was such a lovely child that Li Jing could not believe it was a demon and slaughter it. He carried the baby to his wife, who took to him at once. Indeed they were both delighted.

The next day, his colleagues came to congratulate him on the birth of his third son. When all the guests had gone, Li Jing received the unexpected news that a Taoist had requested to see him. A Taoist himself, Li Jing quickly invited the man in and offered him the seat of honor.

"Master, from which holy mountain and cave do you come? What instructions would you give me?"

"I'm Fairy Primordial from the Golden Light Cave on Qianyuan Mountain. I've come here to congratulate you on your new son. May I see the child?"

Li Jing immediately told a maidservant to bring the baby out. Fairy Primordial held the child and looked at him over closely.

"At what hour was he born?"

"About four yesterday morning."

"That's terrible," Fairy Primordial muttered.

"Do you mean that we may not bring him up, Master?"

"Oh, no! I mean that since he was born at four o'clock in the morning, he's sure to break the commandment on killing. Have you given him a name yet?"

"Not yet, Master."

"Would you let me give him a name and take him for a disciple?"

"We would only be too delighted."

"How many sons do you have, General?"

"Three. The eldest is Jinzha, disciple of Heavenly Master of Outstanding Culture at the High Cloud Cave on the Five Dragon Mountain; the second is Muzha, disciple of Immortal Universal Virtue at the White Crane Cave on the Nine Palace Mountain. As you would have this youngest for a disciple, please give him a name."

"Call him Nezha, as he's the third."

"I greatly appreciate it and thank you very much," Li Jing said, and ordered that a vegetarian feast be prepared for the immortal.

"I've got things to do at Qianyuan Mountain and must return there at once," the immortal declined the offer and left.

One day Li Jing was sitting in his office when news arrived that 400 marquises had rebelled against the king. He issued orders to keep close watch over the pass and other strategic places and to strengthen the defence at the Wild Horse Mountain.

Seasons came and went, and seven years quickly passed. Though it was now the fifth month by the lunar calendar, and the weather was very hot, Li Jing was still training his soldiers vigorously to defend Youhun Pass against Jiang Wenhuan. Irritated by the heat, Nezha, now seven years old and already six feet tall, went to see his mother.

"Mother, won't you let me stroll out beyond the pass? I daren't go there without your permission," he said.

"Only if you bring a guard along, son. But you mustn't

linger there too long. Return before your father does."

Accompanied by a guard, Nezha went out beyond the gates of the pass. By the time they had walked about one *li*, Nezha was so hot that he could go no further.

"There are shady trees ahead. Can we cool ourselves there?" he asked.

The guard rushed over and, walking under the shade of the trees, immediately felt a refreshing breeze. "Master, it's really cool here," he told Nezha.

Nezha happily joined him in the shade. He untied the belt around his gown and stripped to the waist. He was soon cool and comfortable. Looking around him, he caught sight of blue ripples sparkling in a nearby stream. Long, slender willow branches hung low over the water, swaying gracefully in the gentle breeze and small waterfalls gurgled over the rocks. Nezha stood up quickly and strode over to the bank of the stream.

"I got so hot on my way here that I'm bathed in a sweat. I want to have a wash in the stream," he told the guard.

"Don't forget, Master, that you must be home earlier than your father," the guard cautioned him.

"That's no problem," Nezha replied airily and immediately took his clothes off. He sat on a rock and, dipping his Sky Muddling Damask into the water, wiped his body with it.

This stream was the Nine Bend River, and it flowed into the East Sea. As the Sky Muddling Damask was a magic weapon, every time Nezha dipped it in the water, the river turned red, and when he swished it, the river shook violently until the Crystal Palace of the East Sea creaked and groaned.

Ao Guang, the dragon king of the East Sea, was sitting in his own room when the palace began shaking violently. "As there's no earthquake, what's shaking the palace?" he hurriedly asked, and ordered Li Gen, the Yaksha on duty, to find out the cause.

When the Yaksha reached the Nine Bend River, he saw the water there had turned a bright shining red, and a young boy was dipping a red scarf in the water and wiping his body with it.

"Boy! What have you got in your hand that turns the water red and rocks the Crystal Palace?" Li Gen parted the waters and shouted loudly.

Nezha look up and saw a creature with a blue face, red hair, a huge mouth and long protruding tusks, holding a large axe.

"What kind of beast are you? What a wonder that you can speak!" Nezha cried in surprise.

"I'm the Yaksha Sea Patrolman, and I'm here by order of my master. How dare you insult me, calling me a beast," Li Gen said angrily.

He jumped onto the bank, raised his axe and struck at Nezha's head. Nezha, naked and empty-handed, dodged the vicious blow, raised his Universal Ring and struck Li Gen on the head. How could the Yaksha withstand the magic weapon from Fairy Primordial! His skull broke open and he fell dead on the river bank.

"He's soiled my Universal Ring," Nezha laughed, and began to wash it in the stream. This shook the Crystal Palace so violently that it nearly fell down.

"What's going on? It's rocking even more violently! And Li Gen still hasn't returned."

The dragon king was thus wondering when a dragon soldier ran up. "Your Majesty, Li Gen the Yaksha's been killed by a young boy."

Ao Guang was shocked. "Li Gen was appointed by the Jade Emperor in person at the Spiritual Firmament Hall in Heaven. Who's dared to kill him?" He issued an order, "Alert the dragon troops! I'll personally confront the fellow."

As he spoke, Ao Bing, his third son, arrived. "Father, Why are you so angry?"

When Ao Guang told him the whole story, Ao Bing said, "You may rest at ease, father. I'll go and catch the criminal for you."

Mounted on his Water Parting Monster, Ao Bing took a lance and led the dragon soldiers out of the Crystal Palace. As the water parted before them, mighty waves rose high as mountains and crashed onto the shore, flooding the low-lying land.

Nezha was standing there watching the flood when he saw a man in full battle array surface on a marine beast. The man was armed with a lance and displayed valiant bearing.

"Who is it that killed Li Gen, the Yaksha Sea Patrolman?" the man demanded.

"It was me," Nezha answered frankly.

"Who are you?" Ao Bing asked.

"I'm the third son of Commander Li Jing of Chentang Pass. My father's the head of this district. My coming here to bathe in the river had nothing to do with Li Gen, yet he swore at me and acted rudely. Naturally I killed him."

"You damned scoundrel!" swore the third prince, growing angry. "Li Gen was appointed to his post by the Jade Emperor. How dare you beat him to death and then spout such nonsense!"

He raised his lance and ran at Nezha. Having no weapon, Nezha ducked out of the way.

"Wait a moment! Tell me who you are," he called to the dragon prince.

"I'm the third son of Ao Guang, Dragon King of the East Sea. My name's Ao Bing."

Nezha burst into laughter. "Oh! So you're a son of Ao Guang. Don't be so proud. Should you annoy me further, I'll drag out your old loach of a father and skin him alive!"

"You damned scoundrel! You've gone too far this time," the dragon prince roared and lunged at Nezha again.

Nezha became irritated and cast his Sky Muddling Damask into the air at the dragon prince. Thousands of fire balls suddenly appeared, enveloping the third prince and sweeping him from his mount. Nezha rushed over, trod on his neck, and lifting his Universal Ring, struck the prince on the head. The third prince resumed his true form and lay stretched out motionless on the ground.

"What a surprise! I've beaten this young dragon into his true form. I'll take his main tendon and make my father a dragon belt for a present," Nezha said to himself.

When he had taken the tendon from the dead dragon, he left the place at once and returned to the pass. The scene had so terrified the guard that he had gone weak and could scarcely walk.

"My son! Where have you been? Why did it take you so long?" his mother asked him.

"I just wandered out beyond the pass. I forgot the time and so returned late."

Before long, Li Jing returned from the military exercises. He dismissed his attendants, removed his armor and went to the back hall. He sat there worrying about the rebellion of the marquises and the ever-increasing hardship people were suffering.

Ao Guang was waiting in his palace when he got the news of his son's death. He was told that "Nezha, son of Commander Li Jing of Chentang Pass, killed the third prince and cruelly drew out his tendon."

He was shocked. "My son was God of Clouds and Rain and Plant Life, created by the Jade Emperor. Who dares to strike him a mortal blow? Li Jing, we met once when you were studying the Way at West Kunlun Mountain. How could you allow your son to wickedly murder mine? This injustice can never been erased. Your son's got the gall to take the tendon from my son's body! I'm burning with hatred!"

In a great rage and eager to avenge his son, Ao Guang transformed himself into a scholar and made his way directly to Chentang Pass.

Hearing that it was Ao Guang, Li Jing was delighted. "I've been separated from my brother Ao Guang for years and have missed him sorely. It must be a blessing from Heaven that we're to meet today," he said.

He straightened his clothes, hurried out, and invited Ao Guang into the main hall. They greeted each other and sat down. Seeing that Ao Guang was boiling with rage, Li Jing was bemused. He was about to question him when Ao Guang began, "Worthy Brother, how lucky you are to have such a good son!"

Li Jing smiled. "Brother, we haven't seen each other for many years. How happy I am that Heaven's blessed us with this meeting. Why do you speak so abruptly? I've got three sons, Jinzha, Muzha and Nezha, and each has been adopted by a sage as a disciple. Though they're not so good, they're not rascals, either. Please don't get a wrong impression of them."

"Brother, you're the one with the wrong impression! One of your sons took a bath at the Nine Bend River today. Using some magic weapon, he shook the waters until my Crystal Palace nearly collapsed. I sent my Yaksha to find out what was going on, but your son beat him to death. When I sent my third son to see what had happened, he was also beaten to death, and his tendon was cut out. How can you be so unreasonable as to defend his crimes!"

The dragon king was bitter, but Li Jing hurriedly comforted him with a smile. "You've blamed me wrongly, Brother. It couldn't have been one of my sons. My eldest son's at the Five Dragon Mountain, the second at the Nine Palace Mountain. The third is just seven years old and stays indoors all day long. How could any of them have done such a thing?"

"It was your third son, Nezha," Ao Guang said with assurance.

"That's most odd! Don't get impatient, Brother. Let me bring him out here and you can see for yourself."

Without any delay, Li Jing rushed to the back hall to see his wife, who asked, "Who's the visitor in the main hall?"

"My old friend, Ao Guang. He complains that his third son was killed by Nezha. I'll get Nezha to see him, and he'll see that it's not true. Where is Nezha now?"

Madame Yin thought to herself, "This is the first time Nezha went outside to play. How could he have done such a thing?" Not daring to tell him, she said simply, "He's playing in the back garden."

Li Jing entered the back garden. "Where are you, Nezha? Come here at once," he shouted.

Receiving no reply, Li Jing went to Begonia Hall but found the door bolted. He shouted again. Nezha immediately opened the door and came out to meet his father.

"What are you doing here, son?"

"As I had nothing to do today, I went out to the Nine Bend River. It was very hot and so I bathed in the river. Then

Li Gen the Yaksha appeared and swore at me most foully. He ruthlessly chopped at me with his axe. I lost my patience and knocked him off with my Universal Ring. Then some third prince called Ao Bing rushed at me, brandishing a lance, but I captured him with my Sky Muddling Damask. I trod on his neck and knocked him with my Universal Ring. He turned into a dead dragon with just one blow. I've heard that the main tendon of a dragon is very valuable, so I took it to make a dragon tendon belt for you."

Li Jing was stunned and speechless. It was a long time before he cried out, "Woe is me! Don't you know that you've got me into trouble and endless suffering? You'd better come with me to see your uncle and tell him what you did."

"Don't worry, father. As I didn't do it deliberately, I shouldn't be considered guilty. I haven't done anything to his son's tendon yet. It's all here in one piece if he would like to have it. Let me go and see him."

When Nezha reached the main hall with his father, he rushed up and greeted Ao Guang, "Uncle, I've unknowingly committed an error and offended you. I beg you earnestly to forgive me. Here's the tendon in perfect condition. I haven't done anything to it yet."

Looking at it, Ao Guang felt even more grief-stricken. "Your son's so wicked, yet you try to tell me that I'm wrong! Now that he's admitted to his crime, how can you be so cold and unsympathetic? Moreover, my son was a god, and the Yaksha was appointed by the Jade Emperor. How could you take it upon yourselves to murder them in cold blood! I'll report this case to the Jade Emperor tomorrow, and have you both severely dealt with," he threatened, and stormed out in a fury.

Li Jing began to stamp his feet and bewail the great calamity. Hearing his cries, Madame Yin found out from her attendants what had happened and hurried to the main hall herself to comfort him.

When she came to him, Li Jing stopped crying and said, "It was bad luck enough that I failed to become an immortal, but now you've produced this wonderful son! He's going to bring destruction on our whole family! The dragon prince was the god of rain, and now Nezha's murdered him. Ao Guang's bound to report this case to Heaven tomorrow, and within no more than three days we'll all turn to ghosts under the sword."

He began to weep again. Madame Yin also wept. "I suffered for three and a half years to give birth to you! Who would have guessed that you would be the ruin of our family," she pointed at Nezha and accused him.

Nezha felt extremely upset and knelt down before them. "Let me tell you the truth, Father and Mother. I'm not an ordinary mortal, but the disciple of Fairy Primordial at the Golden Light Cave on Qianyuan Mountain, and these weapons were all bestowed on me by him. It would certainly be impossible for Ao Guang to get the better of me. I'll now go straight to Qianyuan Mountain and ask my master how to deal with the matter. He'll surely help us out," he said, then declared, "I've caused all this trouble, and I hold myself responsible for it. I won't get you involved."

He then left the room. Picking up a handful of earth and throwing it into the air, he disappeared. Using his magic powers, he flew on the dust to Qianyuan Mountain. He soon arrived, was ushered in by Golden Haze Lad, and knelt before Fairy Primordial.

"Why don't you stay at Chentang Pass? Why do you come here to see me?" his master asked.

Nezha explained what had happened and begged his master for help.

"Though Nezha killed Ao Bing by mistake, it was in fact destined by fate. Even though Ao Guang is the king of dragons, he's only assigned to gather clouds and distribute the rain. He should understand the celestial phenomena that indicate political trends in the near future. It would be absurd to trouble Heaven with such a minor matter," Fairy Primordial thought, and said, "Come over here, Nezha. Unbutton your coat and shirt."

Nezha did as his master ordered. The immortal drew an Invisibility Charm with his fingers on Nezha's chest and ordered, "Go to the Precious Virtue Gate of the Heavenly Palace and do the following.... When you've finished, return directly to Chentang Pass. Should there be any more trouble, come to see me. I'll always help you. Nothing will happen to your parents. You may go now."

Nezha left Qianyuan Mountain and made his way directly to the Precious Virtue Gate of the Heavenly Palace. Everything in Heaven was different from on earth. Rays of golden light, shining in all directions, produced thousands of beautiful rainbows, and an auspicious purple haze hung in the air.

The South Heavenly Gate was built entirely of green-blue glazed bricks, and was decorated with numerous dazzling precious tripods. On each side of the gate were four huge pillars around which coiled red-bearded dragons whose duty it was to make rain by gathering clouds and fog. Just within the gate were two jade bridges, on each of which stood or danced multicolored phoenixes.

The Heavenly Palace complex contained thirty-six splendid palaces and seventy-two immense halls constructed with massive jade pillars, carved with the images of unicorns. Beneath the numerous terraces were wonderful gardens with exotic grasses and eternal flowers. Among the precious furnaces were the Furnace for Refining the Elixir of Life, the Divination Furnace and the Water-Fire Furnace, in which were planted evergreen fragrant grass. The Hall for Worshiping the Sages was full of officials dressed in brilliant purple silk robes, and standing or kneeling on the stone steps, were numerous officers wearing lotus coronets that glittered in the golden light.

Inside the Spiritual Firmament Hall, golden dragons coiled on the jade doors, while at the Hall for the Worthies, phoenixes danced in front of the pearl gates. Long, winding corridors were exquisitely wrought with wonderful carvings. Pretty birds darted gracefully in and out under the eaves. At the ends of roof-ridges were shining purple gourd-shaped adornments, and just under the roof hung jade bells that rang with sweet tunes in mild breeze. Inside the Heavenly Palace were many rare and precious things. The walls and beams were made of silver, gold and jade. Anyone who had the good fortune to enter the Heavenly Palace would never be polluted by the vulgar world again.

It was still early when Nezha reached the Precious Virtue Gate. Ao Guang had not yet arrived, and the palace gates had not yet opened. He waited at the Gate for the Worthies for a long while before he saw Ao Guang in his official robes striding swiftly towards the South Heavenly Gate.

Finding the gate still closed, Ao Guang said to himself, "I've arrived too early. The heavenly guards haven't come to open the gates yet. I'll have to wait here."

Though Nezha was standing close, he was invisible to the Dragon King because Fairy Primordial had drawn a charm on his chest.

The idea that Ao Guang was to accuse him before the Jade Emperor and have him punished angered Nezha. Rushing over, he raised his Universal Ring and struck Ao Guang a heavy blow on the back. As Ao Guang fell to the ground, Nezha trod on his neck, ready to deal with him.

If you want to know what happened to Ao Guang, you must read the next chapter.

13

COMBAT BETWEEN TWO FAIRIES

Twisting his head, Ao Guang looked round to find out who had knocked him to the ground and was furious to see Nezha. "You audacious scoundrel! You're just a kid and have yet to lose your milk teeth, but you viciously murdered first the Yaksha and then my third son. He wasn't your enemy, yet you had the gall to extract the tendon from his body. The crimes you've committed are really unforgivable, and now you're so barbarous as to beat me, the god of rain, right in front of the Precious Virtue Gate of the Heavenly Palace. You offend Heaven, and even mincing your flesh to bits wouldn't make amends for your crimes," he shouted.

This made Nezha so angry that he longed to beat him to death. But Fairy Primordial had strictly forbidden him to do so. He shifted more weight onto Ao Guang's neck. "Shut up or I'll kill you with my Universal Ring, you old loach! I'm none other than the Pearl Spirit, disciple of Fairy Primordial. By decree of the Jade Emptiness Palace, I was sent down to the world and reincarnated as son of Li Jing at Chentang Pass. Don't you know that the Shang Dynasty won't last long and the Zhou Dynasty will soon take its place? When Jiang Ziya descends from his mountain I'll be leading his vanguard on Zhaoge.

"I took a bath in the Nine Bend River to cool myself down. How could I expect to be insulted by the men you sent? I was so annoyed that I struck the two of them dead. It was only a trivial matter, yet you've come to report me to the Jade Emperor. My master told me that even if I beat you to death like the others, you old fool, it would be of no consequence."

Ao Guang was also exasperated. "You wretched brat! How dare you beat me like this!"

"If you like, I'll hit you again." Nezha immediately lifted his fist and beat Ao Guang until he began to cry out. "You old fool! You're too stubborn. As you're not afraid of my fist, I won't beat you any more. An ancient proverb says, 'A dragon fears having its scales removed, and a tiger fears having its tendon pulled out.'"

He tore away part of Ao Guang's robes, exposing the scales on the dragon king's left side and quickly scratched dozens of them with his thumb and fingers, splashing the ground with the dragon king's blood. The pain was unbearable for Ao Guang, and he began to cry for mercy.

"If you want mercy from me, you must forget about reporting me to the Jade Emperor and follow me back to Chentang Pass. If you don't do as I say, I'll knock you dead with my Universal Ring and let Fairy Primordial deal with the case. I'm not afraid of you in the least."

Confronted with such a wicked fellow, Ao Guang had no choice but to agree, saying, "I'm willing to follow you to Chentang Pass."

Nezha let him get up. They were about to leave for Chentang Pass when Nezha said, "I've heard that dragons have the ability to transform themselves to any size. They can expand their bodies high enough to touch the sky or make themselves as small as a mustard seed. I'm afraid that you'll run away from me and I won't be able to find you again. You'd better transform yourself into a small snake so that I can carry you back with me."

Ao Guang had no choice but to transform himself into a small green snake. Nezha picked him up, put him in one of his sleeves, left the Precious Virtue Gate and made his way directly to Chentang Pass, arriving home moments later. When he heard that Nezha was home, Li Jing felt very unhappy. Nezha noticed his frown. He went up to him respectfully and begged him earnestly for forgiveness.

"Where have you been?" Li Jing asked.

"I went to the South Heavenly Gate to request Uncle Ao

Guang not to make his complaint but to return here with me."

"You lying beast! What makes you qualified to call at the Heavenly Palace? You're just telling a pack of lies to deceive your parents."

"Don't be angry, father. Uncle Ao Guang can verify everything I've said."

"You're absurd. Where's your uncle Ao Guang?"

"He's in my sleeve," Nezha said, immediately took a small green snake from his sleeve and threw it on the ground. In a gust of wind, Ao Guang transformed himself into human form. Li Jing was astonished.

"What's happened, Brother?" Li Jing asked.

In a great rage, Ao Guang told him the whole story: How he was badly beaten and how his scales had been scratched off. He showed Li Jing the wounds on his left side.

"Your son's vicious and wicked! I'm going to summon the dragon kings of all the four seas to go together to the Spiritual Firmament Hall to complain to the Jade Emperor of this injustice. See what you can do about it then," Ao Guang said angrily, turned himself into a light wind and disappeared.

Li Jing stamped his foot with anxiety. "Matters are becoming worse. What shall we do now?"

Nezha walked forward and knelt down. "Father! Mother! You can set your minds at rest. When I asked for help from my master, he told me that it wasn't on my own authority that I was reincarnated here. I was sent down by a decree from the Jade Emptiness Palace on Mount Kunlun. Even if I killed the dragon kings of all the four seas, it would be a trifling matter. My master would take full responsibility for anything really serious. You needn't worry, father," he assured them.

Li Jing had studied the Way, and could understand what Nezha said. Moreover, he realized that since Nezha was able to fly to Heaven and torture Ao Guang at the South Heavenly Gate, he was no ordinary mortal, and must have been sent to the world for a purpose. Madame Yin, however, simply adored her son. Seeing Li Jing still looking angry, she said to Nezha, "Why do you still linger here? Go to the back yard and play."

Nezha went to the back garden as his mother requested, but after sitting there for a while, he felt bored. He left the back garden and mounted the pass wall. He walked up to a tower on top of the wall, intending to enjoy the cool breeze there.

He had never been there before and found the scenery enchanting. The weather was very hot. He saw pedestrians with pearls of sweat on their faces walking under the green willow trees, the sky hanging above them like a burning umbrella. He looked around and noticed a weapon rack with a bow and three arrows. It was the Universal Bow and the Sky Shocking Arrows. Looking at them, he said to himself, "My master told me that I would be in the vanguard in the war against the Shang Dynasty. I shouldn't waste my time. I'll start practising archery now, especially as I've found a bow and arrows here."

He took the bow and one of the arrows in his hand, put the arrow on the string and shot it towards the southwest. It whistled through the air glowing with red light. Little did Nezha know that this arrow was to bring him even more serious trouble. He had no idea that this was the magic bow and arrows and that no one had had the strength to draw since Sage Emperor Xuanyuan used it to subdue his enemies in ancient times. He simply picked up the bow and shot the arrow into the distance.

It flew to the White Bone Cave on Skeleton Mountain. This was the home of a fairy called Lady Rock, who had two young disciples named Blue Cloud Lad and Pretty Cloud Lad. On that day Blue Cloud Lad was picking medicinal herbs when suddenly an arrow struck him in the throat. The lad fell dead to the ground. When Pretty Cloud Lad found his mate dead, he hurried back and reported the matter to his mistress. Lady Rock rushed to where Blue Cloud Lad was lying dead on the edge of a cliff. She pulled the arrow out, looked at it, and recognized at once that it was a Sky Shocking Arrow.

"The arrow's kept at Chentang Pass and must have been shot by Li Jing. Oh, Li Jing, why are you so ungrateful? When you failed to become an immortal, I recommended that your master allow you to leave the mountain in search of riches and power in the world. Now that you've got a high post you don't try to repay my kindness. Instead, you've shot my disciple and returned my kindness with enmity!" she cried bitterly, then ordered her disciple, "Pretty Cloud Lad, look after the cave. I'm going to bring back Li Jing and take my revenge."

Riding a male phoenix, she sped through the air and soon reached Chentang Pass. "Li Jing, come out to see me at once!"

Li Jing rushed out, and upon seeing Lady Rock, knelt down and kowtowed.

"Your disciple Li Jing kowtows before you. I didn't know you were coming. Please forgive me for not coming out sooner," he apologized.

"You've committed an outrage, yet still try to dupe me with cunning words," Lady Rock snapped sharply.

She threw her Cloud Radiance Handkerchief at Li Jing, and ordered her yellow-scarved genie to wrap him up and take him back to the Skeleton Mountain. Back in the cave, Lady Rock sat down on her rush throne and ordered that Li Jing be brought in. Li Jing knelt before her.

"Li Jing! Though you're unable to become an immortal, you've got wealth and position in the world. Have you considered who this is all due to? Now with no thought to reciprocate my kindness, you've wickedly shot my disciple Blue Cloud Lad! What do you have to say for yourself?"

Not knowing what she was talking about, Li Jing was bewildered, "My Lady, what crime have I committed against you?"

"You returned my grace with enmity and shot my disciple. Why pretend that you don't know?" Lady Rock rebuked him.

"Where's the arrow? Show it to me, please."

When Lady Rock showed him the arrow, he was surprised to find that it was a Sky Shocking Arrow kept in the tower at Chentang Pass.

"The Universal Bow and Sky Shocking Arrows were left by the Sage Emperor Xuanyuan and are treasures of Chentang Pass. No one had been able to draw the bow since ancient times," he cried out in astonishment. "It's my ill-fortune that such an extraordinary thing's happened. I hope you'll realize that I'm innocent. If you let me return to Chentang Pass, I'll find out who the real murderer is and bring him here for your judgment."

"If that's so, I'll let you return home. Should you try to run away, I'll ask your master to hand you over to me. You may leave now, Li Jing," Lady Rock said mildly.

Carrying the arrow, Li Jing returned home riding on a dust cloud. He reached his headquarters to find Madame Yin in a state of panic.

"Why were you suddenly seized and carried off? I was worried to death," she cried out.

Li Jing sighed and told her all that had happened, then added, "No one else would be strong enough to draw the Universal Bow. Could it have been Nezha again?"

"That's preposterous! How would he dare to create new trouble when the trouble with Ao Guang's still not settled. Besides, I don't think Nezha could draw that bow."

After pondering for a long time, Li Jing came up with an idea. He sent his men to tell Nezha to see him at once. Soon Nezha arrived, bowed and stood quietly before his father.

"Since your master said you're going to help the sage king against King Zhou, why don't you spend your time learning archery and horsemanship?"

"That's what I've always wanted. A minute ago I was on the pass wall, and I found a bow and three arrows in the tower there. I shot one of the arrows. It flew through the air emitting a red light, and then disappeared," Nezha answered.

Li Jing was furious. "You damned unfilial son! You knocked off the third prince and the trouble isn't over yet. But now you've brought this new calamity upon us."

Madame Yin remained silent, and Nezha, not knowing what his father was talking about, was simply puzzled. He asked innocently, "What do you mean? What has happened?"

"This arrow you shot killed one of Lady Rock's disciples. She took me to her cave and was going to put me to death, but I pleaded my innocence. She sent me back to look for the murderer. How could I have guessed it was you! You must go to see Lady Rock and tell her what you've done!"

"Don't be angry, father. Where does she live? Where was her disciple and how could I have shot him? I won't yield if I've been wrongly accused," Nezha said with a smile.

"She lives at the White Bone Cave on Skeleton Mountain. You've shot her disciple, and you'd better go to see her now," Li Jing said.

"You're right, father. I'll go to this White Bone Cave. But if it turns out that I'm not the killer, I'll knock her off before I return home. Please lead the way," Nezha answered.

Father and son traveled rapidly on the dust to Skeleton Mountain, where Li Jing told Nezha, "Wait for me here while I go in and report to Lady Rock."

Nezha smiled coldly. "I'll be here. See what she can do with me. She's accused me groundlessly."

Li Jing entered the cave and greeted Lady Rock, who asked him, "Have you found out who shot Blue Cloud Lad?"

"It was my unfilial son Nezha. I've brought him here as you ordered."

Lady Rock instantly ordered Pretty Cloud Lad, "Tell him to come in."

Seeing a man coming out of the cave, Nezha thought, "Since there's going to be a fight, I might as well strike the first blow. This is their nest here, and I'm at a disadvantage. I can't let them get the upper hand."

Catching the lad off his guard, Nezha raised his Universal Ring and struck him on the neck. Seriously wounded, he collapsed onto the ground. Hearing the thud of his fall, Lady Rock rushed out from her cave. She saw Pretty Cloud Lad lying there, close to death. "You vile monster! How dare you hurt my other disciple!" She screamed with rage.

She was wearing a gold fish-tail coronet and silk-belted red robes embroidered with the eight diagrams. When Nezha saw her come at him with a sharp sword, he threw up his Universal Ring to strike her.

Recognizing Fairy Primordial's Universal Ring, Lady Rock cried out in surprise, "Oh, so it's you!" Stretching out her hand, she took the ring.

Nezha was greatly frightened and hastily tossed the Sky Muddling Damask into the air in an attempt to wrap her up. Lady Rock laughed uproariously. Lifting one of her arms, she opened her sleeve and the Sky Muddling Damask dropped gently inside it.

"Nezha, take out some more of your master's magic things and see what my magic is like!"

Left empty-handed, Nezha could do nothing but turn and run for life.

"Li Jing, this has nothing to do with you. You're free and can return home now," Lady Rock called pursuing Nezha with the speed of lightning.

In such a desperate situation, Nezha only knew to flee to Qianyuan Mountain. He rushed into the Golden Light Cave and knelt down before his master.

"Why are you so flustered, Nezha?"

"Lady Rock unjustly accuses me of shooting her disciple and is chasing me, trying to kill me. She's taken both your Universal Ring and Sky Muddling Damask. She won't let me alone and is now outside the cave. There's nothing I can do but beg you to save me, Master," Nezha cried.

"You poor devil! Take cover in the peach garden at the back. I'll go out and meet her."

Fairy Primordial went out and leaned on the door waiting. Soon he saw Lady Rock rushing angrily towards his cave brandishing a sword.

"How are you, Brother!" Lady Rock bowed when she saw the master. "I've come to complain that Nezha's killed one of my disciple and seriously wounded the other. He also tried to slay me with the Universal Ring and Sky Muddling Damask. Tell him to come out and see me and the matter can be settled. If you try to protect him, it'll be the worse for you."

"Nezha's in my cave now and I can easily tell him to come out. All you have to do is go to the Jade Emptiness Palace and get an order from my Grand Master. Nezha was reincarnated in this world by his order to support the sage king of the Zhou Dynasty. I'm not acting out of selfish considerations."

Lady Rock smiled. "You're wrong, Brother. How can you force your Grand Master on me? Don't bully me with your words. You must realize that I'm not inferior to you in the least."

"Lady Rock, though you're of Jie Taoism and I of Chan, we come from the same source. We of Chan Taoism cannot purge ourselves of desire although we've studied the Way for 1,500 years. We're fated to break the commandment on killing and have thus been sent down into the world and meet our fate.

"As we all can see, the Shang Dynasty is destined to fall and the Zhou Dynasty will rise to replace. Jiang Ziya will create gods on behalf of the Jade Emptiness Palace and enjoy wealth and power in the world. To this end, not long ago the chiefs of the three religions drew up the List of Creations. I was instructed by my Grand Master to send all my disciples down to the world to join in the war. Nezha's the reincarnation of the Pearl Spirit, and by order of the Jade Emptiness Palace he'll help Jiang Ziya found the new dynasty. All that he's done is destined by fate. Though your disciple has died, he's to be created a god sooner or later. You need know neither worry nor sorrow, neither glory nor humiliation. Why get so emotional and cause a setback in your advance?"

Lady Rock could not control her wrath. "Though we both study the Way, we must find out which is the superior and which the inferior."

"Though we're of the same source, our achievements differ. Don't you think so?" Fairy Primordial said. "I've so refined my spirit under the sun and moon that it's like a pearl now, bright and sparkling. I've magic powers to shake Heaven and earth, and have escaped the cycle of life and death. I've left my footprints over all the four seas. As such I've in this way gained everlasting fame for my accomplishments. Clouds are firm under my feet, and purple divine phoenixes and vermillion cranes meet me where I travel."

This haughty lecture made Lady Rock even more furious. She rushed at him and slashed at his face with her sword, but he evaded the blow and dodged back into his cave. Taking up his sword and a secret weapon, he kowtowed in the direction of the Kunlun Mountain.

"Forgive me, Master, for your disciple will break the commandment on killing on this mountain today," he prayed, then coming out of his cave again, he said, "Your learning's superficial, but how dare you make trouble here on my mountain!"

Lady Rock slashed at him again, and Fairy Primordial parried the blow with his sword crying, "Heaven forbid!" Lady Rock was an uncut rock, but for centuries she had been refining herself with essences from the sun and moon and Heaven and earth, until she had obtained magic powers and human form. But she was not yet an immortal, and so could not avoid the disaster brought about by her rash temper. After a few rounds she threw her Dragon Beard Handkerchief into the air to capture her enemy.

"How can the evil ever conquer the good!" Fairy Primordial said with a smile. He muttered an incantation and pointed at the handkerchief, which dropped to the ground.

Lady Rock was furious. She swung her sword wildly at Fairy Primordial, who leapt out of range and tossed his Nine Dragon Divine Fire Coverlet into the air. It landed neatly on Lady Rock before she had the chance to run away. Glancing towards the cave, Fairy Primordial found that Nezha had stolen out to watch their combat and had taken a great fancy to the wonderful Divine Fire Coverlet. But Fairy Primordial refused to give it to him.

"You must return home right now. The Jade Emperor has already approved the request made by the four dragon kings and has sent his guards to arrest your parents!" the immortal told Nezha, who burst into loud sobs and begged him to think of a way out of the trouble. Fairy Primordial told him what he must do to save them and Nezha rode back on a dust cloud to Chentang Pass.

When Nezha had gone, Fairy Primordial clapped his hands and a fierce fire immediately began to rage within his magic coverlet. Nine fire dragons twisted and coiled upon Lady

Rock, burning her until she resumed her original form— a huge uncut rock.

Meanwhile, Nezha had arrived back home and found the house in an uproar. He confronted the four dragon kings. "I assume full responsibility for what I've done and shall pay with my life. My parents are in no way involved," he announced.

He drew his sword, first cut off his own left arm, then cut open his belly, gouged out his intestines and broke his own bones. He died soon afterwards, and his soul floated on the wind until it reached Qianyuan Mountain.

If you want to know what happened next, you must read the next chapter.

第十四回　哪吒現蓮花化身

REINCARNATION WITH
LOTUS FLOWERS

Golden Haze Lad rushed into the cave. "My fellow disciple's floating about on the wind. He seems to be quite out of control. I don't know what's happened."

Fairy Primordial immediately realized what had happened and hurried out of the cave. "This is no place for you to stay," he told Nezha's soul. "It would be better for you to return to Chentang Pass. Visit your mother in a dream and ask her to build a temple for you on Jade Screen Mountain, about forty *li* from the pass. When you've been worshiped with incense and candles for three years, you'll be reincarnated into human form again, so that you can assist the sage king to found the new dynasty. Go quickly and don't delay."

Nezha left Qianyuan Mountain and went straight to Chentang Pass. In the early hours of the morning, he entered his parents' bed chamber and said, "Dear mother, I'm Nezha. I'm dead now, and have no place to rest my soul. Please take pity on me and build a temple for me on Jade Screen Mountain. If my soul is worshiped, I'll be able to go to Heaven. Your kindness will be appreciated forever."

Madame Yin woke startled from her sleep and wept bitterly. She told Li Jing all that had happened, but Li Jing was furious.

"Why should you weep for him? Haven't you suffered enough because of Nezha? It's often said that a dream is the product of the day's thinking. You must have been thinking of him during the day. You don't need to worry about it!" Li Jing dismissed the dream lightly.

Madame Yin didn't answer. But on the following night,

she dreamt of Nezha again, and yet again the third night. As soon as she closed her eyes, she saw Nezha standing before her, making the same request.

Nezha had a fiery temper when he was alive, and had not changed after his death. After five or six days, Nezha said roughly to his mother, "I've begged for several days already, yet you've completely ignored me! If you don't do as I ask I'll trouble you all the time, making it impossible for the family to live in peace."

After the last dream, Madame Yin didn't have the courage to tell Li Jing but sent a trusted servant directly to Jade Screen Mountain to build a temple. The construction was finished in ten months.

It was a magnificent structure, surrounded by a high white wall. Fir and pine trees were planted both inside and out. Its vermillion gates were fixed with brass ring knockers, while the roofs were beautifully laid with blue-green tiles. Inside the main hall Nezha's image was seated on a pedestal of shining gold, while the silk curtains around it were embroidered with phoenixes and dragons. On either side of Nezha stood the images of secretaries and guards.

Nezha manifested his divine virtue to all people, answered all their prayers and helped them meet their needs. This attracted a steady stream of people from far and near to worship at the temple. Half a year passed in peace and prosperity.

Meanwhile, East Grand Duke Jiang Wenhuan had been leading attacks against Youhun Pass, and General Dou Rong was unable to subdue him. As a result, Li Jing took measures to strengthen this defence and train the soldiers day and night.

One day, when the training was over at Wild Horse Mountain, Li Jing passed Jade Screen Mountain on his way home and was surprised to see all kinds of people, young and old, male and female, passing back and forth before him.

"What are all these people doing here?" he asked his men.

"About six months ago a god appeared here. He grants every request made of him, gives blessings when asked, and answers prayers when there are disasters. The god's loved and attracts worshipers from all over," one of them replied.

"What's the name of this god?"

"God Nezha."

Li Jing was furious. "Halt the army here for a while. I'll go up and have a look," he ordered.

Galloping up the mountain, when he got to the temple he saw a horizontal board on the gate inscribed with "The Temple of God Nezha." He entered and found a lifelike image of his son standing between images of secretaries and guards.

"You beast! You brought suffering to your parents when you were alive and cheat the people when dead," Li Jing swore. He whipped and smashed the image and kicked the secretaries off their pedestals. "Set the temple on fire!" he ordered his men, then told the worshipers, "He's not a real god. You mustn't worship him any more."

Thoroughly frightened, they left the place. Li Jing mounted his horse and returned home, his anger unabated. He dismissed his men and entered the back hall to see his wife.

"The son you bore gave me enough trouble already. How could you have built that temple for him to deceive the public?" he reprimanded her. "You won't be satisfied until I'm dismissed from my post! You know that Fei Zhong and You Hun control the court, and I've never associated with them. Should anyone report to Zhaoge what you did I would certainly be impeached for encouraging the worship of a false god and would be dealt with seriously. All my years of service would come to nothing. How could you do anything so thoughtlessly! I've already burnt down his temple, and I forbid you to rebuild it. I won't forgive you if you repeat your mistake."

On that day, Nezha's soul was not in the temple. When he returned at dusk, he was astonished to find it burnt down. The surrounding land was still smouldering and dense smoke filled the air. Two of his secretaries came forward in tears.

"What happened?"

"Commander Li Jing of Chentang Pass broke your golden image and set fire to the temple. We've got no idea why," the secretaries answered.

"Oh, Li Jing! There's no longer any relationship between us. I've already returned my flesh and bones to you. How could you smash my image and burn my temple, leaving me no place to live?" Nezha cried in annoyance.

He pondered for a long time, and decided to go to Qianyuan Mountain and ask his master to deal with the problem. After months of worship by the people, he had regained some shape and voice. He soon reached the mountain and was led into the cave by Golden Haze Lad.

"Why do you come here? Why don't you stay in your temple?" Fairy Primordial asked him.

Nezha knelt down and told him what had happened and begged his master to save him.

"Li Jing, you've acted wrongly. Nezha returned his flesh and bones to you, and has made no trouble on Jade Screen Mountain, yet you've smashed his image, and made it impossible for him to be reincarnated," the immortal thought. "Time's short, and Jiang Ziya will come down soon. Nezha must be there to cooperate with him. I must do something to help Nezha." He ordered Golden Haze Lad, "Go to the lotus pond and pick two lotus flowers and three lotus leaves for me at once!"

Golden Haze Lad brought the flowers and leaves and placed them on the floor. Fairy Primordial pulled all the petals off and arranged them in three piles: top, middle and bottom. Then he broke the stems into 300 pieces to represent the 300 bones. Finally, he put a lotus leaf on each of the three groups of lotus petals to represent heaven, earth and man. When this was done, he placed a grain of golden elixir in the center and worked his own vital energies into them. Then he grasped Nezha's soul and threw it into the petals, leaves and stems. "What are you waiting for, Nezha? Look, you're a man already," he cried.

There was a tremendous bang, and a boy leapt up before Fairy Primordial. He was young and dashing, with a handsome white face, red lips, shining eyes and a sturdy body sixteen feet tall. Nezha, now reincarnated from lotus flowers, kowtowed to Fairy Primordial in gratitude.

"It was really terrible of Li Jing to have smashed your image in the temple!" His master said to him sympathetically.

"Master, I cannot forgive him. I must take revenge," Nezha said with emotion.

"Come with me to the peach garden, Nezha."

In an open space in the peach garden, Fairy Primordial handed Nezha his Fire-Tip Lance and taught him how to use it. Nezha completely mastered the weapon in a short time, and then made ready to leave Qianyuan Mountain to take his revenge on Li Jing.

"Besides the Fire-Tip Lance, I'll give you two Wind-Fire Wheels. When you stand on them, they'll carry you wherever you wish to go at a fantastic speed. I'll tell you the spells and you can use them as you like," the master said, handing him a leopard-skin bag with the Universal Ring, the Sky Muddling Damask and a gold brick. Bidding Nezha farewell, he said, "You may go to Chentang Pass now."

Nezha kowtowed and thanked him. He then took the Fire-Tip Lance, rode off on the Wind-Fire Wheels and soon arrived at Chentang Pass.

"Li Jing! Come out to see me at once," Nezha shouted loudly.

The guard at the gate rushed in. "The young master's outside. He's riding on a pair of Wind-Fire Wheels and brandishing a Fire-Tip Lance. He demands that you see him."

"Rubbish!" shouted Li Jing. "How can a dead man come alive again."

As he spoke, several more guards rushed in. "If you don't go out quickly, he'll fight his way into your living quarters."

Li Jing was furious. He grabbed his halberd, leapt on his horse and galloped out of his headquarters. He was astonished to see Nezha with his Wind-Fire Wheels and Fire-Tip Lance. He swore loudly, "You damned beast! You caused us endless suffering before your death and now that you've been reborn, you're troubling us again!"

"Li Jing! I returned my flesh and bones to you, and there's no longer any relationship between us. Why did you smash my golden image with your whip and burn down my temple on Jade Screen Mountain? Today I must take my revenge."

He thrust at Li Jing's face, and Li Jing hurriedly parried the blow with his halberd. They fought vigorously. But Nezha had marvelous strength, and after four or five rounds, Li Jing was exhausted. Abandoning the fight, he fled towards the southeast.

"Li Jing! I won't let you off. I won't stop until I've taken your life!" Nezha screamed after him.

As the Wind-Fire Wheels were much faster than Li Jing's gray horse, Nezha soon caught up with him. Panic-stricken, Li Jing jumped down from his horse and mounted a dust cloud.

"There's nothing special for a Taoist to ride invisibly on the five elements. You don't believe you'll get rid of me by riding on the dust, do you?" Nezha said with a smile and rode his Wind-Fire Wheels even faster in pursuit.

Li Jing was frightened. "He'll overtake me soon and kill me with his lance. What shall I do?"

Just at this critical moment, he heard someone approaching, singing a song:

> The moon shines o'er the clear still waters,
> On the bank peach flowers and willows grow.
> This is a scene of no ordinary beauty,
> High in the sky, the dawn clouds glow.

He saw a young Taoist, and immediately recognized to be his second son, Muzha, disciple of the Immortal Universal Virtue.

"Father, Muzha's here."

Seeing him, Li Jing felt relieved. As Nezha rushed up, Muzha moved forward to meet him.

"Stop, you wretch! To murder your father is a capital crime. I'll spare your life only if leave here at once," he threatened.

"Who are you that dares brag so?"

"You don't even recognize me! I'm your elder brother Muzha."

Learning that it was his brother, Nezha hastily said, "Second brother, you don't know the details of what's happened." He told Muzha the whole story, then asked, "Who is right, Li Jing or I?"

"Parents are always right on matters concerning their children!"

"But don't you know that I returned my flesh and bones to him! No relationship exists between us as father and son now," Nezha argued.

At this, Muzha flew into a rage, and cursing him as an unfilial son, slashed at Nezha with his sword. Nezha parried the blow with his lance.

"Muzha! There's no bad feeling between us. Stand back and let me take my revenge on Li Jing."

Muzha swore angrily, "You damned wretch! How dare you be so perverse!"

As Muzha aimed another blow, Nezha sighed. "Things are destined by fate. He's willing to substitute death for life."

He returned the blow with a thrust of his Fire-Tip Lance. Though engaged with his brother, Nezha's mind was on his father. Worried that he might run away, he parried Muzha's blow, took the gold brick from his bag and threw it straight at Muzha. Caught off guard, Muzha was struck on the back and fell to the ground. Nezha turned to Li Jing, who took flight at once.

"Even if you run to the seaside or to an island, I'll get you," Nezha taunted with a laugh.

Li Jing sped along wildly, not knowing whether he was going east, west, south or north. After he had run for a long time, he was exhausted.

"Enough! Enough! I don't know what dreadful sin I must have committed in my previous incarnation that I first failed to become an immortal and then produced such a wicked son. I'd better kill myself so as to avoid further humiliation!" he decided, and was reaching for his weapon when he heard someone call him.

"General Li, stop! I'm coming now," a voice said, and then began to sing:

Warm winds caress the willow trees,

And on the pool sweet petals float.
You ask me where it is I dwell,
I answer "In white clouds remote."

It was Heavenly Master of Outstanding Culture. He approached swiftly with a duster in his hand.

Li Jing cried out, "Master, save my life, I beg of you!"

"Go into my cave at once. I'll wait for him here," the immortal said.

A few moments later, Nezha sped up militantly on his Wind-Fire Wheels. He stopped, spotting the Taoist standing on a slope but no sign of Li Jing.

"Master, have you seen a general pass by?"

"General Li Jing's just gone into my cave. Why do you ask?"

"Master, he's my enemy. You'd better tell him to come out. This matter has nothing to do with you, but if you help him get away, I'll give you a taste of my lance in his place," Nezha said harshly.

"Who are you? Why are you so ferocious as to threaten even me?"

Nezha had no idea who the Taoist was. He answered haughtily, "I'm a disciple of Fairy Primordial on Qianyuan Mountain. My name's Nezha. I'm not to be trifled with!"

"I've never heard of Fairy Primordial's disciple. This isn't the place for you to be blustering about. If you don't behave yourself I'll take you to the peach garden, give you 300 strokes with the cane and hang you there for three years."

Not knowing what was good for him, Nezha lunged at Heavenly Master, who turned and ran towards his cave with Nezha chased close behind. The immortal took out the magic Dragon Bound Stake from his sleeve and threw it into the air. In an instant, fierce winds sprang up, fog filled the sky, and dust billowed through the air. Nezha began to feel faint and his mind became confused. Before he knew what was happening, he found himself tightly bound to a golden stake by golden rings around his neck, arms and legs, unable to move an inch.

The Heavenly Master walked up. "Enough of your impudence, you wicked brat!" he cursed, and then told Jinzha, Nezha's eldest brother, "Fetch me a cane." When it was brought, the Heavenly Master ordered, "Beat him for me."

Jinzha did as he was ordered and gave Nezha a severe beating. After quite a long while, the Heavenly Master said, "All right, that's enough," and the two returned to the cave together.

"What's going on? I not only failed to get Li Jing, but I got myself caught and beaten black and blue in the bargain!" Nezha thought. He gnashed his teeth in fury but could do nothing but wait quietly outside the cave.

Fairy Primordial had planned all this meaning to temper Nezha's violent nature. As Nezha was fuming with rage, he saw his master arrive at High Cloud Cave.

"Master! Master! Please save me," Nezha cried loudly, but Fairy Primordial took no notice of him and went directly into the cave.

When White Cloud Lad reported his arrival, Heavenly Master came out and took his hand. "I've been teaching your disciple a little lesson," he said with a smile.

After they sat down, Fairy Primordial said, "I realized that Nezha's too violent by nature. I sent him here to be tempered. I'm sorry if he's offended you."

"Go and set Nezha free. Tell him to come in," Heavenly Master ordered Jinzha.

Jinzha went up to Nezha. "Your master orders you to see him inside."

"As your master could do nothing with me, he played some trick to make me unable to move. How can you joke with me now?"

Jinzha smiled. "Close your eyes and I'll set you free."

Nezha closed his eyes. Jinzha drew a charm to remove the Dragon Bound Stake. When he opened his eyes, Nezha found that all the rings, together with the stake, had disappeared. Shaking his head, he murmured, "Good Heavens! I've suffered too much today. Let me see my master and find out what I can do."

When Jinzha and Nezha entered the cave, the latter saw

his master sitting on the right and the Taoist on the left.

"Come here. Kneel down and kowtow to your uncle!" Fairy Primordial ordered him.

Nezha didn't dare disobey his master, and so he kowtowed to Heavenly Master. "Thank you for the beating," he said and then kowtowed to his own master.

Fairy Primordial asked Li Jing to come over. When Li Jing knelt before him, he said, "Li Jing! What you did on Jade Screen Mountain was really too narrow-minded. It created this hostility between father and son."

This criticism failed to soothe Nezha. His anger rose so high that he wished secretly to devour Li Jing. The two immortals, however, knew exactly what he was thinking.

"From this day on, there must be no more antagonism between you two. Li Jing, you may leave here first," Fairy Primordial added.

Li Jing thanked the two immortals and left the cave. Nezha seethed with fury but dared not utter a word. He scratched his cheeks, pulled his ears, sighed and groaned. Fairy Primordial laughed inwardly at him.

"You may go too. Go and keep watch on the cave. I'll have a game of chess with your uncle and be back in a minute," he told Nezha.

Nezha was elated. He left the cave immediately and began to pursue Li Jing on his Wind-Fire Wheels. After quite a while, he caught sight of Li Jing hurrying along on the dust. "Li Jing! Stop running! I'm coming to get you!" he called after him.

"How could that Taoist fool me like this? Since I was allowed to leave first, he shouldn't have set him free to chase after me! That immortal had no good intentions at all. What am I to do now?" Li Jing cried out pitifully.

He continued to flee, but time was running out. Just at the critical moment, catching sight of another Taoist on top of a peak leaning casually on a pine tree, he called out for help.

"Is that Li Jing?" the Taoist asked.

"Yes, it's me, Master," Li Jing answered frantically.

"Why are you in such a panic?"

"Nezha's close on my heels. Save me, I beg you."

"Come up here and stand behind me."

Li Jing immediately went up and hid behind the Taoist. Before he could catch his breath, Nezha arrived at the foot of the mountain and saw Li Jing and the unknown Taoist standing on the peak before a pine tree.

"Don't think that I'll come off worst this time," Nezha smiled and rode his Wind-Fire Wheels up the peak.

"Why are you chasing him?" the Taoist asked Nezha.

When Nezha had repeated the whole story, the Taoist said, "Since you agreed to keep peace, why are you pursuing him again? You're breaking your promise!"

"This isn't any of your business. Don't interfere with me. I must get hold of him to vent my hatred."

"If you insist," said the Taoist, and turning to Li Jing, he said, "Go and fight with him while I watch."

"Master! This beast has unbounded strength; I'm surely no match for him," Li Jing answered dejectedly.

The Taoist stood up, spat on him and clapped him on the back, saying, "Go and fight with him. I'm here, so don't worry."

Li Jing had no choice but to lift his halberd and charge into the fight. Nezha met him with his Fire-Tip Lance. Father and son fought violently on the open space of the peak. After fifty or sixty rounds, Nezha was utterly exhausted, his whole body bathed in sweat.

"Li Jing was no match for me, but now he's getting the upper hand. It must be because that Taoist spat on him and clapped him on the back. I'll first stab the Taoist and then deal with Li Jing," he thought to himself and leapt suddenly away from the fight and lunged straight at the Taoist.

The Taoist quickly opened his mouth and spat out a white lotus flower which stopped the lance in mid-air. "You wicked brat! Your fight's with your father. There's no animosity between us. Why did you stab at me with your lance? I would have lost my life if it hadn't been for my white lotus flower. Why are you so savage?"

"Li Jing's never been able to beat me before," Nezha

shouted. "Why did you spit and clap him on the back? There's obviously some trick in it to make me unable to defeat him. That's why!"

"You damned brat! I dare you to stab me again!" the Taoist challenged.

In a burning rage, Nezha lunged forward, aiming his lance straight at the breast of the Taoist. The immortal jumped aside and lifted his sleeves towards the sky. The air was instantly filled with beautiful whirling clouds and a swirling purple mist. An exquisitely wrought pagoda dropped from the sky on top of Nezha, trapping him inside. The Taoist struck the top of the pagoda with both hands, and a fierce fire began to rage within. Nezha was burnt so terribly that he cried out for mercy.

"Are you willing to acknowledge your father now?"

"I do, I do. I acknowledge him." Nezha had to agree.

"Then I'll spare your life," said the Taoist and quickly removed the pagoda.

Looking down at his body, Nezha was astonished to find that he had not a single burn. "How extraordinary," he thought. "This Taoist is playing tricks on me."

"Since you acknowledge Li Jing as your father, you must kowtow to him."

Seeing that if he refused, the Taoist would burn him in the pagoda again, Nezha controlled himself with an effort and kowtowed to Li Jing with an angry expression on his face.

"You must call him 'Father'," the Taoist ordered. When Nezha hesitated, he said, "Since you refuse, you must be still unwilling to acknowledge him. I'll have to burn you again in the pagoda."

This alarmed Nezha so that he hastily cried, "Father! Father! Your son's sinned against you."

The Taoist then told Li Jing to kneel down. "I'll give you this pagoda and teach you how to use it. Should Nezha trouble you again, you can burn him with it."

Hearing this, Nezha realized that it would be impossible for him to get it back at Li Jing. He felt greatly disappointed.

"Henceforth, the two of you must live in harmony. You'll be ministers one day in the same court. You should help the sage king found the new dynasty while cultivating your own proper lives. Nothing more should be said of past events. Nezha, you may go now."

Nezha understood the situation. He left and returned to Qianyuan Mountain.

Li Jing knelt down. "Master, your kindness has saved me from great peril. May I know your honorable name and the cave you live in?"

"I'm Master Burning Lamp from the Prime Consciousness Cave on Mount Divine Hawk. Though you failed to attain the Way, you've enjoyed wealth and power in the world. Now King Zhou rules without virtue and the kingdom is in chaos. You needn't be a garrison commander any longer, but should become a hermit in some mountain valley. Keep away from fame and riches temporarily. When King Wu of the rising Zhou Dynasty launches an attack on King Zhou, you may come out of the mountains and distinguish yourself."

Li Jing kowtowed and returned to Chentang Pass. He gave up his post and became a hermit in the mountains.

Burning Lamp had come at the request of Fairy Primordial to temper Nezha and to effect a reconciliation between father and son.

If you want to know what happened next, you must read the next chapter.

15

JIANG ZIYA
LEAVES MOUNT KUNLUN

Heavenly Primogenitor, the Grand Master of Chan Taoism, lived in the Jade Emptiness Palace on Mount Kunlun. As his disciples were destined to experience the vulgar world and break the commandment on killing, he closed his palace and stopped giving lectures on the Way.

The heads of Chan and Jie Taoism and Confucianism held a meeting, at which it was decided to create 365 gods. They were to be the gods of thunder, fire, plague, constellations, stars, sacred mountains, clouds and rain, virtue, and evil. The creation was destined for the downfall of the Shang and rise of the Zhou when immortals would break the commandment on killing. It was not by chance that Jiang Ziya was to enjoy power and wealth as commander and prime minister.

One day Heavenly Primogenitor ascended his Eight Treasure and Cloud Radiance Throne. "Go to the peach garden and tell Jiang Ziya to see me at once," he told White Crane Lad.

Jiang Ziya hurried into the court and knelt before the Grand Master, saying, "Your disciple Jiang Ziya kowtows."

"How long have you been on Mount Kunlun?"

"I came when I was thirty-two years old, and now I'm seventy-two."

"You were born unlucky. It's difficult for you to become an immortal, and all you can do is enjoy the pleasures of the world. The end of the Shang Dynasty is near at hand, and the House of Zhou is rising. Would you descend the mountain and create gods on my behalf? You're to assist the sage ruler and serve as his commander and prime minister. Your forty years of cultivation here make you ideal for the posts. This isn't the place for you to remain long. You'd better pack up and leave as soon as possible."

"Master," Jiang Ziya begged pitifully, "When I left home, I made up my mind to achieve the Way. I've been at it for so many years. Though the Way is as boundless as the ocean, I hope you might be so compassionate as to guide me to success. I would be glad to continue this effort, and crave for neither riches nor power in the world. I earnestly hope that you'll permit me to remain here and serve you as before."

"This is your destiny, and you must comply with the will of Heaven."

As Jiang Ziya was lingering on, unwilling to leave Mount Kunlun, Immortal of the South Pole came up and urged him, "Ziya! This is an opportunity too good to be missed. Besides, it's destined by Heaven so you'll never get out of it. Though you'll be leaving us, you can come back here when you've achieved success."

Jiang Ziya had no choice but to leave Mount Kunlun. He packed up his books, lute, sword and clothes, and went to take leave of the Grand Master. He knelt before the throne. "I'm leaving as you've ordered, but can you tell me what the outcome will be?" he asked in tears.

"My prophecy is as follows.

> *Live in poverty for twenty years,*
> *Just be patient with your lot.*
> *When fishing at the Panxi Stream,*
> *A sage will seek you from his realm.*
> *A fatherly prime minister to the king,*
> *You'll be commander at ninety-three.*
> *Nobles will meet to found the new dynasty,*
> *At ninety-eight you hold the creation."*

The Grand Master recited, and then added, "Though you're leaving now, you'll return one day."

Jiang Ziya bade him farewell and left the Jade Emptiness Palace carrying his luggage. The Immortal of the South Pole saw him off as far as the Unicorn Cliff.

"Where shall I go now? I've got no relatives. I'm like a bird without a branch to roost on," he wondered as he said farewell to the immortal, but then he remembered. "I have a sworn brother, Song Yiren, at Zhaoge whom I can go to see. Perhaps he'll take me in."

He rode on a dust cloud and soon reached the Song Village, about thirty-five *li* south of Zhaoge. He found Song Yiren's residence the same as before, but he no longer recognized the people there. He approached the gate.

"Is your master in?" he asked.

"May I know your name?" requested the gatekeeper.

"Just tell your master that Jiang Ziya, his old friend, has come to visit him."

Hearing that it was Jiang Ziya, Song Yiren put aside his account book and came out to meet him. The two friends walked arm in arm into the hall, exchanged greetings and then sat down.

"Brother," cried Song Yiren, "I haven't heard from you for decades, but I'm always thinking of you. I'm overjoyed to meet you again today."

"After leaving you I hoped to sever myself from the world and become a supernatural being, but I'm ill-fated and couldn't make it. I'm really delighted to see you, too."

Before lunch was prepared, Song Yiren asked, "Do you take meat or only vegetables?"

"Since I'm a Taoist, how could I drink wine or eat meat? I only eat vegetables."

"Wine's made of precious essences, and I've heard that immortals drink too at the Longevity Peach Banquet. There's no harm in drinking just a little," Song Yiren urged.

"You're right, Brother. I'll do as you say."

While they were drinking, Song Yiren asked, "How long have you been on Mount Kunlun?"

"Forty years."

"How time flies!" sighed Song Yiren. "What have you learned there?"

"I've learned a lot: to carry water, to water the pine trees, to plant peach trees, to tend the fire, and to fan furnaces and refine elixirs."

"These are tasks for servants not worth mentioning. You should start a business or something. You don't want to go back to the monastery, do you? You may stay here with me, so don't look anywhere else for a place to live," Song Yiren suggested warmly.

"Thank you, Brother."

"There's been a saying since ancient times: 'There are three unfilial acts and the most serious one is to have no sons to continue the family line.' As your brother, it's now my duty to find you a wife," Song Yiren added.

Jiang Ziya waved his hand at this in disapproval. "I need to think it over."

Early the next morning, Song Yiren rode a donkey to see Ma Hong, a squire in Ma Village, about the marriage. Ma Hong came out to meet him and showed him into the hall.

"What wind has blown you here today?" Ma Hong asked.

"I'm here as a matchmaker for your daughter."

Ma Hong was delighted. "Who is it, nephew?"

"He's my intimate friend, a native of Xuzhou in the East Sea district," Song replied. "His name is Jiang Shang. He's also known as Jiang Ziya or Jiang Feixiong, the flying bear. It would be an excellent match."

"With you as matchmaker, there can be no mistake," Ma Hong said with satisfaction.

Song Yiren immediately offered him four silver ingots as a betrothal gift, and the latter ordered a sumptuous banquet to entertain him. When Song returned home in the afternoon he met Jiang Ziya in the doorway.

"Where have you been, Brother?" Jiang Ziya asked.

"I must congratulate you."

"On what?"

"I've arranged a marriage for you. An ideal match."

"But it's not an auspicious day today," Jiang Ziya objected.

"Forget about it. Heaven blesses a good man."

"Which family is she from?"

"She's Ma Hong's daughter. Well-educated. At sixty-eight

she's still a virgin," Song Yiren told Jiang Ziya.

As they drank, Song said, "We must choose a lucky date for your wedding."

"I'll never forget your kind regard for me," Jiang said gratefully.

An auspicious day was selected for the marriage. Song Yiren invited relatives, friends and neighbors to attend the wedding feast. The bride was sixty-eight years old and the bridegroom seventy-two.

Though married, Jiang Ziya's mind was still on Mount Kunlun. He had failed to attain the Way and thus failed to become an immortal. He was unhappy and had no interest at all in his family life. Madame Ma didn't know what was on his mind, thinking only that Jiang was impotent and useless.

"Is Song Yiren one of your cousins?" she asked Jiang Ziya one day.

"Oh, no! He's my sworn brother."

"Is that so? Even if he were your brother, the present situation, much like a banquet, can't last long. Now we can live a life of ease under his patronage. But what would we do if he passed away? As the saying goes, 'A person born into this world must be independent and support himself.' I advise you to do some business so that we can cope with any calamity that might befall us in the future."

"You're right, wife."

"What kind of business can you do?"

"At thirty-two I went to Mount Kunlun and know nothing of business. All I can do is make rakes," Jiang Ziya said despondantly.

"O.K., then let's do that. The back garden's full of bamboo. We can cut some down, use the bamboo splints to weave rakes, and then sell them at Zhaoge to make a bit of money. Business is business, no matter what the scale," Madame Ma said with delight.

Jiang Ziya did as his wife suggested: He cut the bamboo and made two loads of bamboo rakes. Carrying them on a shoulder pole, he went to Zhaoge to sell them, but much to his annoyance, he didn't sell a single rake all day. As dusk fell, he decided to go home. He had to walk thirty-two *li* to get home. He came back to the Song Village, tired and hungry, his shoulders sore and swollen under the heavy load.

Madame Ma met him at the doorway and noticed that both baskets were still full. She was about to question him when Jiang Ziya pointed at her and complained, "You're no worthy wife! You're afraid of my being idle at home and send me to sell bamboo rakes. But there can be no doubt that the people of Zhaoge don't use rakes; otherwise how could I have failed to sell a single one all day?"

"Everybody uses rakes. Why don't you admit you don't know how to sell them, instead of grumbling at me!" Madame Ma retorted.

Husband and wife soon began to exchange insults. Hearing their raised voices, Song Yiren rushed over. "Brother, what are you quarreling about?"

When Jiang Ziya told him the whole story, he comforted them. "Don't worry. I could easily support forty people. There's no need for you to do business."

"It's so very kind of you, but we can't be dependent on you for the rest of our lives. We should be self-reliant," Madame Ma argued.

"You may be right, but you'd better give up selling bamboo rakes. We've got so much wheat in our barn that it's beginning to sprout. You can tell the young servants to grind it into flour and my brother can sell it in the market. Selling flour's much better than selling bamboo rakes," Song Yiren proposed.

Jiang Ziya thus put the rakes aside, and the next day, after the servants finished grinding the wheat, he carried the flour to Zhaoge. He went to the market at each of the four gates of the capital, but nobody came to him. The load was heavy, and he was tired and hungry. He went left by the south gate, lay the load on the ground and rested his aching shoulders against the city wall. Feeling down on his luck, he chanted a poem:

At thirty-two I began to study the Way,
But didn't expect that I would fail.

The world's dark, and ugly to see,
How can I shake it off my shoulders.
Having found a branch to roost upon,
Gold shackles now fetter me again.
When shall I fulfil my life's ambition,
And sit on a stream refining my soul.

He was rising from this brief rest when he saw a man approach.

"Flour hawker! Wait a minute."

Jiang Ziya was elated. "Here comes the God of Wealth!" he muttered to himself, and then asked, "How much flour would you like?"

"Just one cent's worth."

Jiang Ziya could not refuse to accept even such a small deal. Not being an experienced hawker, he threw the bamboo pole on the street and let the ropes tying the sacks of flour trail all over the ground.

At this time, 400 marquises in the south and east had already rebelled against the king, and the situation in Zhaoge was tense. Prince Huang Feihu drilled his soldiers everyday. Today, when cannons were fired to signal the end of the training, a horse was startled, got out of control and came galloping down the street.

Busy weighing out the flour, Jiang Ziya did not notice the horse until someone shouted out, "Flour hawker, look out for the horse!" He looked up, but the horse was already upon him. Its hooves caught in the trailing ropes and the sacks were dragged along the street, spilling the flour all over. A strong wind rose and blew all of it away. The disappointed customer left, and Jiang Ziya, covered in flour, returned home with the empty sacks.

Madame Ma was delighted to see him return with empty sacks. "So flour's easy to sell at Zhaoge!"

Jiang Ziya threw down the bamboo pole and the sacks. "It's all your idea, you worthless, meddlesome hussy!" he began to swear at her.

"It's wonderful you've sold all the flour! Why should you

swear at me so absurdly?" his wife protested.

Jiang told her what had happened, and concluded, "You're the cause of all this trouble, you good-for-nothing."

Madame Ma spat angrily in his face. "You're the useless one, yet you grumble at me! You're nothing but a rice bucket and a clothes rack. All you can do is eat and wear out clothes," she retorted.

"You damned bitch! How dare you insult your husband like that!"

Jiang Ziya was furious. The quarrel soon turned to blows, and Song Yiren and his wife Madame Sun hurried over to interfere.

"Brother, what are you quarreling about?" Madame Sun asked.

When Jiang Ziya told them the story, Song smiled. "How can you quarrel about two worthless sacks of flour. Come with me, Brother."

"I really appreciate your help, but I have such bad luck that everything I do ends in failure. I feel terribly ashamed," Jiang Ziya said, sitting down in the study.

"A man's controlled by his destiny, and flowers bloom only when the time's right. The saying goes: 'Even the Yellow River will one day flow with clear water, and every man will meet with good fortune sooner or later.' You needn't worry, Brother," Song comforted him. "I've got about fifty restaurants and wine shops in Zhaoge. You may go to a different one each day and work as an accountant or shopkeeper. Does that sound alright to you?"

Jiang Ziya thanked him saying, "I'm most grateful for your kind help."

On the first day Song Yiren sent Jiang Ziya to a big restaurant at the south gate of Zhaoge, the busiest part of the city. The cooks, waiters and assistants slaughtered pigs and sheep and prepared food and wine for the customers. But as Jiang Ziya was to be the head of the gods and exuded an aura of dignity and power, people avoided him, and no one entered the restaurant from early morning till noon. In the afternoon, there was a heavy rain, and everyone stayed indoors. Even Huang

Feihu had to cancel the military exercises.

As it was hot, the meat and cakes in the restaurant began to go bad and smell, and wine turned sour. Jiang Ziya began to worry, and so he called the staff together saying, "You'd better eat all the food you've prepared before it becomes inedible!" He then wrote a poem to complain about his fate:

> *Heaven begot me in this dusty world,*
> *I spend my time but achieve nothing.*
> *A roc sometimes soars high in the sky,*
> *And in doing so must cross the nine peaks.*

"How was business today?" Song Yiren asked when Jiang Ziya returned home that night.

"I'm ashamed to tell you that we lost a lot of money. We sold nothing at all," Jiang Ziya answered with a sigh.

"Don't be vexed, Brother. A gentleman must know how to wait for his time to come. You haven't lost much in this business. I'll find you something else to do later," Song Yiren said, sighing in agreement.

Fearing that Jiang Ziya would be annoyed, Song Yiren gave him fifty taels of silver as capital and advised him to buy and sell livestock with the assistance of his young servants. "These are living creatures that can't go bad so we won't suffer any further losses," he commented.

Jiang Ziya did as his sworn brother advised and spent several days buying up pigs and sheep. He then drove a large number of them to the market in Zhaoge.

By this time, Daji had already ruthlessly sent numerous innocents to death and the government was monopolized by the wicked, who filled all important offices. Heaven was disgusted and punished the Shang kingdom with floods and droughts. Six months had passed since rain had fallen on the land. Crops in the fields were withered, and the capital was facing starvation. King Zhou and the people began to pray daily for rain.

As Heaven disapproved of the taking of life, slaughtering livestock was strictly prohibited during the rain prayer period. Official proclamations were posted on the walls and gates of the city. All the slaughterhouses were closed and livestock was confiscated. Jiang Ziya, however, didn't know the situation. He drove a herd of pigs and sheep through the city gate, and was immediately stopped by the guards.

"Look! Animals for the slaughterhouse. This is a serious violation of the law. Arrest that man at once!"

Hearing them shout, Jiang Ziya abandoned his pigs and sheep and fled. The guards confiscated all the animals and let him flee empty-handed.

When Song Yiren saw Jiang Ziya return home panic-striken and his face ashen, he asked urgently, "Brother, what's the matter with you?"

Jiang Ziya gave a long sigh. "You're so kind and generous to me, but I'm always ill-fated and fail in everything I try. I've lost a lot of your money already, but I lost even more for you this time. I didn't know the prohibition on slaughtering livestock, and had my pigs and sheep confiscated when I drove them into the city. They tried to arrest me, but I ran away. I'm so ashamed to have lost your capital again that I don't know how to face you. What shall I do, Brother?"

"A few taels of silver confiscated by the government is nothing to worry about. Let's go to the back garden together and drink away our sorrows," Song Yiren said with a smile.

After that, Jiang Ziya's luck took a turn for the better, and he met with success after success.

If you want to know what happened to Jiang Ziya after that, you must read the next chapter.

16

BURNING
THE JADE LUTE SPECTRE

Jiang Ziya found the back garden a very pleasant place. Surrounded by high walls, it was planted with weeping willows on the left side and pine trees on the right. Opposite the Peony Pavilion was the Hall for Enjoying Flowers. Flower beds lay near a swing. In the lotus pond schools of gold fish swam to and fro, while under the arbor pairs of butterflies danced together. The garden looked like a fairyland— an ideal place to enjoy one's retirement.

Jiang Ziya had never been in the garden before. Looking around for a long time, he asked Song Yiren, "Why don't you build a tower on this vacant space?"

"Why build a tower?"

"You've shown me great kindness, but I can give you only a little advice. According to geomancy, a tower here would guarantee that your family will produce thirty-six jade belted ministers and numerous gold belted officials."

"You're also familiar with geomancy!" Song was surprised.

"I know just a little."

"To tell you the truth, I've tried to build here several times, but every time it's been burnt down shortly afterwards. I've lost interest."

"I'll choose a lucky day, and you just take care of the construction. On the day when the beams are raised, you entertain the masons, carpenters and other workers, and I'll stay here to deal with the evil spirits. Nothing serious will happen," Jiang Ziya assured him.

Trusting him, Song Yiren chose an auspicious day on

which he hired laborers and began the construction. At midnight on the day chosen to raise the beams, Song Yiren entertained the workmen in the front hall while Jiang Ziya sat quietly on watch in the Peony Pavilion. Before long, a fierce wind blew up. It was so violent that it sent clouds of sand and dust into the air and scattered stones and rocks over the ground.

In the flickering light of a fire that broke out when the wind came up, Jiang Ziya saw five malignant spirits with faces of five colors, spitting thousands of fiery rays from between their bared fangs. The fire, magnified by the violent wind, became so fierce that it turned the earth red, destroying everything in its path.

Seeing these evil spirits, Jiang Ziya drew his sword and left the pavilion. He waved his sword in the air, pointed at the spirits with the other hand, and then opened his palm. "Come down, you devils!" he shouted.

A thundercrack shook the earth, knocking the spirits onto their knees before him. "Celestial lord! We lower beasts didn't know of your honorable arrival and failed to meet you in time. We beg you to be merciful and spare our lives!" they begged.

"You wicked beasts! You've already burned down the tower here several times, yet your evil knows no end. Now you must all die for it," Jiang Ziya rebuked, and moved forward, sword raised.

The apparitions all kowtowed. "Celestial lord! The Way demands us to be compassionate at all times. We were once animals, but succeeded in becoming spirits. Should you punish us with death today because of our rash mistake, our years of cultivation will all have been in vain. We're sorry to have offended you and beg you to pardon us."

"If you wish to live, you must stop troubling the people here. You five animal spirits must take my order and go straight to Mount Qi. Wait for me there because I'll need you to move earth and clay sometime in the future. When you've accomplished meritorious acts, you'll naturally make spiritual progress along the proper path," Jiang Ziya instructed.

The five spirits kowtowed before him and then set off for Mount Qi at once. All this time, Song Yiren was entertaining the masons and carpenters in the front hall, but Madame Ma and Madame Sun had crept stealthily out to see what Jiang Ziya was doing. When they got to the back garden, they saw him talking into thin air.

"Madame, listen! Jiang Ziya's talking to himself. He's never gotten anywhere in his life. How can a man who speaks a lot of mumbojumbo have any hope of success in the future!" Madame Ma exclaimed, greatly annoyed. She rushed up to Jiang. "Who are you talking to?"

"Oh, you women don't understand. I was just subduing some evil spirits."

"You were just talking mumbojumbo to yourself! Don't give me that rubbish about subduing apparitions!"

"Even if I explained, you wouldn't understand," Jiang Ziya retorted. "Little do you know that I'm not only skilled at geomancy but can predict the future by analyzing the *yin* and *yang*."

"What? You can do fortune-telling?" asked Madame Ma.

"Yes, I'm an outstanding fortune-teller, but I've got no place to open a shop."

As they talked, Song Yiren came up. "Brother, did you see anything during that thunderstorm?"

Jiang Ziya told him the whole story.

"You're so well-versed in magic arts that your years of study were not spent in vain," Song said, admiring him.

"Since he can tell fortunes, it's a pity that no place can be found to open a fortune-teller's shop. We should find a vacant house somewhere for him," Madame Sun urged her husband.

"That's no problem at all. How many rooms do you need? The busiest place in Zhaoge is the south gate district. I'll tell my servants to rent a house there and clean it up," Song Yiren promised.

A few days later, the house in the south gate district was chosen, cleaned and set in order, and a couplet was pasted on the door. On the left was written, "Speaking only of the Way," while the right side read, "Never uttering a word of falsehood." Inside the house was posted a couplet in two long

sentences. On one side was written, "The iron mouth can predict all mortal fortunes and misfortunes" and on the opposite
side, "Two crystal eyes observe the rise and decline of all the
world." A third couplet read, "Inside the sleeves are the immense sky and earth. Within the jug appear the eternal sun
and moon."

When everything was ready, Jiang Ziya selected an auspicious day and opened his fortune-telling shop. But four or five
months slipped by, and not a single customer came to have his
fortune told. One day, a woodcutter named Liu Qian came to
the south gate carrying a shoulder pole laden with firewood.
When he caught sight of the fortune-teller's shop, he put his
load on the ground, read the couplet on the door, and then entered the house. He found Jiang Ziya taking a nap, his head
resting on the desk. Liu Qian banged on the desk, awakening
Jiang Ziya with a start.

Looking up, Jiang Ziya found a man fifteen feet tall glaring at him fiercely. "Do you want me to make a divination by
diagrams or just tell your fortune by the date of your birth?"

"What's your honorable name, sir?" Liu Qian asked.

"My name's Jiang Shang. I'm called Jiang Ziya or
Feixiong."

"Would you tell me what 'Inside the sleeves are the immense sky and earth; within the jug appear the eternal sun and
moon' means?" Liu Qian asked.

"The first sentence means that I'm so profound in my
learning that I know both the past and the future and understand all phenomena in the world. The second means that I'm
in possession of the art of living eternally."

"You brag too much. Since you know both the past and
the future, your prediction should be extremely accurate. Make
a divination for me. If it's accurate, I'll give you twenty coppers for your service, but if it's not, I'll give you the taste of
my fists and close down your shop in the bargain," Liu Qian
said fiercely.

"I've been idle for the last few months, and now that I
finally have a customer, he turns out to be a rogue!" Jiang
Ziya thought to himself, and said, "Pick up one of the

divining slips from the plate and let me work it out for you."

Liu Qian picked out one and handed it to Jiang Ziya. Jiang looked at it.

"My prediction will come true if you do just as I tell you. I'll write three sentences on a sheet of paper, and you may go on your way, but you must make sure to follow their directions."

Liu Qian took the sheet of paper from Jiang Ziya and found the following instructions, "Go straight south. You will find an old man under the willow trees. You will be given 120 coppers, four dishes of refreshments and two bowls of wine."

"How can your prediction possibly come true?" said Liu Qian scornfully. "I've been selling firewood for over twenty years, but never once have I been given refreshments and wine. You're way off the mark!"

"You just go ahead. I guarantee it's accurate," Jiang Ziya insisted.

Liu Qian shouldered his load of firewood and walked directly south. Sure enough, he soon came upon an old man standing in the shade of some willow trees. "Woodcutter, come here a moment," the man shouted to him.

"Good Heavens!" thought Liu Qian, "It's just as he said."

"How much do you want for your firewood?" the old man asked.

Intending to prevent Jiang Ziya's prediction from coming true, Liu Qian answered, "I'll sell it for 100 coppers."

The old man looked the firewood over and said, "It's good firewood, well-dried and tied in large bundles. All right, I'll take it for 100 coppers."

Liu Qian helped the old man take the firewood inside, and being of a tidy nature, swept the ground clean. Then, he waited patiently for his money. When the old man came out to pay him, he saw the ground already swept.

"Brother, it's my son's wedding today. I'm so glad to have met a good fellow like you and got such excellent firewood," he said, and went back inside.

Moments later, a young servant came out with a tray, on

which were four dishes of refreshments, a pot of wine and a bowl. "My master offers you some refreshments. Please help yourself."

Liu Qian gasped in astonishment. "Mr. Jiang must be a celestial being! But I'll play a trick on him. I'll fill the first bowl right up to the brim so that there'll not be wine left to fill up the second. That way his prediction will be rendered untrue," he thought.

He filled the bowl with wine and drank it, then filled it up again. To his surprise the wine filled the bowl exactly to the brim. As he was finishing off the second bowl, the old man came out again carrying two strings of coins. "Here's the money for the firewood," the old man said, giving him the first string, then added, "as it's my son's wedding day today, here's a celebratory tip of twenty coppers to buy wine with."

Shouldering the empty baskets, Liu Qian rushed straight back to the fortune-teller's shop, exclaiming, "A celestial being in Zhaoge!"

Some people had heard Liu Qian's threat that morning. "Liu Qian's not someone to tangle with. You'd better leave in case your prediction doesn't come true," they warned Jiang Ziya.

"There's no need for that," Jiang had answered unperturbed.

Everyone remained there chatting and waiting for Liu Qian's return. Soon Liu Qian came rushing in.

"Was my prediction accurate?" Jiang Ziya asked him.

"You must be a celestial being, sir," Liu Qian cried out. "Everything you said came true. How lucky the people of Zhaoge are to have such a saint with them. They can enjoy happiness and evade all misfortune."

"Since my prediction came true, let me have my pay," Jiang Ziya demanded.

"Twenty coppers is too little for your valuable service," Liu Qian said generously, but did not take his money out.

"If my prediction hadn't come true, you could certainly condemn me, but since it turned out to be accurate, you must pay me now. How can you just give me a lot of empty talk?" Jiang Ziya protested.

"It wouldn't be enough even if I gave you all 120 coppers. Don't get excited. Let me do something for you, sir," Liu Qian said earnestly.

He went outside and stood under the eaves, looking around, and when he caught sight of a man in a cotton shirt with a leather belt rushing up from the south gate, he raced forward and grasped him tightly.

"What do you think you're doing?" the man snapped.

"Oh, nothing. I'm just taking you to see a fortune-teller."

"I'm on business for the yamen, and I'm in a great hurry. I don't want my fortune told."

"But this fortune-teller's really wonderful. All his predictions come true. Besides, don't you know that it's a sign of favor for a person to recommend a good doctor or a good fortune-teller?" Liu Qian urged.

"How funny you are, Brother. It's up to me to decide whether I consult a fortune-teller or not. You can't force me to do it," the man protested.

"If you won't consult the fortune-teller, let's simply jump into the river and end our lives together," Liu Qian said rudely, pulling the man towards the river.

"Friend! Better have your fortune told. Can't you see how sincere Brother Liu is in offering you his recommendations?" the onlookers exhorted the man.

"But I've nothing to ask the fortune-teller, so how can he make any prediction?"

"If his prediction doesn't come true, I'll pay the fee for you, but if it does come true, you buy me a drink," Liu Qian challenged.

The man realized that it was futile to resist, and so he followed Liu reluctantly into the fortune-teller's. He was a clerk in the yamen who was being sent on urgent business, so he had no time to have his fortune told by his birth date. He picked out a divining slip and handed it to Jiang Ziya.

"What do you wish to know, Sir?" Jiang Ziya asked.

"I've been sent to collect the land tax. What do you think will happen?"

"You may verify yourself whether my prediction comes

true or not. Your mission will be easily accomplished. The tax payers are already waiting for you and will pay without delay. You'll collect 103 silver ingots from them," Jiang Ziya said with confidence.

"How much do I owe you, Sir?"

"This is no ordinary fortune-teller's, so the fees are quite high. It's half a tael of silver for each divination," Liu Qian said.

"You're not the fortune-teller. How do you know?" the clerk protested.

"We've got only one price here. At half a tael you're getting it cheap," Liu Qian retorted.

Not having time to argue, the clerk paid and left.

When Liu Qian bade farewell to Jiang Ziya, the latter thanked him sincerely for his help. Many onlookers remained at the fortune-teller's shop eager to witness the results of Jiang's second prediction.

About two hours later, the clerk rushed back. As soon as he reached the door, he shouted loudly, "Oh, sir, you really are an immortal from Heaven. I got 103 ingots, exactly as you predicted. It really is worth half a tael of silver for one prediction!"

After that, news of Jiang Ziya spread like wildfire through Zhaoge, and everyone was eager to pay half a tael of silver to have his fortune told. Jiang's daily income now satisfied his wife, and Song Yiren was naturally delighted. In six months, Jiang Ziya was known throughout the land, and people came from far and wide to consult him.

In the Xuanyuan grave mound south of Zhaoge lived the Jade Lute spectre. Each time she went to the palace to visit Daji, she took the opportunity to devour some of the palace maids under the cover of night and pile the bones under the ornamental Taihu Lake rocks.

One morning she bade farewell to Daji and left the palace on her spectral cloud. Over the south gate, she heard a great clamor below and saw Jiang Ziya making divinations among a big crowd.

"I'll go down and see if he can find out what I am," she

decided, transforming herself into a beautiful young woman in mourning. She moved up gracefully. "Gentlemen, please let me through to have my fortune told," she said in a sweet voice.

People made way for her at once. Jiang Ziya sensed something odd about the woman. Looking at her closely, he realized that she was a spectre.

"The damned beast! How dare she come and test me out! Why wait till later to subdue her? I'll finish her off today!" he decided, and said, "Would you gentlemen please give precedence to the lady? Let her have her fortune told first." When she sat down, he said, "Show me your right hand, please!"

"Do you also tell fortunes by reading palms?" the spectre asked with a smile.

"I'll read your palm first and your birth date later."

The Jade Lute smiled again and gave her hand to Jiang Ziya. He held her wrist tightly, and then transmitting congenital energy to his eyes, he stared at her and fixed her in her seat.

"Why don't you tell my fortune? How dare you grasp my hand like this! Don't you see I'm a lady! Let go at once. How can you explain yourself to all these onlookers?" the spectre cried.

Not understanding what was happening, the onlookers shouted, "Jiang Ziya, you're already an old man. How can you be so bewitched as to lose control of yourself? This is the capital where His Majesty resides. How dare you be so indecent here!"

"Gentlemen," Jiang tried to explain, "this is a spectre, not a human being."

"What nonsense! We're not blind. She's clearly a woman. How can you say she's a spectre?"

As the crowd grew larger, Jiang Ziya thought, "Should I release my hand, the spectre would run away, and I would have no evidence to explain myself. I must subdue her and let my name be known."

He had no weapon, so he picked up a purple stone ink slab from his desk and struck a heavy blow on her temple. Her skull cracked and blood soaked her clothing. Jiang Ziya continued to hold her wrist so that she couldn't transform herself to another form.

"Don't let him run away! The fortune-teller's killed a woman," people cried.

They surrounded the house shouting and cursing. Just then Vice Prime Minister Bi Gan came by on his horse. "Why are they making such a racket here?" he asked his attendants.

But the crowd had already seen him. "Here comes the Prime Minister. Let's take Jiang Ziya to see him."

Bi Gan stopped his horse. "What's the matter here?"

One member of the crowd, exasperated by the atrocity, stepped forward and knelt down. "There's a fortune-teller here named Jiang Shang. Just now a woman asked him to tell her fortune. He took a fancy to her and tried to insult her, but the woman was chaste and resisted him. He became annoyed and killed her with a stone ink slab. It's a terrible shame that this innocent woman should die such a violent death."

Bi Gan became very angry. "Seize him and bring him over," he ordered his guards.

Jiang Ziya was still holding the spectre's wrist. He dragged her over and knelt down.

"You're an aged man, but you ignore the law and attempt to insult this woman in broad daylight. How dare you beat her to death when she refused to comply! Your behavior cannot be tolerated. You must be sent to court for trial and seriously dealt with," Bi Gan swore.

"Please allow me to speak, sir! I've studied the rites since childhood and never dare to break the law. This woman isn't a human being but a spectre. The aura of evil spirits has filled the palace recently, and the kingdom's beset with disaster. Since I'm a citizen of the capital, I have the obligation to wipe out spectres. I hope you can realize that this woman is indeed a spectre."

"She's already dead, so why do you still hold her so tightly?" Bi Gan asked.

"If I release my hand and she runs away, I'll have no evidence to prove my innocence."

Bi Gan saw that people were on the verge of a riot. "The

case cannot be examined here. I'll report it to His Majesty and it can be clarified at the palace," he announced.

Following Bi Gan, Jiang Ziya dragged the spectre to the palace gate. Bi Gan entered the palace and proceeded to the Star Picking Mansion, where he reported to King Zhou what had happened.

Hearing his report, Daji groaned inwardly. "Oh, Sister! Why didn't you go straight home instead of looking for trouble with the fortune-teller! I'll avenge you, Sister," she promised, and immediately presented herself before King Zhou. "Your Majesty! It's really difficult to determine the truth from the Vice Prime Minister's report. Send them and let me see them."

"You're right, Queen," King Zhou agreed and sent for Jiang Ziya and the dead woman.

When Jiang Ziya knelt down and told his story, the king said, "As far as I can see, she's a real woman, not a spectre. How can you prove that she is indeed a spectre?"

"Your Majesty may see her original form by burning her in fire."

When King Zhou gave his approval, Jiang Ziya laid the spectre on the ground, unbuttoned her clothes and stamped a charm on her breast and back, preventing her from running away. Then the guards put her on a great pile of firewood and set it alight. They burned her in the fierce fire for four hours, but she remained unharmed, without even the slightest burn mark on her skin.

"Four hours in the fire hasn't even scorched her. She's undoubtedly a spectre," King Zhou said to Bi Gan.

"Jiang Shang's obviously no ordinary man," replied Bi Gan. "But we still don't know what her real form is."

"Go ask Jiang Shang," the king directed.

If you want to know what became of the spectre, you must read the next chapter.

17

THE SERPENT PIT

As ordinary fire could not hurt the Jade Lute spectre, Jiang Ziya began to spurt divine fire from his mouth, nostrils and eyes. It was produced by tempering breath with vital energies and his own spirit. When this divine fire was applied, the spectre's defences broke down.

She struggled to get up crying, "Jiang Ziya, there's no enmity between us. How can you burn me so ruthlessly?"

Hearing her cries amidst the flames, King Zhou was struck dumb with terror and broke out in a cold sweat.

"Please go inside, Your Majesty. Thunder's approaching," Jiang Ziya directed him, opening both palms towards the sky.

Great thunderbolts crashed and the earth shook. The fire went out and the smoke dispersed, revealing a jade lute lying on the ground.

"Now the spectre's returned to its original form," King Zhou told Daji.

She was devastated by what had happened. "Sister, I must take revenge for you and kill him! He and I cannot exist at the same time," she murmured silently. She then forced a smile and suggested, "Send for the jade lute. When I've strung it, I can play it day and night for Your Majesty's enjoyment. Jiang Ziya's highly talented. You should give him a post so that he can protect you."

"Excellent idea, Queen," King Zhou agreed. He ordered, "Bring the jade lute into the Star Picking Mansion. Jiang Ziya is hereby appointed Junior Minister and Director of the Imperial Observatory."

Jiang Ziya thanked the king for the appointment and returned to Song Yiren's mansion in his official hat and robes. Song Yiren then held a banquet to honor his promotion, inviting his relatives and friends. The celebration lasted several days.

Meanwhile Daji placed the jade lute in the highest part of the Star Picking Mansion so that it could absorb the spiritual essences from Heaven, earth, the sun and the moon. This way, in five years, it would become a spectre again and help Daji bring about the fall of the Shang Dynasty.

One day, King Zhou was drinking in the Star Picking Mansion when Daji began to sing and dance to entertain him. She was applauded by all the concubines and maidservants, except for about seventy palace maids who only shed silent tears. Seeing this, Daji stopped and sent her people to enquire which palace they belonged to. When it was reported that they had been maids of Queen Jiang, Daji was furious.

"Their mistress deserved to die for her treachery. Why are they so deeply sympathetic towards her. They'll be a source of trouble within the palace if they're not dealt with," she cried, and told King Zhou as much.

King Zhou also flared up. "Take them all downstairs and beat them to death with gold hammers," he ordered.

"Your Majesty! There's no need to beat the rebels to death at once. Put them in isolation temporarily while I devise a plan to eradicate this evil from the palace," she said.

The palace maids were taken to the court prison.

Daji told King Zhou, "Dig a pit in front of the Star Picking Mansion, 240 feet in circumference and 50 in depth. Ask for four snakes from each household in the capital and place them in the pit. The palace maids are to be stripped and thrown in the pit among the serpents."

"This wonderful idea of yours is sure to rid the palace of this serious menace," King Zhou praised.

He ordered at once to post a decree on the walls of the capital demanding that serpents be submitted to the Dragon Virtue Hall on the fixed date. It stirred the whole capital into a fever of activity. From morning till night, the streets were crowded with people rushing towards the palace to hand in their serpents. Traffic was disrupted and the city was in chaos. Soon there were no more serpents in the capital, and people rushed to other counties beyond Zhaoge to buy them to meet the king's demands.

One day, Supreme Minister Jiao Ge was reading documents in the secretariat when he saw crowds of people with baskets in their hands hurrying into the palace.

"What's in their baskets?" he asked the Chief of Guards.

"The serpents that the king demands."

He was astonished. "What does His Majesty want them for?"

"Sorry, I don't know, Supreme Minister."

Jiao Ge left his office and walked to the Grand Hall. When people bowed to him, he asked, "What do you have in your baskets?"

"A royal decree posted on the city gates requires that every household contribute four serpents to the palace. We're here to hand them in, but we don't know what His Majesty wants them for."

Jiao Ge had just returned to his office when Prince Huang Feihu, Bi Gan, Wei Zi, Ji Zi, Yang Ren and Yang Xiu arrived unexpectedly. After the customary exchange of greetings, Jiao Ge asked, "Fellow ministers, His Majesty's ordered every household in the capital to contribute four serpents to the palace. Do you know what His Majesty wants them for?"

"When I was returning from the military exercises I heard the people complaining about the royal decree. I've to come here to enquire what it's all about," Huang Feihu replied.

"We know nothing about it either," Bi Gan and Ji Zi said.

"Since none of us knows, let's ask the Chief of Guards," Huang Feihu suggested, and sent for him. "Do as I tell you," he instructed when the Chief of Guards had come. "Try to find out what His Majesty wants the serpents for. If you find out the truth, you'll be well rewarded."

The Chief of Guards departed, and the ministers returned home. Five or six days later, the collection of serpents had been completed.

"The pit's already full of serpents. What do you plan to do with them, my Queen?" the king asked Daji.

"Your Majesty may order that the imprisoned maids be stripped, bound, then pushed into the pit for the serpents to eat alive. Without this drastic punishment, I'm afraid we would find it impossible to eliminate the deep-rooted evil from the palace."

King Zhou praised her ingenuity and gave his orders to the palace guards. The palace maids were led out to the brink of the pit. Looking down at the venomous serpents writhing and spitting below, the poor women were utterly horrified and began to scream and moan.

Jiao Ge was in his office and heard the women's bitter cries. He was on his way to investigate when the Chief of Guards ran up to him.

"Sir, His Majesty's put all the serpents into a huge pit and will feed them on the seventy-two palace maids today. This information's completely accurate. I've made haste to inform you."

The report stunned Jiao Ge. He immediately made his way to the Star Picking Mansion. There he saw the palace maids, bound, naked, sobbing and wailing. It was a horrifying sight.

"This is an outrage. I must admonish His Majesty against it," he roared at the top of his voice.

King Zhou was just about to amuse himself by watching the serpents devour the maids when Jiao Ge unexpectedly requested to see him. He ordered to admit him. As Jiao Ge knelt down, he asked, "What do you have to say?"

Jiao Ge wept. "By using torture, you'll destroy the close relationship between yourself and your ministers, and you'll bring chaos on the kingdom," he began. "The maids are all innocent, yet you're sending them to such a cruel death! Yesterday I saw people coming here with the serpents, and every one was full of complaints. They've suffered from flood and drought and were further compelled to go as far as 100 *li* away for the serpents. Poverty drives them to become outlaw and outlaws endanger the kingdom. In addition, war's ravaging the North Sea district, and hundreds of marquises in the east and south have rebelled. If the country cannot remain in peace, the dynasty is in danger. In spite of all this, Your Majesty refuses to apply benevolent government and commits new atrocities daily. Never since Pan Gu created the world has such a situation prevailed. Which ruler in all of history has ever used this form of torture?"

"The palace maids are wicked. We cannot deal with them by any other means, so we devised this serpent pit."

"They'll suffer unbearable agony. How could you bear to watch, and what pleasure could it give you? Furthermore, they're all women and have served you day and night obeying your orders. They've done nothing to deserve such cruel torture. I beg Your Majesty to forgive them. Let them live as Heaven would desire," Jiao Ge admonished emotionally.

"Though what you've said seems to be reasonable, the conspiracy plotted by these women cannot be dismissed lightly. If they're not punished like this, they're likely to continue their subversive ways."

Jiao Ge grew angry. "The king's the head of a body and his ministers are the limbs. The king should try to be a wise and beloved parent. But you're ruthless and devoid of virtue. You reject wise advice from the loyal and use cruel torture without the slightest remorse. You've murdered the innocent East Grand Duke and South Grand Duke, as well as those who admonished you against the burning pillars. Now you intend to send the guiltless maids into the serpent pit. All you know is drink and lust," he cried. "You must mend your evil ways! Keep your distance from Daji and the minions and turn to the loyal and worthy. Only then can the state be saved and peace be brought to the land. I demand that Your Majesty give this precedence over all else. You mustn't trust the words of women."

King Zhou was furious. "You damned wretch! How dare you insult your monarch like this. You deserve death." He ordered, "Guards, seize this wretch, strip him naked and throw him into the serpent pit."

As the guards moved forward, Jiao Ge shouted, "You damned tyrant! I can't bear to see the Shang Dynasty fall into the hands of somebody else. Though I'll die, I'll find no peace. Furthermore, I hold the post of Supreme Admonishing Minister. How can you unlawfully send me to the serpent pit for admonishing you?" He pointed at King Zhou and swore, "You damned tyrant! You're bound to meet your doom before long."

He ran to a window and threw himself out. His skull smashed on the ground below, and he died in a pool of blood. But King Zhou's wrath remained unabated. "Throw the palace maids and his corpse into the serpent pit to feed the serpents," he ordered.

The maids cried, "Heaven! We've done nothing wrong, but he sends us to a cruel death. Daji, you damned bitch! Though we can't bite your flesh off while alive, we'll devour your soul when we're dead."

King Zhou watched as they were thrown into the pit. The serpents coiled about them, devouring their flesh and boring into their intestines. All died very tragically.

"If we hadn't invented this torture, how could we rid the palace of this scourge," Daji said.

King Zhou patted her on the back and praised her, "This ingenious invention of yours is really too wonderful for words."

"Your Majesty may dig a second pit to the left of this one. Have hills of distiller's grain heaped up inside it, and cover them with a forest of tree branches hung with thin slices of meat. Then you'll have a 'Meat Forest.' Dig a pool to the right of the serpent pit, fill it with wine, and you'll have what's called a 'Wine Pool.' Your Majesty's master of the kingdom and should enjoy boundless wealth and power. Only Your Majesty should be privileged to enjoy the Meat Forest and Wine Pool, nobody else," Daji suggested.

"My dear Queen! You really are wonderful. You can think of such marvelous inventions," the king said admiringly.

Some days later, when both the Meat Forest and Wine Pool had been completed, the king held a feast to enjoy them with Daji. While they were drinking, Daji came up with another suggestion.

"As we're tired of music and dance, let the palace maids wrestle with the eunuchs. The winners may drink from the Wine Pool while the losers, unfit to serve you, must be beaten to death with gold hammers and thrown into the Meat Forest."

King Zhou promptly agreed to her proposal, and ordered that wrestling matches between palace maids and eunuchs be held at once. Great was their suffering, and many of them met cruel deaths.

But why was Daji interested in having the maids and eunuchs murdered and their corpses thrown into the Meat Forest? It was because late every night, the fox sprite assumed her real form and nourished her body and spirit by devouring the flesh and sucking the blood from the corpses.

Adoring Daji to the utmost degree, King Zhou lived extravagantly, neglecting government affairs and wallowing in sexual pleasures. One day, Daji suddenly remembered the humiliation the Jade Lute spectre had suffered at the hands of Jiang Ziya, and devised a plot to have him put to death. She designed a magnificent building complex and showed her drawing to the tipsy king when they were drinking at the Star Picking Mansion. It was a huge terrace forty-nine feet high, on which stood splendid jeweled halls and towers, with jade beams and agate railings that shone brightly in the darkness. She named it "The Happy Terrace."

As King Zhou was looking over the design, Daji said, "Your Majesty's the ruler of the country and the son of Heaven. Nothing other than this magnificent construction is sufficient to manifest your prestige and dignity. The terrace would be exactly like a jade palace in the Penglai fairyland. When you hold feasts there, celestial beings would come down from Heaven to participate. By meeting them you could attain longevity and unbounded power and happiness. You and I can then live happily together, enjoying all the riches and honors of this world."

"Who would be qualified to oversee the construction of such an immense complex?"

"The overseer must not only be an architect, but also have

a thorough understanding of *yin* and *yang*. As I can see it, no one but Jiang Shang is qualified to undertake the task," Daji said unhesitatingly.

King Zhou promptly ordered, "Send for Jiang Shang."

The royal messenger found Jiang Ziya in Bi Gan's office. Jiang Ziya received the royal order, expressed his thanks for the honor of meeting His Majesty, and then told the messenger, "You may leave for the palace first. I'll be there shortly."

After the messenger left, Jiang Ziya quickly made a divination and found to his surprise that great danger was imminent. He bade farewell to Bi Gan, saying, "I'll always appreciate your kindness and help. I'm sorry that I don't know when I'll have the opportunity to see you again."

"Why do you say that?"

"I just made a divination and found that today I'll encounter a misfortune which I'll be unable to avoid."

"But you aren't an appointed admonitor, and it's a good sign that he's about to receive you. Just do as he instructs, and there can be no danger at all."

"I've written a note and placed it under your ink slab. If you face a calamity in the future and cannot find a way out, you may read it. It will help you to avert the disaster. I'm sorry there's nothing more I can do to return your kindness."

Jiang Ziya rode to the palace gate and then made his way to the Star Picking Mansion to see King Zhou.

"I've appointed you to oversee the construction of the Happy Terrace for me. As soon as it's completed, I'll reward you with a promotion," the king said, showing him the project.

Jiang Ziya looked over the design. "As Zhaoge's not the place for me to stay long, I must try my best to admonish this tyrant. It's certain that he won't listen to me but will fly into a rage and try to hurt me. I must get out of here and hide myself," he decided.

If you want to know what became of Jiang Ziya, you must read the next chapter.

18

FLIGHT FROM ZHAOGE

As Jiang Ziya looked at the project, King Zhou asked, "How long do you need for the construction, Jiang Shang?"

"It's a huge project, forty-nine feet high and with halls and towers of jade and agate. It'll take a great amount of labor and I think at least thirty-five years."

King Zhou turned to Daji. "My dear Queen! Jiang Shang says it'll take thirty-five years to complete the Happy Terrace. Time flies swiftly and pleasures are best enjoyed when young. If it takes so long, we'll be too old to enjoy it. There seems to be no point in having it built at all."

"Jiang Shang's a sorcerer and speaks only nonsense. How can it take so long! He's deceiving you and should be punished with the burning pillar."

"You're right, Queen. Guards, seize him and execute him by the burning pillar."

"Your Majesty, I must point out that the labor required for this project is enormous. It'll exhaust the people and waste a lot of money. Your Majesty must abandon the whole idea," Jiang Ziya told the king. "We're constantly troubled by war, floods and drought, and the royal treasury's empty. The people are living in dire poverty. Your Majesty doesn't consider how to help them and bring them peace but spends time on wine and women. You've estranged the loyal and trust only the wicked. You murder the faithful, breed discontent among the people and anger Heaven. Now another project at the instigation of that enchantress, and it'll be your own ruin. As I've received your favor, I'm duty-bound to risk death and make this frank admonition. I can't bear to watch the state change hands."

"You damned fool! How dare you insult me!" King Zhou ordered his guards, "Seize him and slice him in pieces."

As the palace guards moved up to arrest him, Jiang Ziya turned and ran downstairs.

"Look at that old wretch! He ran off the moment he heard the word 'seize,' completely ignoring the protocol. Have you ever seen anything like it?" King Zhou was angry but also amused.

The guards chased Jiang Ziya past the Dragon Virtue Hall to the Nine Dragon Bridge. He was caught there at bay.

"Guards! There's no need to chase me. I'll take my own life," Jiang Ziya called, and vaulting over the railings, he threw himself into the river and sank beneath the surface.

The guards ran onto the bridge and gazed into the water but could see no trace of him. Little did they know that Jiang Ziya had mounted an invisible water cloud and flown away.

"The old clod got off lightly," King Zhou commented when he learned that Jiang Ziya had drowned himself.

Four guards were leaning over the bridge gazing and sighing when Supreme Minister Yang Ren entered the palace and saw them.

"What are you looking at?" he asked.

"Junior Minister Jiang Shang just drowned himself in the water here."

"Why?" Yang Ren asked again.

"We don't know, sir."

Yang Ren went on to his office in the palace to read documents and reports. Meanwhile, King Zhou was still discussing with Daji as to who should be the overseer of the Happy Terrace.

"I should think that no one's fully qualified to take up the task except Chong Houhu," Daji said thoughtfully.

King Zhou immediately approved the recommendation and ordered the secretariat to summon Chong Houhu to Zhaoge.

When the messenger reached the secretariat, he met Yang Ren.

"What did Jiang Shang do to have offended the king that

compelled him to commit suicide?" Yang Ren asked.

"His Majesty appointed him to supervise the construction of the Happy Terrace, but Jiang spoke against him, and he ordered Jiang's arrest. When the palace guards tried to seize him he ran and drowned himself in the river."

"What's this Happy Terrace?"

"It's a project designed by Lady Su. Extravagant buildings are to be constructed on a terrace forty-nine feet high. His Majesty's now appointed Chong Houhu as supervisor. I can't bear to see him behave like an ancient tyrant and the country fall into ruin. I hope you'll petition him to give up this project. If you can save the people from the project and relieve the merchants from crippling exactions, your kindness will never be forgotten."

"Don't publish the appointment for the time being. Wait until I've seen His Majesty. We'll see what we can do then," Yang Ren said.

He went to the Star Picking Mansion, and was ordered to go upstairs.

"What memorial do you wish to present?"

"Your Majesty must realize that we're faced with three calamities from without and one from within. As for the calamities from without: First, there's Jiang Wenhuan who's rebelled in revenge for his father. He's besieged Youhu Pass for three years, amd we've suffered several defeats. Second, there's E Shun who's also rebelled in revenge for his father. General Deng Jiugong's been fighting him at Sanshan Pass in a bitter war that's emptied the national treasury. Both the people and soldiers have lost hope. Third, Grand Tutor Wen Zhong's expedition to the North Sea district has already lasted ten years without achieving a final victory. As for the calamity from within, it's clearly seen by all. You're completely bewitched by your concubine and deceived by the minions. As a result many of the loyal have met cruel deaths. Now you're planning to carry out a massive project that will only further threaten the peace of the country. I beg you to give it up and please the people. Otherwise, you'll lose their support and inevitably be

faced with doom. What a pity it would be for the 600-year-old
Shang Dynasty to fall into the hands of someone else," Yang
Ren said bluntly.

On hearing this petition, King Zhou cursed furiously,
"You damned wretch! How dare you insult me so!" He immediately ordered, "Royal guards! Take him downstairs and
gouge his eyes out. Out of consideration for his past service to
me, I'll let him off lightly this time."

"Though I can bear the agony of having my eyes gouged
out," Yang Ren warned him, "I'm afraid that the marquises
of the kingdom may be unable to bear the sight of my suffering."

Carrying out the orders, the guards took Yang Ren downstairs, gouged out his eyes and presented them on a tray to the
king.

Yang Ren was a very loyal minister. Even though he had
lost his eyes, his loyalty remained unchanged. His bitterness
rose to the sky and drifted to Master Virtue of the Pure Void
in the Purple Sun Cave on Mount Green Peak. The master realized what had happened and immediately ordered his yellow-
scarved genie, "Rescue Yang Ren and bring him here at
once."

The genie flew straight to the Star Picking Mansion and,
using three gusts of fragrant magic wind, raised a violent dust
storm. Yang Ren's body disappeared in the whirl of dust. King
Zhou had run inside to protect himself from the sand and
stones. When the wind subsided, the royal guards came to report that Yang Ren's body had disappeared during the storm.

"The same thing happened when I was about to execute
the two princes. It's a commonplace occurrence nowadays and
nothing to wonder at," King Zhou said, and turning, said to
Daji, "Yang Ren deserved death for his insolent admonitions.
Chong Houhu must receive my order of appointment with all
speed."

When Yang Ren's corpse was brought to the Purple Sun
Cave, Master Virtue of the Pure Void came out. He placed
two celestial elixirs into the empty eye sockets and then blew a
celestial breath into Yang Ren's face. "Yang Ren! Rise

up!" he shouted.

Yang Ren came right back to life. From his empty eye sockets sprouted two small hands, each with an eye in the center of the palm that enabled him to see the scenes and secrets of Heaven and earth and everything in the world of men. He stood before the cave for a long while, pondering over his new form, before he noticed a Taoist beside him.

"Your Reverence! Is this the world of the dead?" he asked.

"No," the immortal replied. "This is the Purple Sun Cave on Mount Green Peak, and my name's Virtue of the Pure Void. As you bravely confronted King Zhou in order to save the people from suffering, I took pity on you, brought you here and restored you to life, so that you can help found the new Zhou Dynasty."

Yang Ren bowed and thanked him, saying, "You're so kind. I'll never forget your generosity. Allow me to be your disciple and serve you throughout my life."

After that, Yang Ren stayed on Mount Green Peak until he was sent down to break the Plague Trap.

King Zhou, meanwhile, had appointed Chong Houhu to supervise the building of the Happy Terrace. The project required a vast amount of labor, huge sums of money and an enormous quantity of materials. Armies of laborers had to be conscripted from all over the land to transport timber, clay, tiles, bricks and other materials. The rich could hire substitute laborers, but the poor had no choice but to endure exhaustion and even death. The people lived in fear and uncertainty, and many fled the country to settle elsewhere. In addition, Chong Houhu treated people so cruelly that vast numbers of young and old died of exhaustion and were buried in the foundations of the Happy Terrace.

But let's now talk of Jiang Ziya. Fleeing the palace, he returned to Song Yiren's mansion and met his wife. "Welcome home, my husband minister!" she greeted him joyfully.

"I've already given up my post," he told her bluntly and explained what had happened. He added, "I don't consider King Zhou my real master. Let's go to West Qi and wait there for my luck to turn. When the time comes I'll be appointed to the highest rank and be able to use my genius and talent to its fullest."

"It's only by luck that you were made a junior minister. You should have appreciated the great favor bestowed on you by His Majesty and exerted yourself in the construction of the Happy Terrace. Moreover, as supervisor, you would have had plenty of money and material at your disposal to bring some home from time to time. How could you have opposed the king so recklessly? You're simply destined to be nothing but a paltry magician," Madame Ma said contemptuously.

"Wife! Take it easy! In that junior post I couldn't make use of my talent nor achieve my life's ambition. You'd better pack up and come with me to West Qi. I'll soon be made prime minister, and you'll be a first-ranking lady, wearing jade pendants and a pearl coronet."

Madame Ma laughed. "You're talking a lot of unrealistic nonsense. You couldn't even keep the post you had, yet you're expecting to go somewhere else empty-handed and be made a high official! Day-dreaming will get you nowhere! What makes you think you'll be made prime minister in West Qi? You failed to see His Majesty's deep concern for you when he chose you to supervise the building of the Happy Terrace. Why play the upright official when everyone else just goes along with the current situation?" she mocked him.

"Wife, you don't understand that Heaven's fixed a tune for everything. We'll enjoy a good future in West Qi. Come with me now, Dear. You'll soon be blessed with riches and happiness."

"Jiang Ziya, our predestined marriage comes to an end right here! I'm a native of Zhaoge, and I won't go to a strange land. From now on, you do what you like, and I'll do as I please. There's no other alternative," Madame Ma said resolutely.

"You're wrong! 'A woman must follow her husband.' How can we be separated?"

"I was born in Zhaoge, and I'm unwilling to leave this place. Ziya, you must allow me to divorce you. Please write me a note to make it formal, and we can go our own ways. I absolutely refuse to go with you."

"Come with me, Dear, and we'll enjoy riches and power together."

"It's my fate. I'm really not destined to enjoy riches and power. You go and be your prime minister; I'll stay here and endure my poverty. You can marry some other lucky woman."

"You won't regret it afterwards?"

"No, this is my destiny."

"Since you married me, how can you leave me? I insist that you come with me," Jiang Ziya protested.

Madame Ma became angry. "Jiang Ziya! If you agree with me, we can separate in peace. Otherwise, I'll tell my father and brother. We can go together to Zhaoge and get justice from the king."

As they quarreled, Song Yiren and his wife came in.

"Brother! I was the one who arranged this marriage. Since she's unwilling to go with you, you'd better write her a note of divorce. As a man of talent you'll have no trouble finding a new wife. Why are you so reluctant? As the saying goes, 'Once the heart's gone, it's not easy to retain the body.' Nothing good can be achieved by force," Song Yiren advised.

"But Brother, ever since she married me, she hasn't enjoyed any happiness, and I feel uneasy to leave her like this. But as she's made up her mind, I'll write her a note of divorce."

When the note was written, Jiang Ziya held it in his hand and said, "Wife! We're husband and wife as long as this note remains in my hand, but once you accept it, we must part forever."

Madame Ma stretched out her hand without the least hesitation. Jiang Ziya sighed. "The fangs of a snake and the sting of a yellow wasp are nothing when compared to her heart," he commented.

Madame Ma packed her bags and returned home to marry someone else. When Jiang Ziya was ready to leave, Song Yiren invited him to have a few farewell drinks. He escorted him on the first part of his journey.

"Where will you go, Brother?"

"I appreciate very much the deep concern you've shown for me and never expected to be leaving you today. I plan to seek a career in West Qi."

"If you meet with success, let me know, and I'll be able to set my mind at rest," Song Yiren urged.

The two men parted in tears.

After leaving the Song Village, Jiang Ziya made his way westwards to Mengjin, crossed the Yellow River, passed through Mianchi County and approached Lintong Pass. There he came upon several hundred refugees, weeping and crying in a deplorable state.

"Are you all from Zhaoge?" Jiang Ziya asked.

Some of the refugees recognized him. "Yes, Mr. Jiang, We're all from Zhaoge." They explained, "King Zhou's ordered the building of the Happy Terrace, and appointed Chong Houhu to be supervisor. Two out of every three able-bodied men must do corvee labor on the terrace and tens of thousands have already died of exhaustion. Their corpses are buried in the foundation. We can't bear such suffering and want to flee beyond the five passes, but the garrison commander won't let us through. If we're taken back, we're sure to die violent deaths. That's why we're weeping here."

"Don't despair. I'll go to see him and talk him into letting you all through the pass," Jiang Ziya promised.

"It's kind of you to bless us with such Heavenly grace. You'll help us to escape death," they thanked him.

Jiang Ziya left his lugguage with them and went to see Zhang Feng, the garrison commander. When questioned where he was from, Jiang told the guards, "I'm Jiang Shang, a junior minister from the capital."

"He's a civil official close to the palace, while I'm a military commander far away from the central government," Zhang Feng thought when he heard the report. "If I establish a good relationship with him it'll make things easier for me in Zhaoge." He quickly ordered that Jiang Ziya be admitted, but grew doubtful when he saw Jiang Ziya in Taoist robes. "Who are you?" he asked.

"I'm Junior Minister Jiang Shang."

"Why do you come wearing Taoist robes?"

Jiang Ziya explained about the Happy Terrace and his flight from Zhaoge, then added, "When I got here I found a crowd of refugees in despair because they're unable to pass through. Should those poor people be taken back to Zhaoge, they're bound to be put to death either on the burning pillar or in the serpent pit. I beg that you let them through and grant them life. It's by the mercy of Heaven that I've met with a man of your boundless kindness and compassion today. You'll surely grant this favor."

Zhang Feng became very angry. "You're only a common sorcerer. Having gained wealth and honor, you should have striven to return the grace bestowed on you by the king. How dare you venture to deceive me with your cunning words! Those fleeing people are not loyal citizens, and I would be an unloyal official if I granted your request and let them through. If I were really to do my duty, I would arrest all of them and send them back to be dealt with. But I have merely stopped them from getting through, compelling them to return to Zhaoge of their own accord, and giving them a chance to live. According to the law, I should take you back to Zhaoge to be punished along with them, but I'll let you off, because this is the first time we've ever met," he said and ordered his guards to throw Jiang Ziya out.

When they saw Jiang Ziya return from the meeting with the garrison commander, the refugees rushed forward. "Will he permit us through the pass?" they asked.

"No, he won't. He wants to take all of us, including me, back to Zhaoge to be severely dealt with," Jiang Ziya said dejectedly.

At this, all the refugees began to wail and lament, their crying echoing across the wilderness.

Jiang Ziya couldn't bear to see such a pitiful scene. "Don't cry," he comforted them. "I can help you get out of here, but you must do exactly as I tell you. At dusk, I'll order all of you to close your eyes tightly. You may hear the sound of rushing wind, but on no account should you open your eyes. If you do, you'll fall to death."

In the early evening, Jiang Ziya kowtowed towards Mount Kunlun and began to recite incantations. There was a great crash, and the refugees felt the wind whistling past their ears. Traveling on the dust, they crossed Lintong Pass, Tongguan Pass, Chuanyun Pass, Jiepai Pass and Sishui Pass as far as the Golden Chicken Ranges. All the refugees landed safely on the ground. "You can open your eyes now," Jiang Ziya said. "You're now in the Golden Chicken Ranges beyond Sishui Pass, in the West Grand Dukedom. You may go now. Good luck!"

The refugees kowtowed to express their heartfelt gratitude and then set out for West Qi City, capital of the Dukedom.

When Supreme Minister San Yisheng received a petition from the refugees from Zhaoge, he immediately reported the case to Bo Yikao, acting ruler of the dukedom.

"They must be taken care of in every way," Bo Yikao decided. "Distribute silver among them, so that the bachelors can marry, and all may set up new homes. Widows, widowers, orphans and old people without support may register at the granary and receive free grain rations." He then asked San Yisheng, "My father's been confined in Youli for seven years already. I wish to go to Zhaoge to atone for his crime. What do you think?"

"At his departure, he warned us not to do anything rash. He said he would return as soon as the period of adversity is over. You shouldn't go, Prince."

Bo Yikao sighed and said, "As a son, I can't bear to have my father confined to a strange land for so long without any member of his family there to comfort him. What use are we ninety-nine sons? I'll take the three precious family heirlooms and present them to the king in order to obtain my father's release."

What was the result of Bo Yikao's journey to Zhaoge? If you want to know, you must read to the next chapter.

GIFTS TO THE KING

Bo Yikao was unwilling to give up his plan, even though it was strongly opposed by San Yisheng. He went into the inner palace to bid farewell to Tai Ji, his mother.

"If you leave here, who's to rule the dukedom?" Tai ji asked.

"I've entrusted Ji Fa with all domestic affairs, San Yisheng with all external affairs and General Nangong Kuo with military affairs. In the name of offering tribute, I'm going to Zhaoge to see the king in order to redeem my father."

Seeing that Bo Yikao was so determined, Tai Ji gave her reluctant consent, but she cautioned him, "You must be very careful."

Bo Yikao then left his mother and went to the front palace to see his younger brother Ji Fa. "Remain in harmony with your brothers and don't change any customs or regulations. It'll be two or three months before I come back," he instructed.

He prepared the items for tribute and selected an auspicious day on which to start his journey. When the day arrived, Ji Fa and his other ninety-seven brothers, as well as all the civil and military officials escorted Bo Yikao to Changting Pavilion ten *li* from the city, where they parted after farewell toasts.

Traveling quickly, Bo Yikao and his party reached Sishui Pass after a single journey. When the guards saw the procession of horses, chariots and especially the penants indicating "Tribute to His Majesty from the West Grand Duke," they rushed in and reported to Commander Han Rong, who ordered that the gates be opened at once. Bo Yikao went through the

five passes in this way without any trouble. He reached Mianchi County, where he crossed the Yellow River by ferry to Mengjin and finally entered Zhaoge. He put up there in an official hostel.

The next morning, he dressed up, took his memorial and went to the palace gate. When he got there, he saw no one about, and as he dared not enter without authorization, he returned to his lodgings. On the fifth day he finally saw a minister approaching the palace gate on horseback. It was Vice Prime Minister Bi Gan. He went up and knelt down before him.

"Who is the gentleman kneeling before me?" Bi Gan asked.

"I'm Bo Yikao, son of Ji Chang, the convict."

Bi Gan quickly dismounted and raised Bo Yikao to his feet, saying, "Please get up, Prince. What brings you here?"

"When my father offended His Majesty, he was only saved from death by your appeal to the throne. My family will never forget this overwhelming kindness you have shown us. Nevertheless, my father's been confined in Youli for seven years already, and we've worried about him constantly. I'm sure His Majesty must remember how honest and loyal my father has always been and wouldn't do anything to him. I discussed the matter with San Yisheng and decided to offer some precious family heirlooms as tribute to His Majesty in order to redeem my father. I hope you'll sympathize with us and help my father return to his native land. The people of West Qi would be eternally grateful."

"What's the tribute you're offering?" Bi Gan inquired.

"There's the Seven Fragrance Carriage, a sobriety carpet, a white-faced monkey, and ten beautiful maids," Bo Yikao answered.

"Why's the Seven Fragrance Carriage regarded as precious?"

"This Seven Fragrance Carriage was left by the ancient sage emperor Xuanyuan, who used it to defeat his enemies in the North Sea district. The carriage needs neither driver nor horses, and runs automatically according to the will of the rider. The sobriety carpet is also very valuable. Any drunkard who lies on the carpet quickly becomes sober. As for the white-faced monkey, though it's not human, it's a great musician. It knows 3,000 folksongs and 800 classical pieces. He can sing at banquets and dance gracefully upon one's palm."

"Though they're truly wonderful, they won't help His Majesty mend his ways. He's lost all virtue and may possibly become worse if you present him with these playthings. But you're doing this out of true filial concern for your father, so I'll report your arrival to His Majesty so as not to thwart your good intentions."

King Zhou quickly admitted Bi Gan and asked him what he wished to report.

"Bo Yikao, son of Ji Chang, the West Grand Duke, has arrived with tributes hoping to redeem his father."

"What's he offering?"

Bi Gan presented Bo Yikao's memorial, and after reading it, the king ordered that Bo Yikao be admitted. When Bo Yikao entered, he fell down and walked on his knees towards the throne.

"The son of your criminal minister ventures to seek an audience with Your Majesty," he said.

"Ji Chang committed a serious crime, but you're a filial son to offer precious tributes to redeem him."

"Our whole family greatly appreciates the boundless grace Your Majesty showed in sparing my father's life. I venture to redeem him so that he may be reunited with his family. If you would grant this favor, your mercy and great virtue would be remembered and admired for 10,000 years."

King Zhou was deeply moved by Bo Yikao's filial piety and his sincere and courteous manner. He ordered that he get up and stand beyond the rail of the court. Daji peeped at Bo Yikao from behind the curtain and was captivated by his handsome appearance and refined manners. Unable to restrain herself, she ordered her attendants to raise the curtain.

"Queen! Bo Yikao, son of the West Grand Duke, has brought gifts to atone for his father's crime. He really is rather pitiful," King Zhou addressed her.

"I've heard that Bo Yikao is a great musician. His skill

in playing the zither is unrivaled anywhere in the world," Daji told King Zhou.

"How do you know that, my dear?"

"When I was still at home I heard from my parents that Bo Yikao was good at music and especially skilled at playing the zither. You may see for yourself."

The king believed every word she said and ordered Bo Yikao to enter and meet Daji.

"I've heard that you play the zither well. Would you play a tune for me now?" Daji asked, after he had kowtowed.

"Your Majesty! The saying goes that 'when parents are not in good health, their sons dare not dress comfortably or eat in comfort.' As my father's suffered for seven years, how could I be so unconcerned about him as to take pleasure in music! In addition, my heart's broken, and I cannot play in tune. My performance would be an insult to you," Bo Yikao said sadly.

"Yikao," said King Zhou genially, "play a tune for us here. If your skill's outstanding, I'll set both you and your father free."

Bo Yikao was delighted and thanked the king profusely. When a zither was brought in, he sat crosslegged on the floor, rested it on his knees, and began to play a tune entitled "The Breeze in the Pine Forest":

> Delicate willows tremble in the morning breeze,
> Half-opened peach blossoms reflect the sun.
> Heedless of the carriages running east and west,
> Fragrant grass covers the earth with brocade.

Bo Yikao played enchantingly, and the notes fell now like the tinkling of jade and pearls, and now like the rustling of pines in a secluded gorge. Everyone felt cleansed and uplifted as if they had visited paradise and heard its Heavenly music. King Zhou was greatly pleased. "You're right, Queen. Bo Yikao's playing is perfection itself."

"His skill is renowned throughout the kingdom, but as we've just seen, not even his reputation does justice to his talent," Daji replied.

Even more pleased, King Zhou ordered a banquet at the Star Picking Mansion in honor of Bo Yikao. At the table, Daji watched Bo Yikao surreptitiously and found him very fascinating. She noticed his full, handsome face, elegant manner and charming behavior. Looking then at King Zhou, she found him in contrast to be old, withered and unattractive. Since ancient times, beautiful young women have always preferred handsome youths, and Daji was no exception, particularly as she was, in fact, a lewd fox sprite!

"I must keep him here on the pretext of having him teach me to play the zither," she thought. "Then I'll take the opportunity to play with him in bed. Since he's a young man he can satisfy me more than that old guy," she mused, and thought up a plan. "Though your kindness would be boundless as the heavens should you set his father free, Bo Yikao's the only person in the world so skilled in playing the zither. Zhaoge would regret his absence if he leaves here. What a pity it would be!" she said to King Zhou.

"What should we do then?"

"I have a perfect solution."

"What ingenious idea have you come up with now, dear?"

"You may set Ji Chang free, but keep Bo Yikao here to teach me the zither. He can attend to you all day and entertain you with his music. Both the West Grand Duke and his son would be overwhelmed by your kindness while Zhaoge wouldn't miss his sweet music," Daji said excitedly.

King Zhou patted her on the shoulder. "Darling, you've come up with a solution to please everybody," he said admiringly, then ordered, "Let Bo Yikao stay at the Star Picking Mansion to give zither lessons."

Daji was secretly overjoyed. "I must get King Zhou drunk and put him to bed and out of the way, so that I can make it with Bo Yikao," she thought, ordering the palace attendants to prepare another feast. King Zhou assumed it was a sign of her deep love for him, never imagining that she dared to offend public decency and violate the ethical code by committing adultery.

She raised a gold goblet and toasted King Zhou again and again. "Long live Your Majesty! Bottoms up!"

Believing that she loved him deeply, the king drank freely and soon became intoxicated. Daji ordered the palace maids to help him to bed and then asked Bo Yikao to begin teaching.

When the palace maids fetched two zithers, Bo Yikao began, "Your Majesty, I'll start with a description of the zither. It's composed of five parts, and can be played on six pentatonic scales. When playing, the fingers of the left hand should assume the shape of a dragon's eye and those of the right, the shape of a phoenix's eye. There are eight types of fingering: downward stroke, upward stroke, picking, scraping, casting, holding, pressing and beating. But one should never play when in one of six frames of mind and or in seven kinds of situations."

"What are these?" Daji asked.

"When one's affected by sounds of mourning; when one cries; when one's mind is heavy; when one is angry; when one's sexually aroused; and when one's frightened. The seven situations are: thunderstorms, great grief, untidy appearance, drunkenness, when there's no incense, ignorance in music, and dirty environment. The zither is inherited from the remote past and enhances elegance as no other instrument can. There're eighty-one majors, fifty-one minors and thirty-six enharmonics."

At the end of his introduction, Bo Yikao moved his fingers across the strings, producing resonant notes of indescribable beauty. Nevertheless, from the start, Daji had not had her mind on the zither, but on Bo Yikao's handsome appearance. She tried all she could to seduce him, endeavoring to rouse him with smiles, amorous glances and sweet words.

However, Bo Yikao was son of a sage and had risked his life in coming to Zhaoge for the sole purpose of redeeming his father and bringing him home. His heart was like ice, his will inflexible. He did not even glance at Daji and concentrated solely on his teaching.

When she realized that she was getting nowhere, Daji ordered her maids to prepare a feast and invited Bo Yikao to take a seat beside her. Bo Yikao was frightened out of his wits and knelt down before her.

"I'm the son of a convict. I greatly appreciate your kindness in permitting me to live. In your lofty position as Queen, you're respected by all as mother of the kingdom. If I should dare to sit beside you, I ought to be punished with 10,000 deaths," he said, and knelt there, daring not to raise his head.

"Bo Yikao! You're wrong. As a subject, you're certainly not qualified to sit beside the queen, but as a tutor, there's nothing wrong for you to sit beside your pupil."

Bo Yikao gnashed his teeth. "This heap hussy takes me for one at once disloyal, unfilial, unrighteous and lacking in propriety, virtue and wisdom," he thought and made up his mind. "I must think of my ancestors who have been loyal officials since the time of Emperor Yao and never allow myself to fall into her trap. I never imagined that she would violate the sacred code and be so cheap. It's an insult to the king! I would rather be cut into 1,000 pieces than sully my ancestral name."

Daji was disappointed to see him kneeling before her in silence. She could do nothing, but she was unwilling to give him up at once.

"Though I love him deeply, he's not in the least interested in me. What can I do next?" she wondered. "Ah! I'll use another trick to seduce him, one that cannot fail to make him mine." She ordered her maids to clear the table, then turned to Bo Yikao. "Since you're determined not to drink, let's continue with the lessons."

Bo Yikao dared not disobey her orders and began to demonstrate the techniques to her.

"We're too far away from each other. I can't see properly and keep playing the wrong notes," Daji suddenly cut him short. "It's too inconvenient, and I'll never be able to learn quickly. If we sit close together I can learn much faster. You sit in my place, and I'll sit on your lap. Then you can hold my hand and guide it across the strings. That way I'll make rapid progress and you needn't spend years teaching me."

Bo Yikao was terrified. "This has been destined by fate, and it'll be difficult to get out of her trap. But I would rather be a chaste ghost than do anything contrary to my father's teachings. I'll risk my life to admonish her, for it's better to die than live in dishonor," he decided, and addressed Daji seriously, "Your Majesty! If I did as you've suggested, I would be a loathsome beast. Your Majesty is mother to the country, honored by the nobles and people alike, and respected as the head of the fairer sex in the palace. It's most indecorous that under the pretext of learning to play the zither, you should lower yourself to this extent. Should this matter be known beyond the palace walls, how could future generations believe in your chastity? Please don't be so impatient, or people will hold you in contempt."

Daji blushed with shame. At a loss for words, she ordered him to return to his lodgings. She was now filled with hatred for Bo Yikao. "That bloody wretch! How dare he disdain me like this. I offered him my heart, but all he gave me was a mouthful of insults. I won't be satisfied until I've had him torn to pieces and pulverized," she swore angrily before she went back to King Zhou.

The next morning, King Zhou asked her, "Did Bo Yikao teach you well last night?"

Daji seized the opportunity to lie, saying, "I should report to you that Bo Yikao didn't have his mind on teaching me at all but did all he could to seduce me. He uncouthly violated the rites that govern the relationships, between queen and subject."

King Zhou was furious. He got up, dressed and breakfasted, then ordered, "Tell Bo Yikao to see me at once."

Entering the Star Picking Mansion, Bo Yikao knelt down and kowtowed before the king.

"Why were you so slack in teaching last night? Why did you try to prolong the time it will take for the queen to become thoroughly skilled?" King Zhou demanded.

"Patience and sincerity are required to learn the zither. It cannot be learned thoroughly in a short time," Bo Yikao replied.

Daji, who was sitting beside King Zhou, interrupted, "Playing the zither isn't really complicated. If you had given me a detailed explanation, I certainly could have mastered it without any difficulty. It's just that you weren't diligent, and explained nothing clearly. How could I be expected to make good progress?"

King Zhou felt it inconvenient to mention what Daji told him in bed about Bo Yikao, so he ordered, "Play us another tune so I can see how good you really are, Yikao."

Bo Yikao sat on the floor and began to move his fingers across the strings. He was determined to play a tune full of loyal admonitions:

> *My loyalty reaches to the heavens,*
> *May His Majesty live forever!*
> *And be blessed with timely rain and breeze,*
> *May the kingdom be united and last long.*

King Zhou listened attentively and understood that the tune was loyal and patriotic, without a hint of slander or ridicule. It would be groundless to find fault with Bo Yikao.

Daji understood what was in his mind and proposed, "The white-faced monkey can sing very well. Have you ever heard it, Your Majesty?"

"No, I haven't. I was so busy enjoying the zither last night that I didn't have the time. I'll order Bo Yikao to bring it in now and make it sing for us. What do you say to that?"

Bo Yikao and his men carried the monkey upstairs in its red cage. Bo let it out and handed it two hardwood clappers with which to keep time while it sang. The white-faced monkey was really a good musician. It beat the clappers and sang in a bewitching and soothing tone that made every listener forget his anxiety and sorrow. King Zhou forgot his anger and Daji became intoxicated with its beauty.

As the monkey sang on, Daji became so enchanted that she forgot herself, and her spirit flew out in its true form.

Now this was a magic monkey that had cultivated itself for a thousand years. It could not only sing sweetly but could also tell demons and ghosts. As soon as it saw the fox sprite, it threw down the clappers and darted at Daji, attempting to scratch her with its nails. Daji immediately leapt backwards to evade it, and King Zhou knocked it dead to the ground.

As the palace maids helped Daji up, she wept and said, "This is clearly a plot. Pretending to amuse you with the monkey, he intended to murder me. If you hadn't graciously saved my life, I would be dead by now!"

The king was outraged and shouted, "Guards! Take Bo Yikao out and throw him into the serpent pit."

As the palace guards dragged him out, Bo Yikao cried, "I'm wronged. I beg for justice!"

Hearing this, King Zhou had him brought back and swore, "You damned wretch! Everybody saw that monkey try to murder the queen. You deserve to be severely dealt with. Why do you still claim you've been wronged?"

Bo Yikao wept. "Monkeys are wild animals. Though this one is familiar with human beings and can understand us well, it hasn't been completely tamed. Besides, monkeys and apes like to eat fruit and dislike cooked food. When it saw the wonderful fruits on your table, it threw down its clappers and tried to snatch some of them. Moreover, the ape was completely unarmed. How could it murder the queen? Your servant has received great favor from Your Majesty and would never be so ungrateful as to commit murder. If you will consider this matter I can die in peace, though my body is sliced into a thousand pieces."

King Zhou considered his statement for a long and gradually his wrath turned to joy. He said to Daji, "What he said is quite reasonable. Monkeys and apes are wild animals difficult to be fully domesticated. Moreover, there was no knife in its hand, and it couldn't have hurt you."

King Zhou thus pardoned Bo Yikao, who thanked him profusely for his grace.

"Since you've generously forgiven him, let him play the zither again. If he plays a tune expressing loyalty and sincerity, then you can let him off. But if there's any hint of danger in his words, he must on no account be pardoned."

"A brilliant idea, my Queen."

At this proposal, Bo Yikao thought, "It looks as if I

won't be able to escape her trap this time. Let me sacrifice my body for my loyalty, and let history record that every generation of the Ji family is loyal and upright."

He sat on the floor and began to play:

> A good king's always virtuous,
> Never will he use cruel torture.
> Hot pillars turn flesh to ashes,
> While serpents devour intestines.
> The Wine Sea's full of human blood,
> The Meat Forest's hung with corpses.
> Women's looms are empty,
> But the Happy Terrace is full.
> Men's ploughs are broken,
> Yet royal granaries rot.
> May the king expel minions,
> And restore peace to the nation.

King Zhou did not understand the meaning implicit in the tune, but Daji understood it perfectly. She shouted angrily, "You damned wretch! How dare you insidiously slander His Majesty with your tunes! You're a sly devil and deserve death!"

As she explained the meaning, King Zhou became enraged. "Get hold of him, guards!"

"I haven't finished the final verse," said Bo Yikao calmly. "Please listen to it."

> May the king keep from lust,
> And abandon that queen,
> If only for the nation's sake.
> When the evil's gone,
> The nobles will gladly submit.
> When lust is cleansed,
> The kingdom will live in peace.
> I dread not a cruel death,
> But eliminate Daji
> To clear your name.

When he finished, Bo Yikao hurled the zither across the table at Daji sending plates and dishes flying. Daji leapt out of the way and tumbled to the ground.

King Zhou roared, "You damned wretch! Attempting to murder Her Majesty with the zither is an unpardonable capital crime. Guards, take him away and throw him into the serpent pit at once!"

"Your Majesty, wait. Take him downstairs, and let me deal with him myself," Daji begged.

She ordered the executioners to nail Bo Yikao's hands and feet to a board and then had the flesh sliced from him piece by piece. Bo Yikao swore at her until his last breath was spent.

When Bo Yikao's flesh had been minced, the king ordered that it be fed to the serpents. Daji, however, suggested, "Let's test Ji Chang with pies made of his son's flesh. If he eats them, he's none other than an ordinary man. You may set him free and display your kindness. If he won't, he's a real sage. We must then put him to death at once to guard against future trouble."

This suggestion was approved by the king, and Bo's flesh was sent to the kitchen, made into pies and sent to Ji Chang in Youli.

If you want to know what happened to Ji Chang, you must read the next chapter.

SAN YISHENG BRIBES
THE CORRUPT COURTIERS

Ji Chang had been imprisoned at Youli for seven years. He stayed quietly behind closed doors and did his utmost to repent of his crime. In addition, he studied the theory of the eight diagrams which Fuxi had invented, and expanded it greatly until it became the basis of *The Book of Change*. He multiplied the eight diagrams until they grew into sixty-four. He based them on the *yin* and *yang* theory and modeled them on the zodiac so that they contained 360 explications.

One day, with little else to do, the duke picked up his zither and idly began to play. Suddenly he was alerted by the undertone of death coming from the thickest string. He stopped playing and made a divination by throwing gold coins. Reading the results, he began to weep.

"Ah! My poor son! You failed to obey my instructions," he mourned. "Now if I refuse to eat your flesh, I cannot avoid death either. But how can I bear to devour my own son's flesh! I feel as if my heart's been pierced with a sword, but I mustn't be mournful and weep for I wouldn't be able to protect myself if I let my knowledge of the matter known."

Before long a palace messenger arrived with the king's order. Ji Chang knelt down and listened to it. When the messenger finished reading, he handed Ji Chang the casket of pies.

"As you've been imprisoned here for so long, His Majesty is deeply concerned," he announced. "He shot some deer on a hunt yesterday and ordered that pies be made and presented to you."

Still on his knees, Ji Chang opened the casket. "His Majesty exhausted himself with the rigors of hunting, yet bestows upon his convict minister the pleasure of tasting the fruits of his labor! Long live His Majesty!" he exclaimed.

After expressing his gratitude, he took a pie and ate it appreciatively. He ate a second and then a third, and finally replaced the lid of the casket.

The messenger sighed, "Everyone says that Ji Chang can foretell fortunes, yet he's eaten the flesh of his own son without knowing it. He found it so delicious that he ate three pies in a row! He certainly isn't a prophet. What he says is all nonsense!"

Ji Chang knew well that he had eaten his son's flesh, but he had to hide his sorrow. He dared not show it and pretended delight. "Sir, I'm sorry that I cannot directly offer my gratitude to His Majesty for this special grace," he said. "But I would venture to trouble you to pass my thanks on to him." He knelt down before the messenger. "I thank His Majesty for his great favor. The light of his grace shines brightly over Youli today."

The messenger bade him farewell and returned to Zhaoge. Ji Chang grieved deeply for his son and could not eat or sleep. King Zhou was playing chess with Fei Zhong and You Hun at Celebration Hall when the messenger returned from Youli and requested an audience. When the king gave the order, he entered and knelt before the king.

"By order of Your Majesty, I took the pies to Ji Chang. He immediately expressed his gratitude, saying, 'I should have been put to death for the crime I committed, but I was forgiven and allowed to live by the great kindness of His Majesty. This is more than I could have hoped for. Now, His Majesty is so kind as to grant me another great favor by bestowing upon me these deer pies. His grace is boundless, and my gratitude knows no limits!' Still kneeling on the ground, he opened the casket and ate three pies with great enjoyment. Then he kowtowed in gratitude and said again, 'Your convict minister regrets being unable to thank Your Majesty in person.' After kowtowing again, he begged me to pass his words on to you."

Hearing the account, King Zhou said to Fei Zhong, "Ji Chang is known to all for his virtue and for his accuracy of pre-

diction. But today he's eaten the flesh of his own son without
knowing it! His reputation is clearly unfounded. As he's been
imprisoned for seven years, I would like now to forgive him
and let him return home. What do you think?"

"Ji Chang never makes mistakes in his divinations. He certainly knew he was eating the flesh of his own son, but realized that if he didn't, he would lose his own life. He forced
himself to eat those pies, expecting you to be generous enough
to set him free. You'd better consider the matter carefully.
Don't be deceived by him," Fei Zhong warned.

"Ji Chang would certainly have refused to eat the pies if
he knew they were made of his son's flesh. He's a saint and
no saint could bear to eat his son's flesh," King Zhou argued.

"Ji Chang's a hypocrite. Outwardly he's loyal and honest, but inwardly treacherous and dishonest. Everyone's been
fooled by him. You don't have to kill him, but you'd better
continue to confine him to curb his ambition, much like keeping a tiger in a trap or locking a hawk in a cage. What's
more, the rebellions in the east and south haven't yet been suppressed. If you allowed him to return to the west, you would
be just bringing more trouble on yourself. I beg you to think it
over carefully," Fei Zhong persisted.

"You may be right, Minister," King Zhou agreed at last.

Learning that Bo Yikao had been killed, his entourage fled
Zhaoge by night and reached West Qi just as Ji Fa was holding court. When they knelt before him weeping, Ji Fa was greatly startled and asked the reason.

"Our master didn't go to Youli to see the Grand Duke,
but first went to present his tribute to King Zhou. For some
reason unknown to us, the king cruelly murdered him, mincing
his body."

Ji Fa burst into sobs at the news and nearly fainted.

"Prince Bo Yikao was the young master of the West Grand
Dukedom. How could King Zhou have slayed him so cruelly
when he went to offer tribute! Though our old master's been
imprisoned for so long, we've remained loyal ministers to the
king, despite his tyrannical behavior. Now this butchering's
broken the sacred code between king and ministers," Nangong

Kuo cried from among the generals. "We can't wait patiently any longer. We must take action as the East Grand Duke and South Grand Duke are doing. We must send an army to Zhaoge and replace this tyrant with a virtuous ruler. This is the only way to restore peace in the country."

"General Nangong Kuo's right," the ranks of generals roared their agreement.

They ground their teeth and glared angrily, filling the court with the clamor of their voices. Not even Ji Fa could maintain his composure.

Just then San Yisheng came forward. "Master, please calm down and hear me speak. First of all, you should have General Nangong Kuo beheaded at the gate. Then we can discuss how to deal with this emergency."

"Why do you want to have General Nangong beheaded? You'd better have a good reason to convince our generals," Ji Fa demanded.

"Because what he proposes would endanger the old master. Our generals are very brave, but not thoughtful," San Yisheng began. "They're ignorant of the fact that the old master's always been loyal to the king. He's never complained, even though he's been confined for such a long time. If you take reckless action, he'll certainly be executed before we even reach the five passes. They're all talking nonsense. That's why I say first behead General Nangong Kuo before we discuss the situation."

Ji Fa and his ministers fell silent, and General Nangong also lowered his head, not saying a word.

"Prince Bo Yikao didn't heed my advice and has lost his life. I still remember clearly that on the day of his departure, our old master made a divination and found that he would suffer there for seven years but would return of his own accord as soon as his time was up. He warned us not to send anyone to meet him," San Yisheng continued. "Yet Prince Bo Yikao didn't obey him and met with disaster. Besides, he didn't notice that Fei Zhong and You Hun are the favorites of King Zhou. On his arrival at Zhaoge he should have bribed them. To meet the present situation, I propose that we send two messengers secretly to Zhaoge and bribe the two with valuable presents. That way we'll have secret aid within the court when we try to do something officially from here. I'll write letters to Fei Zhong and You Hun, begging for their help. If they accept our bribes, they'll be sure to speak to King Zhou on our behalf and secure our old master's release. Once he's returned, we can march on the tyrant in alliance with the other dukes. The whole kingdom will naturally support us in our efforts to eliminate the tyrant and enthrone a virtuous ruler. If we act otherwise, we'll be the laughingstock of the country for generations to come."

"You've taught us an excellent lesson today. But tell me, please, what kind of present should we send and who should we entrust with this mission?" Ji Fa inquired.

"We should send pearls, jade, satin, gold, silver and jade belts. I suggest that General Tai Dian go to see Fei Zhong and General Hong Yao go to see You Hun. They must travel secretly in the guise of merchants. If the presents are accepted, our old master will soon return home."

Ji Fa was overjoyed. When the presents were ready, he immediately sent Tai Dian and Hong Yao to Zhaoge. Disguised as traders, Tai Dian and Hong Yao carried the presents concealed in their luggage and got through all five passes without a hitch. After passing through Mianchi County, they crossed the Yellow River by ferry to Mengjin and soon reached Zhaoge. They dared not stay in the government hostel, taking up lodgings at a small inn.

Fei Zhong returned home from the palace at dusk, and was sitting in his study when the gateman came to report, "A messenger with a letter from San Yisheng, Supreme Minister of the West Grand Dukedom, requests to see you."

Fei Zhong smiled and said, "It's just a little late, but bring him in."

Entering the hall, General Tai Dian greeted Fei Zhong.

"Who are you? Why do you come at this late hour?"

"I'm Tai Dian, General of Divine Prowess of the West Grand Dukedom. At the request of Supreme Minister San Yisheng, I've come with a letter and some gifts as a small token of our gratitude for your saving the life of our master. You've done us a great favor, yet we've done nothing to repay you. I've been sent here today bearing our warmest regards," Tai Dian replied courteously.

Fei Zhong told Tai Dian to rise, then read over the letter from San Yisheng:

> Most Gracious Supreme Minister Fei Zhong: I have long had deep admiration for your lofty virtue, but to my regret, have never had the good fortune to meet you and offer my sincere service. Our master Ji Chang tactlessly offended His Majesty, committing an unpardonable error. Nevertheless, due to your kindness, he was granted life, though he is still confined at Youli. You bestowed on him the possibility to live out the natural term of his life. What more could we have hoped for? We are far away and can do nothing to express our profound gratitude, but pray night and day for your good health and longevity. Now we have asked General Tai Dian to present you with two pairs of white jade disks, 2,400 taels of gold and four rolls of satin as an insufficient expression of the gratitude of the people and officials of this grand dukedom. We constantly worry about our master, as he is old and weak and has been confined at Youli for such a long time. In addition, he still has an old mother and young children who night and day anxiously await his return. His situation is truly pitiable. We beseech you to show your great compassion and benevolence by speaking to the king on his behalf and secure his release. Such an act of virtue would be remembered by the people of the West Grand Dukedom forever.

"These presents are really valuable, worth 10,000 taels of silver. What can I do for him?" Fei Zhong thought for a while, then instructed Tai Dian, "You'd better return to West Qi straightway. Convey to Supreme Minister San Yisheng my best regards and thanks. It's not convenient now for me to write a reply, but I'll take the earliest opportunity to secure your old master's release and safe return home. I won't disappoint your supreme minister, I guarantee."

General Tai Dian thanked Fei Zhong, bade him farewell and returned to his lodgings. Soon afterwards, Hong Yao returned from his visit to You Hun. Exchanging stories, the two found their results had been identical. Delighted with their success, they packed up and returned to the West Grand Dukedom without the least delay.

Though Fei Zhong had accepted San Yisheng's gifts, he mentioned nothing to You Hun. You Hun likewise kept his gift a secret. One day, King Zhou played chess with Fei Zhong and You Hun at the Star Picking Mansion. Two successive wins put the king in excellent spirits, and he ordered that a feast be given and that the two of them join him. After a few rounds, King Zhou mentioned how skillfully Bo Yikao had played the zither and how sweetly the white-faced monkey had sung.

"Since Ji Chang ate the flesh of his son, it's obvious that his divinations are simply nonsense. He knows nothing about fate and is no prophet at all," he remarked.

Fei Zhong seized the chance. "I was always wary of Ji Chang, as I often heard that he was treacherous. Nevertheless, a few days ago I sent some trustworthy men to Youli to find out the truth. They reported that Ji Chang is righteous and loyal. On the first and fifteenth day of every month he burns incense and prays for Your Majesty's health, for the peace of the nation and for the tribes on the borders to refrain from further disturbances, so that the people can enjoy a better life and the nation can prosper. Though he's been confined for seven years, he's never complained once. It seems to me that Ji Chang's a genuinely loyal minister."

"But the other day you said that Ji Chang was outwardly loyal and honest, but inwardly treacherous and dishonest. Why do you speak of him so differently today?" King Zhou pointed out.

"People speak of Ji Chang differently; some say he's dishonest, while others say he's loyal. That's why I sent my men to find out the truth. Now I know he's really loyal and trustworthy. As the proverb says, 'It takes a long time to know the real moral integrity of a man,'" Fei Zhong replied.

"What do you think, Supreme Minister You Hun?" the king asked.

"I can assure you that Fei Zhong's report is true," You Hun replied. "I've heard that, though confined for so long, Ji Chang's been teaching the people of Youli to be loyal to Your Majesty and to refrain from doing anything to harm the country. The people there are virtuous and happy, and honor him as a sage. I dare not lie to you. I would have reported this even if Fei Zhong hadn't mentioned it just now."

"Since you two are of the same opinion, Ji Chang must be a good man after all. I would like to pardon him and set him free. What do you think?"

"I dare not express any opinion as to whether Ji Chang should be pardoned or not, but one point is important. Since Ji Chang's so loyal and filial that he hasn't murmured a single word of complaint, even though he's been imprisoned for so long, he would be all the more grateful if you set him free and let him return home. I can assure you that he would serve you faithfully for the rest of his life," Fei Zhong replied.

Hearing Fei Zhong speak so favorably of Ji Chang, You Hun clearly understood that he too had received generous gifts from the West Grand Dukedom. "I can't let him do all the favors," he thought. "I must do something to make Ji Chang even more grateful to me." He left his seat. "Your Majesty shows great magnanimity in pardoning Ji Chang, but if you bestow further favors on him, you can naturally be even more assured of his loyalty to the country. We've been fighting to suppress rebellions by the East and South Grand Dukes for seven years already, and there are uprisings all over the country. Since Ji Chang's highly respected by the other dukes I suggest that he be granted the title of prince and thus obliged to suppress the rebels on your behalf. Once they know of his appointment, the South and East Grand Dukes would withdraw their forces of their own accord."

King Zhou was delighted with the suggestion. "I'm so glad to see that You Hun's both wise and talented, and Fei Zhong's skilled at selecting outstanding men."

Fei Zhong and You Hun thanked the king, who immediately issued a decree pardoning Ji Chang and freeing him from his confinement. Amid the joyous cries of the ministers, a palace messenger set out for Youli with the royal pardon.

The West Grand Duke was still thinking bitterly about the cruel death of his son when a strange wind arose. It blew with such force that two tiles flew off the roof and smashed on the ground. He realized that it was an omen and immediately burnt incense and made a divination with gold coins. "Today the king will pardon me!"

He had just ordered his attendants to pack up his luggage when the palace messenger arrived. He knelt down as the messenger officially announced the pardon. The duke offered his thanks and then made ready to leave for Zhaoge.

Hearing that the duke was going to leave them, the people of Youli crowded into the streets to present him with wine and mutton as a token of their gratitude.

"Dear Duke, today you're free to return home, like a dragon to the sea, a tiger to the mountains or a phoenix to the forests. You've educated us for seven years on how to be loyal and chaste and taught us good customs and behavior. All of us deeply appreciate your great kindness and are grieved that after our parting today we can no longer receive your guidance," they said weeping.

The duke also wept, "I've been confined here for seven years, and I'm ashamed that I haven't done anything to help you. When I see you send me off with wine and mutton I feel most unworthy. I hope you may all continue to live as I've taught you, so that you may achieve success in all things and enjoy the blessings of peace."

The people escorted him ten *li* from Youli and finally bade him farewell in tears. When the West Grand Duke reached the palace gate at Zhaoge he found Wei Zi, Ji Zi, Bi Gan, Huang Feihu and many other officials waiting there to meet him. He hastily dismounted.

"It's been seven years since we last met. But now, thanks to your kindness and grace, I've been generously forgiven by His Majesty," he said bowing.

All the officials were delighted to find that though the duke had aged, he was still healthy and vigorous. Just then an order arrived from the Dragon Virtue Court summoning Ji Chang to see the king.

Dressed in white as a convict, Ji Chang kowtowed before the king. "The convict Ji Chang committed a grave fault punishable by death, but Your Majesty has been so kind as to forgive me and grant me life. How can I ever return such a great favor! May Your Majesty live 10,000 years!"

"You accepted your confinement at Youli for seven years without a complaint and prayed only that our kingdom would enjoy lasting peace and the people would live in happiness. You've proven your loyalty. Today I'll not only grant you a pardon, but also appoint you as chief of all the dukes, authorized to undertake military operations in times of need. I bestow on you the yak-tail pennant and yellow axe, crown you prince and increase your monthly allowance of rice by 1,000 piculs. Before you return home in honor, I'll hold a banquet for you at the Dragon Virtue Court and grant you the privilege of parading in the streets for three days," King Zhou announced.

Ji Chang kowtowed again to thank King Zhou for the favors generously bestowed on him. When the king had withdrawn, Ji Chang changed into his official robes and joined the other ministers at a sumptuous banquet, drinking and eating amidst sweet music. Bi Gan, Wei Zi, Ji Zi and all the other ministers were glad to see him out of trouble.

After the banquet, Ji Chang, or Prince Wen, as he was known later on, paraded through the streets and markets to demonstrate his glory before the people. The residents of the capital lined the streets to see him.

"The loyal minister's released from his cage at last. The virtuous and worthy duke should be free from all calamity now," they commented.

Late in the afternoon of the second day of his parade, a long procession of pennant-bearers and armed guards suddenly approached from the opposite direction. Prince Wen reined in his horse and asked, "What's that procession in front of us?"

When he was told that it was Prince Huang Feihu returning from the military exercises, he quickly dismounted and bowed at the side of the road. When Huang Feihu saw him standing at the roadside waiting for him, he jumped down from his ox, and taking Ji Chang's hands, said, "I've blocked your path, please forgive me." He then added in a low voice, "I'm delighted that you'll return home in honor. I'd like to have a chat with you in private. My home's not far from here. Would you care to come for a couple of drinks?"

Prince Wen was a sincere and honest man, incapable of making polite refusals, so he said, "Anything Your Highness pleases. I'd be delighted to hear any advice from you."

Reaching Huang Feihu's residence, the two walked arm in arm into the hall. A feast was soon prepared, and the two men drank and talked until dusk fell. Candles were then lit, and ordering his attendants to withdraw, Huang turned to Prince Wen.

"Your Highness! You're blessed with happiness today, but can't you see that King Zhou blindly trusts the minions and ignores the loyal? He spends all his time drinking and lusting. He neglects state affairs and doesn't read any official documents. He sends loyal ministers to the burning pillars and silences admonitors with the serpent pit. The virtuous cannot live in peace, and revolts have broken out all over. Of the 800 marquises, 400 in the east and south have already risen against us. Though you're a virtuous man, you've still had to suffer in prison for seven years. Now that you've been freed by special pardon, you're like a dragon returning to the sea, a tiger going back to the mountains or a turtle getting off a hook. How can you fail to see reality!" Huang Feihu reminded him. "Don't you know that the state is deteriorating day by day? Things'll never be put in good order. What glory and honor can you derive from parading for three days? Why don't you fly from this cage as soon as possible and return to your own dukedom, to your wife, sons, relatives and ministers? There's no need for you to remain in this web where nothing you do can have predictable results!"

Prince Wen felt as if awakening from a dream. He got up from his seat, bowed and thanked Huang Feihu, saying, "Your advice is really valuable. I don't know how I'll ever be able to repay your kindness. But though I would like to leave Zhaoge, I've no way of getting through the five passes. What can I do?"

"That's no problem," replied Huang. "I've all the military tallies here, and I'll give you enough to get through." He took some of the tallies from his office, then added, "Your Highness, take these, and disguise yourself as a royal patrolman. You'll get through the five passes without any trouble."

Prince Wen bowed and thanked Huang Feihu again. "The kindness you've shown me is that of parents giving new life. I don't know how I can thank you enough."

Early that same evening, Huang Feihu ordered Long Huan and Wu Yan to open the west gate of Zhaoge and secretly escort Prince Wen out of the capital.

What became of the West Grand Duke? If you want to know, you must turn to the next chapter.

21

FLIGHT THROUGH THE FIVE PASSES

With the help of Huang Feihu, Prince Wen secretly left Zhaoge and crossed the Yellow River on the same night. He made his way through Mianchi County towards Lintong Pass.

At the hostel, the officials became extremely anxious when he failed to return all night. They hurriedly reported the situation to Fei Zhong.

"What shall I do now? If I'm held responsible, it could cause me a lot of trouble," Fei Zhong hesitated as he got the news, and then immediately sent for You Hun to discuss the matter. When You Hun arrived he told him of the situation.

"On your recommendation, His Majesty created Ji Chang prince. As a special favor, he was also permitted to parade through the streets for three days. But yesterday, on only the second day, he ran away without the permission of His Majesty. He's obviously up to no good. This is really serious. We're already trying to cope with the south and east, and now his flight may mean another crisis. Who's going to assume responsibility? What shall we do?" Fei Zhong asked.

"Don't worry, Brother! I don't think this is any trouble. Let's talk to His Majesty and advise him to send men after Ji Chang. When he's brought back, we'll behead him in the market for insulting the king. We've got nothing to worry about."

Reaching agreement on the matter, Fei Zhong and You Hun went to see King Zhou at the Star Picking Mansion.

"What do you have to report to me, Ministers?"

"We must inform Your Majesty that Ji Chang's so ungrateful that he's disobeyed your orders and stealthily ran away on just the second day of his celebratory parade. He's

likely to rebel after returning to his dukedom. We wrongly recommended him and must assume responsibility for it. We
await your decision," they reported carefully.

King Zhou was infuriated. "It's only on your recommendations that I decided to pardon him. What's happened today is
entirely your responsibility!"

"Human hearts have never been easy to fathom. A man
may appear obedient, yet nurses treachery in his heart. As the
saying goes: 'When the sea dries up one can see the bottom,
but not even when a man dies can one know his heart.' Ji
Chang can't have gotten very far. Your Majesty may send Generals Yin Pobai and Lei Kai after him. When they bring him
back, deal with him according to the law," You Hun suggested.

King Zhou gave his immediate approval, and in no time at
all, Generals Yin and Lei, leading 3,000 hand-picked
cavalrymen, left the west gate in hot pursuit.

Prince Wen, meanwhile, was taking his time. He was
riding leisurely through Mianchi County when he heard the sudden clamor of men and horses behind him. Looking back, he
saw a trail of dust rising in the air, and realizing that the
king's men were after him, he was terrified.

He gazed at the heavens. "Though Prince Huang was kind
to me, I've been careless. The king's bound to find out that
I've fled the capital and has sent troops after me. If I'm
caught this time, I'll be a dead man. All I can do is ride as
fast as I can and try to escape danger," he quickly decided.

He galloped wildly, not knowing where he was going. He
cried out to Heaven for help, but there was no response. He ap-
pealed to the earth, but the earth was silent. At about twenty *li*
from Lintong Pass, the pursuing troops were almost upon him.
Prince Wen was in a critical situation!

But now let's return to Master of the Clouds, who was
just then meditating on his Green Touring Bed. All of a sudden he felt a surge of uneasiness pass through him, and he
quickly made a divination on his fingers.

"Oh!" he exclaimed. "The West Grand Duke's escaped
one calamity only to run into another. I must fulfil the promise

I made on Mount Yan and allow father and son to meet again today," he told himself, then shouted, "Where are you, Golden Haze Lad? Go to the peach garden and bring Thunderbolt here at once."

Thunderbolt came and knelt before him. "I await your instructions, Master."

"Disciple! Disaster is about to befall your father. You'd better go and rescue him."

"Who's my father?"

"Ji Chang, the West Grand Duke. He's facing danger now near Lintong Pass. You'd better go to the Tiger Cliff and find yourself a weapon. I'll teach you how to handle it so that you can go to his rescue."

On these orders, Thunderbolt left the Jade Pillar Cave and went straight to the Tiger Cliff. He looked all around but could not find anything that looked like a weapon. "I was careless not to have asked my master for more details. I've heard that there are many kinds of weapons, like spears, cutlasses, swords, halberds, whips, axes and hammers, but I don't know which kind my master meant. I'd better go back and ask him."

As he turned to go, an exotic fragrance suddenly filled his nostrils. He followed the scent and found a stream rushing down a hillside of exquisite beauty. Creeper-entwined cypress and pine trees and swaying bamboos covered the slopes. Foxes and hares ran about freely; deer and cranes wandered amongst the trees. Fairy mushrooms peeped out from behind green grass, and tree branches bowed low under the weight of juicy plums.

Although drunk with this lovely scene, he noticed two beautiful red apricots hanging on a leafy bough. The sight filled him with delight and regardless of danger, he struggled up the steep slope clinging to vines and creepers, to pick the fruit. He was tempted by the exotic fragrance.

"I'll eat one of them and take the other to my master," he decided.

But he found the first so delicious that he couldn't resist eating the other as well. He devoured them both.

He was going to resume his search for a weapon when there was a sudden explosion. A long wing grew from under his left armpit and hung to the ground.

"Oh! Woe is me! What shall I do now?" he cried in terror.

He was trying to rip the wing off when another one spray out from under his right arm. At a total loss what to do, he sank to the ground. What terrified him most was not the wings but that his whole body had been transformed. His nose had grown high, his face had turned indigo, his hair had turned red, his eyes had become swollen balls, his teeth had become tusks and his trunk had grown twenty feet tall.

As he sat stupefied, Golden Haze Lad came up and called to him, "Brother, Master orders you to return at once."

"Look at me, Brother! How can I go and see him like this?" Thunderbolt said despondently.

But Golden Haze Lad shouted, "You'd better come quickly! Master's waiting for you."

Thunderbolt walked back dejectedly, feeling ugly and awkward, his two long wings dragging on the ground like a defeated cock. Master of the Clouds was standing outside the cave. When he saw Thunderbolt, he clapped his hands, exclaiming, "How wonderful! How wonderful!" and then ordered, "Come with me."

Thunderbolt followed him into the peach garden. The Taoist took up a golden cudgel, handed it to him and taught him how to use it. He learned to whirl it until it whistled like the wind, to advance and retreat like a darting serpent, to turn like a savage tiger and to rise like a dragon from the sea. The whirling cudgel filled the air with bright light, and at its flying tip formed beautiful brocades and myriads of dancing flowers.

As soon as Thunderbolt had thoroughly mastered the weapon, Master of the Clouds wrote "wind" on his left wing and "thunder" on his right. And when he muttered a magic charm, Thunderbolt spread his wings and soared high into the sky, the beating of his wings producing a roar like thunder.

Dropping back down to the ground, Thunderbolt knelt before Master of the Clouds and thanked him, saying,

"Master, I'm so grateful to you for passing on such miraculous skills to me and enabling me to rescue my father. You couldn't have shown me greater kindness."

"You'd better go to Lintong Pass now and rescue your father," replied Master of the Clouds. "Go quickly, and return without delay. You may escort your father through the five passes, but you're not permitted to go to West Qi with him. Neither may you hurt any general or soldier. After fulfilling this mission, you must return to Mount Zhongnan at once and continue to cultivate yourself with me. I'll let you meet your brothers in the near future."

Thunderbolt left the Jade Pillar Cave on wing and reached Lintong Pass in the twinkling of an eye. Alighting on a peak, he looked around carefully, but could not see any sign of his father.

"I was really careless not to have asked my master what my father looks like. How am I going to recognize him?" he wondered. Just then, a man in a black shirt and green felt hat galloped swiftly towards him on a white horse. "Is that the West Grand Duke at the foot of the hill?" he shouted.

Hearing a voice, Prince Wen reined in his horse and looked up, but could see no one. He sighed to himself. "My life's nearly over! Why else would I hear a voice, yet see no one! It must be a ghost or a devil fooling with me."

Since Thunderbolt had a blue face and green body, he blended in with the colors of the mountain, so Prince Wen could not see him at a distance. Thunderbolt saw the man stop his horse, look around, and then continue on his way.

"Is that His Highness the West Grand Duke Ji Chang?" he shouted again.

Prince Wen lifted his head again, and when he caught sight of Thunderbolt's indigo face and red hair, he was scared out of his wits. "If he were a ghost, he wouldn't be able to speak. Since I've no way to evade him, I may as well climb the mountain and find out who he is," he reasoned, and urged his horse up the mountain.

"Who's that hero? How do you know my name?" he asked in return.

Hearing his words, Thunderbolt fell to the ground and kowtowed. "Forgive me, father! I've arrived late and caused you great alarm."

"You're wrong, hero. I've never met you before. Why do you call me father?"

"I'm Thunderbolt, you adopted me on Mount Yan seven years ago."

"My son, how is it that you've grown up to look like this? It's been exactly seven years since Master of the Clouds took you into his care. How did you come here today?"

"By order of my master, I've come here to help you out of trouble. I'll escort you through the five passes and repel the soldiers for you ."

"I fled the capital and have committed a crime against King Zhou," Prince Wen thought. "This chap looks pretty rough. If he kills anyone, my crime will become much more serious. I must convince him not to use violence."

"Thunderbolt, my dear boy! You must be careful not to hurt the generals or soldiers. I fled Zhaoge, expressing gross ingratitude towards His Majesty. Should you hurt any of them, you wouldn't be saving my life but would place me in a much worse situation."

"Don't worry, father!" Thunderbolt assured him. "My master also instructed me not to hurt any of King Zhou's men. My duty is to rescue you, take you through the five passes, and then go straight back to the mountain. I'll go now and pursuade the troops to return to Zhaoge in peace."

Thunderbolt discovered that the pursuing troops were close upon them. Their flags fluttered bravely in the air, drums and gongs sounded noisily, and dust filled the sky, blocking out the sun.

With a flap of his wings, Thunderbolt soared into the sky, brandishing his cudgel. Prince Wen was so shocked that he tumbled to the ground. Thunderbolt circled up into the sky and landed right in front of the soldiers. He stood the golden cudgel on the palm of his hand and roared, "Don't you dare come any further!"

The soldiers were astonished to see him, and rushed back

to Yin Pobai and Lei Kai crying, "There's an evil god blocking the path ahead. He looks a ferocious, brutal fellow."

Yin and Lei angrily ordered them away, and spurring their horses forward, advanced to engage Thunderbolt.

What became of them? If you want to know, you must read the next chapter.

RETURN OF THE GRAND DUKE

Despite Thunderbolt's appearance, Generals Yin Pobai and Lei Kai bravely advanced, challenging him with "Who are you that dare to block our path?"

"I'm Thunderbolt, the one-hundredth son of Prince Wen. My father's a virtuous gentleman. He serves King Zhou loyally and his parents filially, treats his friends faithfully and his ministers righteously. He rules according to the rites and acts according to the doctrines. He upholds the law and makes all efforts to be a good minister. He was imprisoned for seven years without a word of complaint and waited patiently for His Majesty's pardon. The king has set him free, so why does he send you after him again? His Majesty's dealt with matters most irregularly. Hence, by order of my master, I left Mount Zhongnan to meet my father and help him return to his native dukedom. You may return to Zhaoge in peace. There's no need to display your courage. As my master forbids me to hurt you, you may just go back straightway."

General Yin Pobai burst into laughter. "You ugly beast! How dare you brag so! How dare you deceive my men and denigrate my valor."

He spurred his horse forward and slashed at Thunderbolt with his cutlass.

Thunderbolt parried the blow with his golden cudgel. "Stop, stop! I would be quite happy to have a bout with you, but I must obey the instructions of my master and father. Here, let me show you what I can do so that you can cool off," he said, and soared up into the sky, his wings roaring like thunder. He alighted on a nearby mountain and pointing

第二面　西伯侯文王吐子

to a crag protruding from the mountainside to the west, he called to General Yin, "Watch me knock that crag off."

Raising his golden cudgel, Thunderbolt struck half the crag away with a single blow. He then flew back to the two generals.

"Do you think your heads are tougher than that rock?" he demanded.

Witness to his ferocity and miraculous strength, both generals were terrified. They realized that they could not possibly defeat him, and unwilling to lose their lives, they ordered their troops to return to Zhaoge.

When Thunderbolt returned, he found Prince Wen still on the ground in a faint.

"I've repulsed the pursuing troops in peace as you ordered. I pursuaded Yin Pobai and Lei Kai with mild words to return to Zhaoge. Now that they're gone, I'll take you through the five passes."

"I have military tallies with me. The pass guards will let me through without any trouble."

"There's no need for you to do that, Father. You're bound to be delayed if you use them, and the situation's still serious. What shall we do if King Zhou sends more troops to pursue us? Let me carry you on my back and we'll fly over the five passes to avoid any further trouble," Thunderbolt urged him.

"You've got a good plan, but what about my horse? How can it get through the passes?" Prince Wen asked.

"The horse is not important. You've got to worry about getting yourself through, Father!"

"This horse has served me faithfully for seven years. How can I bear to abandon it now?" Prince Wen said sadly.

"We've got no choice. We have to sacrifice trifles in order to accomplish great deeds," Thunderbolt reasoned.

Prince Wen patted the horse on the head and sighed. "I don't like to be unkind and leave you here, but I'm afraid that the soldiers will come again. Go where you will and find yourself another master," he said beginning to weep.

"Hurry, Father! We mustn't delay any longer,"

Thunderbolt urged him.

"Take care when you're carrying me," Prince Wen exhorted his son.

He climbed up on Thunderbolt's back and closed his eyes tightly. The wind whistled past his ears as they flew swiftly over the five passes to the Golden Chicken Range, where Thunderbolt alighted on firm ground.

"Father, we're arrived beyond the five passes already."

Prince Wen opened his eyes, looked around, and recognizing his native land, cried in delight, "My son! It's all due to your effort that I am home again. I must thank you."

"Take care on the road ahead, Father! I will leave you here."

"But why do you leave me half way, Son?"

"My master instructed me to return straight to Mount Zhongnan once I had carried you beyond the passes. I dare not disobey him. You may return to your dukedom first, and I'll follow when I've obtained greater magic powers," Thunderbolt explained.

He knelt down, kowtowed to Prince Wen, and then tearfully left for Mount Zhongnan.

Having no horse to ride, Prince Wen set out on foot and walked all day long. He was an old man, and the traveling exhausted him. At dusk he put up at an inn, and the next morning when he was about to leave the inn, he discovered that he had no money to pay for his food and lodgings.

"How can you stay at our inn and eat our food without the money to pay for it?" the assistant protested.

"I'm sorry, but I arrived without any money on hand. Could you temporarily give me credit? I'll pay the debt with interest as soon as I reach West Qi City," he begged.

The assistant was angry. "This is West Qi, and no one gets away with dishonesty. You see, the West Grand Duke rules his people with kindness and righteousness. No one picks up articles others have lost on the street, and no one has to lock up at night. All live in peace and happiness. Pay your bill and I'll let you go. Otherwise, we'll take you to the capital to see Supreme Minister San Yisheng. It'll be too late to be sorry then."

"I won't break my word. Please trust me," Prince Wen begged.

Hearing their quarrel, the innkeeper came out and questioned them, "What's the matter? What are you arguing about?"

When the assistant explained that the guest had no money to pay his bill, the innkeeper noticed that though Prince Wen was old, he had a noble, dignified bearing.

"What brings you to West Qi? Why didn't you bring any money to cover your expenses? As we don't know you, how can we allow you credit! If you explain yourself clearly perhaps we can agree to give you credit and let you go," he said.

"Master! I'm none other than the West Grand Duke. I was confined at Youli for seven years, and on my way home I was pursued by royal troops, but luckily my son Thunderbolt carried me through the five passes. That's why I have no money and must ask you to allow me a few days' credit. I'll send a messenger and pay you as soon as I reach the capital. I promise I'll keep my word."

Hearing that he was the West Grand Duke, the innkeeper knelt down and kowtowed before him, saying, "I beg your forgiveness, Your Highness. My vulgar eyes failed to recognize you. Please come in and have some tea. I'll personally escort you back to the capital."

"What's your name, innkeeper?" Prince Wen asked.

"My name's Shen Jie. My family has lived here for five generations."

Prince Wen was delighted. "Have you a horse here? Lend me for my journey, and I'll reward you handsomely when I reach the capital."

"Since no one here is very wealthy, how could we own a horse? All we have is the donkey used to grind flour. I'll saddle it up and go along to look after you," Shen Jie said sincerely.

Filled with joy, Prince Wen left the inn, crossed the Golden Chicken Range and Mount Shouyang, and traveled several more days. He rode by day and put up by night. It was late autumn, and the wind blew chill, leaves falling from the trees. The maples were turning red, and birds chirped sadly as the cold weather set in. Prince Wen had been away from his native land for seven years, and the desolate autumn scenery made him homesick. He longed for the comfort of his family, and for the happy reunion with his mother and wife.

Meanwhile, his mother, Tai Jiang, was sitting in her room thinking of her son when three sudden gusts of wind swept through the palace, howling strangely. She quickly burned incense and made a divination, finding to her delight that her son would reach the capital at a certain hour on a certain day. She thereby ordered her grandsons and the ministers to go and meet the grand duke. Everyone was overjoyed by the news. Every household in the city burned incense, and the people prepared mutton and wine to welcome the return of their beloved duke.

Setting foot on his native soil and seeing once more the familiar hills and plains, Prince Wen could not help feeling melancholy.

"It's been seven years since disaster befell me, but now I'm home again. The rivers and mountains remain the same, but the people have all changed," he thought sighing sadly, but then he saw a long procession of men, horses, banners and flags approaching from the opposite direction and heard the ringing of cannon shots. He cheered up at once. "These must be my ministers coming to meet me."

Soon he saw General Nagong Kuo and Supreme Minister San Yisheng as well as Xin Jia, Xin Mian, Tai Dian, Hong Yao, Qi Gong and Yin Ji, all kneeling down before him at the roadside.

Ji Fa came forward, knelt down before the donkey and kowtowed. "You were imprisoned for a long time, but your children did nothing to alleviate your suffering. Our crime is monstrous. We beg your generous forgiveness. Your safe return today makes us unspeakably relieved."

Seeing so many ministers come to meet him, Prince Wen wept. "I'm now home again in my dukedom with all my ministers. This is more than I dared to hope for when I was imprisoned. I never thought that I would have the opportunity to meet you all again. I'm overjoyed but can't help feeling a little sad at the same time," he replied.

"History records that King Tang, the first ruler of this dynasty, was once imprisoned at Xiatai, but as soon as he was set free, he started a revolution to overthrow the old regime. He united the whole country and founded the Shang Dynasty. Now, Master, you're back home again. You can administer the country in a more virtuous way, help the people prosper and take action when the time's ripe. Perhaps today's Youli may become another Xiatai," Supreme Minister San Yisheng tried to comfort him.

"What you've said has no meaning for me, as a proper subject would never act that way. I committed a crime, but His Majesty spared my life and showed great mercy by confining me for only seven years. Now His Majesty has set me free, created me prince, and conferred on me the privilege to subjugate the rebels. Never in this life shall I turn against him. How can you compare Youli with Xiatai, Supreme Minister! That isn't what I would hope for. I beg you to never speak like that again," Prince Wen refuted him.

All the ministers were convinced by his speech. Ji Fa then moved forward and asked him to change into his official robes and mount a coach. All along the way, the procession was warmly welcomed by the people playing music, burning fragrant incense, cheering, singing and dancing.

As the prince passed by, people cried out, "We haven't seen Your Highness for seven years, but now that you've returned, we're overjoyed and greatly comforted." When he heard this Prince Wen left his coach and rode on horseback. Everyone cheered thunderously, "Now we have a master again!"

When he got to Mount Small Dragon, Prince Wen saw all his civil and military officials and his ninety-eight sons lining the road. Everyone was there except Bo Yikao. He remembered his son's death, and how he had eaten the pies. His tears fell like rain and he covered his face with his sleeve, chanting:

Obeying the summons, I went to court,
To right his conduct, I advised my lord.
Framed by minions, I was thrown in jail,
Without complaint, I suffered my misery.
Then filial Bo Yikao pleaded my suit,
Innocent, he died playing the zither.
Compelled to eat his flesh, my heart broke,
Till I was set free, and a prince made.
Fleeing, I lived for Thunderbolt's effort,
Alive, I happily return to my native land.
Reunited with my family after many a year,
It grieves my heart as Bo Yikao's disappeared.

At the end of his song, he screamed in agony and tumbled from his horse onto the ground, his face white as paper. All his sons and ministers rushed up, and raising him from the ground, they gave him some tea. All of a sudden his belly grumbled and he vomited up a piece of meat. As it rolled across the ground, it grew four feet and two long ears. It then ran towards the west and disappeared. Prince Wen threw up three pieces of flesh, which all turned into rabbits and ran west.

The ministers helped him onto the coach and brought him back to the city, where he was examined by the palace doctors and rested several days. When he had fully recovered, he told his ministers how he had been released from Youli, created prince, and fled back to West Qi with the help of Thunderbolt and the innkeeper Shen Jie. "Shen Jie should be handsomely rewarded before he returns home," Prince Wen concluded.

Supreme Minister San Yisheng knelt down. "Master, your virtue's known throughout the country and your benevolence felt everywhere. Two-thirds of the kingdom have already turned over to us. Your people live in peace and love you dearly. As the proverb says, 'The virtuous are blessed with a hundred happinesses while the wicked plagued with a hundred calamities.' You've returned home, just as a dragon returns to the sea and a tiger to the mountains. We should prepare to take action while the time's ripe. Four hundred marquises have already declared independence in rebellion against King Zhou's atrocities. I should think that Zhaoge will be taken by someone else before long...."

Before he had the chance to finish speaking, General Nangong Kuo added, "My Lord! Now that you're home, you should take action at once to avenge the death of Prince Bo Yikao. We've got 400,000 soldiers and sixty brave generals. We ought to attack and take over the five passes, besiege Zhaoge, and have Fei Zhong and Daji beheaded in the marketplace. We can dethrone the tyrant and set up a good ruler to pacify the people."

Prince Wen was displeased by their suggestions, "I've always depended on both of you as loyal subjects, but you've spoken most disloyally today. How dare you mention vengeance! The king's the head of the state. Even if he commits errors, a minister should dare not mention it. A minister should be loyal above all else, just as a son should be filial before all things. He must not offend his king or father with thoughtless words," he said, then continued, "I committed the error of admonishing His Majesty. Though I suffered much in those seven years, it was all my own fault. I don't have a word of complaint against His Majesty. As the proverb says, 'A gentleman should be true to his fate and never try to avoid hardship.' I was made a prince and came back home in glory. I'm grateful for this. As a loyal subject, I pray day and night for blessings on His Majesty. I wish only that the rebels might lay down their arms, and that the people may live in prosperity. I earnestly hope that you'll never again say things that violate the ethics and run contrary to commonsense. They'll only make you the subject of ridicule for generations to come."

"But Prince Bo Yikao held no treacherous intentions when he went to redeem his father. How could he have been cut to pieces so cruelly? That is intolerable. We must get rid of the tyrant and put the country back in order as all the people wish," General Nangong Kuo argued.

"My son brought about his own death. Before I left for Zhaoge, I predicted that I would suffer for seven years. I told you all not to send anyone to me, as I would return in glory at the end of the seventh year. Bo Yikao, however, disobeyed my instructions. He acted rashly, not understanding how to deal with the matter and not realizing the paucity of his own virtue and talent. His pride eventually cost him his life. I must deal with things according to the law and do my best to be a loyal and obedient subject. The marquises have already expressed the public opinion on the misconduct of King Zhou. There's no need for us to be the first to stir up the ranks. That would only bring about our own downfall. Now that I've returned to my native land, I should encourage virtue and raise the living standard of the people, so that they can live in security and prosperity. Then we can all enjoy peace and won't have to worry about victories and defeats. That is true happiness. We shouldn's burden the people and impoverish the land by provoking a war," Prince Wen said decisively.

Both San Yisheng and Nangong Kuo kowtowed, acknowledging his instructions.

"I wish to build a terrace to the south of the city which could be used to foretell disasters. It would be called the Spiritual Terrace. I'm afraid, however, that it would trouble the people and waste too much money."

"Since the terrace will be used to serve the people and not for pleasure-seeking, I'm sure there will be no trouble. Besides, you're so good to the people that there's no one who's not grateful to you, and they'll certainly be glad to help. If you feel uneasy about it, you may pay them in silver and allow them to come and go as they please," San Yisheng suggested.

Prince Wen was delighted with this idea, and acting on San Yisheng's advice, he issued a notice without delay.

If you want to know what happened next, you must read the next chapter.

DREAM OF A FLYING BEAR

Prince Wen accepted San Yisheng's proposal and had notices posted on every gate of the city. It read:

> Prince Wen hereby declares to both the people and the military that although West Qi is a land of virtue without war and with few lawsuits, and although people live in peace and produce is abundant, floods and droughts have frequently occurred here. As there is no observatory to foretell natural disasters, a piece of government land to the west of the city has been selected, where I wish to build a Spiritual Terrace to forecast the weather and guard against natural disasters. Fearing that corvee labor would be a burden to the people, I have decided to pay every worker one-tenth of a tael of silver per day. Everyone has the right to join the labor force and may quit as they wish. Those who wish to join should register their names immidiately for the convenience of payment. Those who do not wish to offer their service may continue to do their own business, free from any compulsion....

Those who read the announcement cried happily in one voice, "The grace of our prince is as great as Heaven. Due to his kindness, we're happily employed during the day and rest at home after sunset. Now that he wishes to construct a Spiritual Terrace, he doesn't conscript us into forced labor but will pay us daily in silver. We'll be glad to work our fingers to the bone for him. Besides, as the terrace will be for the welfare of the people, how could we accept wages for it?"

Everyone was willing to work himself wholeheartedly on the project. When San Yisheng reported the situation to Prince Wen, he said, "Since both the people and soldiers are glad to contribute to the building of the terrace, issue their wages at once."

An auspicious day was chosen on which to start the project, and everyone set to work, carrying earth or cutting wood. In less than ten months, the supervisor came to report that the Spiritual Terrace had been completed. Greatly delighted, Prince Wen led the civil and military officials beyond the city on an inspection tour. Looking around the twenty-foot high terrace, Prince Wen fell silent.

San Yisheng noticed his silence and asked, "Your Highness, we're all delighted with the terrace, but why are you, on the contrary, so displeased?"

"I'm not displeased at all. It's just that it needs a pool beside it to meet the requirements of the *yin-yang* theory. I don't want to trouble the people for extra labor so I'm a little depressed."

"Though the terrace was a massive project, it was completed in a very short time. It would be a simple matter to add a pool beside it." San Yisheng told him, and then passed his words onto the people.

"What's so difficult about digging a little pool! Don't be distressed, Your Highness. We'll do it at once," they cried.

As they dug, they found a skeleton buried in the ground and casually disposed of the bones. Watching them work from the terrace, Prince Wen asked, "What did they throw away over there?"

"The bones of a skeleton," someone replied.

"Bring the bones here. Put them in a small coffin and bury them on a hill. It would be a crime to leave them exposed just because I'm digging a pool," Prince Wen ordered.

"What divine virtue! The kindness of our lord extends even to the bones of the dead. His benevolence is felt everywhere, and his every action accords with the will of Heaven. The prince of West Qi truly cares for his people," everyone commented when they heard the order.

Dusk fell as he watched the excavation work, and as it was too late for him to return home a feast was prepared on the terrace. After he and his officials enjoyed a pleasant meal together, the prince retired to a room on the terrace.

He had a strange dream: a fierce winged tiger with a white forehead suddenly flew up from the southeast and threw itself at the curtains of his bed. Greatly alarmed, Prince Wen began to call for his attendants when there was an explosion at the back of the terrace and brilliant light shot into the sky. He woke up bathed in sweat. As he pondered over the dream, he heard the watchman sounding the third watch and decided to wait until daybreak to discuss the dream with his officials.

When he met them the next morning, he asked, "Where's Supreme Minister San Yisheng? I would like to see him at once."

When San Yisheng stepped before him, the prince told him about the dream and asked him what it meant.

San Yisheng bowed. "This dream is a very auspicious omen for you, Your Highness. You'll get a highly talented minister, the pillar of the government. He'll serve you like the famed Prime Ministers Feng Hou and Yi Yin of the past."

"What makes you say that?"

"King Gao Zong of the Shang Dynasty got Prime Minister Fu Yue after he dreamed of a flying bear. What you saw in your dream wasn't a tiger but a flying bear. The brilliant light you saw behind the terrace signifies the future prosperity of the house of Zhou."

The ministers burst into applause and offered their congratulations. Prince Wen then gave the order to return to the palace, determined to find the talented assistant as he had dreamed.

But now let's turn to Jiang Ziya. Leaving the refugees, he went to a hermitage near Panxi Stream, where he spent much of his time fishing. While waiting for his destiny to be fulfilled, he recited Taoist scriptures and strove to become enlightened by the Truth. When he felt bored, he fished, leaning against a willow tree, but his mind was always on his master and he never forgot the Way.

One day, as he sat fishing, he sighed to himself and chanted:

> *Since I left Kunlun,*
> *Eight years have passed.*
> *I rebuked the king,*
> *And had to flee at last.*
> *Coming to the western land,*
> *I fish at Panxi Stream.*
> *When shall I meet a sagely king,*
> *To fulfil my destiny?*

He sat under the hanging branches of a willow tree and watched the water flowing endlessly towards the east. He reflected on the transience of human life compared to the mountains and streams, and was sighing to himself when he heard someone singing a song:

> *Up the slopes and over the peaks,*
> *The air rings with the sound of my axe.*
> *I carry it with me all the time,*
> *To slash down creepers in my way.*
> *Down the cliff run wild hares,*
> *Behind the hill young doves croon.*
> *Over the treetops fly rare birds,*
> *In the willows sing yellow orioles.*
> *In pine, cypress, plum and peach trees,*
> *A merry woodcutter I'll stay!*
> *I won't be a millionaire anyday.*
> *Three pints of rice for a load of wood,*
> *Vegetables galore, and wine that's good.*
> *The moon's my companion as I drink*
> *Beneath the trees in the quietude*
> *Of hills and valleys.*
> *Exotic plants delight my heart,*
> *A carefree life is all I want!*

When the woodcutter finished his song, he put down his

load of firewood and sat down beside Jiang Ziya.

"Venerable elder," he said, "I often see you fishing here. May I have a chat with you?"

"What about?"

"A chat between fishermen and woodcutters like in the old stories."

Jiang Ziya was delighted. "Splendid! A chat between a fisherman and a woodcutter."

"What's your lofty name and your honorable birthplace? Why have you come here?" the woodcutter asked.

"I'm a native of Xuzhou on the shore of the East Sea. My family name's Jiang, my name's Shang, and I'm called Ziya. I've also got another name, Fei Xiong the Flying Bear."

The woodcutter burst into loud laughter.

"What's your name?" Jiang Ziya asked.

"My name's Wu Ji. I'm a native of West Qi."

"Why did you burst into laughter when you heard my name?"

"I couldn't help laughing when I heard 'Fei Xiong the Flying Bear'."

"Everyone's given a second name. What's there to laugh at?" Jiang Ziya objected.

"Only sages and worthies like Feng Hou, Lao Peng, Yi Yin and Fu Yue, virtuous, talented, and prominent in rank, are qualified to have that name, but you're a nobody. That's why I couldn't help laughing. You do nothing but sit and fish and lean against that tree all day long. You're like the man who sits waiting by a tree stump in the hope that a rabbit will run into it and knock itself out. You don't look particularly brilliant to me. How can you call yourself 'Fei Xiong'?" Wu Ji asked.

He walked over and picked up Jiang Ziya's fishing rod from the bank. He found that a needle and not a hook was fixed to the end of the line. Clapping and laughing, he shook his head at Jiang Ziya.

"Talent cannot be measured by a man's years. Some may live to be 100 but have no common sense at all," he commented. "Why do you fish with a straight needle instead of a hook? Let me show you how to do it: Heat the needle till it's red hot, and bend it into a hook. Then attach some tasty bait to the hook, and fasten a float to the line. As soon as a fish swallows the bait, you'll see the float move. You must lift the rod as quickly as possible to catch the fish. If you use your own method you won't catch a fish in a hundred years. It just shows how stupid you are. How can you have the impudence to call yourself Flying Bear?"

Jiang Ziya remained unperturbed. "You only know half the story. Though I'm ostensibly fishing here, I don't really care about the fish. I'm merely killing time while I wait for my chance to attain lofty heights. How could I deign to make a hook to catch fish? It's not what a true man should do. I prefer to achieve success with the straight needle and am unwilling to obtain what I want with the crooked. I'm not really out to catch a fish, but a duke or a king."

Wu Ji burst into laughter again. "So you want to be a duke or a king as well! You look more like a monkey to me!" He laughed sarcastically.

Jiang Ziya had to smile. "I may not look like a duke or a king, but as far as I can see, your face doesn't augur well for you either."

"Well, at least it's better than yours. Though only a woodcutter, I'm happier than you: I enjoy the peach and apricot flowers in spring, lotus flowers in summer, yellow chrysanthemums in autumn and plum flowers in winter," Wu Ji retorted.

"That's not what I mean. I mean the destiny revealed in your face isn't auspicious."

"How can you tell?"

"Your left eye's greenish and your right red. That means you'll kill a man in the city today," Jiang Ziya explained.

"We were just joking with each other. Why suddenly turn nasty and say such damaging things?" Wu Ji swore in anger.

He immediately shouldered his load of firewood and set off for the city to sell it on the market. He got to the south gate just as Prince Wen was leaving the city for the Spiritual Terrace. The royal guards were shouting "Clear the way! His

Highness is coming!"

Wu Ji dodged into a narrow lane. As he swung his carrying pole with its load of firewood from one shoulder to the other, the sharp end of a thick dried branch accidentally struck Wang Xiang, a city guard, in the temple, killing him instantly.

"A woodcutter's killed a city guard," people around him cried out, and Wu Ji was arrested and taken before Prince Wen.

"Who is this man? What has he done?"

"Your Highness! For some unknown reason, this woodcutter just killed the city guard Wang Xiang."

The prince remained seated on his horse. "What's the woodcutter's name? Why did he kill Wang Xiang?"

"Your Highness! I'm a decent citizen of West Qi named Wu Ji. When I saw you coming, I turned into a narrow lane, and Wang Xiang was killed accidentally when I swung my carrying pole from one shoulder to the other."

"Since Wu Ji killed Wang Xiang, he should pay with his life." Prince Wen said.

He had his men draw a large circle on the ground near the south gate and stand a log inside it as a warder. Wu Ji was then imprisoned inside the circle.

Imprisoning convicts in a circle drawn on the ground was only done in West Qi during the reign of King Zhou. As Prince Wen could predict accurately by divination, a convict confined within the circle dared not run away. Any convict who tried to flee could be located by divination and taken back to face more severe punishment, so even the sly and crafty strictly observed the law.

Now Wu Ji had been imprisoned in the circle for three days. "Mother's alone and without support. She must lean on the door looking for me all day long, wondering what's happened to me. She must be terribly worried. What shall I do?"

Thinking of his mother, he burst into loud sobs. Pedestrians were gathering round to look at him when San Yisheng passed by on his way to the Spiritual Terrace. He heard Wu Ji weeping. "Aren't you the one who killed Wang Xiang a few days ago? It's the usual practice for a murderer to pay with his life. Why are you crying so?"

"It was my ill-fortune to meet with this mishap. Wang Xiang was killed by accident. I know I should pay with my life and have no complaint about that. However, I've got an aged mother of over seventy. I'm unmarried and have no brothers. There's no one to look after her while I'm kept here. She'll starve to death and her bones will remain unburied. If the son dies, the mother will perish too. She's raised me in vain. The thought of it breaks my heart, so I can't help crying bitterly. I didn't know of your arrival and failed to suppress my tears. Please forgive me."

"Since Wu Ji didn't kill Wang Xiang on purpose, he shouldn't pay with his life," San Yisheng thought, and said to Wu Ji, "Don't cry. I'll see His Highness about it. I hope he'll set you free to prepare food, clothing, and a coffin in case she dies. You may come back in the autumn to receive your punishment."

Wu Ji immediately kowtowed in gratitude for the kind help.

The following day, San Yisheng reported Wu Ji's case to Prince Wen and suggested, "His mother's a widow. As she cannot survive alone and doesn't know about her son's plight, I think it would be better to let Wu Ji return home temporarily to take care of her and make arrangements for a funeral in case of her death. When everything's been arranged satisfactorily, he may come back to receive punishment for the Wang Xiang case. I beg you to give it your consideration."

Prince Wen approved his proposal and granted Wu Ji temporary freedom. As soon as he was freed, Wu Ji rushed back home, where he found his old mother at the gate watching eagerly for his return. "My dear boy! Where have you been these last few days? I've been terrified that you might have been wounded or killed by wolves and tigers in the high mountains. I've been so worried that I haven't been able to eat or sleep. Only now can I rest at ease. What happened to you?"

When Wu Ji related what had happened in the city, she began to weep and wail and bemoan her fate.

"A few days ago I saw an old man fishing in a stream

using not a hook but a straight needle. I asked him why he
didn't bend his needle into a hook and attach a piece of tasty
bait, and he answered that he would achieve success with
straightness, not crookedness. He said he wasn't looking for
fish with beautiful scales but for a duke or king. When I said
sarcastically that he looked more like a monkey than a duke,
he told me my appearance wasn't good, either, because having
one green eye and one red, I would kill a man that day. He's
wicked and his mouth was poisonous for, sure enough, it was
on that day that I killed Wang Xiang."

"What's the old man's name?"

"Jiang Shang or Jiang Ziya, and his alternative name's
Fei Xiong the Flying Bear," Wu Ji answered.

"He must be a prophet, a highly talented man. You'd better go and beg him to save you," she said.

On her orders, Wu Ji went to Panxi Stream to look for
Jiang Ziya.

If you want to know what happened next, you must read
the next chapter.

第三十四圖　渭水文王聘子牙

24

FROM FISHERMAN
TO PRIME MINISTER

At Panxi Stream, Wu Ji found Jiang Ziya still fishing under the willow tree. As his bamboo rod floated on the blue ripples, he amused himself by singing a song. Wu Ji walked up behind him.

"Venerable master."

Looking round, Jiang Ziya asked, "Aren't you the woodcutter I met here the other day?"

"Yes, sir. I am."

"Did you kill someone that day?"

Wu Ji fell on his knees, sobbing. "I'm a vulgar man who lives in the mountains. I know only how to use an axe and understand nothing of profound mysteries. I failed to recognize you as a highly cultured recluse. I offended you with my foolish words. I beg you to pardon my ignorance." he apologized, and went on to relate all that had happened since he left Jiang. He concluded, "In the autumn, I must go back to be punished for Wang Xiang's death, and the lives of my mother and myself are still in danger. Today I've come to pay you my respects and beg you to take pity on us and save us. We'll never forget your kindness."

"This is all determined by fate, and fate is difficult to change. Since you caused the death of another person, you have to pay with your life. What can I do to save you?" Jiang Ziya replied.

Wu Ji fell to the ground weeping bitterly. "Have compassion, sir!" he pleaded. "If you save our lives, we will be eternally grateful."

Jiang Ziya knew that Wu Ji had an outstanding future. He

relented. "I'll save you from death only if you acknowledge me as your teacher."

Wu Ji immediately knelt down and kowtowed in acknowledgment.

"Now that you're my disciple, I'm obliged to help you. Return home at once and dig a pit before your bed four feet deep and long enough for you to lie in. Sleep in it tonight with lighted lamps at your head and feet. Your mother must scatter a few handfuls of cooked or uncooked rice on your body and cover you with hay. Tomorrow you may get up and go about your business as usual. You'll have no more trouble from then on."

When Wu Ji returned home and told his mother what had happened, she was overjoyed, and immediately directed him to dig the pit and prepare lamps. Late that night, Jiang Ziya loosened his hair, took a sword and walked in a square reciting charms to cover up Wu Ji's star and make it disappear from Heaven.

Early the next morning, Wu Ji came to see him. He knelt down and kowtowed. "Master," he greeted Jiang Ziya.

"Since you're my disciple now, you must always obey my instructions. It's not a good idea to spend all your time cutting wood. You may go to the market and sell firewood before noon and come here in the afternoon for lessons on military theories and stratagems. Do you know that four hundred marquises have declared independence and rebelled against King Zhou?"

"Master, which four hundred marquises?"

"Jiang Wenhuan commands 400,000 men and is waging a fierce battle at Youhun Pass. E Shun's attacking Sanshan Pass with 300,000 men. A few days ago I observed the celestial phenomena and saw that West Qi will be affected by war soon. Military talents are needed. You'd better spend your time and effort learning weapon skills and military stratagems. If you offer outstanding service on the battlefield, you'll be made a minister in the government. An old proverb says, 'No one is born a general or prime minister, a man must make himself strong and able.' Another proverb says, 'Sell your civil and military talents to the king.' As your teacher, I must help you to have a good future."

On his instructions, Wu Ji studied military techniques diligently day and night. One day, however, San Yisheng recollected the Wu Ji affair, and wondered why he failed to come back to gaol.

"Though Wu Ji killed Wang Xiang, I set him free temporarily with your approval as he had an old mother unable to live alone at home," he spoke to Prince Wen. "I told him to return to gaol when he had made the necessary arrangements for her. However, he hasn't come back to receive the penalty deserved. He must be a sly and deceitful fellow. Perhaps Your Highness should make a divination to determine what's happened to him."

"Yes, you're right," Prince Wen answered. He picked up his gold coins and made a divination. He groaned as he shook his head. "Wu Ji's neither sly nor deceitful. Out of fear of punishment, he committed suicide by throwing himself into a deep pool. According to the law, he ought not to be sentenced to death as he didn't kill Wang on purpose, but he's lost his life nonetheless. It's a great pity."

Sighing deeply, Prince and minister withdrew from the court. Time passed swiftly, and soon spring came again. Flowers blossomed on the willows, and peach and plum trees exploded with color.

"The scenery's lovely. Everything's bursting with new life. It's hard not to feel cheerful and vigorous. Let's take a trip to the southern outskirts and enjoy a few days of nature," Prince Wen proposed to his ministers.

San Yisheng came forward. "Your Highness! You dreamed of a flying bear when you slept on the Spiritual Terrace. The dream signifies that West Qi will get a capable man, a pillar of the state, and you'll gain a talented assistant. We shouldn't only enjoy the spring scenery but should also try to find him somewhere in the wilderness. We ministers will accompany you, and General Nangong Kuo and General Xin Jia can act as guards. We can enjoy ourselves with the people just as the sage emperors Yao and Shun did."

Delighted with the idea, Prince Wen announced that they would set off early the following day. The next morning, General Nangong Kuo took five hundred royal guards to the south of the city and closed off a hunting zone there. Prince Wen and his ministers followed on horseback admiring the scenery. Brilliant flowers and fragrant grass waved in the warm gentle breeze. In the forest, orioles and cuckoos welcomed the spring. Young cowherds with bamboo flutes piped merry tunes on the backs of oxen. Farmers were busy ploughing their fields, while young girls picked tea and mulberry leaves. Mandarin ducks played in pairs on the gentle blue current of a passing stream. The beauty of the spring scenery was indeed a captivating sight!

When Prince Wen reached the hill on which the hunting ground had been enclosed, he saw many guards with iron forks, hawks and hounds. In a very short time, deer, leopards and foxes fell before them as prey, staining the earth red with their blood and filling the air with their death cries.

Prince Wen was distressed by the scene of slaughter. "Why did you establish a hunting zone on this hill?" he asked San Yisheng.

"As Your Highness is taking a spring outing with us here, General Nangong Kuo closed off this area so that Your Highness could enjoy the pleasures of the hunt."

"You're wrong, Minister!" Prince Wen replied solemnly. "In ancient times, Fu Xi was respected as a sage emperor because he never ate meat. Once when his Prime Minister Feng Hou entertained him with meat, he refused to eat it, saying, 'People eat the flesh of animals when hungry and drink their blood when thirsty, but I want them to live. I can't bear to have them killed. I would rather eat grain so that all creatures may live in peace. Isn't that as Heaven would wish?' Fu Xi lived in times less civilized than today. They didn't have the many different grains that we have now, but he still refused to eat meat. We're here to enjoy the spring scenery. How can we hunt down innocent animals? Besides, it's now the beginning of spring when everything's reproducing and growing, and to slaughter is most distressing to a benevolent man. The ancients didn't hunt animals in their periods of reproduction and growth, and neither should we. Make haste and tell General Nangong Kuo to open up the place at once." When the order had been carried out, Prince Wen proposed, "Let's drink and make merry on horseback."

They saw men and women, old and young, coming through the fields and meadows to enjoy the spring scenery, some drinking by the stream and others singing. Both the prince and his ministers were glad to see their people living in contentment as in the days of the sage emperor Yao. Just then, they spotted a group of fishermen singing:

> *Remember how King Tang felled the tyrant,*
> *Rose as he did in the town of Ge?*
> *It's the people's will and Heaven's,*
> *That he raised the banner and*
> *Restored peace to the land.*
> *That was 600 years ago, and the glories*
> *Are things of the past.*
> *Wine, women, and atrocities,*
> *The new tyrant wallows in evil.*
> *Happy Terrace built in thick blood,*
> *Lust and pleasure trips all day,*
> *While his citizens suffer bitterly.*
> *A hermit among the blue waters,*
> *I wash my ears clean of*
> *Anything to do with power and wealth.*
> *Singing on the surging waves,*
> *I spend my days fishing,*
> *And nights observing celestial phenomena.*
> *Alone, I remain aloof from the world,*
> *All my life I'll be carefree*
> *Until my hair turns white.*

"That song's written so well that it must be the work of some sagely recluse who lives here," Prince Wen commented, and ordered Xin Jia, "Go and ask the ideal man that wrote that song to come and see me."

The general whipped his horse forward. "Will the ideal

man please come and see His Highness?"

Misunderstanding him, all the fishermen knelt down and replied, "All of us are idle men."

"How can you all be ideal men?" Xin Jia demanded.

"Because we fish early in the morning and have nothing to do the rest of the day. We're all idle."

Just then Prince Wen came up on his horse.

"Your Highness, they're all ordinary fishermen. There's no ideal man here," Xin Jia told him.

"The song's so excellent that there must be a talented man among you," the prince insisted.

"We didn't write the song, Your Highness. Thirty-five *li* from here is Panxi Stream. This song was composed by an old man who lives there. As we have often heard him sing it, we all became familiar with it as well."

"You may go then. I'm sorry to have troubled you," Prince Wen said with disappointment.

After they had gone, Prince Wen kept thinking about the song, particularly the line "I wash my ears clean of anything to do with power and wealth."

"What does that line mean? Is there any story to it?" San Yisheng asked.

"It refers to the story of how the sage emperor Yao sought out Shun as his successor. Yao was a virtuous ruler, but he had a worthless son. Not to disappoint his people, Yao often made secret trips in an attempt to find a good and talented man to succeed him. One day Yao was walking through some remote mountains when he saw a man twirling a gourd ladle in a stream. He was intrigued and asked, 'Why do you twirl your gourd ladle about in the water?'

"The man smiled and answered, 'I've freed myself from worldly burdens. I've forsaken fame, riches, and family. I wish only to live here in the forests, eating salted vegetables and drinking from the springs. I'll be content to pass my life this way.'

"Yao was delighted with the reply and thought, 'This man dislikes the riches and glories of the world, and distances himself from worldly disputes. He's a man of outstanding caliber, and just the man I should choose as my successor.' He said, 'I'm none other than Emperor Yao. As I can see that you're so virtuous, I would like to abdicate in your favor. Would you accept the throne?'

"Hearing his words, the man immediately stood up, threw his gourd ladle on the ground and stamped on it, smashing it to pieces. Then he covered his ears with his hands and rushed to the stream where he began to wash his ears vigorously.

"As he washed, another man came up, leading an ox to the stream. 'Sir, I must water my ox,' the man called, but he just went on washing his ears. Perplexed, the man demanded, 'How much dirt is in your ears that it takes you this long?'

"It was a long while before he finished washing and finally replied, 'Emperor Yao asked me to succeed him to the throne and polluted my ears dreadfully. I had to wash them in the stream. I'm sorry I delayed you watering your ox.'

"The man immediately led his ox upstream. 'Why do you take it up there?' the ear-washer asked.

"The man replied, 'By washing your ears, you've polluted the water. I don't want to pollute the mouth of my ox!'

"This story of the lofty and pure is the origin of that line," Prince Wen concluded the story.

The party continued on its way enjoying the spring scenery. Soon they saw a group of woodcutters coming towards them singing:

> There're certainly phoenixes and unicorns,
> But no ruler's virtuous enough to see them.
> When the dragon rises clouds appear,
> And with the tiger comes the wind,
> But no one cares to seek out the talented.
>
> Remember Yi Yin that toiled in the fields,
> He thought of Yao and Shun beside the plough.
> Without the three visits from King Tang,
> He would have remained a recluse like hermit Zuo.
>
> Look at Fu Yue the mason, unknown and poor,

Content to brave hardship in his cape of straw.
Had King Gaozong not dreamed of him that year,
He would have worked on stone all his life.

Ever since the ancient times,
Some have attained glory
While others remained in obscurity.
I'm not the only one
Who might spend his life on
The banks of a stream.

I play my flute in the sunshine,
And urge on the ox under white clouds,
While kings, dukes, and the powerful,
All fall as fate decrees.
Unconcerned, I smile on the heavens
While awaiting an enlightened ruler.

Prince Wen found the song to be extremely well written, and once more thought there must be a talented man among the crowd. He ordered General Xin Jia to go and find him out. Xin Jia rode over. "Is there a talented man among you? If so, please come forward and see my master."

The woodcutters laid their loads on the ground. "Sorry, there's no talented man amongst us, General," they replied.

"They say 'there's no such man among them, Your Highness,'" Xin Jia told Prince Wen.

"How can that be?" Prince Wen asked them. "The song's excellent."

"We didn't write the song, Your Highness," one of the woodcutters replied. "About ten *li* from here at Panxi Stream there's an old man who fishes all day. When we return from woodcutting and rest there, we always hear him sing this song. We didn't realize Your Highness was coming. Please forgive us."

"If that's the case, you may all go," Prince Wen directed.

Riding along, he couldn't let the matter drop from his mind. Then a woodcutter appeared, carrying two loads of firewood on a shoulder-pole. He was singing happily:

> *Spring waters flow endlessly,*
> *Spring flowers are gay.*
> *Meeting no opportunity,*
> *A hermit I'll stay.*
> *No one knows my ideals,*
> *They see a mere fisherman*
> *Casting his line all day.*

Hearing the song, Prince Wen sighed. "This at last must be the worthy man I'm seeking."

But San Yisheng looked at the woodcutter and exclaimed, "Your Highness, he looks just like Wu Ji, the man who killed Wang Xiang!"

"You must be wrong, Minister. My divination showed clearly that Wu Ji committed suicide. How can he still be alive?" Prince Wen objected.

San Yisheng looked at the woodcutter closely and was convinced that it was Wu Ji. He ordered that Wu Ji be arrested at once. Having come so unexpectedly upon the prince, Wu Ji had no time to dodge aside and hide himself. He could only put down his load and kneel before the general. As soon as Xin Mian ascertained his identity, he seized him and brought him before Prince Wen. The prince went scarlet with anger.

"You damned rascal! How dare you practice such deception on me!" he shouted, then said to San Yisheng, "Supreme Minister! Such a dishonest citizen must be sent to court for trial. He's a murderer and has cheated the government. He must be seriously dealt with. He's held my divination in contempt! He must be severely punished as a warning to others."

Wu Ji kowtowed on the ground, weeping. "I've always strictly obeyed the law and have never dared to break it. I killed Wang Xiang accidentally. When I was set free, I went to Panxi Stream about three *li* from here and sought help from an old man called Jiang Shang or Jiang Ziya. His alternative name is Flying Bear. He took me as his disciple, then told me to go home and carry out the instructions he gave me. This freed me from any trouble and allowed me to live and work as usual. Your Highness! Even ants and worms struggle to live as long as they can, and men certainly cherish their lives even more. I beg you to forgive me."

San Yisheng immediately turned to Prince Wen. "I should congratulate you, Your Highness! The Flying Bear that Wu Ji just mentioned is the very same that you dreamed of on the Spiritual Terrace. King Gaozong was blessed with Fu Yue as his prime minister after dreaming of a flying bear. Now you've had a similar dream. I suggest that you forgive Wu Ji and let him lead the way to your new minister."

Prince Wen approved San Yisheng's proposal and set Wu Ji free. The woodcutter kowtowed in gratitude then hurried to the forest in search of Jiang Ziya. When they arrived at the forest, Prince Wen and his party dismounted so as not to startle the worthy recluse whom they were seeking. Accompanied by San Yisheng, Prince Wen continued on into the forest on foot.

Wu Ji grew flustered when he couldn't find his master anywhere.

"Is your master here?" San Yisheng asked.

"He was here just a moment ago, but I can't find him now."

"Where does he live?" Prince Wen asked.

"In a cottage not far from here."

Wu Ji led them to the cottage, and Prince Wen knocked gently on the door. A young boy came out to meet them.

"Is your teacher at home," Prince Wen asked with a smile.

"No, he's not. He went out to stroll in the forest with a friend."

"Do you know when he'll be back?"

"He never returns at a definite time. Sometimes he returns in a few minutes, but sometimes he doesn't come back for days. He never has a fixed destination. He tours the lakes and streams or wanders in the deep mountains, or discusses the Way with his teachers and friends. It's impossible to know when he'll be back."

"Your Highness," said San Yisheng, "to engage a worthy man, one must be single-minded and sincere. Today we're on a pleasure trip and came here only by chance, so naturally we've failed to meet him. As we know from history, when Emperor Shen Nong called on Chang Sang, when Emperor Xuan Yuan called on Lao Peng, when Emperor Huang Di called on Feng Hou and when King Tang called on Yi Yin, they were all sincere and earnest. They abstained from meat, washed themselves thoroughly and chose an auspicious date for the visit. These are the rites that should be observed in order to show due respect to the talented. We had better return home now, choose a lucky date and come back here later."

"You're right, Minister," Prince Wen agreed, then ordered Wu Ji to come with him back to the palace.

When they got back to the stream, he composed a poem:

> *To rule, I need a long-term plan,*
> *And the assistance of a talented man.*
> *Today I've failed to see the sage,*
> *But when to meet him and end the misery?*

When he saw Jiang Ziya's fishing rod still floating on the water, Prince Wen felt even more upset. He chanted:

> *I expected the sage,*
> *But I see only his rod.*
> *The green thread floats*
> *Beneath the verdant willow,*
> *And the stream sparkles,*
> *While its waters flow in vain.*

Prince Wen lingered on, unwilling to leave, but San Yisheng finally persuaded him to return to the capital. Arriving at the palace at dusk, Prince Wen ordered that his ministers stay in the palace for three days to purify themselves, in preparation for the second visit.

General Nangong Kuo, however, voiced his disapproval. "The old fisherman may have a false reputation. How can we treat him with honor and glory without ascertaining the truth? If he's not as talented as we've been led to believe, Your Highness will be made a fool. As I see it, there's no need to take such pains. I'll go there tomorrow and ask him to come here to see you. If he's as talented as they say, it still won't be too late then to treat him with honor. Otherwise you may dismiss him. There's no need for you to fast and bathe."

"General! This matter cannot be dealt with like that. The state's in turmoil, and the people cannot live in peace. Many highly talented men have secluded themselves in the mountains. Our master's dream about the flying bear shows clearly that Heaven will bestow upon us a highly talented man to help us in our cause. We must follow the example of the ancient sage emperors and secure his service with exceptional sincerity. At a time like this, no talented man will voluntarily offer his service. General, you mustn't say such things and slacken our efforts," San Yisheng refuted him.

Prince Wen was very pleased with San Yisheng's rebuttal and said, "You're quite right. I'm of exactly the same mind."

All the ministers remained in the palace for three days, cleansing their hearts and bodies. On the fourth day, they bathed, dressed in official robes and accompanied Prince Wen in his phoenix carriage at the head of a long caravan.

Wu Ji, now General of Military Virtue, led the whole procession down the streets lined with flute players. The whole city surged out to watch them.

They traveled thirty-five *li* to the forest. Prince Wen ordered his soldiers to halt and wait quietly outside the forest so as not to startle the sage. He himself dismounted and went on foot with San Yisheng. To his great delight, they came upon Jiang Ziya sitting beside the stream. Prince Wen walked up quietly and stood behind him. As he approached, Jiang Ziya deliberately began to sing:

> The west wind blows and white clouds fly,
> Where shall I be when the year comes to an end?
> Five phoenixes sing as my true master appears,
> Few realize my talent as I sit here fishing.

When his song was over, Prince Wen asked softly, "Are

you happy, my worthy man?"

Looking back and seeing the prince, Jiang Ziya instantly threw his fishing rod aside and knelt down. "Please forgive me. I didn't know Your Highness was approaching and failed to welcome you."

Prince Wen hastily helped him up and bowed. "I've admired you for a long time, but not having shown you sufficient respect, failed to meet you on my first visit. Now I've fasted in order to express my sincerity, and I'm happy that I have the honor to meet you today," he replied.

"I am old and lack talent. I can neither administer the country so that the people may live in peace nor subjugate the frontier tribes with the little knowledge I possess of civil or military affairs. I'm ashamed that you should have wasted your time in coming here."

"You mustn't be so modest," said San Yisheng. "To show our sincerity we've fasted and bathed in the hope that you'll accept an appointment by His Highness. At present the nation's disturbed and divided, and there's no one to bring an end to the chaos. King Zhou distances good ministers and maintains a close relationship with the minions. He wallows in wine and women and treats his subjects brutally. As a result, the marquises have rebelled and the people are unable to live in peace. My master worries about it all the time, unable to eat or sleep properly. He's long admired your virtue and comes with gifts today in the hope that you'll help him rule the nation. If you accept, Prince Wen and the people will be overjoyed. Why not use your talents to lift the people from their suffering? The future generations will be forever grateful."

San Yisheng laid out the gifts they had brought, and Jiang Ziya accepted them. He expressed his thanks, and told his boy servant to take them to the inner room. San Yisheng drove Prince Wen's carriage to the cottage and invited Jiang Ziya to board it.

Jiang knelt down. "Your Highness, I'm deeply grateful for the great favor you've shown me. How could I dare to exceed the bounds of what's proper for a man of my status and ride in the prince's carriage? I would never dare do such a thing!"

"I arranged the carriage especially for you. You must ride in it so as not to thwart my good intentions," Prince Wen urged him.

But Jiang Ziya still refused to board the coach.

"Since the worthy man won't take your carriage, you may let him ride your horse while you yourself take the coach," San Yisheng suggested.

"That would belie the sincerity I've shown in the last several days," Prince Wen disapproved of the idea.

After more urging and more polite refusals, Prince Wen finally yielded. He took the carriage while Jiang Ziya rode on his horse. Guarded by infantry and cavalry men, Jiang Ziya was warmly greeted all along the way to the palace.

Fortune smiled on Jiang Ziya at the age of eighty. Reaching the palace, Prince Wen immediately held court. After the exchange of usual courtesies, he appointed Jiang Ziya prime minister of the West Grand Dukedom. Jiang Ziya expressed his thanks and then attended a banquet in his honor. All the ministers offered their congratulations.

Jiang Ziya ruled with discipline, law, and virtue, and the dukedom prospered. Work was begun on a new Prime Minister's mansion in the capital.

News of the developments in West Qi soon reached the five passes, and Commander Han Rong of Sishui Pass immediately sent a messenger to Zhaoge.

If you want to know what became of Jiang Ziya, you must read the next chapter.

25

A BANQUET FOR SPECTRES
IN THE PALACE

The messenger arrived at Zhaoge a few days later, and presented the report to Bi Gan. As he read, Bi Gan groaned and fell silent. He looked towards Heaven with a sigh.

"Jiang Ziya is so talented and has such great ambitions, he's bound to be a serious threat to us. I must report this to His Majesty at once," he decided. He took the report and went to the Star Picking Mansion. King Zhou summoned him to step forward.

"What do you wish to report, Uncle?" King Zhou asked.

"Han Rong has sent an urgent report that the West Grand Duke Ji Chang has appointed Jiang Shang as his prime minister to realize his treacherous ambitions. The East Grand Duke's already rebelling in East Lu and the South Grand Duke's attacking Sanshan Pass. Should Ji Chang rise in revolt as well, the whole nation would be ravaged by war and the people may be incited to join the uprisings, endangering our safety. Besides, we've been often troubled lately by floods and drought. The people are impoverished, the army is exhausted and the royal treasury is empty. Finally, Grand Tutor Wen is still fighting rebels in the northern district without any notable success. This is a critical moment for the nation, and we should consider things very carefully."

"I shall hold court and discuss matters with all the high officials," King Zhou answered.

Just then a royal attendant reported, "Chong Houhu requests an audience with the king." King Zhou ordered that he be admitted. "What do you have to report, Duke?" King Zhou asked when Chong Houhu entered.

第一五回 妹妲己請妖赴宴

"By your order, I've been overseeing the construction of the Happy Terrace. Now after two years and four months, it's nearly completed. I'm here to tell you the good news," Chong Houhu said proudly.

King Zhou was delighted. "Without your effort, the Happy Terrace could never have been finished so quickly."

"I've been diligent, not permitting the slightest axation on the part of the workers."

"Han Rong of Sishui Pass has reported that Ji Chang's appointed Jiang Shang as his prime minister. What should I do to eradicate this threat?" the king asked.

"What ability does Ji Chang have? What's Jiang Shang to worry about? They're frogs at the bottom of a well, very limited in their outlook, or glow-worms, capable of only an insignificant glimmer of light. Though Jiang Shang's prime minister, he'll soon be a winter cicada on a withered willow tree. You needn't worry about it. All the nobles in the country would laugh at you should you send your troops. They can do you no harm."

"You're quite right," King Zhou said, then added, "Since the Happy Terrace has been completed, I would like to look it over."

"We're awaiting your inspection."

"You and Bi Gan may both withdraw. My queen and I will go straightway to the terrace."

King Zhou and Daji rode together in the Seven-Fragrance Coach, followed by a long procession of maids and servants. On arrival, they found to their delight that the Happy Terrace was really magnificent. When they alighted and had been helped up to the terrace, they looked round, pleased to find that it was just like the Purple Palace in a fairyland.

Its outer walls were made entirely of marble and agate. Elegant towers and halls with blue-tiled roofs and exquisitely carved eaves led onto gorgeous pavilions and terraces. The center of the ceiling in each hall was inlaid with bright pearls that glowed brilliantly in the dark, turning night into day. All the furniture and ornaments were made of the finest jade and gold.

A member of the inspection party, Bi Gan thought only of the enormous cost of the construction, and how the people had suffered to provide such luxuries. How many ghosts of those who died in its construction must be lingering about the terrace! Watching King Zhou, with Daji on his arm, enter the inner hall, he sighed deeply. The tyrant had forced the whole country to work solely for him. The people suffered merely to satisfy his personal whims.

King Zhou ordered music and a feast and kept Bi Gan and Chong Houhu with them to celebrate. When both men had left, the king continued drinking with Daji. "My dear love! Do you remember telling me that once the Happy Terrace was completed, immortals and fairies would come and enjoy themselves with us? Now the terrace has been finished. Can you tell me when they'll come?"

Daji had said this only to deceive the king and destroy Jiang Ziya in revenge for the Lute spectre. She never imagined that he would remember what she had said. All she could do was answer vaguely, "Immortals and fairies are all pure, modest and virtuous. They'll come here only when the moon's full and bright and the sky's clear."

"It's the tenth day of the month. On the fifteenth there'll be a full moon and the night will be bright. Arrange for me to meet them then. How about it, dear?"

Daji dared not argue and promised to arrange it.

King Zhou wallowed in unrestrained sexual pleasure with Daji on the Happy Terrace. Since ancient times, the virtuous have lived long while debauchers have met an early death. King Zhou, however, held no misgivings and spent day and night in the arms of the fox sprite.

But Daji was most uneasy. She had to think of a way to satisfy his desire for beautiful fairies. On the night of the thirteenth day, when King Zhou was sound asleep, she resumed her original form and traveled on a gust of wind beyond the south gate of Zhaoge to the grave mound of Emperor Xuanyuan. She was welcomed by the nine-headed pheasant.

"What makes you come here?" the pheasant spectre asked. "You enjoy boundless pleasure in the palace. What made you remember us, desolate and lonely in this bleak place?"

"Oh, Sister! I've never forgotten you all, though I serve the king day and night and enjoy endless pleasures. The king has built a Happy Terrace and wants to meet beautiful fairies there. I've thought of a plan involving all of you. Those of you who can must transform into immortals and fairies and attend the banquet on the Happy Terrace. Those who cannot must be content to stay here."

"I myself can't be there, as I've some important business to attend to. There are only thirty-nine here who will be able to transform themselves," the pheasant spectre said.

After a detailed discussion, Daji returned to the palace on a gust of wind and lay down again beside the king, who was still in a drunken stupor.

The next day, King Zhou remembered Daji's promise. "It'll be fifteenth tomorrow, and the moon will be full. Are you sure the immortals will come?"

"Set thirty-nine seats for the immortals. Your Majesty will enjoy a long life if you meet them."

King Zhou was overjoyed. "Shall we assign an official to serve them?"

"Only a high ranking minister with a large capacity for wine is qualified," Daji replied.

"The only minister who can drink a great deal is Bi Gan," King Zhou said and immediately summoned him. When Bi Gan came to the Happy Terrace, King Zhou told him, "Uncle, I would like you to come here tomorrow evening to meet fairies and immortals. You should be here as soon as the moon rises."

The order left Bi Gan totally bemused. He gazed towards the heavens. "Stupid tyrant! The dynasty's in critical danger and on the brink of collapse, yet he idiotically dreams of meeting fairies! He's been listening to rubbish again. It's not a good omen for the kingdom!"

He sighed, and returned home dejectedly, not knowing what to do.

On the following day, King Zhou ordered, "Prepare for

the feast. There should be thirty-nine seats for the fairy guests. They're to be in three rows, thirteen seats each."

When everything was ready, King Zhou was anxious and excited, longing for the sun to set and the moon to rise. At dusk Bi Gan put on his official robes and made his way to the Happy Terrace as the king had ordered. Seeing the moon finally rising in the east, King Zhou was as happy as if he had gained a treasure house of pearls and jade. He took Daji on his arm and ascended the terrace, where the tables were laid with all kinds of delicacies and fine wine. King Zhou and Daji went into the banquet hall to drink and wait for the arrival of the fairies.

"Your Majesty! You shouldn't be present when they arrive. If their divine way is known, they won't visit here again," Daji warned him.

"You're right, Queen."

Just then they heard a great wind howling around them and realized that the immortals had already arrived. The foxes living in the gravemound of Emperor Xuanyuan had absorbed the essences of Heaven, earth, the sun and moon for hundreds of years, and were now capable of assuming the likenesses of immortals. As they traveled through the air, the moon was hidden by their spectral emanations, and a strong wind howled like the cry of an angry tiger. As they floated down onto the terrace one by one, the moon gradually came back into sight.

Daji said quietly, "Look, here come the fairies."

King Zhou became so excited that he couldn't resist peeping at them through the curtain. He heard one of the immortals saying, "Greetings, my Taoist friends."

"Greetings," the others replied. "Today we're honored to attend this banquet, so graciously prepared by King Zhou. May this dynasty last 1,000 years!"

"Bi Gan, mount the terrace," Daji ordered.

Bi Gan went upstairs and looked around under the bright moon. There, sure enough, he saw a crowd of elegant beings with the appearance and demeanor of celestials. He wondered to himself, "This is really very strange. They look like real fairies in human form. I must go forward and greet them."

"Who're you, sir?" one of the Taoists asked Bi Gan.

"I'm Vice Prime Minister Bi Gan. I'm here to serve you."

"Since you're destined to meet us, I'll grant you 1,000 years of life," the Taoist immortal said generously.

Bi Gan poured out wine and toasted each of them. Though he was vice prime minister, he didn't realize that the guests were not fairies but spectres. Holding the gold pitcher in his arms, he waited on them.

In human form, the fox sprites moved about freely. But though they were dressed smartly in flowing robes and Taoist coronets, they could find no way to change the foul smell of their bodies. Bi Gan smelt the vile odor.

"Immortals are always pure in heart, unpolluted by the effects of the six sensations, and their bodies are clean and fragrant. How can these fairies smell so?" he wondered, and sighed inwardly. "The king's unprincipled, and spectres are able to appear wherever they like. It's an omen of ill fortune for the state."

As he was deep in thought, Daji ordered him to start the second round of toasts. Bi Gan filled each of the thirty-nine cups and once more drained a cup with each fairy. He had a wonderful capacity and drank two rounds without even getting tipsy. But the fox sprites had never before tasted the strong fragrant wine stored in the palace. Those with a good capacity could manage to control themselves, but others could not withstand its effects and began to lose their power of transformation. As they became drunk, their fox tails reappeared, hanging down behind them.

Daji did not realize at first what was happening, and just wanted the members of her family to drink their fill. Bi Gan was serving in the second row and clearly saw the fox tails hanging down from the guests in the first row. He was filled with remorse.

"What a great humiliation! I'm a prime minister but I've bowed to these beasts," he groaned inwardly.

He ground his teeth in shame and anger at the vile stench. From behind the curtain, Daji realized that some of the younger fox sprites were getting drunk and in danger of revealing their true forms.

"Bi Gan may leave the terrace. No more drinking and the immortals may return home as they please," she ordered hurriedly.

Bi Gan was extremely unhappy. He left the terrace and walked through the heavily guarded palace to the gate, where he mounted his horse and set out behind two attendants carrying lanterns. After about two *li*, he saw a long column of torches and lanterns coming from the opposite direction. It was Prince Huang Feihu on night patrol. As Bi Gan rode forward, Huang Feihu dismounted.

"What urgent matter makes you leave the palace at this late hour?" Prince Huang asked.

Bi Gan stamped his foot, and said with regret, "Your Highness! With the state in chaos and on the point of collapse, spectres are making havoc in the palace. What shall we do? I was ordered by His Majesty to serve the so-called immortals on the Happy Terrace. I got there and ascended the terrace as the moon rose in the east. There I saw a number of Taoists dressed in blue, yellow, red, white and black robes. I never guessed that they were all fox spectres. But they were not good drinkers, and as they became drunk their tails reappeared. I could see them clearly in the moonlight. What shall we do now?"

"You needn't worry, Prime Minister. Go home and rest. I'll deal with it tomorrow," Huang Feihu answered.

After Bi Gan departed, Huang Feihu ordered Huang Ming, Zhou Ji, Long Huan and Wu Qian, "Each of you take 24 men and patrol the districts around the east, west, north and south gates. When those Taoists leave, follow them back to their lair. When you've found where they live, come back and report to me immediately."

Intoxicated with the strong wine, the fox sprites found it difficult to fly on the wind. Though they tried their hardest, they had just passed the palace gate when they dropped to the ground. From there they dragged themselves along, stumbling and bumping into each other, to the south gate, which was opened at dawn.

They were clearly seen there by General Zhou Ji. He followed them and saw them stop at the gravemound of Emperor Xuanyuan. They then crawled one by one into a large hole and disappeared from sight.

The next day when Huang Feihu came to his office, General Zhou Ji reported what he had seen the previous night. He immediately ordered Zhou Ji to take 300 soldiers, each with a load of firewood, to the gravemound, set fire to the hole and then block the entrance. He demanded a report of the results that afternoon.

That same morning Bi Gan called on Huang Feihu. After tea was served, Prince Huang told him what he had ordered Zhou Ji to do. The two men then discussed state affairs and drank together until afternoon. When Zhou Ji came to report the success of his mission, they went together to inspect the scene.

At the gravemound, they found the fire still burning. Prince Huang ordered his men to put out the fire and take out the corpses of the fox sprites. The acrid smell of burnt fur and flesh filled the air.

"Pick out those with unscorched fur and skin them. I'll make a fur robe for His Majesty. It'll be a good warning to Daji and help His Majesty to his senses. It'll show how loyal we are," Bi Gan suggested.

They returned home in high spirits, drank their fill and then parted. There is an old saying, "Mind your own business and you'll remain free from trouble; meddlers bring disaster upon themselves."

If you want to know what happened next, read the next chapter.

Daji Plots Revenge

Bi Gan had the skins tanned and a robe made. Soon winter came. One day, dark clouds covered the sky and a strong north wind rose up. A heavy snow fell over Zhaoge like silvery pearls or fluffy willow catkins. Pedestrians waved their sleeves to fend off the snowflakes. Nobles sat around a stove or before a fireplace enjoying delicious food.

King Zhou and Daji were drinking happily when an attendant came to report, "Bi Gan requests to see you."

When Bi Gan had offered his respects, King Zhou asked him, "It's snowing so heavily. Why don't you stay indoors, Uncle? What's so urgent that you must see me in this weather?"

"The Happy Terrace's so high that it touches the clouds and must be cold in the winter. I'm worried about your health, and have come to present you this fur robe as a small token of my loyalty."

"You're getting on in years and should keep it for yourself. That you should present it to me is real proof of your loyalty and affection," King Zhou said appreciatively.

Bi Gan then went downstairs, collected the tray on which the robe was placed and reascended the terrace holding it high above his head. He then helped the king on with the scarlet satin fox fur-lined robe.

"Though I'm the king and own everything in the country, I have never had such an excellent fur robe for the winter. Uncle, you cannot have done me a greater service," King Zhou praised him with a smile, and asked Bi Gan to sit down to wine.

Peeping out from behind a curtain, Daji realized that all the fur was stripped from her relatives. She felt as if her heart was being pierced by a sword, but could pour out her grief to no one. She hated Bi Gan bitterly.

"You old bastard! What business is it of yours that I entertained my family! You're deliberately insulting me by displaying the fur before my very eyes. If I don't gouge your heart out, I won't remain queen of this palace!" she swore, tears pouring like rain.

After a few drinks Bi Gan thanked the king and then left the palace. King Zhou entered, still wearing his new robe. Daji came out to meet him.

"The Happy Terrace is so cold in winter, and I'm delighted to have this fur robe," the king said with satisfaction.

"I see things differently," said Daji. "I do hope that you'll consider my foolish opinion. Your Majesty's the dragon incarnate. How can you wear a robe of fur stripped from so mean an animal as the fox! This is not suitable and beneath your dignity."

"You're right, Queen," King Zhou said.

He immediately took off the robe and sent it to the royal treasure house. Daji had said this because she could not bear to see the king wearing the skins of her relatives.

"In order to avenge my sister, I proposed the building of the Happy Terrace. How could I have foreseen that it would lead to the slaughter of all my relatives," Daji thought, burning with hatred.

She made up her mind to destroy Bi Gan, but could not think of a way to achieve her aim. One day, Daji was drinking with King Zhou on the Happy Terrace when an idea sprang into her mind. With her magical power of transformation, she greatly reduced her beauty. She had been as beautiful as newly opened peonies or begonia flowers radiant in the morning sun, but now she retained only a fraction of her original beauty. The king noticed it. He stared in wonder at her for a long time without uttering a word.

"Why do you stare at me in silence, Your Majesty?" Daji asked.

"Because I find you as lovely as flowers. I long to hold you in my arms and never let you go," King Zhou said insincerely.

"I'm not as pretty as you say," protested Daji. "As you love me very much, I appear beautiful in your eyes. But I've a sworn sister, Hu Ximei, a nun in the Purple Sky Nunnery. She's at least a hundred times more beautiful than I."

King Zhou could never resist women and wine. He was delighted to hear Daji's description and asked with a smile, "Would you let me have the chance of meeting her, my love?"

"She's a virgin maid. She's studied the Way since her childhood with a nun in the Purple Sky Nunnery. It won't be easy to get her to come here."

"By your grace, you have to let me meet her once. I won't be ungrateful for your service, my dear," King Zhou begged.

"When I was at Jizhou, Hu Ximei and I lived in the same chamber and learned needlework together. When she left home to become a nun, I wept. But she comforted me and said, 'If I ever learn the art of riding on the five elements, I'll send some incense to you. Should you wish to see me, just burn the incense and I'll come to you at once.' She kept her promise and sent me the incense a year later. Yet I've never tried it, as soon after I was granted the divine favor of serving you in the palace. If you hadn't suggested meeting her, I would never have dared to mention the matter," Daji told him.

"Why don't you get the incense and burn it straightway?" King Zhou urged.

"It's still early. Hu Ximei's a celestial, not an ordinary woman of this vulgar world. Let me do it tomorrow. I'll wash my body clean and set tea and fruit on a table in the moonlight. Then I'll burn the incense."

"You're right. We cannot blaspheme her," King Zhou agreed.

Late that night, King Zhou slept soundly. Daji took the opportunity to resume her true form and went directly to the gravemound of Emperor Xuanyuan. She was met by the pheasant spectre.

"Sister! Don't you know that the royal feast you offered resulted in the slaughter of all your family! Some of them even had their skins stripped off!"

Daji wept too. "I shall avenge them, Sister. I've thought of a way to deal with the old bastard. I won't be satisfied until I have the heart taken from his breast. Let's help each other. All you have to do is.... You must be lonely here all by yourself. Why not take this chance to enjoy the pleasures of the palace? We can be together night and day. What could be better?"

"You're doing me a great favor. How could I refuse? I'll be there right on time tomorrow evening," the pheasant spectre said gratefully.

Having arranged everything, Daji made her way back to the palace and returned to King Zhou's side without disturbing him. The king got up at daybreak, excited at the thought of meeting Hu Ximei that night. He waited impatiently all day, and when the moon finally rose, he wrote a poem to express his delight:

> Over the East Sea shines the moon,
> The universe clear and transparent.
> Like a jade disc hanging in the sky,
> It radiates rainbows of hope and joy.

On the Happy Terrace, King Zhou urged Daji to burn the incense at once. Daji assented, but advised him, "You'd better conceal yourself, for Hu Ximei's a celestial. I'm afraid she might be offended by the presence of a mortal man. She might leave at once and never come here again. I'll have to tell her about you first."

"As you like, my dear love," King Zhou wholly agreed.

Daji then began to complete her trap. She washed her hands and burned the incense. At about the first watch, the wind began to whistle, dark clouds covered the moon and a murky fog filled the air. In an instant, the sky became dim and a bitter chill penetrated every corner of the palace.

"What a dreadful wind! It's creating havoc!" King Zhou

cried in alarm.

"It's Hu Ximei riding here on the cloud and wind," Daji explained.

Just then, they heard the sweet tinkling of jade pendants and a thud as if someone was dropping from the air. Daji hurriedly urged King Zhou to conceal himself in the inner chamber. "Here comes Hu Ximei. Let me talk with her first."

King Zhou had no choice but to hide in an inner room, but he peeped out through the curtains. The wind soon dropped, and under the brilliant moon, he saw a Taoist nun, dressed in a pink robe, a silk belt and a pair of hemp shoes.

As the saying goes, "A woman looks much more beautiful under the soft moon than in the strong sunshine." The king found her extraordinarily charming: her skin white as snow, her face like a begonia at dawn, her small cherry mouth and peach cheeks alluring, her bearing graceful and her manner sweet.

Daji moved forward and greeted her, "Sister, you've come!"

"Elder sister, how are you?" Hu Ximei replied.

Daji led her into an inner chamber. They exchanged courtesies and then sat down.

As they sipped tea, Daji said, "I burned the incense, and you've kept your promise. I appreciate it very much."

"I came as soon as I smelt the incense. I apologize for intruding," Hu Ximei answered courteously.

Comparing the two, King Zhou saw that Hu Ximei was a divine beauty and Daji a mere pretty mortal. He felt his heart quicken and his blood race.

"If I could sleep with Hu Ximei, I wouldn't even regret losing my throne," he said to himself.

"Do you eat vegetables or meat, Sister?" Daji asked.

"I prefer vegetables."

Daji ordered a vegetarian banquet, and the two gossiped warmly and, knowing the king was watching them, behaved alluringly. The more he watched Hu from behind the curtain, the more the king felt she was a celestial come down from the moon palace. He longed to sit beside her, talk with her and embrace her. He pulled his ears and scratched his cheeks in frustration, unable to sit still for a second. Finally, he lost his patience and coughed meaningfully to indicate to Daji that he could not tolerate the situation any longer.

Daji understood clearly what it meant. She signaled to Hu with her eyes. "I've something to ask of you, Sister. I don't know whether you'll agree or not."

"I'll do whatever you instruct me to, Sister."

"I've mentioned you to His Majesty several times, telling him of your great virtue. His Majesty greatly admires you and would like very much to meet you. Now that you're here, would you agree to see His Majesty? He didn't dare intrude without your prior consent and asked me to consult you first. What do you think, Sister?"

"I'm a woman; moreover, I'm a nun. I think it's indecorous for me to meet a man, especially a stranger. Custom forbids anything to be passed by hand between a man and a woman. How could I meet and sit with him at the same table? It would surely be a violation of the rites," Hu Ximei refused resolutely.

"Not at all," Daji refuted. "Since you're a nun, you've already transcended the vulgar world. How can you still talk of differences between men and women? Besides, the king's the son of Heaven. He rules over millions of people and owns all the riches in the land. He has the privilege to meet whomever he wishes. As we're sworn sisters, he's your brother-in-law. There's nothing wrong with you meeting a close relative!"

"Then I'll do as you bid. I would be glad to meet His Majesty," Hu Ximei agreed at last.

Hearing that Hu Ximei did not object to meeting him, King Zhou rushed out at once. He bowed to the nun, and she returned his greeting. "Please take a seat, Your Majesty."

King Zhou sat down on the side, letting Daji and Hu Ximei take the seats of honor. In the bright lamplight, King Zhou was bewitched by Hu Ximei's sweet cherry lips and fragrant breath. She gazed at him seductively until he found it difficult to control his passion. Daji saw it all and stood up.

"Your Majesty, please accompany my sister for a while. I

must go and change my clothes," she excused herself.

After Daji left, King Zhou poured Hu Ximei a cup of wine, fixing her with an amorous glance while the nun smiled and blushed. When the king passed her the cup, Hu Ximei reached out for it, murmuring, "You're too kind, Your Majesty."

The king immediately seized the chance to fondle her wrist. Hu Ximei said nothing, and the king was ecstatic, his soul soaring to the heavens. As Hu Ximei offered no resistance, he became more audacious and proposed a stroll on the terrace.

"As you wish, Your Majesty."

They walked out arm in arm to enjoy the moon. The king ventured his hand on her shoulder, and she leaned on him enticingly. The king felt encouraged.

"My dear fairy! Won't you forsake your nunnery and live with your sister in the palace? You can enjoy wealth, power, and pleasure all year long and leave your bleak, lonely life behind. As life's so short, don't make yourself suffer like this. What do you think?"

He put out feelers, but Hu Ximei remained silent.

Seeing that she expressed no objection, King Zhou began to stroke her breasts and belly. She still offered no resistance. He seized her in his arms, carried her to a side court, laid her on a bed and fully indulged his passions. They were straightening their clothes when Daji reappeared, and saw Hu Ximei's dishevelled hair and heaving breast.

"What have you been doing to get yourself into this state?" Daji joked happily.

"I won't deceive you," said King Zhou. "I just made love to Hu Ximei as predestined by Heaven. Henceforth, the two of you will serve me together. I won't forget the great service you've done me by recommending her."

He ordered another banquet, feasted, and then bedded down with them both.

The adultery between the king and Hu Ximei was not known to the ministers beyond the palace. King Zhou cared nothing about his government but devoted himself entirely to Daji and Hu Ximei.

Though Huang Feihu commanded 480,000 soldiers, even he had no chance to see the king. One day news arrived that Jiang Wenhuan was attacking Wild Horse Mountain with the intention of capturing Chentang Pass. He immediately sent General Lu Xiong to reinforce the front with 100,000 soldiers.

Ever since he obtained Hu Ximei, King Zhou spent day and night making love, drinking and singing. One day, they were eating breakfast when Daji shrieked and fell to the ground, spitting blood. Her face turned purple.

"In all her years with me, she's never had such an affliction. What's wrong with her today?" King Zhou cried, frightened to see his love in such a state.

Hu Ximei replied with a sigh, "Oh, how awful it is! The old disease is attacking her."

"How do you know it's an old disease, my beauty?"

"Back in Jizhou, she suffered often from heart attacks and nearly died. The doctor Zhang Yuan cured her with a soup made from a human heart with seven fine outlets."

"Send for Dr. Zhang Yuan at once," the king ordered.

"Oh, that won't do, Your Majesty," cried Hu Ximei. "Jizhou's so far away that it would be at least a month before he could get here. She'll die unless we can find a man in Zhaoge with such a heart."

"How can we do that?"

"I can find him by divination, Your Majesty."

Greatly delighted, King Zhou ordered her to make the divination at once. Hu then moved her fingers as if she were divining.

"There's only one man with such a heart, a high-ranking minister. But I don't think he would be willing to give it up." she told him.

"Who is this man? Tell me quickly," King Zhou demanded.

"Only Vice Prime Minister Bi Gan possesses the heart that can save my sister."

"Bi Gan's my uncle. He should be generous enough to give up a piece of his heart to let my queen live. Send for him immediately," the king ordered.

Bi Gan was at home that day, deliberating the deplorable state of the kingdom when the decree arrived summoning him to see the king. Within a few minutes another four urgent decrees arrived with the same order. Bi Gan was perplexed, and when the sixth royal messenger arrived, he asked him what had happened. The messenger told him the whole story about Hu Ximei and her prescription for Daji's strange illness. Bi Gan was very much frightened, but could not disobey the royal orders. He dismissed the messenger and went to bid farewell to his wife, Madam Meng.

"Wife! Take good care of our children. After my death you must observe the rules I've laid down for the family and do nothing to violate the law. It's a pity that there will be nobody to take my place in the government," he said in tears.

Madam Meng was greatly alarmed. "Why do you speak so inauspiciously, my lord?"

"Daji's ill, and the tyrant wants to use my heart to cure her disease. How can I return home again alive?" Bi Gan replied sadly.

Madam Meng burst into tears. "But you're a loyal prime minister. You've never cheated the king, nor the people, nor the soldiers. You are innocent. How can you be sent to such a cruel death!"

His son You Zi, weeping, comforted him. "Don't worry, Father. Jiang Ziya said you would meet ill fortune and left that note in your study. He said it would help you out of harm in case of emergency."

Bi Gan rushed to his study, found the note and hastily read it through. Following the instructions, he burned the charm drawn on it and drank the ashes mixed with water. He then donned his robes and rode on horseback to the palace.

The news spread quickly in the capital, and all the ministers were shocked. Bi Gan was met by Huang Feihu and many other ministers at the palace gate. They besieged him with questions as he dismounted.

"According to the royal messenger," he explained, "His Majesty's in need of my heart to cure Daji. But I don't know the real reason."

On the Happy Terrace, King Zhou told Bi Gan, "Uncle! My queen's suffering from a serious heart disease. She can only be cured by a piece of flesh from a heart with seven fine outlets. As you've got such a heart, you may lend me a piece of it. If she's cured, your merit will be unsurpassed."

"The heart is the major organ of the body. How can I live if my heart's damaged? Your mind is befuddled by wine and sex. If you finish me off, nothing will save the state," Bi Gan shouted angrily.

King Zhou was furious. "When the king demands your death, you must die. If you don't obey my orders, I'll order my guards to take your heart out by force."

"Daji, you cheap hussy! I'll feel no shame when I meet the deceased kings after my death," Bi Gan swore and called for a sword. When it was handed to him, he kowtowed towards the Ancestral Temple and wept. "Royal ancestors! Little did you know that your dynasty would perish at the hand of your twenty-eighth generation descendant! But it's not because I, your servant, was disloyal. There's nothing I can do anymore."

He loosened his clothes and thrust the sword into his chest, opening a wide cavity. He reached his hand inside, pulled his heart out and threw it on the ground. Not a single drop of blood flowed from the wound. His face ashen, he straightened his robes and left the terrace without a word.

When the ministers waiting in front of the palace heard his footsteps and saw him striding towards them, they were overjoyed. Huang Feihu rushed forward. "Your Highness, how did it go?"

Bi Gan did not reply. As his colleagues came forward to meet him, he lowered his head, passed by them with swift steps and walked rapidly to the palace gate. There he took the reins from his attendant, mounted his horse and rode towards the north gate of the capital.

If you want to know what became of him, you must read the next chapter.

27

RETURN OF THE GRAND TUTOR

When Bi Gan strode through the palace gate in complete silence, Huang Feihu ordered General Zhou Ji and Huang Ming to follow him.

Bi Gan set off at a fast gallop, the wind whistling in his ears. He had traveled about five *li* when he heard a woman hawker at the side of the road selling heartless cabbages. "The cabbage I'm selling has no heart in it, sir."

"What if a man has no heart?" Bi Gan asked her.

"A man with no heart will die at once," the hawker replied.

Bi Gan uttered a loud cry and fell from his horse, blood pouring from his chest. The woman hawker was terrified and fled the scene immediately. Arriving moments later, Generals Huang Ming and Zhou Ji found Bi Gan lying dead under his horse, his robes stained with blood. They were puzzled, not knowing what had happened.

Before his departure from Bi Gan's residence, Jiang Ziya had written a note, on which a charm was drawn and his seal was stamped. Once Bi Gan drank the ashes, his internal organs were protected from harm. Even when his heart had been removed, Bi Gan was still able to ride out of the north gate. Had the woman hawker replied "A man can live even without a heart," Bi Gan could have continued on his way. It was the miraculous charm that allowed Bi Gan to pull his heart out, leave the palace, and ride out of the north gate without losing a drop of blood.

Huang Ming and Zhou Ji returned to the palace and reported to Huang Feihu what had happened. All the other ministers were heartbroken.

"The tyrant's unjustly killed his uncle, violating both the law and the ethics. I'm going to see him right now," Xia Zhao, a junior minister, cried.

He did not wait for the king's permission but made his way straight onto the Happy Terrace, where King Zhou was waiting anxiously for the heart soup. Xia Zhao approached scowling. He did not kneel down or offer greetings.

"Xia Zhao, why do you intrude without an order for admission?" King Zhou demanded.

"I've come to kill you!" Xia Zhou cried.

King Zhou burst into laughter. "There's never been any provision in the rites for a minister to kill a king."

"You damned tyrant! You know clearly that there's no provision in the rites for a minister to kill a king, but is there any provision in the world for a nephew to kill his uncle without cause? Bi Gan's your uncle, the younger brother of your father. How could you have conspired with that enchantress Daji to have his heart taken out! As you killed your uncle, I will kill you now," Xia Zhao said.

He grabbed the flying-cloud sword that was hanging on the wall and rushed forward to stab King Zhou. The king was highly skilled in martial arts. He dodged to one side, and Xia Zhao's blow landed in mid-air.

"Guards, seize him!"

As the guards ran forward, Xia Zhao yelled: "Don't touch me! The tyrant's killed his uncle, and it's only natural that I kill him."

When the guards were almost on him, Xia Zhao bravely threw himself off the Happy Terrace, dying instantly. Hearing of the tragedy, the ministers were deeply grieved. They had helped bring back Bi Gan's corpse from beyond the north gate, and his relatives began to enact the funeral rites. As the funeral was in progress, news came that Grand Tutor Wen was returning to Zhaoge after a great victory. All the ministers immediately mounted and rode ten *li* out of the capital to meet him.

When they reached the camp gate, Grand Tutor Wen sent

word that he would meet his fellow colleagues at the palace gate. They hurried back to the palace gate. Grand Tutor Wen set out too on his pure black unicorn. At the north gate, he caught sight of the paper penants of a funeral procession. "Whose funeral is this?"

"It's for Bi Gan," they replied.

Grand Tutor Wen was astonished. He entered the capital and saw the gorgeous Happy Terrace towering above the other buildings. His colleagues lined the roadside at the palace gate to meet him. He dismounted.

"Venerable colleagues! I've been away for many years. I find everything's changed here in the capital," he said with a smile.

"Grand Tutor, have you heard about the rebellions and the situation here when you were in the north?" Huang Feihu asked.

"I was well informed from month to month and I read all the reports, but I was occupied on the front. Only by the grace of Heaven and the fortune of His Majesty was I able to destroy the enemy. How I longed to have wings to fly back to the capital and discuss these matters with the king!"

Entering the Grand Hall, Grand Tutor Wen wondered at its bleak silence and the thick dust on the king's desk. He noticed the tall, yellow pillars standing on the east side of the hall.

"What are those big, yellow pillars for? Why are they standing in the royal court?" he asked the guards.

"Grand Tutor, it's a new torture invented by His Majesty. They're burning pillars."

"What's a burning pillar?" Grand Tutor Wen inquired further.

Huang Feihu moved forward. "Grand Tutor, the burning pillar's made of brass with three fire channels. Any minister who dares to point out the faults committed by His Majesty is subjected to this torture. Charcoal and wood are used to heat the pillar red hot. Then the victim's bound hand and foot to the pillar and burnt to ashes. This torture makes the loyal retire to hermitage and the good and talented resign their posts.

Many have left the capital, and many have sacrificed their lives in vain."

Grand Tutor Wen was greatly enraged. His three eyes flashed angrily, and the divine third eye in the middle of his forehead emitted a powerful white light. He ordered the royal guards: "Strike the bells and ask His Majesty to ascend the throne at once."

The officials were delighted.

After drinking the soup made from Bi Gan's heart, Daji had completely recovered. She was dallying with King Zhou when an attendant came in. "The bells are ringing at the Grand Hall to announce the victorious return of Grand Tutor Wen. He demands your presence."

King Zhou was silent for a long time then ordered: "Prepare the royal carriage. I'll go straightway." After greetings were over, he said: "Grand Tutor Wen! You went through a lot in the North Sea district. You've achieved victory and your service to the state's truly meritorious."

Grand Tutor Wen knelt on the ground and reported: "Thanks to your good fortune, I've been able to eliminate all the rebels in the North Sea district. I was always ready to sacrifice my body for the state to return the kindness shown me by the late king. However, when I was on the front I heard that the palace was in chaos and the dukedoms beyond the capital had rebelled. I was deeply worried and longed to fly back. Now that I'm back, I'm eager to know all the facts."

"Both Jiang Huanchu and E Chongyu were sentenced to death, as Jiang conspired to slay me and E was in a plot to rebel against the government. Moreover, their sons are treacherous and lawless. They've risen in rebellion and threaten our passes," King Zhou explained.

"Who are the witnesses to prove that Jiang Huanchu conspired to seize the throne and E Chongyu plotted to rebel against the government?" Grand Tutor Wen inquired.

King Zhou remained silent, unable to give an answer.

The Grand Tutor went forward and snapped: "When I was fighting the rebels, you didn't reign with virtue. You devoted yourself to wine and women. You slaughtered the loyal.

What are those yellow things standing there?"

"The ministers insulted me with wicked lies. I was forced to deal with them with those burning pillars," the king murmured.

The Grand Tutor asked further: "When I entered the city I saw a lofty building. What is it?"

"In the hot summer days I suffered from the heat and had no cool place to rest, so I had to build it. Not only can I relax there, but I can also see into the distance and keep in touch with the outside world. I named it the Happy Terrace for this reason."

Grand Tutor Wen was very upset. "Why is the state in disorder? Why are the numerous nobles in rebellion? You've failed in your duty towards them! You rule without benevolence, and won't listen to them. You associate with the minions and keep away from the loyal. You indulge yourself in wine and women day and night. You make people suffer through large construction projects. You're the cause behind their rebellions! I remember clearly the reign of our late king. All the frontier tribes offered allegiance to us, foreign countries made obeisance and people lived in peace and prosperity. But what have you done? I hope you'll give the situation deep thought. Since I've returned to the capital, I'll endeavor to set the country in order. I'll report to you later what I plan to do. Please return to your apartments for the time being, Your Majesty."

The king had nothing to say in his own defence. All he could do was leave the court and return to his apartments.

Grand Tutor Wen, however, remained in his position. "Fellow colleagues! Please don't return home yet. I would like you all to come to my residence." he said.

They all followed him back to his home.

"Fellow colleagues! I've been away from the capital a long time," he addressed them when they were all seated in the Silver Peace Hall. "That's made it impossible for me to pay any attention to state affairs. However, I was entrusted by the late king on his deathbed with the care of his successor. I cannot break my promise. I'm sorry to learn that he rules without law and virtue. I would like all of you to give me the truth so that I can find a way to deal with the situation."

"Grand Tutor!" Su Rong began. "It's not convenient for all of us to speak at the same time. I venture to propose that Prince Huang Feihu tell you the whole story, from beginning to end. Then you may hear it without interruption."

"A good suggestion," Grand Tutor Wen agreed. "General Huang, I'm listening with rapt attention. Please tell me everything."

Huang Feihu bowed and related in detail all that had happened, from Daji's entry into the palace to the death of Bi Gan. At the end of his report, Grand Tutor Wen let out a roar of anger.

"It's all because I was away for so long! I've let down the late king and ruined the state through my negligence. You may all return home now. I'll appear before His Majesty in four days' time and present my memorial for the improvement of state affairs," he told them, and escorted them out of his mansion.

He then ordered that the gates be sealed for three days, during which time no documents were to be delivered and no visitors admitted. After three days of painstaking work, he completed a memorial containing ten proposals for reform to present to the king in the presence of all the ministers.

On the fourth day, King Zhou ascended the throne. After he was greeted by his ministers, he asked: "Are there any memorials for me to consider? If not, this session can be closed."

"I have a memorial to be submitted to Your Majesty," Grand Tutor Wen moved forward.

King Zhou laid it on the desk in front of him and read it over carefully. It enumerated his failings and put forward ten proposals:

(1) Demolish the Happy Terrace to pacify the people;

(2) Destroy the burning pillars to encourage the ministers;

(3) Fill in the Serpent Pit to right the palace of its wrongs;

(4) Fill in the Wine Pool and destroy the Meat Forest to pacify the nobles;

(5) Depose Daji to put an end to her conspiracies to ruin

the state;

(6) Behead Fei Zhong and You Hun to warn the flatterers;

(7) Open the granaries to relieve the poor and the starving;

(8) Send representatives to the East Grand Dukedom and the South Grand Dukedom for peace negotiations;

(9) Look for talented hermits in the mountains and forests; and

(10) Encourage freedom of speech, let everyone have the chance to voice opinions publicly without fear.

The Grand Tutor stood beside the royal desk. He ground the ink slab, dipped the writing brush in the ink and handed it to King Zhou. "Your Majesty, please sign your name."

Looking through the ten proposals again, the king found the first one much against his will. "We've spent a great deal of labor and money. It would be a great pity if it were pulled down. This needs further consideration," he said. "Though I agree to destroying the burning pillars, filling in the Serpent Pit and the Wine Pool, and removing the Meat Forest, it won't do to depose Queen Daji. She's virtuous and chaste. This must be discussed further too." He then added: "As for the sixth proposal, it's unjust to execute Fei Zhong and You Hun. They've served me well and committed no crime. How can you call them flatterers? I approve all your proposals, except the first, fifth and sixth."

But Grand Tutor Wen insisted. "The Happy Terrace has wasted much money and the people have suffered greatly for it. They won't stop grumbling until you pull it down. Your queen invented the burning pillars, angering Heaven and hell. The ghosts of the innocent weep at the injustices done. Unless she's deposed, neither the gods nor ghosts will be satisfied. Fei Zhong and You Hun must be beheaded so that the court may be cleansed. I hope you'll implement all ten proposals promptly. Any delay would be harmful to the state."

At a loss what to do, King Zhou stood up. "I can only approve seven of the proposals. As to the first, fifth and sixth, we ought to have more time to discuss them before making a final decision."

"Your Majesty," warned Grand Tutor Wen, "Don't regard those three as unimportant. They're closely related to the future of your state. Whether the dynasty revives or falls depends on this decision. Seize the chance and don't let it slip by."

Fei Zhong did not realize the seriousness of the situation. He ignored Grand Tutor Wen and moved forward to speak to King Zhou. Grand Tutor Wen did not know him. "Who are you?"

"I'm Fei Zhong" was the answer.

"Oh! So you're Fei Zhong! What do you wish to say?"

"Though you're higher in rank, you've violated the rites. You're insulting His Majesty by forcing him to give his approval to your proposals. By demanding that His Majesty depose his queen, you're failing to behave as a minister. It's lawless to compel His Majesty to execute innocent officials, and is an insult by an inferior to a superior."

Fei Zhong's words infuriated the Grand Tutor. He glared at Fei Zhong with his divine third eye. "You wretch! How dare you deceive the king with your cunning words!" he cried, and with a blow from his immense fist, he knocked Fei Zhong down the steps.

Seeing Fei Zhong lying on the floor, his face bruised and swollen, You Hun rushed forward. "The Grand Tutor's committed a grave fault by beating a royal minister right before His Majesty's eyes. It's the equivalent of beating His Majesty himself," he said.

"Who're you?" Grand Tutor Wen demanded.

"I'm You Hun" was the reply.

The Grand Tutor burst into laughter. "So it's you! You two mishandle state affairs with your dirty tricks and conspiracies. You're in collusion with each other."

He ran forward, raised his fist again and knocked You Hun down the steps and several yards across the floor. He ordered the guards to seize both Fei Zhong and You Hun and take them to the palace gate to await execution.

As he vented his wrath, King Zhou remained completely silent. "They've no idea how to behave in the present situation, and have brought this humiliation on themselves," he thought

to himself. When Grand Tutor Wen urged him to behead Fei
Zhong and You Hun, he stubbornly refused. "Everything in
your memorial's correct. But I can't approve the first, fifth
and sixth proposals before I've considered them carefully.
Though Fei Zhong and You Hun foolishly offended you, it
isn't a serious case. They'll be sent to court and tried according to law. They can't complain about receiving the penalties
they deserve."

Observing the king's frightened manner, the Grand Tutor
relented. "Though I've acted out of loyalty, to make him frightened of me is a crime," he thought, kneeling down before
King Zhou. "I hope only that your state may have peace on
all frontiers, that your people enjoy happiness, and that the nobles submit peacefully to us. This is all I desire and nothing
else."

"Send Fei Zhong and You Hun to gaol to await trial. The
seven proposals are approved but the remaining three are to be
carefully discussed and dealt with later," King Zhou ordered,
and then dismissed the court.

When a kingdom is in decline, disasters never cease. As
Grand Tutor Wen was about to succeed in the effort for political reform, news arrived that King Ping Ling had declared the
independence of the East Sea district. On receiving the report,
the Grand Tutor left his residence to visit Huang Feihu at
once.

After the formal greetings were over, Grand Tutor Wen
asked, "General, this rebellion must be quelled at once. But
who should head the expedition, you or I?"

"Whatever you think best," Huang answered promptly.

After careful consideration, Grand Tutor Wen said:
"You'd better stay here to guard the palace. I'll take 200,000
soldiers to the East Sea district. I'll deal with the state administration after my return."

Early the next morning, Grand Tutor Wen reported the
emergency to King Zhou.

"What shall we do? Who's to subdue the rebellion?" the
king exclaimed in alarm.

"My loyalty compels me to go personally. General Huang

Feihu can stay here to protect the capital. The three proposals can be dealt with after my return from the front," Grand Tutor Wen replied.

Greatly delighted at the prospect of the Grand Tutor leaving the capital, King Zhou immediately ordered the mobilization of the army. He escorted the Grand Tutor beyond the east gate of Zhaoge. He toasted Grand Tutor Wen with a cup of wine in farewell, but the latter turned and passed the cup on to Huang Feihu. "Let General Huang drink first. I entrust you with the care of state affairs. I ask that you speak frankly about anything improper. To keep one's mouth shut isn't the way for a loyal minister to act."

Huang Feihu could not very well refuse. He emptied the cup in one draught. Grand Tutor Wen then turned to King Zhou. "I hope you'll pay more attention to the fate of your kingdom, listen to the loyal, and do nothing more to aggravate the situation. I won't be away long, a year at most."

After the farewell drinks, Grand Tutor Wen set out to the roar of cannons.

If you want to know how events developed, you must read the next chapter.

PUNITIVE EXPEDITION AGAINST THE NORTH GRAND DUKEDOM

King Zhou returned to the Grand Hall in great delight. He held court and immediately ordered that Fei Zhong and You Hun be released from prison.

At this Wei Zi moved forward. "They're awaiting trial. How can they be set free in such a hurry when the Grand Tutor's just left the capital? Please consider the matter, Your Majesty."

"They're innocent. I'm well aware that they were wrongly accused. Don't be so prejudiced against the loyal," King Zhou refuted.

Wei Zi left the court without another word. Before long Fei Zhong and You Hun entered and were restored to their original ranks. King Zhou was delighted: the Grand Tutor had left the palace for the front, leaving him completely free to enjoy himself, without the slightest misgivings.

It was spring. In the royal garden lovely peonies and other spring flowers were blooming. Thinking that the spring scenery would soon be gone, King Zhou ordered a party for himself and his ministers in the royal garden, as had been done in prosperous times during the reigns of Yao and Shun.

The officials found the royal garden as pretty as the Penglai fairyland. The fragrance of pink peach blossoms and white plum blossoms filled the air, while slender green willow branches trembled in the breeze. Bamboos stood gracefully beside the golden doors, and beneath jade windows grew two rows of majestic pines. The Brocade Hall was purple with exquisitely painted decorative beams and the lofty tower attached to it had carved eaves of a beautiful deep blue. Lovely palace maids walked to and fro by the Peony Pavilion or wandered amongst the begonia beds not far from where green water flowed under a golden bridge. On a white stone path stood two carved dragons and on the balustrades to its left and right were sculptured red phoenixes flying and dancing in the sunshine. The Jadeite Pavilion shone in rays of golden light and over the royal library hung variegated clouds. The king was enraptured by a mynah bird that talked like a man and a parrot that sang like a musician. In a clear pool, goldfish frolicked in the water and within a white-walled enclosure deer and cranes lived peacefully together. Little paths wound around enchanting hills of corals, and butterflies danced happily among the flowers. Purple swallows darted in and out under the eaves, frogs croaked at the waterside, and the songs of spring birds could be heard wherever one went.

The banquet was held in the Peony Pavilion, where all the ministers took seats according to rank. King Zhou, however, set his own table in the royal library where Daji and Hu Ximei joined him.

As they ate Prince Huang Feihu said sadly to Wei Zi and Ji Zi, "I haven't the heart to enjoy this grand party today. The country's torn by rebellions. At such a time how can we enjoy the peonies? Should His Majesty repent of his behavior, we may hope to quell the rebels, and live happily as in the days of Yao and Shun. If His Majesty refuses to change his ways I'm afraid the days of this dynasty are numbered!"

Wei Zi and Ji Zi nodded and sighed. The banquet ended at midday. The officials went to the royal library to thank King Zhou and take their leave.

"We should make the most of these pleasant spring days and enjoy ourselves to the fullest. Why are you leaving? I'll come down and drink with you," the king said.

As the king had joined them, the ministers had no choice but to remain in their seats. When dusk fell, the king ordered that candles be lit so that the drinking, singing, and dancing could continue.

In the royal library, Daji and Hu Ximei became completely drunk and lay down in the king's dragon bed. But Daji could control herself no longer. She resumed her true form and rushed out to look for human flesh, flying on a gust of wind that filled the air with dust and rocked the Peony Pavilion. The officials did not understand what was happening until some attendants cried out, "A spectre's coming!"

Hearing the shouts, Huang Feihu, who was half drunk, left his seat hurriedly. He looked around and saw something horrible rushing at him from the ground. Having no weapon, he broke a railing from the pavilion and struck at the fox sprite, which dodged and then turned to make a second attack.

"Hurry! Hurry! Fetch me the hunting hawk with golden eyes," Huang ordered.

His guards immediately fetched the cage and set out the hawk. It soared high into the sky, fixed its eyes on the fox sprite, then swooped down and clawed the fox sprite with its talons. The fox sprite gave a cry of pain and crawled swiftly into the rocks of an artificial hill. Seeing where it had fled, King Zhou ordered his attendants to dig out the stones and earth in the hope of capturing it.

They dug three feet into the earth, and found no fox sprite but a huge pile of half-eaten corpses. The king was horrified. "Many officials have reported that a spectral air permeates the palace and stars of disaster are seen in the sky. I've never believed it, yet it's evident that it must be true," he thought.

He felt extremely unhappy. The ministers got up, thanked the king and returned home. Daji, meanwhile, had been startled out of her intoxication by the hawk, and returned to bed with a badly scratched face, regretting her own folly.

The next morning, the king saw the wound. "My dear queen, how did you hurt yourself like that?" he asked in alarm.

"When you left to drink with the ministers, I went strolling alone in the royal garden. I walked into an overhanging branch and scratched my face badly," she replied, still in bed.

"From now on you mustn't wander about in the royal garden alone. It's true that there are spectres hiding in the palace." King Zhou said, and told Daji the whole story, never imagining that he had been sleeping with that same fox sprite for several years.

Daji was now filled with hatred for Huang Feihu. "You damned bastard, Huang Feihu! I've never offended you. Why should you try to hurt me? We're enemies now! You won't find it easy to escape my revenge."

But now let us turn to Jiang Ziya. One day he received the report that King Ping Ling had started a rebellion against King Zhou, that Grand Tutor Wen had been sent to suppress him, and that King Zhou still indulged himself with women and wine and placed his trust in the minions. A second report informed Jiang Ziya how Chong Houhu deceived the king, framed high-ranking ministers, inflicted great suffering on the people and colluded with Fei Zhong and You Hun to manipulate state affairs.

"If we don't get rid of that scoundrel straightway, he'll bring greater disaster on the state!" he thought.

The following morning, Prince Wen asked him, "Prime Minister, did you get any information about Zhaoge from the reports you read yesterday?"

Jiang Ziya moved forward. "According to the reports, King Zhou took out Bi Gan's heart and used it as medicine to cure Daji of an illness. In addition. Chong Houhu's throwing state affairs into chaos. He insults ministers, deceives the king and tyrannizes the people, yet the victims dare not complain. He's wicked and greedy. If he's permitted to remain at His Majesty's side, he's bound to bring disaster to the dynasty. In my opinion, we must get rid of this rogue and give the king a chance to repent and turn over a new leaf. You're fully authorized by His Majesty to wage punitive expeditions against traitors and rebels and would be letting him down if you don't do so. If you could help His Majesty become a good ruler like Yao or Shun, memory of your great service would last forever."

Prince Wen was delighted to hear that he could help King Zhou become a sage ruler like Yao or Shun. "If we launch an attack against Chong Houhu, who'll be the commander of the army?" he inquired.

"I offer to be the commander of the army on your behalf," Jiang Ziya replied immediately.

But Prince Wen was worried that he might be too severe. "It's better that I go with him," he decided, then said, "I'll go with you to the front so that we can discuss important matters together."

Jiang Ziya was happy with this decision. "If you personally command the expedition, all the nobles of the kingdom will support your cause."

They chose an auspicious date to set out. Prince Wen took the white ox-tail hammer and yellow axe that symbolized the authority bestowed on him by the sovereign and left the capital with 100,000 soldiers. Nangong Kuo was commander of the vanguard and Xin Jia his deputy. Four worthy and eight eminent men were appointed as military attaches.

The army started off amid the roaring of cannons and was cheered by the people all along the way for its perfect discipline. They were delighted that the soldiers were advancing on Chong Houhu. The army reached Chong City a few days later and set up camp outside the city walls.

Chong Houhu was away at Zhaoge and Chong City was under the command of his son Chong Yingbiao. When he learned about the arrival of Prince Wen's army, Chong Yingbiao immediately summoned his generals. "Ji Chang acts far beyond the bounds of his duty. He fled Zhaoge a couple of years ago and His Majesty's long intended to punish him. Rather than repenting for his previous mistakes he's come here to attack us, without the least provocation! Since he wants to throw away his life, I don't intend to let him off lightly," Chong Yingbiao exclaimed.

He organized his army with Huang Yuanji, Chen Jizhen, Mei De and Jin Cheng as leaders. "Capture the rebels and take them to Zhaoge," he declared.

On the day after their arrival, Jiang Ziya sent General Nangong Kuo to do the first battle. Nangong Kuo arranged his troops in battle formation. "Chong Houhu, you rogue, come out and meet your death," he challenged.

Before he had a chance to finish, cannons roared, the city

gates opened wide, and a contingent of soldiers rushed out, with Flying Tiger General Huang Yuanji at their head.

"Huang Yuanji! There's no need for you to come here. Call Chong Houhu out. I'll put him to death and appease men and Heaven, and then the fighting can stop," Nangong Kuo yelled.

Huang Yuanji angrily urged his horse forward, and brandishing his cutlass, rushed in to attack. Nangong Kuo raised his cutlass to meet the challenge. They fought vigorously, their horses circling close together and their cutlasses ringing with the force of their blows.

But Huang Yuanji was no match for the famed Nangong Kuo. After thirty rounds he was exhausted. He tried to flee, but was blocked by a blow from Nangong Kuo's cutlass. He tried a second time, and was knocked from his horse. Nangong's soldiers decapitated him, and the victorious general returned to the West Qi camp, where he presented the head to Jiang Ziya.

Learning that Huang Yuanji's head was now hanging over Jiang Ziya's camp gate, Chong Yingbiao pounded his desk in a fury. "You damned traitor, Ji Chang! A rebel, and now you've slained a general appointed by His Majesty. Your crimes are beyond measure. I won't give up until I've cut your head off," he cried, and ordered, "Alert the whole army. Tomorrow we'll engage Ji Chang in mortal combat!"

Early the next morning, the city gate opened wide and a huge army rushed out amidst the roar of cannons. They cried for Ji Chang and Jiang Ziya.

At the request of Jiang Ziya, Prince Wen made his appearance at the battlefield. Behind him, the army arrayed itself for combat.

Chong Yingbiao saw an old man, dressed as a Taoist, ride out among the numerous brave generals. He wore a gold hat and a satin robe embroidered with cranes and carried a shining sword in his hand. His silvery-white hair and long white beard gave him a dignified air, like an immortal coming down from Heaven.

Jiang Ziya shouted, "The commander meet me at once."

Chong Yingbiao, wearing a coiling-dragon hat and gold armor over a scarlet robe, galloped forward. "Who're you that dare to invade my territory?" he yelled.

"I'm Jiang Ziya, prime minister of His Highness Prince Wen. You extort money from the people, deceive His Majesty and persecute the faithful. Everyone in the country, down to the smallest child, hates you bitterly. My master's here to eradicate this gang of criminals. He's fulfilling his duty to the king, who has authorized him to launch such punitive expeditions."

Chong Yingbiao immediately yelled back, "You're just a useless, decaying old dodderer from Panxi Stream. How dare you brag so much!" He turned to his generals. "Who'll take the old scoundrel for me?"

Prince Wen lost his patience. He galloped forward. "Chong Yingbiao! There's no need for violence, I'm coming now."

Seeing Prince Wen before him, Chong Yingbiao became even more angry. He pointed at him and swore, "Ji Chang! Why don't you behave yourself and serve His Majesty? Don't you realize that you're committing a crime by opposing the government and invading my land!"

"As both you and your father have committed crimes against the people, you'd better get down from your horse at once. We'll bring you back to West Qi, erect an altar, and inform Heaven of our deed, and then have both of you put to death without having to involve the people of Chong City."

Chong Yingbiao yelled, "Who'll take that bloody traitor for me?"

General Chen Jizhen answered the call. He rushed out at Prince Wen but was met by Xin Jia, brandishing his axe. Their two horses in close contact, they wielded lance and axe vigorously against each other. After twenty rounds, Chong Yingbiao realized that Chen Jizhen could not defeat Xin Jia, and immediately sent Jin Cheng and Mei De to join the battle. To meet the situation, Jiang Ziya ordered Sui, the Duke of Mao; Dan, the Duke of Zhou; Shi, the Duke of Shao; Wang, the Duke of Lu, Xin Mian and Nagong Kuo to go to Xin Jia's aid. The reinforcements from both sides intensified the battle.

As his men were outnumbered, Chong Yingbiao spurred his horse forward and threw himself into the fray. After a long and bitter fight, the Duke of Lu inflicted a fatal wound on Mei De with his lance. Mei De fell from his horse and died instantly. A blow from Xin Jia's axe finished off Jin Cheng.

Having lost two generals, Chong Yingbiao hurriedly took flight with his army back into Chong City. Jiang Ziya ordered that gongs and drums be beaten to summon the soldiers back to the Zhou camp.

Back in the city, Chong Yingbiao ordered that the city gates be closed. He then called an urgent meeting to discuss how to repel the enemy forces. However, all could see clearly that the Zhou army was strong and brave. None of them knew what to do. The meeting proved fruitless.

Jiang Ziya wanted to order an immediate attack on Chong City, but Prince Wen opposed the idea. "The people of Chong City are innocent. They've nothing to do with Chong Houhu and his son. If we attack the city, 'jade' and 'stone' would be destroyed together. My purpose is to rescue them. How can we do anything to hurt them? On no account shall we attack the city."

Jiang Ziya realized that Prince Wen placed benevolence before all else, and dared not oppose his wishes. "My master's as virtuous as Yao and Shun and won't permit the use of force. I'd better send Nangong Kuo to Caozhou with a letter to Black Tiger Chong Heihu. We might take over the city with his aid," he decided.

He took no immediate military action and awaited the reply from Black Tiger.

If you want to know what became of Chong Houhu, you must read the next chapter.

DEATH OF TWO GRAND DUKES

Nangong Kuo left with all speed for Caozhou. When he got there, he took up lodgings in an official hostel, and went to see Black Tiger Chong Heihu the following morning. Chong Heihu was in his office when a guard came in. He immediately went out to meet Nangong Kuo.

"What news do you have, General?" he asked Nangong Kuo.

"By order of Prince Wen and Prime Minister Jiang Ziya, I'm here to pay respects to Your Lordship and bring you a letter."

Chong Heihu took the letter and began to read:

Dear Chong Heihu:

A minister should serve his king with loyalty, offering him advice so that the people and the state may rest in peace and prosperity. He should not pander to the wickedness of the king, be the cause of suffering to the people, or enrich himself in the name of the king. Yet this is exactly what your brother Chong Houhu has been doing. Due to the crimes he has committed, he is regarded as a fierce tiger and hated by the people and gods. He is forsaken by the nobles of the whole country.

Though my master, the West Grand Duke, is empowered to start a punitive expedition, we are greatly concerned that despite your virtue, you would be involved in this calamity. We have given the matter much consideration and have sent General Nangong Kuo with a letter, in the hope that you will act righteousnessly, seize Chong

Houhu and bring him to the Zhou camp as all desire. You
may, in this way, distinguish yourself from the wicked.
Otherwise, people will condemn you as they do your brother, without distinguishing the jade from the stone. What a
pity that would be! I earnestly hope that you will consider
this matter and reply to us at your earliest convenience.

> Jiang Shang,
> Prime Minister

Chong Heihu read the letter over and over again, then
nodded to himself. "What Jiang Ziya says is certainly correct.
I would rather offend my ancestors than the people and be condemned for generations to come. Even a filial son would find it
impossible to cover up for my brother. If I turn him in and
apologize to my parents after my death, I'll be able to save my
own family and save the Chong clan from complete destruction."

He reasoned thus with himself, nodding and muttering.
General Nangong dared not utter a word. But then Chong
Heihu turned to him. "I'll be glad to comply with the prime
minister. There's no need for me to write a reply. Please go
back and offer my respects to your prince and prime minister
and tell them that I'll seize my brother and place him at their
disposal."

He then entertained Nangong Kuo and saw him off the
next day. Black Tiger Chong Heihu ordered Gao Ding and
Shen Gang to choose 3,000 Flying Tiger soldiers to march with
him to Chong City. He told his son Chong Yingluan to guard
the city of Caozhou during his absence and then departed.
When Chong Yingbiao learned of his arrival, he came out to
meet his uncle beyond the city gate.

"Forgive me, Uncle! My armor prevents me from offering
you a full salutation," Chong Yingbiao said, greeting Chong
Heihu with a bow.

"Worthy nephew! I heard that Ji Chang was attacking
Chong City and I've come with reinforcements."

Chong Yingbiao ushered him into the city with gratitude.
When they were seated in the main hall, Chong Heihu asked

his nephew why Ji Chang had come to attack the city.

"I don't know why. I engaged them once but lost generals and men. It's indeed fortunate that you've come with reinforcements, Uncle."

At dawn the next day Black Tiger Chong Heihu took his 3,000 Flying Tiger soldiers out of the city and challenged the Zhou army.

As General Nangong Kuo had already returned, Jiang Ziya understood the situation. He sent Nangong Kuo to meet the challenge.

On the battlefield, Nangong Kuo saw Chong Heihu in a nine-cloud coronet and gold armor over a scarlet robe embroidered with dragons. Chong Heihu rode on a fiery-eyed monster. His face was as black as the bottom of a cauldron, his eyebrows were yellow, his eyes were golden, and a red beard hung down below his chin. Chong Heihu galloped up, brandishing two short-handled axes. "You've invaded our land without reason. Why are you so savage? You aren't an army of justice at all."

"Chong Heihu! Don't you know that your brother's committed all manner of crimes! He's framed the loyal and mal-treated the good. As the old saying goes, everyone has the right to get rid of rogues," Nangong Kuo yelled back.

Without further delay, he lifted his cutlass and slashed at Chong Heihu, who returned the blow with his axes. When they had fought twenty rounds, Chong Heihu said quietly to Nangong, "I'll just fight this one last bout. See you again when I've seized my brother. You may give up ground now as a pretext to end the combat."

"I'll do as you order."

Nangong Kuo made a feint with his cutlass, then pulled his horse round and fled, yelling, "Chong Heihu, I'm no match for you! Don't come after me!"

Chong Heihu did not chase him, but returned to the city. Chong Yingbiao saw from the watchtower that Nangong Kuo had fled but his uncle failed to chase him. Hurrying down the tower, he rushed to meet Chong Heihu.

"Uncle! Why didn't you send your magic eagle to capture him?"

"My dear nephew! You're young and don't know that Jiang Ziya's a well-known sorcerer from Mount Kunlun. He would certainly have destroyed my eagle had I used it today. That would be a great pity. We've won, and we can now work out the next step."

At Yingbiao's office the two men dismounted and entered the main hall to discuss stratagems.

"You'd better report to the king about what's happened. I'll write to your father, asking him to come back," Chong Heihu suggested.

Chong Yingbiao did as his uncle suggested and sent Sun Rong to Zhaoge with the report and the letter. Sun Rong started off at once. After crossing the Yellow River, he passed through Mengjin and rushed directly to Zhaoge. He went to see Chong Houhu first and presented the letter. As he read the letter, Chong Houhu pounded his desk. "You old scoundrel Ji Chang! You insulted His Majesty, and would have died then! But I was generous. I help you out of trouble every time the king wants to send troops to West Qi. How can you be so ungrateful! I won't return here until I've cut off your head!" he cried.

He dressed in his official robes and went to see King Zhou.

"What do you wish to report to me, Duke?" the king asked.

"Ji Chang's ambitious. Unwilling to live in peace, he's sent a so-called punitive expedition to my land, slandering me with abominable insults. I beg that Your Majesty direct me as how to deal with the case."

"He showed ingratitude fleeing the capital. Now he has the gall to bully my minister. You may return home first. I'll send men soon and help you seize the treacherous rogue," King Zhou reassured him.

Chong Houhu took 3,000 men and hurried straight to Chong City, arriving in just a few days. As soon as he learned of his brother's arrival, Chong Heihu gave secret orders, "Gao Ding! Take twenty men and wait in ambush inside the city gate. As soon as you hear the rattling of my sword, seize Chong Houhu and take him to the Zhou camp." He then turned to General Shen Gang, "When I leave the city to meet my brother, arrest his family and take them to the Zhou camp."

He then set out with Chong Yingbiao. They came to Chong Houhu's camp about three *li* beyond the city. Delighted that his brother and son had come to meet him, Chong Houhu came out at once to see them. "I'm glad to see you here, Brother," he said with a smile.

Upon entering the city gate with the father and son, Black Tiger pulled his sword from the scabbard and put it back with a loud rattle. The soldiers immediately rushed out to seize and bind both Chong Houhu and Chong Yingbiao.

"Good brother! Why do you tie us up?" Chong Houhu cried.

"Brother! You're not a virtuous minister. You flatter His Majesty and inflict suffering on the people. You demand huge bribes and put the innocent to death. You're hated by all the kingdom, and the people demand the death of our clan. I'm grateful to Prince Wen. He kindly makes a demarcation between the good and the wicked. I dare not reject his goodwill. I'd rather offend the ancestors than hurt the feelings of the people and see the Chong clan face total destruction. I have no other alternative than to take you to Prince Wen," Chong Heihu replied.

Chong Houhu let out a long sigh and remained silent. Father and son were brought to the Zhou camp, where Chong Houhu saw his wife and daughter already held there. They wept bitterly.

"Who would have imagined that my brother would be so cruel as to send all my family to death!" Chong Houhu cried.

At the camp gate, Black Tiger Chong Heihu dismounted and was invited into Zhou headquarters.

"Worthy Marquis!" Jiang Ziya greeted him. "You're most noble to sacrifice private relationships in the interests of public welfare. You're the real hero of this country."

Chong Heihu bowed. "I'm grateful for your favor. I've complied with your orders, and my brother's here for your judgment."

Prince Wen was surprised to see Chong Heihu. "What
brings you here?"

"My brother's committed crimes against Heaven. I've
seized him and brought him here for trial."

Prince Wen was displeased. "He's your elder brother!
How can you be so ruthless?"

Jiang Ziya understood what Ji Chang was thinking.
"Chong Houhu's ruthless. That Heihu puts aside family ties
only shows that he's truly a loyal minister," he put in.
"People hate Chong Houhu and demand his death. Even small
children gnash their teeth when they hear his name. They may
know now that Chong Heihu is virtuous. The virtuous in a
family are now distinguished from the wicked." He then ordered, "Bring them over."

Prince Wen took a seat in the middle with Jiang Ziya on
his left and Chong Heihu on the right. Chong Houhu and his
son were brought in and were forced to kneel down before
them.

"Chong Houhu, your crimes are too many to speak of!
You should be put to death as a punishment from Heaven today. What do you have to say for yourself?" Jiang Ziya demanded.

Prince Wen, however, had not the least intention of
putting them to death. But Jiang Ziya was resolute. "Guards!
Take them out and cut their heads off," he ordered.

Soon the executioners returned with two heads in their
hands to show that the order had been carried out. Prince Wen
had never before seen a human head just severed from its
body. The sight frightened him so much that he covered his
eyes with one of his sleeves. "Horrible! Horrible! I will also
surely die!" he cried out.

Jiang Ziya ordered his guards to hang the heads beyond
the camp gate as a warning to the wicked. Chong Heihu asked
him how to deal with Chong Houhu's wife and daughter.

"The wicked doings of your brother have nothing to do
with his wife and daughter. They're innocent. You should
show concern for them and supply them with food, clothing
and other necessities. You should allow them to live in their

own quarters in your residence. You may take command of Chong City."

Black Tiger Chong Heihu did as Jiang Ziya proposed. He released his sister-in-law and asked Prince Wen to inspect Chong City. But Prince Wen refused. "You're head of the city. I needn't go there. I'll bid you farewell without further delay."

Prince Wen felt melancholy on the way back to West Qi. He was in no mood for food or drink and could neither sit nor sleep. Every time he closed his eyes, he seemed to see Chong Houhu standing right before him, demanding his life back. The sight alarmed and distracted him. When the army reached West Qi, all the civil and military officials came out to meet him. Doctors were summoned but all their medicines proved futile.

After the death of Chong Houhu, all his territory was given to Chong Heihu, and as a result became independent of Zhaoge. When news of it reached the secretariat in the capital, Wei Zi felt both pleased and worried at the same time. He was overjoyed at the execution of Chong Houhu, but he was worried that Chong Heihu now had control over all that vast area in the north, and that since Ji Chang had dared to use violence without royal permission, he would one day attack Zhaoge. He decided the matter was serious enough to be reported to King Zhou immediately, and so he requested to see King Zhou.

The king was infuriated by the news. "Chong Houhu served me with outstanding merit on numerous occasions, but he should die at their hands! The matter must be dealt with severely," he said, and gave the order, "Send troops to West Qi, and bring Ji Chang and Chong Heihu back for trial."

Li Ren moved forward and knelt down. "Though Chong Houhu served Your Majesty well, he was hated by the people for his cruelty and greediness. Many ministers were dissatisfied with your special favor for him, and to revenge him would be unavoidably opposed by all of them. It might be better to deal with the matter later on. If you take action now, you'll have to cope with your civil and military officials first. They would think that you favor only the minions and pay no attention to the loyal. The death of Chong Houhu is just like a skin disease, not a serious problem. But the uprisings in the east and south are truly of grave concern. I hope you'll give the matter careful consideration, Your Majesty."

King Zhou pondered over this advice for a long time and abandoned the idea of attacking Chong Heihu.

Back in West Qi, Prince Wen's health worsened daily. Lying on his sick bed, he was frequently visited by his ministers asking after his health, but there was no sign of recovery. One day, Jiang Ziya was summoned to the inner apartments.

Kneeling down before the bed, Jiang Ziya asked, "Your aged subject, Jiang Shang, is here at your command. Do you feel better today, Your Highness?"

"I've asked you to come and see me as I would like to tell you something very important. I'm deeply grateful for the favor His Majesty showed by creating me West Grand Duke at the head of 200 marquises. Though there are rebellions, we should maintain harmony with the central government and offer better service to His Majesty. I greatly regret putting Chong Houhu to death without obtaining royal approval. I am clearly in the wrong. I'm too dictatorial, as he and I were of the same rank, I didn't have the authority to try him. I'm guilty of a serious crime. I often hear him weeping and see him standing before my bed when I close my eyes. I believe that I can't live long. After my death, you mustn't listen to the nobles and rise against the king, even though his behavior degenerates daily. Should you ignore what I tell you now, you'll find it awkward to meet me in the afterworld."

As he spoke, Prince Wen was so overcome by emotion that tears poured down his face. Still kneeling, Jiang Ziya replied, "It's by your grace that I was made prime minister. How dare I not to obey your instructions. Should I disobey you, I would prove myself a disloyal minister."

The king and prime minister were talking when Ji Fa came in to see how his father was.

"My boy! I was just expecting you," Prince Wen said happily. "After my death, you'll take my place. You're still young but must never accept anyone's advice against King

Zhou. Even though he's not virtuous, as his subject you should never rebel. Come here now and kneel before the prime minister. Bow before him and acknowledge him as your father. You must always listen to his advice."

Ji Fa asked Jiang Ziya to take the seat of honor, then knelt down and kowtowed before him. Sobbing bitterly, Jiang Ziya turned to kneel at Prince Wen's bedside. "Even if my brains and innards were smeared on the ground and my bones pulverized, it wouldn't be enough to return one-thousandth of the favor you've shown me. You needn't feel anxious about me, Your Highness. You should take care of your health and make an early recovery."

Prince Wen then turned to Ji Fa. "King Zhou lacks virtue, but as subjects we're obliged to stay loyal. You must carry out the duties of your office, and on no account exceed the bounds of them, lest you be criticized by future generations. Love your brothers, and be kind and helpful to the people. I'll die in peace if you obey my wishes." He then warned, "You mustn't become lax about doing good nor hesitate to act righteously. Abstain from all that's wrong. This is the proper way to cultivate yourself. It's the only way to rule."

Ji Fa kowtowed his acceptance.

"I was favored by King Zhou with special grace. Alas! I'll never again be able to look on his divine visage and offer my advice. Nor shall I have the chance to make divinations at Youli and educate the people there."

He stopped speaking and breathed his last. He died at the age of 97 and was posthumously given the title of King Wen of Zhou.

After King Wen's funeral, a conference was held at the White Tiger Hall, attended by all the ministers. Jiang Ziya, on behalf of his colleagues, proposed that Ji Fa succeed his father as the West Grand Duke and declare himself King Wu (the Military King). King Wu honored Jiang Ziya as "Shangfu" or the Adopted Father and promoted all the officials by one grade. Before long the 200 marquises and frontier tribes of the district all came and paid their obeisance to him.

Commander Han Rong of Sishui Pass was surprised to

learn that the West Grand Duke had died and Jiang Ziya had made Ji Fa his successor. He sent a messenger to Zhaoge. When the palace secretariat received the report, Minister Yao Zhong consulted Prince Wei Zi about the matter. They realized that Ji Fa was ambitious and would surely rise against the government. The situation was grave. Nevertheless, Prince Wei Zi thought that the tyrant would not consider it urgent, and it would be useless to deliver the report. Yao Zhong, however, motivated by his sense of loyalty, decided that he must see the king, whatever the result might be. He went at once to the Star Picking Mansion.

If you want to know what resulted from the visit, you must read the next chapter.

INCIDENTS LEADING TO A REBELLION

When Yao Zhong was ushered into the Star Picking Mansion, he kowtowed to the king. "Ji Chang's dead. His son Ji Fa has succeeded him and has given himself the title of King Wu. Many nobles have already acknowledged him. This is going to cause a lot of trouble in the future. I'm extremely worried by this news and suggest that you send a punitive force. If you don't take action in time, the others will follow suit," he warned the king.

"What can Ji Fa do? He's just a young whippersnapper scarcely off his mother's milk," King Zhou said scornfully.

"Though he's young, Jiang Ziya's thoughtful, San Yisheng's highly educated and Nangong Kuo's very brave. We must be on our guard against them," Yao Zhong argued.

"You may be right, but Jiang Ziya's only a sorcerer. He can do nothing," King Zhou said, dismissing his words.

Yao Zhong left the Star Picking Mansion, sighing deeply, "Ji Fa will surely be the man who brings this dynasty to an end!"

Time passed swiftly, and it was soon New Year's Day of the 21st year of the reign of King Zhou. It was a day of celebration when all the ministers entered the palace to extend their greetings to the king, and their wives offered their greetings to Queen Daji.

When the officials and their wives completed the congratulatory formalities and withdrew from the palace, trouble began.

Lady Jia, wife of Huang Feihu, had entered the palace to offer her greetings to Daji. Huang Feihu's sister was Concu-

bine Huang of the West Palace, and as the two women could only meet this once each year, they always spent several hours talking together. As usual, Lady Jia first went to see Daji before visiting her sister-in-law.

When a palace maid reported, "Your Majesty! Lady Jia's awaiting your permission to enter." Daji asked, "Who's Lady Jia?"

"Lady Jia's the wife of Huang Feihu."

Daji nodded to herself. "Huang Feihu! You set your wild eagle on me and scratched my face, but today your wife will walk straight into my trap!" She ordered, "Admit Lady Jia."

After the greetings, Daji asked Lady Jia to sit down. "How old are you, Lady Jia?"

"I'm thirty-six, Your Majesty."

"You're eight years older than I. You should be my elder sister. Would you agree to becoming my sworn sister?"

"Oh, Your Majesty! How dare I? You're the queen while I'm only an ordinary woman. A peasant in the wilderness certainly cannot be a match for a beautiful phoenix," Lady Jia protested.

"You're too modest, my lady. Although I am queen, I'm only the daughter of Marquis Su Hu, while you're wife of a prince, relative of His Majesty. You're a member of the aristocracy, not an ordinary woman."

She entertained Lady Jia. They had drunk four or five cups of wine when a palace maid reported, "His Majesty approaches."

Lady Jia was flustered. "Where shall I go to avoid him?"

"Don't worry, Sister. You may take cover in the rear hall."

When Lady Jia had hidden herself in the rear hall, Daji welcomed the king in. He saw the cups and dishes on the table. "Who were you drinking with?"

"Lady Jia, wife of Prince Huang Feihu."

The table was cleared and set again. King Zhou toasted Daji, but she asked, "Have you ever seen Lady Jia, Your Majesty?"

"How can you ask such a thing! According to the rites,

the king may not see the wife of his subject."

"You're right, Your Majesty. But Huang Feihu's sister is your concubine. Lady Jia's your relative. As her brother-in-law, you may see her without violating the rites. This is quite in keeping with ordinary customs. You may leave here temporarily. I'll induce Lady Jia to ascend the Star Picking Mansion. You can go there and take her by surprise so that she hasn't the chance to avoid you. She's extraordinarily beautiful."

King Zhou retired to a side court in great delight, and Daji called Lady Jia to come out. Lady Jia thanked Daji and bade her farewell, but Daji said very earnestly, "We meet each other only once a year. How can you leave me so soon? Come with me to the Star Picking Mansion and look at the beautiful scenery. Won't you come, Sister?"

Lady Jia had no choice but to follow Daji to the Star Picking Mansion. As she walked along the upper balcony, Lady Jia looked down and saw the writhing serpents and piles of human skeletons. An eerie wind blew from the wine pool and a chill rose from beneath the meat forest. She was scared.

"Your Majesty, what's that pit down there for?" she asked.

"In order to maintain discipline, I invented this serpent pit as a means of punishment. Anyone who violates the palace discipline is stripped and bound and thrown into the pit to feed the serpents."

Daji's explanation frightened Lady Jia. She wanted to leave at once but Daji ordered that wine be brought in.

"I know you're going to the West Palace to see your sister-in-law, but do sit down and have a few more cups first, and then I'll see you off."

Lady Jia could do nothing but comply.

In the West Palace, Concubine Huang had been waiting for her sister-in-law but received word that Lady Jia was being entertained by Daji in the Star Picking Mansion. She was greatly alarmed. "Daji's an extremely jealous and evil woman. How can my sister be drinking with her?" she wondered and sent her maid to obtain further news.

As Daji and Lady Jia drank, a palace maid announced the arrival of His Majesty. Lady Jia looked around in fright.

"Don't panic, Sister. Wait for me out on the balcony. As soon as His Majesty's gone, you may leave. You needn't worry so much," Daji soothed her.

The king entered the hall and took a seat at Daji's side. "Who's that standing outside by the rail?"

"That is the wife of Prince Huang Feihu," Daji replied.

Forced now to make an appearance, Lady Jia had to bow before King Zhou. The king looked at Lady Jia with his lustful eyes and found her really beautiful.

"Please take a seat," he ordered.

"Your Majesty," she replied. "You're the king. How could I dare sit in your presence!"

"Sister, there's nothing wrong with you taking a seat," Daji urged.

"Why do you call her sister?" King Zhou asked.

"Lady Jia's my sworn sister and your sister-in-law. She can certainly sit down before you," Daji explained.

Lady Jia could see the situation clearly. "So I've fallen into her trap," she thought. She knelt down and said, "I came to the palace to offer my greetings out of respect to my superiors. I beg Your Majesty to observe the rites and allow me to leave here at once."

"Don't be so modest, Sister. If you don't sit down, then I'll have to stand up and toast you," King Zhou said encouragingly.

Lady Jia flushed with anger, feeling humiliated. "My husband's a noble and great man. How can I endure insult from the tyrant like this?" she thought and decided that she could not possibly leave the palace alive.

King Zhou poured a cup of wine and offered it to Lady Jia with an alluring smile. Lady Jia had no room to retreat. She grabbed the cup and threw it straight in the king's face.

"Tyrant! My husband's served for your kingdom well, yet without rewarding him, you try to insult his wife!" she cursed. "Tyrant, you and Daji are bound to meet your doom before long."

In great wrath, King Zhou ordered, "Seize her at once."

"No one dare touch me!" Lady Jia screamed, then turned and ran to the balcony railings. "Husband! I'll protect the honor of your name and my chastity with my life. Alas, my poor children. There'll be no one to take care of you!" she cried and leapt.

King Zhou felt great remorse, but it was already too late. News soon reached the West Palace, and Concubine Huang wept bitterly. "Daji, you cheap bitch! You hate my brother and take revenge on his wife!"

She rushed to the Star Picking Mansion and went straight upstairs to see King Zhou. "You damned tyrant!" she swore, pointing her finger at him. "To whom do you owe the peace and security of your kingdom? My brother's repulsed the pirates on the sea in the east and subdued the savage tribes in the south. My father Huang Gun's commander at Jiepai Pass. He trains his troops day and night for the security of your rule. Every member of the Huang family is loyal to you. Today Lady Jia came to the palace to offer her greetings. But you, you tyrant, were encouraged by that cheap hussy to cheat her into coming up here. You're so lustful that you totally disregard the ethic governing human relationships. You're a humiliation to your deceased ancestors, and your name'll be dirt in the history books of the future!"

Concubine Huang's curses left King Zhou dumbstruck. Seeing Daji beside him, she then pointed her finger at her. "You cheap bitch! You turn the palace into chaos and poison His Majesty's mind. My sister died tragically as the result of your dirty trick!"

She rushed over, seized Daji and struck her. As the daughter of a general, she was very strong. She knocked Daji to the ground, and the punches rained down. Though Daji was a spectre and could beat Concubine Huang with ease, she could not do it before King Zhou.

"Help! Help! Your Majesty," she pleaded pitifully.

The king rushed over to mediate. "It had nothing to do with Daji. Your sister offended me so much that she felt scared and killed herself by leaping from the balcony. It's not

Daji's fault," he explained.

But in her anger, Concubine Huang acted without thinking and landed a punch in King Zhou's face. "You tyrant!" she screamed. "You're still trying to defend the bitch. I'll beat her to death to pay for the life of my sister."

King Zhou was furious. "How dare you strike me, you wretched woman!"

He grabbed her hair with one hand and her robes with the other, lifted her up and hurled her from the balcony. She died at once. King Zhou then sat down in silence. Though he was filled with remorse, he was unwilling to reproach Daji.

Meanwhile the attendants who had accompanied Lady Jia to the palace were still waiting for her in the Nine Chamber Hall. They waited until dusk, but she failed to return. A maid appeared from the inner palace and asked them who they were.

"We're from the mansion of Prince Huang Feihu. We're waiting for Lady Jia," they replied.

"You'd better return home. Lady Jia's committed suicide by throwing herself from the Star Picking Mansion. Concubine Huang then had an argument with His Majesty, and he threw her off the building too."

Huang Feihu was enjoying the New Year's feast with his brothers Huang Feibiao and Huang Feibao, his generals, Huang Ming, Zhou Ji, Long Huan and Wu Qian, and his three sons, Huang Tianlu, Huang Tianjue and Huang Tianxiang when Lady Jia's attendants returned.

"Your Highness! Disaster's befallen us!" they reported in great fright.

"What happened?" Huang Feihu asked hurriedly.

The attendants knelt down. "We don't know why, but our mistress Lady Jia threw herself from the Star Picking Mansion and Concubine Huang of the West Palace was thrown off the building by His Majesty. Both are dead."

Huang Tianlu, aged fourteen, Huang Tianjue, twelve, and Huang Tianxiang, seven, immediately burst into tears. But Huang Feihu remained silent at the news.

"Don't hesitate, Brother!" Huang Ming urged him. "The tyrant must have been fascinated by Sister's beauty and attempted to insult her. She defended her chastity by suicide. Concubine Huang must have learned of her tragic death and protested, so he threw her off the mansion. This is undoubtedly what happened. The old proverb teaches us that 'Should the monarch rule improperly, his subjects may seek a new master.' Look! We're brave and loyal, fighting for the king in the north, south, east, and west. If we remain indifferent to such a serious matter, we'll be ridiculed by the heroes. Since the king insults his subjects, we can only rebel. There's no other choice."

The four generals took up their weapons, mounted their horses and rode out of the mansion. Seeing them leave, ready to take action, Huang Feihu hesitated. "How can I rebel just for a woman's sake? How will I be able to defend my position when the rebellion is known to all?"

He ran outside and shouted to the four generals, "Come back, Brothers! Let's discuss what to do and where to go. We'll have to prepare carts for our luggage. How can you four leave here alone?"

The four generals turned back and went inside with Huang Feihu. Unexpectedly, Huang Feihu raised his sword in his hand. "You rogues! You don't repay royal favor but take action detrimental to my whole family! What's the death of my wife got to do with you? Have you ever thought that the Huang family has served the dynasty faithfully for seven generations, enjoying royal favor for more than two hundred years? How can we declare a rebellion against the government just because a woman has died! You're just using this as an excuse to plunder Zhaoge. You forget that you're high military officials, wearing the golden belts of office!"

The generals were momentarily dumbstruck, but then General Huang Ming laughed. "Brother! You're absolutely right. The matter has nothing to do with us at all. Why should we be angry about it?"

They sat down again to the feast, eating, drinking and laughing incessantly. But Huang Feihu's heart was boiling. His three sons' bitter sobbing resounded in his ears. "What makes you four so happy?" he demanded.

"Brother! You're in trouble, we're not. This is New Year's Day. We ought to enjoy ourselves. It has nothing to do with you," Huang Ming replied.

Huang Feihu exploded with rage, "How can you laugh when I'm in such distress?"

"To tell you the truth, Brother, we're all laughing at you," General Zhou Ji said coldly.

"Am I a laughingstock? I'm the highest official in the kingdom. I'm the head of all the ministers. What's there to be laughed at?" Huang Feihu demanded.

"Brother, you're quite right. You enjoy high rank. Those who know, of course, realize that the service you've rendered the kingdom fully qualifies you for such glory. But those who don't would think that your power and riches are only due to the king's appreciation of your wife's beauty," General Zhou Ji answered.

Zhou Ji's acute answer made Huang Feihu boil with rage. He ordered his guards, "Pack up the luggage and get ready to fight our way out of Zhaoge!"

As his elder brother was determined to rebel, Huang Feibiao organized 1,000 soldiers and 400 carts, all loaded with gold, silver, pearls and other valuables in preparation for the journey.

Huang Feihu doubtfully asked his three sons, two brothers and four trusted generals. "But where shall we go?"

"Brother! Don't you know the ancient proverb that the talented choose only a virtuous master? King Wu in West Qi already has political influence over two-thirds of the kingdom. Let's go to him. What could be better?" General Huang Ming suggested, as he thought, "I've incited him to rebel, but he might regret it and change his mind. I must make it impossible for him to turn back." He said, "Revenge for Lady Jia and Concubine Huang will be slow if we wait till we've fought our way through the five passes and asked King Wu for troops. We ought to challenge King Zhou to battle before we leave. What do you think, Brother?"

Huang Feihu agreed without thinking. He put on his armor, mounted his divine ox, and then rode with his brothers and generals to the palace gate. His sons, under the protection of family guards, left the capital through the west gate along with the luggage carts. Dawn was just breaking when they reached the palace gate.

"Tell the tyrant to come out and explain himself without delay," General Zhou Ji shouted. "If he's slow about it, we'll break into the palace. It'll be too late to regret it then."

After the death of Lady Jia and Concubine Huang, King Zhou was filled with remorse. He was sitting alone in the Dragon Virtue Hall when a guard rushed in. "Huang Feihu's rebelled. He challenges you at the palace gate."

King Zhou was furious and took the opportunity to vent his frustration. "The bloody bastard! How dare he!"

He put on his armor, took a cutlass and rode out on his Jaunty Horse, followed by the palace army. Though Huang Feihu was determined to rebel, he felt ashamed to meet him. Zhou Ji read it from his expression.

"Tyrant! You mishandle administration and have insulted the wife of your minister. You're wanton and barbarous," he shouted. Raising his axe, he rode his horse at King Zhou. The king lifted his big cutlass to parry the blow. Without losing any time, Huang Ming urged his horse forward to join the attack.

Huang Feihu said nothing, but he was displeased. "They rushed into fight without giving me a chance to clarify the facts with the king."

He had no choice but to spur his divine ox forward to join the combat. It was like a fight between a dragon and three tigers. King Zhou played his cutlass with skill, but he could not withstand the combined attack of the three generals. After thirty rounds he had to give up ground and flee back through the palace gate. Huang Ming wanted to follow in pursuit, but Huang Feihu stopped him. They left Zhaoge through the west gate, quickly caught up with the rest of the family, and went on together towards Mengjin.

After his defeat, King Zhou fled into the palace and sat in his court brooding remorsefully, but it was too late. At the news of the rebellion of Prince Huang Feihu, the people of the capital closed their doors and few ventured out onto the streets. When the ministers heard about the battle, they appeared before the king to comfort him.

"What made Huang Feihu rebel against Your Majesty?" they asked.

King Zhou was naturally unwilling to admit his guilt. "When Lady Jia entered the palace to offer New Year's Day greetings, she offended my queen and then committed suicide by throwing herself off a balcony. Concubine Huang relied on the power of her brother and tried to get away with insulting Her Majesty. She was accidentally pushed off the building. I really don't understand why Huang Feihu has rebelled. Tell me quickly how I should deal with the matter."

The ministers remained silent, no one daring to speak first. As everyone pondered in silence, news came that the Grand Tutor had returned from the East Sea district. Cheered by the news, they left the palace and rode out of the city to meet the Grand Tutor.

As was the usual custom, Grand Tutor Wen asked his fellow colleagues to meet him at the palace gate. Grand Tutor Wen then dismounted from his black unicorn, greeted the ministers and walked to the Nine Chamber Hall. He kowtowed to the king, got up and looked round. There was no sign of Prince Huang Feihu.

"Your Majesty, why's Huang Feihu absent today?" the Grand Tutor asked.

"Huang Feihu's rebelled!"

"How can that be? Why did he rebel?" the Grand Tutor asked in surprise.

King Zhou repeated his version of the story and then added, "I never imagined that Huang Feihu would have the gall to attack me at the palace gate. I was lucky to escape unharmed. Huang Feihu and his gang have already left the capital through the west gate. I hope that you'll bring them back to be dealt with according to the law."

The king's fabrications angered the Grand Tutor. "It seems to me that this has been caused solely by your illtreatment of him. Huang Feihu's always been loyal and patriotic. Lady Jia entered the palace to offer New Year greetings in fulfillment of the ritual duty of a subject. How could she commit suicide without cause? Moreover, the Star Picking Mansion are your private living quarters, not the central palace. Why did Lady Jia go up there?" he demanded sternly. "Someone must have tricked her into doing so in order to push you into a trap. Why didn't you consider it carefully and refrain from insulting her? Concubine Huang learned that her sister-in-law died so tragically, and must have rushed upstairs to protest to you and Daji. But in your partiality for Daji, you ruthlessly threw her off the balcony. The fault doesn't lie with them! As the proverb says, 'should the monarch rule improperly, his subjects may seek a new master.' Huang Feihu must have felt frustrated. For although he's loyal and has served you with great merit, he's been unable to bring honor and happiness to his wife and children. On the contrary, his wife and sister have died tragically! Your Majesty, you should forgive him for all his transgressions. I'll go after him and ask him to return to the capital so that peace may be protected."

When he finished, he was applauded by all the ministers. "Your Majesty! The Grand Tutor's right. We earnestly hope that you'll issue a decree forgiving Huang Feihu and his followers for the sake of the state," they cried in one voice.

Grand Tutor Wen spoke again, "We should forgive Huang Feihu because His Majesty didn't treat him properly. But on the other hand, we ought to consider whether Huang Feihu's committed any crime against His Majesty, lest we make a wrong decision on the matter."

Xu Rong, a junior minister, moved forward. "The king was certainly not right to have insulted the wife of his subject and to have thrown Concubine Huang to her death, but Huang Feihu was wrong to attack the palace gate with his men. He showed gross disrespect for His Majesty."

"You're all dim and dull today, speaking only of the faults committed by His Majesty and not of Huang Feihu's treachery," Grand Tutor Wen reprimanded his colleagues and then ordered General Ji Li and Yu Qing, "Send urgent orders to Lintong, the Good Dream and the Green Dragon passes that they must on no account allow the rebels through. That way I'll have sufficient time to trace them."

How did events develop? If you want to know you must read the next chapter.

FLIGHT AND PURSUIT

Grand Tutor Wen's army left Zhaoge with flags flying and amidst the clamor of gongs and drums, in pursuit of Huang Feihu.

Huang Feihu's party, meanwhile, had passed through Mengjin, crossed the Yellow River and reached Mianchi County. As Commander Zhang Kui of the local garrison was a fierce fighter, Huang Feihu dared not go through the county seat. He skirted around it and made his way directly to Lintong Pass. Near the White Oriole Forest, they heard shouts and saw clouds of dust rising in the air behind them. Huang Feihu looked back. He touched his saddle and sighed.

"Grand Tutor Wen! How can I resist him with this small force! All I can do is wait for my death," he thought. He looked at his youngest son Tianxiang, who was only seven years old, and moaned inwardly. "The boy's so young, yet he'll also meet with disaster."

Just then, a general galloped up and told him that an army had appeared on the left. Looking into the distance, Huang Feihu saw Zhang Guifang of the Green Dragon Pass approaching at the head of his troops. Two more reports arrived soon: the four Mo generals had arrived from the Good Dream Pass on the right, and General Zhang Feng had come from Lintong Pass. Huang Feihu found that he was surrounded on all sides and escape was impossible. He exhaled a sigh so deep that it penetrated far into the heavens above.

But now let us turn to the immortal, Virtue of the Pure Void. As the immortals were going to break the commandment on killing, lectures in the Jade Emptiness Palace were put off until Jiang Ziya finished creating the gods and life had returned to normal. The immortals were thus idle, spending their leisure time touring the sacred mountains.

Today Virtue of the Pure Void was traveling over Lintong Pass when cloud he was stopped by the emanation of anger and despair from Huang Feihu. The immortal pushed open the cloud and looked down. "So, it's Prince Huang Feihu. If I don't rescue him, nobody will." He ordered his yellow-scarved genie, "Wrap them up in my Universe Muddling Pennant and hide them in the mountains. I'll see that the soldiers go back to Zhaoge before I send Prince Huang on through the passes."

The genie immediately carried out the order.

Catching Grand Tutor Wen in hot pursuit, a patrolman from the vanguard rode up. "Commander Zhang Guifang of the Green Dragon Pass awaits your orders."

When Zhang Guifang came alongside, Grand Tutor Wen asked, "Huang Feihu must have fled this way. Have you seen them?"

"No, I haven't."

"Then, you must go back at once and guard your pass carefully," Grand Tutor Wen ordered.

Before long, a second messenger reported, "The Mo generals await your orders, Grand Tutor."

Soon the four generals approached.

"Has Huang Feihu been to the Good Dream Pass?" Grand Tutor Wen asked.

"No, not yet."

"Alright. You'd better return at once and guard the pass lest the rebels get a chance to flee."

Grand Tutor Wen then asked Commander Zhang Feng of Lintong Pass the same question. Zhang gave the same answer and received the same order.

As he rode along on his pure black unicorn, the Grand Tutor felt puzzled. "Everyone says that Huang Feihu left Zhaoge through the west gate and passed through Mengjin. How can I possibly have missed him? How odd! We came in from all four directions yet none of us has seen him! I must halt my men here and find out the truth."

The immortal watching from the air saw that Grand Tutor Wen had stopped. "If I don't send him back to Zhaoge, how can Huang Feihu get by the five passes? I must do something else," he decided.

He took the lid off his gourd, poured out a handful of magic sand and threw it towards the southeast. A short time later, patrolmen hurried in. "Grand Tutor, Huang Feihu is on his way back to Zhaoge."

Grand Tutor Wen immediately ordered his army to set off in hasty pursuit. All along the route, he could see a company of armed men rushing swiftly along in front of him. He urged his men on at top speed, but reached Mengjin without being able to catch up with them.

When he saw that Grand Tutor Wen had left, Virtue of the Pure Void ordered the genie to bring Huang Feihu and his men back on to the highway. The party rubbed their eyes as if waking from a dream. Looking around, they found that the pursuing soldiers had completely disappeared.

"The good are certainly blessed by Heaven," Huang Ming commented.

"Brothers," said Huang Feihu. "Since Grand Tutor Wen's gone, let's make haste to get through Lintong Pass."

Close to the pass, Huang Feihu was stopped by Zhang Feng, who had received the report of his arrival and came out to meet him, leading his troops. "Huang Feihu, listen to me. Your father and I are sworn brothers. As an important minister and relative of King Zhou, why do you humiliate your ancestors? Your father's a supreme commander, and you're a prince. How can you turn against your monarch just because of a woman? You're just a rat in my trap. When I heard what you had done I felt ashamed for you. Take my advice, get down from your beast, and let me take you back to Zhaoge. There must be ministers who will ask for mercy for you. Your whole family may be pardoned from the death penalty. If you don't come to your senses now, it'll be too late for you to regret it."

"Uncle!" Huang Feihu replied politely. "You know me well. King Zhou spends all his time lusting and drinking. He listens only to the minions, keeps away from the loyal, and mishandles state affairs. Moreover, he's violated the ethic that governs human relationships. I subdued the East Sea district, performed more than 200 great feats for him, and brought peace and security to the kingdom. How can he now forget all my merits and insult me, yet expect me to remain loyal? I hope that you'll be kind enough to let us through. We would all greatly appreciate your kindness and be sure to return it in the near future. What do you say, Uncle?"

Zhang Feng was furious. "You traitor! How dare you try to deceive me with your slander."

He raised his cutlass and swung at Huang Feihu, but Huang blocked the blow with his lance.

"Don't be angry, Uncle," Huang pleaded. "We're both ministers under the same ruler. If you had been wronged, you would surely take the same action. As the proverb says, 'Subjects may take asylum elsewhere if their ruler doesn't govern properly.' It's clearly true. Why be so over-conscientious in my case!"

Zhang Feng did not relent. "You rebellious rogue! How dare you try your cunning tongue on me!"

He struck again. At this second blow, Huang Feihu lost his temper and urged his divine ox in to attack. After thirty rounds of bitter fighting, the aged Zhang Feng was exhausted. He turned his horse and fled. Huang Feihu chased after him.

Zhang Feng heard Huang Feihu close behind him. He stealthily hung his cutlass on his saddle and took a small stringed hammer from inside his robes. He swung round suddenly and flung the small, yet deadly, weapon straight at his pursuer. Huang Feihu was an experienced fighter. As fast as lightning, he struck upwards with his sword, cutting the hammer's string and catching the small round hammer in his hand.

Zhang Feng was unnerved and fled back to the pass. Huang Feihu did not pursue him further. He ordered his men to place the luggage carts in a circle around their camp and then sat down with his brothers and generals to discuss how to get through.

Zhang Feng sat alone in his office at this very same time.

"I'm old and weak, but Huang Feihu's brave and strong. How can I ever seize him? If he gets through the pass, I'll be guilty and punished. What shall I do now?" he wondered, and then asked, "Where's General Xiao Yin?"

"I await your orders."

"Huang Feihu's a fearsome opponent; he's not only defeated me, but also taken my stringed hammer. We can't beat him by force. Late tonight, take 3,000 archers and surround his camp. When I beat the bamboo slats, the archers must shoot simultaneously and kill every one of the rebels. We'll cut their heads off and send them to Zhaoge as evidence," Zhang Feng ordered.

Xiao Yin received the order and left. But he reasoned with himself. "Several years ago I was under the command of Huang Feihu at Zhaoge. He promoted me to general and posted me here as deputy commander. How can I be so ungrateful as to forget his kindness at such a critical moment and see his whole family massacred!"

He disguised himself and secretly made his way through the darkness to Huang Feihu's camp. Huang Feihu ordered his patrol to escort him in.

Xiao Yin knelt. "I used to be under your command. You appointed me here as deputy commander several years ago. Zhang Feng's given me a secret order to surround you with archers and shoot you all late tonight. But to forget the kindness you've shown me would be a crime against Heaven, so I've come here to give you a warning."

Huang Feihu was shocked by the news. "Many, many thanks for your great virtue. If not for you, every member of the Huang family would meet a cruel end. You've saved our lives, and we'll never forget it. But can you do anything to rescue us from this critical situation, General?"

"Mount your divine ox immediately and fight your way through the pass. I'll open the gates and wait for you there. There should be no delay lest word leak out," Xiao Yin answered.

Huang Feihu and his group mounted their steeds and galloped towards the pass roaring ferociously. As it was already dark, the guards at the pass were totally unprepared and had no chance of coping with the emergency. As soon as Xiao Yin opened the gates, Huang Feihu rushed through at once.

Zhang Feng was sleeping when he received the report that Huang Feihu had gotten through the pass. "It was my mistake to have trusted the wrong person. Xiao Yin served under Huang Feihu," he reproached himself.

He immediately mounted his horse and set off in pursuit. But he never imagined that Xiao Yin was waiting for him in the darkness. As Zhang Feng rode through the gates, Xiao Yin caught him off guard and struck him off his horse. When he was sure that Zhang Feng was dead, Xiao Yin galloped after Huang Feihu. "General Huang! Take your time. I've already killed Zhang Feng. I'll go back and block up the pass so that the king's men will be delayed long enough for you to get well out of their reach. I'm sorry that we must part. Who knows when we may meet again!"

"I don't know when I can return the kindness you've shown me today!" Huang Feihu thanked him with great sincerity, and they bade farewell to each other.

When they reached Tongguan Pass, about eighty *li* from Lintong Pass, Huang Feihu's party halted and set up camp. Commander Chen Tong of Tongguan Pass had already learned of his arrival.

"Huang Feihu, you fancied that you could hold your princeship for 1,000 years, but you've really come down in the world now," he muttered to himself, smiling sarcastically. He ordered, "Take the soldiers out and confront Huang Feihu."

He donned his armor and made ready for battle.

"Who's the commander here?" Huang Feihu asked.

"Chen Tong," Zhou Ji answered.

Huang Feihu was silent for some time and then said with a sigh. "Chen Tong was under my command. Once when he disobeyed my orders I sentenced him to death, but then pardoned him at the request of other generals. He holds a grudge against me. As commander here, he's sure to seize this opportunity to get revenge. What should we do?"

As he pondered over the problem, he heard a great clamor

outside. He mounted his ox and rode out of the camp to find Chen Tong flourishing his weapon in a great display of prowess.

Chen Tong pointed at Huang Feihu with this halberd. "How do you do, General Huang! You used to enjoy a high position, but why do you flee through the passes today? On Grand Tutor Wen's orders, I've been waiting for you here for a long time. Get down from your beast at once, and I'll take you back to the capital. There's no other choice for you."

"You're wrong, General Chen," Huang Feihu replied. "Ups and downs are common in this world. You were once under my command, and I treated you like my own brother. When you were court-martialed I exempted you from capital punishment at the request of other generals. By insulting me today, could you be trying to get revenge on me? Ride forward then. I'll dismount and surrender at once if you can beat me in three rounds of combat."

Huang Feihu raised his lance and charged straight at Chen Tong, who flourished his halberd to meet the challenge. They fought desperately back and forth for more than twenty rounds. Chen Tong was far from being a match for Huang Feihu. He pulled his horse out of the fight and began to flee.

Huang Feihu yelled angrily, "Get hold of that scoundrel; we can't give him up!"

He set off in hot pursuit, but when he was almost on his opponent, Chen stealthily took the halberd in his left hand and threw out his small, light Fire Dragon Javelin. This was a magic javelin from an immortal, which never missed its mark. Huang Feihu was struck beneath the armpit and toppled from his mount with a sharp cry.

Seeing him fall, Huang Ming and Zhou Ji rushed out. "Don't you dare to hurt our commander," they shouted and engaged Chen Tong.

As the battle raged, Huang Feibiao brought his brother back from the battlefield only to find that he was already dead.

Huang Ming and Zhou Ji fought Chen Tong with such ferocity that he was forced to flee again. To avenge their commander, Huang Ming and Zhou Ji galloped after him, determined to chop him to mincemeat.

Hurling the javelin a second time, Chen Tong brought Zhou Ji down from his horse, but when he circled back to decapitate him, Huang Ming intercepted him. As he had won twice, Chen Tong was unwilling to continue the fight with Huang Ming. He left the battlefield and returned to the pass.

When Huang Feibiao returned with their father's corpse, Huang Feihu's three sons burst into tears. Huang Ming brought Zhou Ji's corpse back to the camp as well and laid it on the grass. There was not a single man in the camp who was not filled with grief. Having lost two generals, they knew neither where to go nor what to do next.

Meanwhile, Virtue of the Pure Void was meditating on his Green Cloud Bed when he felt his heart jump in alarm. He made a divination on his fingers and found out that Huang Feihu had suffered a great calamity.

"Tell your fellow disciple to come at once," he ordered White Cloud Lad.

Before long, White Cloud Lad brought in a youth, who was nine feet tall, and had smooth creamy skin, two bright eyes and a powerful body. His hair was coiled and he wore a robe tied with a hemp belt and a pair of straw sandals. The youth bowed before the immortal. "You wish to see me, Master?" he asked the immortal.

"Your father's in trouble. Go and rescue him."

"Who's my father, Master?"

"Your father's Huang Feihu, a prince of the Shang Dynasty. He's been killed by a Fire Dragon Javelin at Tongguan Pass. First revive him and then introduce yourself. In the future you'll serve together in the founding of the Zhou Dynasty."

"How did I come here?" the youth asked further.

"Thirteen years ago I was riding on a cloud to Mount Kunlun when my path was blocked by a strong beam of light emanating from your skull. I looked down to find you an uncommon child, destined to have a brilliant future. I brought you here as my disciple. Your name's Huang Tianhua. I'm obliged to save your father from this disaster."

The immortal gave Huang Tianhua a sword and a flower

basket and taught him how to deal with Chen Tong's magic javelins. He cautioned the youth, "You must return as soon as your father gets out of Tongguan Pass. You're not to accompany him to West Qi. You'll meet him again in the future."

Huang Tianhua knelt down and kowtowed to his master, and then left the Purple Sun Cave. He picked up a handful of dust, threw it in the air and traveled swiftly on it to Tongguan Pass.

If you want to know what happened to Huang Feihu next, you must read the next chapter.

HUANG TIANHUA MEETS HIS FATHER

Huang Tianhua arrived Tongguan before dawn. He landed near a crowd of men and horses clustered around a dim lamp hanging on a pole. He could hear bitter weeping. As Huang Tianhua moved nearer to them, someone challenged him through the darkness. "Who are you? A spy?"

"No, I'm a Taoist from the Purple Sun Cave on Mount Green Peak. Your commander's in trouble, and I've come to help him. Go quickly and announce my arrival," Huang Tianhua answered.

At the report, Huang Feibiao hastily went to the camp gate, where he saw a neatly dressed young Taoist, holding an unusual flower basket and carrying a sword on his back. The youth bore a striking resemblance to Huang Feihu.

After the youth had met all the generals and exchanged greetings, Huang Feibiao said, "We greatly appreciate your honorable presence. If you revive my brother, you'll be like a parent giving him new life."

"Where's His Highness?" Huang Tianhua asked.

He was led to the back of the camp and saw his father lying on a carpet, pale and motionless, his eyes tightly closed.

"Oh, Father!" he silently sighed. "Where's your glory now? Where's your power now? You held the highest rank among the ministers, but why are you in such desperate straits now?" He then saw another dead man, and asked, "Who's that?"

"He was our sworn brother. He was also killed by Chen Tong's javelin," Huang Feibiao answered.

Huang Tianhua asked for some water from a stream.

When the water was brought to him, he took elixir pills from his flower basket and dissolved them in it. He forced open Huang Feihu's lips with his sword and poured the liquid down his throat. The elixir ran into all his internal organs and limbs and reached every pore.

An hour or two later, Huang Feihu gave a loud cry of pain and opened his eyes. "Is this the afterlife? How did this young immortal get here?" he wondered, when he saw Huang Tianhua.

"If not for him, you couldn't have been brought back to life," Huang Feibiao told him.

Huang Feihu immediately got up and thanked Tianhua, saying, "I'm most fortunate that you should take pity on me and restore me to life."

Huang Tianhua wept and knelt down on the ground. "Father, I'm none other than Huang Tianhua!"

Everyone was greatly astonished. Huang Feihu cried happily, "So it's you, my son Huang Tianhua! You've been missing for thirteen years!" He then asked, "Where are you studying the Way, my son?"

"At the Purple Sun Cave on Mount Green Peak. My master's Virtue of the Pure Void. When he realized that I was destined to study the Way, he took me to that high mountain. Yes, it's already been thirteen years. Time's passed swiftly," Huang Tianhua answered, still weeping.

He then moved forward to meet his two uncles and three brothers, and when the greetings finished he brought Zhou Ji back to life. He saw everyone except his mother, Lady Jia. He had a fiery temper, and he turned red with anger. "Father! How can you be so hard-hearted?"

"My son! Why do you say such a thing when we've just met?"

"You brought your brothers, sons and generals from Zhaoge, but why didn't you bring my mother? She's a woman, and if she's captured by the tyrant and exposed in the streets and markets, all your dignity as prince will be gone!"

Huang Feihu wept and told him of the tragic fate of his mother and aunt. Huang Tianhua uttered a cry of grief and fell to the ground in a faint. When he came to, he wept bitterly. "Father, I won't return to Mount Green Peak. I'll fight my way to Zhaoge and take revenge on the tyrant for my mother's death!" he decided, grinding his teeth and sobbing.

"Chen Tong is challenging us," a messenger came to report.

Huang Feihu turned pale. Seeing that his father was flustered, Tianhua stopped weeping. "Father! Go out and meet the challenge. You needn't worry. I'll protect you."

Huang Feihu put on his armor, mounted his magic ox, and rode from the camp. "Chen Tong, I'm coming to take revenge."

When he saw Huang Feihu as strong and healthy as before, Chen Tong was puzzled, but he dared not question him. He shouted, "Come on! You rebel!"

"You wretch! Though you hit me with your javelin, Heaven wouldn't let you end my life," Huang Feihu swore.

Huang Feihu raised his lance and charged in to attack. Chen Tong returned the blow with his halberd. After fifteen rounds, Chen Tong once more pulled his horse around and ran away. Huang Feihu dared not pursue him.

"Father! Chase the wretch. I'm right here, and you've nothing to fear," Tianhua urged him on.

Seeing Huang Feihu close behind, Chen Tong threw a javelin at him. But Huang Tianhua secretly pointed his flower basket towards the javelin, and it flew harmlessly inside. Before long, all of Chen Tong's javelins had been caught inside the flower basket. Chen Tong was enraged. He turned his horse and thundered back to reengage Huang Feihu. Huang Tianhua immediately galloped forward to join the fight.

"You wretch, Chen Tong! I'm coming to deal with you," he shouted.

Finding a Taoist coming to Huang Feihu's aid, Chen Tong shouted, "Ah! So it's you that took my javelins! I won't let you get away with it."

Brandishing his halberd, he charged straight at Tianhua. Huang Tianhua hastily drew his sword and pointed it at Chen Tong. A beam of brilliant light as wide as a cup flew out from the tip, and as it struck Chen Tong in the face, his head rolled off and fell to the ground.

Huang Tianhua's sword was the magic Moye Sword, which Virtue of the Pure Void used to protect Mount Green Peak. Anyone hit by the sword's magic light would be instantly decapitated.

With Chen Tong out of the way, Huang Feihu and his men charged on the pass. They smashed the locks, broke open the gates and soon left the pass behind. Huang Tianhua then bade farewell to his father, uncles and brothers. "Be careful as you go, and look after yourselves," he told them.

"My son, why don't you come with us?" Huang Feihu asked.

"I dare not disobey my master's orders. I must return to Mount Green Peak without delay," Tianhua answered sadly.

Huang Feihu was unwilling to see his son leave. "Our meeting's late, but our separation comes too soon. What a pity it is! When shall we see each other again?"

"We'll meet again in West Qi in the near future. Don't worry, Father."

They parted in tears.

About eighty *li* from Tongguan, Huang Feihu came to Chuanyun Pass. The commander was Chen Wu, Chen Tong's brother. When Chen Wu learned of the fall of Tongguan Pass and the death of his brother, he was furious. He summoned all his generals and advisors to discuss how to beat the enemy and take revenge for his brother.

General He Shen warned him, "We must be careful, Commander. Huang Feihu is brave and skillful. We should learn a lesson from your brother and take them by cunning, not by force. If we meet them in open battle, we're uncertain of victory and may even run into unforeseen disaster."

"You're right, but tell me what we should do," Chen Wu asked.

"We must .... That way we can get the whole Huang family without using even a single arrow!"

Chen Wu was delighted with the idea. When Huang Feihu arrived, he went out immediately to meet the party, beating drums and gongs. Huang Feihu saw that he wore no armor and carried no arms.

"Welcome, Your Highness," Chen Wu and his men shouted.

Huang Feihu saluted from the back of his ox. "I'm a mere refugee and have committed a crime against the royal government. I deeply appreciate your great kindness, but I'm sorry to say that your brother lost his life as he blocked my path yesterday. If you would let us through, we'll never forget the great favor," he said.

Chen Wu answered courteously from his horse, "I know well that you've been loyal to the king for many generations. It's King Zhou who's mistreated you, and you're totally innocent. My brother was ignorant of the situation and failed to distinguish between justice and injustice. He deserved his death. Won't you have a short rest, Your Highness, and join us at a feast. I would be most honored if you accept."

Huang Feihu sighed deeply. "The same mother may give birth to two entirely different sons, just as the same tree may produce fruit sweet and sour. How superior Chen Wu is to his brother Chen Tong!" he told himself.

Both parties dismounted. Chen Wu invited Huang and his men to the main hall. When all were seated, Chen Wu ordered his men to bring in the meal.

When they had finished eating, Huang Feihu got up. "If you take pity on us, General, I would trouble you to open the pass gate for us. We'll assuredly return your great kindness in the near future."

Chen Wu smiled. "I know that you must be going to West Qi to offer your service to a new illustrious master. I've already prepared wine as a token of my respect. Do have a few drinks, Your Highness. Please trust my sincerity."

"We're all warriors, rough and uncultured," Huang Feihu replied. "And you must take pity on us, as we've been wronged and are fighting for our lives. Please forgive us should we have done anything to displease you. As you've prepared wine, how could we dare to refuse!"

As they ate and drank, time flew by, and the sun set be-

fore they knew it. Huang Feihu stood up to bid Chen Wu farewell, saying, "Your kindness is as high as Mount Taishan. If I
ever have the slightest chance to repay your favor, I'll certainly
not forget to do it."

"Rest assured, Your Highness. I know you must be exhausted after such a tiring journey. It's already dark. Won't
you all take a good rest here tonight? You can start off early
tomorrow morning. What could be wrong with that?" Chen
Wu suggested.

"Though it's not a bad idea, this is not a good place to
spend the night," Huang Feihu hesitated.

"Since General Chen's so sincere, there's no harm if we
leave here tomorrow," Huang Ming put in.

Huang unwillingly agreed.

With great satisfaction, Chen Wu added, "I'll trouble you
no longer. You haven't slept well for many days and must be
tired. I'll retire now so that you can get sufficient rest before
traveling on tomorrow."

After Chen Wu left the place, Huang Feihu told his men
to move the luggage carts into the corridors. After their difficult journey, everyone slept soundly, but Huang Feihu was restless. He could neither sit nor lie down at ease. His thoughts
raced at random. "Oh Heaven! The Huang family has served
this dynasty loyally for seven generations. How could we
expect that today we would end up as rebels! Only Heaven
knows that my heart's loyal. I hate that tyrant for insulting
my wife and murdering my sister. If King Wu lends me troops,
I'll certainly launch an attack on that wicked tyrant!"

He sat thinking late into the night but still felt no desire
to sleep. The first watch sounded and then the second.
"Where's my grand mansion now? Where's my finely fur-
nished hall and my lofty towers? Where are my power and riches now?" he thought. Hearing the third watch strike, he wondered, "Why can't I sleep tonight?" He was puzzling over his
fate when he heard a strong wind whirl up the steps and
straight into the hall. Huang Feihu was so startled that he
broke out in a cold sweat. From the center of the whirlwind
an arm suddenly appeared and snuffed out his candle.

He heard a voice calling him. "My lord! Don't be afraid!
I'm not a spectre, but your wife Lady Jia. I've followed you
here. You're in danger now! A great fire will be lit to burn all
of you to death. Tell everyone to get up. Take care of my
three motherless children, my lord. Get up quickly. I'm going
now."

As the candle light gleamed bright again, Huang Feihu
came to his senses with a start. He pounded a desk and
shouted, "Get up everyone! Get up!"

Huang Ming, Zhou Ji and the others woke up instantly
and jumped to their feet. "What's the matter, Brother?"

After Huang Feihu had told them of Lady Jia's warning,
Huang Feibiao said, "We should believe her."

Huang Ming walked over to the door and found it locked
from the outside. He cried out, "Something's wrong here."

Long Huan and Wu Qian broke open the door with axes
and found heaps of firewood piled high before it. Long Huan
and Zhou Ji immediately ordered that the luggage carts be
pushed out of the building. Everyone mounted their horses and
quickly left the place. They had not gone far when they saw
Chen Wu and his generals carrying torches towards their residence, but it was Heaven's will that he arrived too late.

Chen Wu was furious when he learned that Huang Feihu
and his men had already left their quarters with their luggage
carts. He shouted, "We're late. Hurry, hurry! Catch them!"

"Chen Wu!" Huang Feihu addressed him sternly when
the soldiers were almost upon them, "The kindness you offered
us yesterday was insincere. Why did you act that way when
there's no enmity between us?"

Now that his plot was known, Chen Wu swore, "You rebel. I truly hoped to kill you and your whole family, but you
were cunning enough to escape my trap. Even so, you won't
find it easy to get out of this alive."

He spurred his horse forward, brandishing his lance charged at Huang Ming. Huang Ming struck at him with his axe.
In the pitch darkness, they fought up and down with desperate
ferocity. Huang Feihu spurred his ox forward to join the combat, and Chen Wu came to meet him. After only a few rounds,

Huang Feihu stabbed him through the heart, toppling him from his horse.

The battle raged desperately until many of the garrison troops were slain. Huang Feihu won a complete victory. Smashing down the gates, they fought their way out of Chuanyun Pass just as dawn was breaking.

On the way to Jiepai Pass, Huang Ming commented, "We won't have to fight at Jiepai. The commander's old Huang Gun, Huang Feihu's father."

The party hurried eighty *li* before they came to Jiepai Pass.

General Huang Gun had been greatly annoyed by the report that his eldest son, Huang Feihu, had rebelled against the king, fought his way out of Zhaoge, and slaughtered generals and soldiers on his way west. As soon as he received the report that Huang Feihu was approaching, he took 3,000 soldiers out to wait for his arrival. He had ten prison carts prepared, ready to arrest his sons and grandsons and bring them back to Zhaoge.

If you want to learn what happened next to Huang Feihu, you must read the next chapter.

第三十二回　黄飛虎泗水大戰

THE BATTLE AT SISHUI PASS

As Huang Gun arrayed his troops in front of the pass, Huang Ming said to Long Huan, "Things don't look optimistic here. Look at the combat formation, and the prison carts!"

"Let's first see Huang Gun and hear what he has to say," Long Huan answered.

The Huangs trotted forward and Huang Feihu bowed on the back of his ox. "Father, your unfilial son begs your pardon for being unable to kowtow before you."

"Who're you?" Huang Gun demanded.

"I'm your eldest son, Huang Feihu. Why do you ask me such a question?"

Huang Gun roared at him, "My family's been honored by monarchs for seven generations, and all are loyal, filial and just. None are treacherous, deceitful or wicked. No one has ever broken the law and no woman ever remarried after the death of her husband. But what have you done now? Just for a woman's sake, you've forsaken the monarch, abandoned your posts, and rebelled! You've committed a capital crime by slaying, plundering, and storming the passes. You've humiliated your ancestors in the afterworld and your father in this one. You damned beast! You've held a high rank in vain! You only implicate me in this disaster, I wonder that you should dare to face me."

Huang Feihu was completely dumbstruck.

"Beast! Are you going to be a loyal subject and a filial son or not?" Huang Gun demanded.

"What do you mean, Father?" Huang Feihu asked.

"If you want to be a loyal subject and filial son, just dismount. I'll take you to Zhaoge. That way I'll have performed a service of great merit and have the chance to live. You'll die a minister of this dynasty. That would make you both filial and loyal. Otherwise, your rebellion's already shown your disloyalty, and you have only to stab me to prove your unfiliality. I guess then you'll go to West Qi. When I die, you can do as you like, and I'll see and hear nothing. I hope that you won't leave me alive to be shackled and executed in public for your crimes. People would point at me and say 'He's beheaded because his son rebelled.' I'm willing to die under your sword, and I'm sure you must be willing to kill me," Huang Gun said emotionally.

"Don't say anymore, Father. You may take me to Zhaoge now," Huang Feihu cried out and was about to get down from his ox.

"Brother, don't!" Huang Ming stopped him. "King Zhou's a tyrant. Since he's immoral, why should we be loyal? We've braved innumerable hardships to get this far, struggling with death on each occasion. Why commit suicide for the single reason given by the old general? How pitiful it is to die without clearing our names of that great injustice!"

Thinking that what Huang Ming said was right, Huang Feihu sat on his ox, lowered his head and kept silent.

"Huang Ming, you bastard! I'm sure my son had no intention of rebelling against the government. It's unfilial and disloyal wretches like you that incited him to it. How dare you stop him from surrendering to me!" Huang Gun cried.

He spurred his horse forward and slashed at Huang Ming with his cutlass. Huang Ming parried the blow with his axe. "General, listen to me! Huang Feihu's your son and Huang Tianlu your grandson, but I'm neither. You can't expect to get us into your prison carts?" he began. "General, you're wrong. Even a fierce tiger wouldn't devour its own son! How can you be so cruel as to send your own children to death? Your daughter-in-law was insulted by the tyrant and committed suicide and your own daughter was murdered. Why don't you avenge their deaths? As the proverb goes, 'If a ruler isn't virtuous, his subjects may seek a new master; if a father's unkind, his son may oppose him'."

With great wrath, Huang Gun shouted, "Scoundrel! Your sophistry infuriates me!"

He slashed at Huang Ming again. Huang Ming once more parried the blow. "Old chap! Why not enjoy the sunny days but foolishly awaiting the rainy weather? As a general, you're totally blind to the current situation. You forget that there are no eyes in my axes and one slip would mean the end of your life of fame! How could I dare to do such a thing!"

Even more infuriated, Huang Gun rushed forward to attack him again.

Zhou Ji shouted, "General! I'm afraid I'll have to offend you now. I can't control my temper any longer!"

Instantly, Huang Ming, Zhou Ji, Long Huan and Wu Qian surrounded Huang Gun, halberd clashing on axe as the horses sprang in and out of combat. Watching them do battle with his old father, Huang Feihu felt his anger rise. "How dare they insult my father before my very eyes!"

But Huang Ming shouted, "Brother, we've got the old general tied down here. Why don't you get out of the pass as fast as you can? Are you waiting for an invitation?"

Huang Feihu, Huang Feibiao, Huang Feibao, Huang Tianlu, Huang Tianjue and Huang Tianxiang rushed swiftly out of the pass. When he saw that his sons and grandsons had escaped, Huang Gun toppled from his horse and tried to commit suicide. Huang Ming instantly leapt down and seized his arms.

"Sir! You needn't do that!" he told Huang Gun.

Huang Gun only stared at him. "You stupid bandit. You let them get away. Now you're trying new tricks on me."

"It's hard to explain things briefly," said Huang Ming. "It's really a case of having nowhere to air my grievances. I've been repeatedly insulted by your son. He was determined to rebel and tried more than once to put us to death when we advised him against it. The four of us consulted together and decided to come with him to Jiepai Pass where we could help you take him back to Zhaoge. When we met, I tried to signal to you with my eyes, but you were so engrossed in idle talk

that you didn't notice. I couldn't say anything lest our plan be
uncovered."

"Then what do you suggest?" Huang Gun asked.

"General! You must go quickly and catch up with Huang
Feihu. Tell him 'Huang Ming's right. Even a cruel tiger
wouldn't devour its son. You may all come back. I'll come
with you to West Qi.' What do you say?"

Huang Gun smiled. "You beast! You talk so sweetly, but
how do I know that you're not deceiving me?"

"Of course we won't really go. We'll simply lure him
back, and you'll entertain them. We'll get a hold of them as
soon as you give us the signal by ringing a bell. Then you may
put your three sons and three grandsons in the prison carts and
escort them back to Zhaoge to be punished. As for the four of
us, we hope only that you would kindly forgive us and keep us
in our current ranks."

Huang Gun sighed deeply. "General Huang, you're a
good man after all!"

He mounted his horse and chased after Huang Feihu.
"My sons," he called, "Huang Ming's right. After consider-
ing it, I've decided to come with you all to West Qi."

"Why's father suddenly changed his mind?" Huang
Feihu wondered.

"It must be a trick thought up by Huang Ming. We'd better return at once and go along with his plan," Huang Feibiao
said perceptively.

Returning to the pass, Huang Feihu kowtowed before his
father. Huang Gun said, "You must be weary after your journey. Let's have some food and wine first, and then we'll start
off to West Qi together."

When five cups of wine had been downed, Huang Gun
struck his gold bell several times, but Huang Ming paid no attention to it. Long Huan secretly asked Huang Ming, "What
shall we do now?"

"You two pack all his private belongings on the luggage
carts and set fire to the barns and warehouses. Then we'll all
mount and leave. I'll answer any questions the old general
asks."

When Huang Ming did not respond to his signal, Huang Gun called him over. "Why didn't you make a move when I rang the bell?"

"The men aren't ready yet. It would be dreadful if we acted prematurely and they got away," Huang Ming answered dishonestly.

Meanwhile, Long Huan and Wu Qian packed all the old general's private belongings onto the carts and set the barns and warehouses on fire. When Huang Gun learned of the news, and then saw Huang Feihu's men getting out of the pass, he groaned. "I've been taken in!"

"General!" urged Huang Ming, "Let me tell you the truth. King Zhou's a wicked tyrant, and King Wu's a sagely ruler. We're going to ask him for an army to revenge the wrongs we've suffered. We welcome you to join us. If you don't, you'll certainly meet your death in Zhaoge, as your barns have been burnt and taxes lost. You'd better come with us to see King Wu. It's the best path for you to take."

Huang Gun pondered for a while, and then sighed, "I cannot oppose public opinion. My family's been loyal for seven generations, but we are rebels now!"

He knelt down, kowtowed towards Zhaoge eight times, and hung the seal of his office in his Silver Security Court. Then he extinguished the fire, and took 3,000 soldiers and 1,000 guards out of Jiepai Pass.

"Huang Ming! As far as I can see, you offer no help to my son. On the contrary, you're bringing the whole Huang family to its death. About eighty *li* from here is Sishui Pass under the command of Han Rong. Beneath him there's Yu Hua, a sorcerer. He's nicknamed the 'seven-headed general.' He rides on a fiery golden-eyed monster and has never lost a battle. If I had taken you all as prisoners to Zhaoge, I could have saved my own life at least, but now we'll all share the same fate. This must be the will of Heaven, and I must accept my destiny," Huang Gun told Huang Ming as they rode along. He felt even more grieved when he saw that his seven year old grandson was weeping. "What crime have you committed against Heaven that you should suffer the same cruel fate as ours!"

He sighed and groaned all the way to Sishui Pass where the party came to a halt.

When Han Rong learned that Huang Gun and Huang Feihu had arrived at Sishui Pass, he fell silent. "General Huang! What a great pity! As marshal, you're of the top rank. How could you be so dull as to go along with your son?" He ordered that the drums be beaten to summon his generals. When they all arrived, he announced, "Huang Gun's joined his son. They're already here so we must decide what to do."

They decided to block the pass and prepare for combat. Meanwhile Huang Gun sat in his tent looking at his sons and grandsons. He nodded his head. "You all stand here now, but which one of you will be missing tomorrow?"

The following day, General Yu Hua came out and challenged the Huangs.

"Who would like to answer the first challenge?" Huang Gun asked.

"I'll go first," Huang Feihu answered.

He mounted his divine ox, took his lance, and rushed onto the battlefield. Yu Hua had a golden face, red hair, a red beard, and two sparkling eyes. But Yu Hua had never met Huang Feihu. He saw a general with a long five-tufted beard, phoenix eyes and silkworm eyebrows.

"Who's that coming?" he shouted.

"I'm Prince Huang Feihu. As King Zhou is a wicked tyrant, I've abandoned him and will take shelter in West Qi, and who are you, General?"

"I'm Yu Hua. I'm sorry that I've never had the opportunity to meet Your Highness before. You were of the top rank. Why did you rebel?"

"It's difficult to tell the whole story in just a few words. According to the code, a ruler should respect his subjects, while his subjects should be loyal. But now everyone knows that King Zhou is a cruel tyrant and feels ashamed to be his subject. All know of the virtue of West Qi, and two-thirds of the Shang kingdom is already under Zhou influence. Man can do nothing to change the will of Heaven. I hope that you'll be kind enough to let us through. We would appreciate the favor forever."

Yu Hua sighed. "Your Highness, you're not right. I'm obliged to fulfil my duty and guard this pass. Were you not a rebel, I would certainly welcome you warmly. But you're a rebel now, and that makes us enemies, so I can't possibly let you through. I advise you to dismount, and I'll take you back to Zhaoge. The ministers are bound to plead on your behalf, and King Zhou may consider your past service and pardon you. It's absolutely impossible for you to get out of this pass."

"I've gotten through four of the five passes already. What can you do to stop me at this last one? Come forward and let's see who'll win the day."

He raised his lance and charged in to attack. Yu Hua met him with his halberd. Huang fought with such speed and skill that his lance seemed to be a silver python coiling itself around Yu Hua and rendering him helpless. Utterly exhausted, Yu Hua feinted with his halberd and fled.

Huang Feihu gave chase, but as he closed in, Yu Hua opened his robe and drew out the Soul Killing Pennant, a magic weapon from the immortal Primal Ether of Penglai Island. As soon as he raised the pennant in the air, it emitted a black cloud that engulfed Huang Feihu and threw him to the ground. Huang Feihu was taken prisoner and pushed before Han Rong.

"What did the government do that made you rebel?"

Refusing to kneel, Huang Feihu answered with a cold laugh, "A powerful position here, eh? But in fact you just use the awe inspired by the throne to suppress this area. How could you understand why state affairs are in complete disorder, and the ministers in revolt? Now that you've got me, I'll merely be executed and that'll be the end of it. What's the point of lengthy explanations?"

"As commander here, I'm merely doing my duty by arresting you rebels. I don't want to argue with you either. I'll put you in gaol and take you to Zhaoge when I've captured the rest of your gang," Han Rong said.

Hearing that Huang Feihu had been taken, Huang Gun

said, "Beast! You didn't listen to my advice. What a pity that the merit for capturing you has now fallen into Han Rong's hands!"

The night passed. The next morning Yu Hua galloped out and challenged again.

"Who'll go?" Huang Gun asked.

"I'll go," Huang Ming and Zhou Ji answered together.

They got on their horses, took their battle-axes, and left the camp. "Yu Hua, we'll get revenge for our brother," they shouted.

They raced forward, whirling their axes. Yu Hua defended himself with his halberd. After about thirty rounds Yu Hua pulled his horse around and fled. When Huang Ming and Zhou Ji pursued him, he lifted his Soul Killing Pennant again and took them both. They were put in gaol with Huang Feihu.

Huang Gun lowered his head in silence when he heard of their capture. He then asked again, "Who will go out to meet Yu Hua this time?"

Huang Feibiao and Huang Feibao answered, "We would like to meet him."

They took their lances and galloped out. As before, Yu Hua took flight after twenty rounds and captured both Huang Feibiao and Huang Feibao with his pennant.

When he learned of their capture, Huang Gun was very upset. The following day, Yu Hua challenged again and Long Huan and Wu Qian volunteered, "We're not intimidated by his sorcery. We'll go and meet him."

They galloped onto the battlefield. "You damned wretch! How dare you use your dirty sorcery. We'll knock your block off."

However, after thirty rounds, Long Huan and Wu Qian were also taken, brought before Han Rong, and sent to prison. In four encounters, Yu Hua had taken seven generals. Han Rong held a banquet to honor him.

Meanwhile, Huang Gun sat alone, feeling very discouraged. He looked sadly at his three grandsons standing beside him and shook his head. "My children, you're so young. Why should you have to suffer the same fate as we do?"

Just then a guard reported that Yu Hua had challenged once again. Huang Tianlu, Huang Gun's second grandson, bowed and said, "Your grandson wishes to answer the challenge to avenge my father and uncles."

"You must be very careful," Huang Gun warned him.

Huang Tianlu fought bravely. Though he was young, he was born into a warrior's family and had been well-trained since childhood. His lance darted in and out like lightning and before long he scored a hit, stabbing Yu Hua through the left thigh. Nursing his wound, Yu Hua took flight, and Huang Tianlu plunged after him. Though defeated, Yu Hua still had his magic, and in a wink of the eye, Tianlu was captured and thrown into prison with his father.

Huang Feihu was already distressed to see so many of his men captured and brought to prison. When he saw his son, he could not restrain his tears.

Huang Gun felt utterly desolate when he heard that Huang Tianlu had also been lost, but he could think of no way to deal with the matter. How could they get out of the net that entrapped them? He was too old, and his grandsons were too young.

He pounded his desk heavily. "We're finished, finished!" he cried, and ordered his men, "Present all the jewels, gold and silver on the carts to Han Rong, and he'll allow you to get out of the pass. As for me and my grandsons, we won't live much longer."

His 3,000 soldiers fell on their knees and comforted him, "Don't be so upset. 'Heaven helps good men out of trouble.' You mustn't despair."

"Yu Hua's a sorcerer, skilled in all sorts of magic arts. How can I ever beat him? If I were captured as well, my reputation would be ruined." He wept when he saw his grandsons standing before him with tears in their eyes. "Children, I don't know whether you will be lucky or not. I'll beg Han Rong to show mercy on you and set you free."

He took off his helmet, jade belt and robes, and put on mourning. Then he took his grandsons directly to Han Rong's headquarters. As he had made up his mind to surrender, none of his men dared to say a word.

At Han Rong's headquarters, Huang Gun said to the gatemen, "Would you please report to your commander that Huang Gun requests to see him?"

Han Rong smiled at the report. "It's already too late. There's no use in you coming to see me now."

He ordered his soldiers to stand on guard to the left and right, and with his generals on either side of him, strode out to the gate. He saw Huang Gun dressed in mourning kneeling at the gate with Huang Tianjue and Huang Tianxiang.

What became of them? If you want to know, read the next chapter.

34

HUANG FEIHU
MEETS THE PRIME MINISTER

Huang Gun crawled towards Han Rong on his knees, saying humbly, "The criminal Huang Gun is here to see Your Excellency."

Han Rong hurriedly returned his salutation. "Venerable General! This matter's so important that I cannot make any decision on my own authority. But what do you wish to see me about?"

"For the crimes committed, the Huang family should all be dealt with according to the law. Nevertheless, I beg you to show mercy on just one of us. We would appreciate it even after my sons and I had gone to the netherworld," Huang Guan pleaded pitifully.

"Tell me what you have in mind, sir," Han Rong answered politely.

"I've no complaints about dying for my son's crimes. Nevertheless, the Huang family has served the kingdom for seven generations. What a pity it is that all my descendants will be ruthlessly massacred. Here on my knees, I beg you to take pity on my seven year old grandson. Let him out of this pass so that the Huang family may not be extinguished. Would you kindly consider it, General?"

"You're mistaken, General. As commander here, I'm obliged to carry out my duty and cannot act out of personal consideration. Every member of your family enjoyed wealth and noble status. You've received great favor, but you've never appreciated it. I must take you all, including your children, to Zhaoge for trial. The court will distinguish the innocent from the guilty. No one should be dissatisfied as it'll all be done through the lawful channels. Should I comply with your wishes, I would be colluding with you to deceive the king. I would be taking the burden of your crimes onto my own shoulders. I can't do it."

"Commander!" Huang Gun pleaded. "Though the Huangs have broken the law, there're still many good people in the Huang family. What harm could there be in sparing a small child? As the saying goes, 'every person has a sense of compassion.' You shouldn't be so stubborn as to refuse us such a small favor. The ancient proverb says, 'to withhold help when one has the power to give it is like returning from a treasure mountain empty-handed.' No one can be certain that nothing will happen to him in his life. Besides, the Huang family has done the king great service, and it's not been our wish to rebel. We were wronged and forced into it. I beg you to show compassion. We'll never forget your kindness."

"General! I couldn't set him free unless I were to rebel and follow you to West Qi. But that's out of the question," Han Rong refused bluntly.

With great wrath, Huang Gun said to his two grandsons, "I'm a marshal. How can I degrade myself so pitifully before him. Since the general refuses to be merciful, let's throw ourselves fearlessly into his gaol."

He took the two boys to the gaol and was locked inside. When he saw his father and sons arrive together, Huang Feihu burst into loud sobs. "I never thought that everything you said would come true. I'm the most unfilial son that has ever lived!"

"As things have already reached this stage, feeling sorry isn't of any use. I begged you to let me live, but you didn't take me seriously. Why grumble now?" Huang Gun said coolly.

It was such a great feat to have captured Huang Feihu's entire family as well as his gold, silver and jewels, so his generals held a banquet to offer Han Rong their congratulations. As they drank, they discussed who should escort the prisoners to Zhaoge.

"Only if I go personally can we be assured of security," Yu Hua said proudly.

"I won't feel at ease unless you accompany them," Han Rong replied with satisfaction.

The following day, Yu Hua took 3,000 soldiers and set off for Zhaoge with the eleven prisoners. After traveling eighty *li*, the group reached Jiepai Pass. Huang Gun saw that his headquarters and mansion were in the same condition as before. But he was now a convict in a prison cart. He felt so distressed that he couldn't restrain his tears.

In the Golden Light Cave on Qianyuan Mountain, Fairy Primordial was meditating on his bed when he felt his heart pounding abnormally. As a celestial, his heart could only be stirred by events of great significance. He made a divination on his fingers and found that Huang Feihu and his family were in grave danger.

He ordered Golden Haze Lad, "Bring your fellow disciple here at once."

Golden Haze Lad found Nezha practising the lance in the peach garden and called out to him, "Master wants you to see him at once, Brother."

Nezha put down his lance, went to his master, and bowed. "Master, what orders do you have for your disciple?"

"Huang Feihu and his father are in great trouble. Go down the mountain and rescue them. Just help them get out of Sishui Pass and then return without delay. In the future you'll all be ministers in the same court."

Nezha was an active youth and was delighted to be given the mission. Grasping his Fire-Tip Lance, he sped on his Wind-Fire Wheels towards Chuanyun Pass. He alighted on a mountain near the pass. He waited a long time before he saw an army marching smartly towards him with flags and pennants fluttering gaily and swords and halberds gleaming in the sun.

"How can I go at them without a reason?" Nezha thought. "I must pick a quarrel with them first."

He took up his position on a narrow stretch of the road and began to sing:

So long have I lived that my age I've forgot,

> *I answer to my master, but Heaven I fear not.*
> *Even when monarchs pass this way,*
> *A fat gold ingot they must pay.*

A patrolman reported to Yu Hua, "General, there's a funny fellow standing on two wheels, singing in the middle of the road."

Yu Hua ordered his men to halt and rode out on his fiery golden-eyed monster to find Nezha blocking the way on a pair of Wind-Fire Wheels.

"Who're you?" he asked.

"I've lived here for many years. Anyone who passes, whether an official or even an emperor, has to pay me a road toll. Wherever you're going today, you'd better pay up fast, and I'll let you continue your journey without delay," Nezha declared.

Yu Hua burst into laughter. "I'm a general under Han Rong, commander of Sishui Pass. I'm taking the rebels Huang Feihu and his family to Zhaoge. How dare you stop me! Get out of the way if you want to live."

"So, you've achieved great merit, capturing a bunch of rebel generals. Okay then, just pay me ten gold ingots and I'll let you pass."

Yu Hua was furious. He spurred his mount forward and struck at Nezha with his halberd. Nezha returned the blow with his lance. How could Yu Hua stand up to Nezha, who had been trained by an immortal in martial arts unknown to mortal man? Exhausted, he made a faint at his opponent, then turned and fled. As Nezha pursued him, he waved the Soul Killing Pennant, but Nezha only laughed at the black vapor.

"So this is the Soul Killing Pennant! What's so extraordinary about it?" he cried mockingly. He beckoned to it and it flew into his hand. He then slipped it into his leopard skin bag. "How many do you have altogether? You'd better give them all to me now."

As he had lost his magic weapon, Yu Hua turned his mount to engage Nezha.

"My master sent me here to rescue Huang Feihu. If Yu

Hua discovers my plan, he may kill them. I can't delay any longer," Nezha thought. He parried Yu Hua's blows with his left hand and took out his gold brick with his right. He tossed it into the sky. "Quick! Quick!"

Shining brilliantly, the gold brick flew high into the air and then dropped down swiftly, striking Yu Hua on the head and knocking him flat across his saddle. Bleeding profusely, he galloped off dragging his halberd behind him.

Nezha followed in pursuit, but then thought better. "My master sent me here to rescue Huang Feihu. If I keep pursuing Yu Hua, I'll just be delaying my mission."

Turning back, he threw his gold brick into the air, sending Yu Hua's men fleeing. He then looked at the dirty, ragged men in the prison carts.

"Which of you is General Huang?" he asked.

"Who's the gentleman riding on the wheels?" Huang Feihu asked in return.

"I'm Nezha, surnamed Li, a disciple of Fairy Primordial. My master realized that you were in trouble and sent me from the mountain to rescue you all." The prince was delighted. Nezha broke open the prison carts and released them. As Huang Feihu prostrated himself in gratitude, Nezha said, "Take your time, General. I'll go first and hold Sishui Pass for you. I'll wait for you all there and help you get through."

Thanking Nezha again and again, they picked up their weapons and started off after Nezha to Sishui Pass.

Han Rong was drinking with his generals when Yu Hua's return was announced. "Something must be wrong," he said with alarm, and asked anxiously when Yu Hua entered the hall. "Why have you returned, General? You look pale. Are you wounded?"

Yu Hua related his encounter with Nezha.

"What about Huang Feihu and his family?"

"I don't know."

Han Rong stamped his foot. "All our hard work has been in vain. If His Majesty learns that I'm responsible for the rebel's escape, he'll never forgive me!"

"Huang Feihu's still in an impossible situation. He can't

get through this pass, and he can't retreat to Zhaoge either. We can just guard the pass and block his advance," a general suggested.

They were still discussing what to do when a scout came in. "A man riding a pair of wheels is here. He wants to challenge the 'Seven-headed General'."

"That's the man who beat me," Yu Hua cried.

Han Rong angrily ordered his men to mount, ready for battle. "I'll personally capture this wretch," he pledged.

When he took his generals out of the pass, he saw Nezha on his wheels, still demanding, "Come out, Yu Hua, I'll finish you off!"

"Who are you?" demanded Han Rong, galloping ahead of his generals.

Nezha looked at Han Rong in his gold helmet, gold armor and red battle robes and answered, "I'm none other than Li Nezha, disciple of Fairy Primordial. By order of my master, I came here to rescue Huang Feihu. Unfortunately, I failed to kill Yu Hua just now. I've come here to get hold of him."

"You released the convicts wanted by the imperial government and still have the gall to come here causing trouble," Han Rong cursed.

"The Shang Dynasty's destined to end soon, and a sagely ruler's already appeared in West Qi. Heaven has determined that the Huang family will be a pillar of the rising Zhou kingdom. Why are you so stupid as to act against the will of Heaven and bring disaster on yourselves?"

Han Rong furiously spurred his horse forward and stabbed at Nezha with his lance. Nezha returned the blow with his own. After several rounds, Han's generals joined in, and a fierce battle unfolded.

As disciple of an immortal, Nezha thrust like a pouncing silver dragon and parried like a streak of lightning. As he darted amongst them on his Wind-Fire Wheels, Han Rong's generals were felled from their horses one after another. Unable to withstand the onslaught, they all fled for their lives.

Regardless of the danger, Han Rong resisted with all his strength. As the battle reached a peak, Huang Ming, Zhou Ji,

Long Huan, Wu Qian, Huang Feibao and Huang Feibiao galloped up from behind. "Don't let Han Rong get away! We must take our revenge on him."

Yu Hua could not hesitate any longer. He mounted his monster and charged out of the pass to join the fray.

The arrival of Huang Feihu's generals gave Nezha the chance to take out his gold brick and toss it into the air. It dropped down and struck Han Rong directly in the heart, wounding him badly. He fled.

"Li Nezha, don't touch my commander!" Yu Hua cried.

He spurred his monster forward to intercept Nezha. After three or four rounds, Nezha blocked his halberd and took his Universal Ring from the leopard skin bag. With one blow, he broke Yu Hua's arm. Almost falling from his beast, Yu Hua took flight towards the northeast. Nezha took Sishui Pass, while Huang Ming and the other five generals cleaned up the enemy soldiers in the area.

Huang Feihu and Huang Gun arrived the following day. They ordered their men to load the gold, silver, and other valuables from Han Rong's mansion back onto the carts and when all was prepared, they left Sishui Pass. Nezha saw them as far as the Golden Chicken Range and then bade them farewell.

Huang Gun thanked him sincerely. "We deeply appreciate your kindness in rescuing us from death. It was quite beyond our expectations. We're sorry that you must go now. We don't know when we'll meet again and return your great grace!"

"Take care of yourselves, Generals," Nezha replied. "We'll see each other in West Qi in the future."

Nezha returned to Qianyuan Mountain without further delay.

Huang Feihu's party continued on its way, climbing high mountains and crossing deep rivers. They passed Mount Shouyang, Peach Blossom Peak and Mount Yan, and days later reached Mount Qi only seventy *li* from West Qi City. Huang Feihu ordered his men to halt.

"Father, I think I should go alone to West Qi and pay my respects to Prime Minister Jiang. If he accepts us, we can all enter the city. If not, we can discuss the matter further," he suggested.

"You're right, my son," Huang Gun agreed.

Huang Feihu, dressed in plain clothes, rode to West Qi City. He found that the people there were very honest. The pedestrians were polite and treated each other in accordance with the rites. The markets were full of produce, and every household was prosperous.

"It really is a land of sages," he thought to himself. "People are happy, and there are abundant supplies. It's just like in the days of Yao and Shun." He asked a passer-by, "Where's the mansion of Prime Minister Jiang located?"

"Near the end of the Lesser Gold Bridge, sir."

When he found the place, Huang Feihu said to the gateman, "Please report to the Prime Minister that Huang Feihu from Zhaoge is here to see him."

"Huang Feihu's a prince. What makes him come here to see me?" Jiang Ziya wondered.

Huang Feihu was ushered in. Jiang Ziya, dressed in his official robes, went out to meet him as an honored guest. When they had exchanged salutations, Jiang Ziya apologized, "Please forgive me for not riding out beyond the city gates to meet Your Highness."

"I'm a poor refugee now. I've forsaken the Shang and hope to take shelter in Zhou. I'm just a bird that has lost its nest and seeks a new branch to perch on. I would greatly appreciate it if you would kindly take me in," Huang Feihu said, kneeling before Jiang Ziya. And when the prime minister tried to help him up and to a seat, he said humbly, "I'm a rebel against the Shang Dynasty. How dare I sit beside you!"

"You're too modest, Your Highness. Though I am prime minister, I was an official under you. Please don't stand on ceremony."

Huang Feihu finally took a seat. Jiang Ziya then bowed and asked, "Why did you forsake the Shang Dynasty?"

Huang Feihu explained the situation in Zhaoge and the reason for his revolt, and then concluded, "I hope to take shelter here and offer you our faithful service. You could do us no greater favor than to accept us."

Jiang Ziya was overjoyed. "King Wu will be delighted to have you assist him. He's sure to accept you. Please rest at the state hostel while I go to see him," he assured Huang Feihu.

He rode to the palace and requested to see the king. When the greetings were finished, the king asked, "What do you wish to see me about, Prime Minister?"

"Your Highness! Congratulations! Huang Feihu, Prince for National Pacification and of Military Prowess has forsaken King Zhou and is here to offer his service. This is a good omen for this west land," Jiang told him.

"Is Huang Feihu a relative of the king?"

"Yes, he is. Our late king mentioned the great favor Huang Feihu had shown him. Now that he's come, we should treat him with great courtesy according to the rites."

King Wu then sent for Huang Feihu, and when courtesies had been exchanged, he asked Jiang Ziya, "What rank did General Huang hold under the Shang?"

"He was Prince for National Pacification and of Military Prowess."

"Then I'll just change his tittle by one word. I'll create him Prince for National Founding and of Military Prowess, in the hope that he'll be one of the founders of the new dynasty."

Huang Feihu thanked King Wu sincerely, and the king ordered a banquet in his honor. As they ate and drank, Huang Feihu told King Wu and Jiang Ziya of King Zhou's mismanagement of state affairs.

"Though he doesn't behave himself, his subjects should still respect and serve him loyally. Let each side try to fulfil his own duty," King Wu said, and then told Jiang Ziya, "Choose an auspicious day to lay the foundation for Prince Huang's new mansion."

The next day, Huang Feihu went to the Celebration Court to see King Wu. "My father Huang Gun, my brothers Huang Feibao and Huang Feibiao, my sons Huang Tianlu, Huang Tianjue and Huang Tianxiang, my sworn brothers Huang Ming, Zhou Ji, Long Huan and Wu Qian, 1,000 guards and

3,000 soldiers are all waiting at Mount Qi. They dare not enter the city without your permission. Tell me what to do with them."

"Please bring them to the city. Each retains his old rank and position without any changes whatsoever," King Wu replied.

After Huang Feihu went to serve in West Qi, war soon threatened the whole land.

If you want to know how events developed, you must read the next chapter.

THE SURRENDER OF TWO GENERALS

When he chased Huang Feihu to Lintong Pass, Grand
Tutor Wen was tricked by Virtue of the Pure Void, mistaking
his sands for Huang Feihu's party. He rushed back to the capital to protect the palace.

How could he have been so easily deceived? The Grand
Tutor was a disciple of Mother Golden Spirit at the Green
Touring Palace. He was skilled in the art of riding invisibly on
metal, wood, water, fire and earth, and could stir up the seas
and move mountains. He could predict victory or defeat by
smelling the wind and ascertain a situation by sniffing the
ground. It was probably because fate already favored West Qi
that he made a critical miscalculation.

When the Grand Tutor returned, the ministers asked him
about his pursuit of Huang Feihu. After he told them what
had happened, they fell silent.

"Even though Huang Feihu got out of Zhaoge, we've got
General Zhang Guifang on the left, the Mo brothers on the
right and the five passes in the center. All are strong enough to
stop him. It's impossible for him to get through of these passes
even if he grows wings," the Grand Tutor thought, though
still puzzled over the matter.

Just then, news arrived that Xiao Yin at Lintong Pass had
killed Commander Zhang Feng, and Huang Feihu had gotten
through. The Grand Tutor did not utter a word.

Soon news came from Tongguan Pass that Huang Feihu
had killed Chen Tong and gotten through the second pass as
well, and before long it was reported that Huang Feihu had
killed Chen Wu and gotten through Chuanyun Pass. This was

followed by the report that Huang Gun of Jiepai Pass had joined his son and left for West Qi. Finally a message from Han Rong arrived requesting urgent reinforcements.

As he listened to the reports, Grand Tutor Wen became infuriated. "I was entrusted by the late king to assist the present monarch, but I never expected that His Majesty would so maladminister state affairs that trouble breaks out everywhere," he thought. "First, the East and South dukedoms declared their independence, and now we've lost such an important minister. I'm sorry that I wasn't able to catch up with him and bring him back. It must have been destined by fate. I don't know whether we will prosper again, or whether this dynasty's heading towards complete destruction. Nevertheless, I can't forget the late king's instructions and must fulfil my duty as a minister even if it means sacrificing my life." He silently made up his mind.

He ordered that the drums be beaten to summon the generals. "Generals, Huang Feihu has rebelled and defected to Ji Fa," he announced when all were present. "This is bound to bring disaster upon us. We must take action at once. What do you think we should do?"

General Lu Xiong stood up. "Grand Tutor, Jiang Wenhuan's been fighting us at Youhun Pass for several years already, and Commander Dou Rong's exhausted, physically and mentally. E Shun's likewise waged war against us for years, and General Deng Jiugong never gets a good night's sleep. Though Huang Feihu has fled to West Qi, we have only to guard the strategic points. Should Ji Fa take any action, we've got the five passes in the middle, the Green Dragon Pass on the left and the Good Dream Pass on the right. Even with his great talent, what can Huang Feihu do? You needn't worry, Grand Tutor. As we're already coping with wars on two fronts, we mustn't create another one to make more trouble for ourselves. Besides, our coffers are almost empty. We don't have sufficient money, food or supplies for a new war. As the old proverb goes, 'Only when a general understands when to advance and when to retreat can he bring peace to the state'."

"You may be right, General, but I'm afraid that West Qi

might be unwilling to live in peace. We have to be well prepared to meet any emergency. West Qi has a courageous general in Nangong Kuo, an experienced strategist in San Yisheng, and Jiang Shang is versed in magic. 'It'll be too late to dig the well when we're thirsty'," the Grand Tutor argued.

"If you can't decide what to do, Grand Tutor, you may send one or two generals to find out the real situation in West Qi. If they intend to take action, we'll attack them at once; otherwise, we should maintain peace for the time being," General Lu Xiong said again.

"You're right, General, but who will undertake this mission for me?"

"I'll go, Grand Tutor. I'll find out the real situation and attack them if necessary," Chao Tian volunteered.

Grand Tutor Wen gave his consent, and the Chao brothers left for the frontier with 30,000 soldiers that same day. They crossed the Yellow River and marched through the five passes, halting near the west gate of West Qi City.

Jiang Ziya heard the sudden roaring of cannons. Scouts soon returned with the news that an army had arrived from Zhaoge and had camped near the west gate. He was puzzled. Why did King Zhou send an army to West Qi? He ordered that the drums be beaten to summon the generals.

In the Shang camp, Chao Tian and Chao Lei were also engaged in a heated discussion.

"We're here to find out what the leaders of West Qi intend to do, but I'm at a loss where to begin. How about a challenge?" Chao Tian asked.

"That seems reasonable, Brother," Chao Lei agreed.

He mounted his horse, took his cutlass and rode towards the city, shouting his challenge.

Jiang Ziya was still in conference when a guard came in. "A general from their camp has given a challenge."

"Who would like to meet the challenge?" Jiang Ziya asked.

"Let me go, Prime Minister," General Nangong Kuo answered at once.

Nangong Kuo took his men out of the city, discovering the

challenger to be General Chao Lei. "Take it easy, General Chao," he called. "Why do you come here?"

"By order of His Majesty and Grand Tutor Wen, I've come here to call Ji Fa to account. He has set himself up as a king without the authority of His Majesty, and he has dared to take in that rebel, Huang Feihu! You'd better return to the city and tell your master to bind up the rebel, and hand him over to me. Otherwise, the people here will all suffer for these crimes and it'll be too late for you to regret it then."

Nangong Kuo smiled. "Chao Lei, don't you know that King Zhou is a wicked tyrant? He slices his ministers to mincemeat, burns them on the burning pillars, feeds them to vile serpents; he took the heart from his uncle to cure Daji's disease, built the Happy Terrace, and insulted the wife of his minister. Yet here in West Qi, my benevolent master rules according to the law. He respects his subjects and enables his people to live in peace and prosperity. We've won the support of two-thirds of the kingdom already. You're simply humiliating yourself coming as the king's representative today."

Filled with fury, Chao Lei spurred his horse forward to slash at Nangong Kuo with his cutlass. Nangong met the blow with his weapon. After thirty rounds, Chao Lei was exhausted, and he was taken alive. He was tied up and brought to the city. When he was pushed before Jiang Ziya, Chao Lei defiantly refused to kneel.

"Chao Lei, why don't you kneel and ask for mercy?" Jiang Ziya asked.

Chao Lei glared at him and said sarcastically, "You sold flour and wove bamboo baskets, but I'm a ranking general. I'm unlucky to have been taken, but I'm ready to die. How could I be willing to kneel before you?"

"Take him outside and cut his head off at once," Jiang Ziya ordered.

When Chao Lei ridiculed his origins, the generals standing on either side could not help smiling, but Jiang Ziya understood their reaction. "Chao Lei was telling the truth. We know from history that Yi Yin was once a poor tiller of the fields, yet he became prime minister to the first king of the

Shang Dynasty. Fate destines that some achieve greatness early and others late," he explained, and ordered again, "Execute him."

But Huang Feihu moved forward. "Prime Minister, Chao Lei is a loyal minister in that he acknowledges only King Zhou as his master. Let me talk with him and bring him over to our side. He may be useful to us in the future."

Jiang Ziya gave his approval. Huang Feihu hurried over and found Chao Lei kneeling and awaiting his end.

"General Chao," he called.

When he saw that it was Huang Feihu, Chao Lei lowered his head in silence.

"General! Why are you so ignorant of the will of Heaven and the people? Two-thirds of the kingdom already belongs to West Qi. Though King Zhou has the upper hand at the moment, it's just like a cold spell in spring that cannot last long. The whole kingdom knows how wicked he is. The country's now ravaged by war, and his future's hopeless. King Wu, on the other hand, is virtuous. Only he can restore peace to the kingdom. I've retained my princeship under him with only one word changed in my title. It's no exaggeration to say he's as virtuous as Yao and Shun. I did all I could to recommend you to the prime minister and beg him for a pardon. He's agreed to let you retain your old position and rank. Don't hesitate as it may endanger your life," Huang Feihu said earnestly.

Chao Lei knew that he was telling the truth. "But I've gravely offended Jiang Ziya. I'm afraid he won't be willing to pardon me."

"If you agree to come over, I'll guarantee your life."

"As you're showing me such great favor, I don't dare refuse."

Huang Feihu returned to the hall and reported the matter to Jiang Ziya.

"It's wrong to execute one who's surrendered," Jiang Ziya said and ordered that General Chao Lei be set free and ushered in.

Chao Lei came in and knelt down. "I've uncouthly offended you and deserve to be executed. I'm most grateful that you've so generously pardoned me."

"Since you agree to come over, we're all ministers in the same government. Bring in your troops now," Jiang Ziya replied.

"My brother Chao Tian's beyond the city. Let me go and persuade him to join us."

Jiang Ziya gave his consent.

Meanwhile, back in their camp, Chao Tian was worrying about his brother. "We're supposed to ascertain the situation, but he's been taken in the very first battle."

He was thus musing when a guard came in with the news of his brother's return.

"How did you get back here, Brother?" Chao Tian asked when Chao Lei entered the tent.

"When I was taken before Jiang Ziya, I didn't yield in the least. I insulted him, and he ordered my execution. But then Prince Huang Feihu came to see me and persuaded me to go over. I've made up my mind to defect to Zhou. Let's go to the city together," Chao Lei explained.

"You damned fool! How can you believe their sweet words? You're a rebel yourself now. How can you face Grand Tutor Wen again! " Chao Tian flew into a rage.

"You don't know, Brother. I'm not the only one pledging allegiance to Zhou. Most of the kingdom's already willingly submitted," Chao Lei replied.

"Of course I know it, but our parents, wives, sons and daughters are all at Zhaoge. We may be safe here, but they'll be slaughtered. How would you feel then?"

"Then what shall we do?"

"Ride back to the city and.... That way we can return to Zhaoge with feathers in our caps," Chao Tian said.

Chao Lei entered the city to see Jiang Ziya. "My brother's willing to come over, but as a general appointed by King Zhou, he demands respect. He hopes you'll send a general to meet him."

"So he'll come over only at my invitation. That can be easily arranged," Jiang Ziya said happily. He asked, "Who would like to go and bring Chao Tian back here on my behalf?"

"Let me go, Prime Minister," Huang Feihu volunteered.

As soon as Huang Feihu and Chao Lei had gone, Jiang Ziya gave secret orders to generals Xin Jia, Xin Mian and Nangong Kuo, and they also left immediately.

At the camp of the Shang army, Chao Tian met Huang Feihu and his brother at the gate with a bow of welcome, "Please come in, Your Highness." But when Huang Feihu entered the gate, he yelled, "Seize him!"

In an instant, the men lying in ambush leapt out, seized Huang Feihu, stripped him of his robes and bound his hands and feet.

"You rogues! So this is how you return my kindness!"

Chao Tian, however, answered slyly, "It's just as the proverb says, 'We couldn't find you even if we wore out iron shoes looking for you, yet now we've caught you without expending the least effort!' You came just at the right time. We'll escort you to Zhaoge at once."

They left West Qi immediately, traveling in complete silence. No talking was allowed. They traveled thirty-five *li* and had almost gotten to Mount Dragon when they unexpectedly found two generals blocking their way.

"Chao Tian! Release General Huang Feihu at once. On Prime Minister Jiang's orders, we've already been waiting here for you for a long time," a voice said.

"I didn't hurt any general or soldier of West Qi. How dare you try to kidnap an important prisoner from us!" Chao Tian said angrily.

Whirling his cutlass, he charged in to attack, and Xin Jia rose to the challenge. After they had fought twenty vigorous rounds, Xin Mian observed that Xin Jia was gaining the upper hand. "Since I've been sent here to rescue General Huang, I should join the battle at once," he thought. Wielding his axe, he fought his way into the Shang line-up. Chao Lei rushed on him, but after only a few rounds, Chao Lei realized that he was trapped in an ambush. He pulled his horse around and fled into the wilderness. Xin Mian fought on until all of King Zhou's soldiers had dispersed. He then freed Huang Feihu.

After a hasty thanks, Huang Feihu leapt on a horse and galloped out of the camp. He saw Chao Tian still fighting with Xin Jia.

"You ungrateful wretch, Chao Tian!" he shouted.

Huang Feihu rushed towards Chao Tian and took him in only a few rounds. "You deceived me, but you never suspected that Prime Minister Jiang was one step ahead of you."

Chao Lei escaped from the battlefield, but he was not familiar with the area. Though he tried the right and then the left, he could not find his way out of West Qi district. Around midnight, he finally found the highway, but saw ahead of him a night patrol carrying lanterns. He heard the sudden firing of cannons and saw a general blocking his path. In the dim light of the lanterns, he found it was General Nangong Kuo.

"General Nangong! Grant me a chance to live. I won't be ungrateful," Chao Lei begged.

"Stop blathering. Get down from your horse and let me bind you up."

Chao Lei plunged into combat, but he was no match for Nangong Kuo. He was taken alive.

It was near dawn when Huang Feihu and Nangong Kuo arrived back at the Prime Minister's mansion. Xin Jia had also returned with his prisoner, Chao Tian.

Huang Feihu moved forward. "If you hadn't saved me, I would have surely died in their hands," he told Jiang Ziya.

"I grew suspicious when Chao Lei told me of his brother's demands. I sent three generals to wait for them at two strategic points. The result was exactly as I had predicted," Jiang Ziya explained.

Then General Nangong Kuo came forward. "By your order, I waited at Mount Qi, and I was able to capture Chao Lei."

Jiang Ziya ordered that Chao Tian and Chao Lei be brought before him. "You traitors! How could you ever fool me!" He ordered, "Guards, drag them out and cut their heads off."

As they were being pushed out, Chao Lei cried, "This is not justice."

Jiang Ziya immediately ordered his guards to bring him back. "Why do you complain of injustice?"

"Prime Minister, everyone knows that West Qi's won the hearts of the people. However, as my brother pointed out, our parents, wives and children are all at Zhaoge. If we pledge allegiance to King Wu, they're bound to meet with disaster. We were only trying to save ourselves with that paltry trick."

"Why didn't you tell me about this earlier? I could have done something to help you. Why did you instead try such a dirty trick?" Jiang Ziya demanded.

"We're stupid and short-sighted. This wouldn't have happened if we had reported the problem to you at first," Chao Lei said with tears on his face.

"Are you telling the truth?"

"If I was lying, General Huang could expose me," Chao Lei answered.

"General Huang, is it true that their parents are at Zhaoge?" Jiang Ziya asked Huang Feihu.

"Yes, it is, Prime Minister."

"Then I'll believe you." When the Chao brothers knelt before him, Jiang Ziya ordered, "Chao Tian is to be kept here as a hostage. Chao Lei may return to the capital with my secret instructions and bring both your families to West Qi."

Chao Lei set out for Zhaoge at once.

If you want to know what happened to him, please read the next chapter.

第三十六回 張桂芳奉詔西征

36

FIRST EXPEDITION AGAINST WEST QI

According to Jiang Ziya's instructions, Chao Lei left West Qi and went back to Zhaoge. He went directly to see Grand Tutor Wen. The Grand Tutor was alone in his office when a guard announced, "General Chao Lei begs to see you."

As soon as Chao Lei entered, Grand Tutor Wen asked him anxiously, "What's the situation in West Qi, General Chao Lei?"

"When we arrived, Nangong Kuo challenged us. I went out to meet him, but after thirty rounds neither of us had gained the upperhand. The next day Chao Tian fought Xin Jia and defeated him. The fighting continued for several days without a definite victor. But Commander Han Rong of Sishui Pass refuses to supply us with rations and fodder, and the whole army is beginning to fall into disorder. Without supplies, the army cannot survive. There's nothing we could do to relieve the situation. That's why I've returned in all haste to see you."

When he heard Chao Lei's report, Grand Tutor Wen fell silent, then said, "I commanded Han Rong to supply you with rations and fodder. Why didn't he do as ordered? General Chao, take 3,000 more soldiers and 1,000 piculs of rice and return to the front without delay. I'll send another experienced general to help you."

Following his orders, Chao Lei took the soldiers and rice, and set out for West Qi, secretly taking the entire Chao family with him. Three days later, Grand Tutor Wen suddenly felt uneasy. Why was Han Rong unwilling to supply the front with food rations? There must be some reason, he mused. He burned incense and made a divination. When he found out the truth, he pounded his desk. "Because of my carelessness, that scoundrel's gotten away with his whole family!"

But it was too late for him to pursue Chao Lei. He asked his disciples Ji Li and Yu Qing, "Whom should I send to West Qi now?"

"As far as we can see, there's no one better than General Zhang Guifang."

The Grand Tutor agreed and immediately sent a messenger to the Green Dragon Pass with the order. He appointed Qiu Yin, General of Divine Dignity, to take over command of the pass.

Meanwhile Chao Lei had crossed the five passes and returned to West Qi. He kowtowed before Jiang Ziya. "Acting on your brilliant instructions, I've successfully brought our parents, wives and children from Zhaoge. We'll never forget this great favor, Prime Minister."

He gave an account of his conversation with the Grand Tutor. "Grand Tutor Wen isn't likely to let us live in peace. War's unavoidable, and we must be well-prepared," Jiang Ziya told his generals.

On Grand Tutor Wen's order, Zhang Guifang handed his post over to Qiu Yin and assumed command of the 100,000-strong army. He appointed Feng Lin commander of the vanguard. When all the preparations had been completed, he set out towards West Qi, reaching the city after several days' march. He camped about five *li* from the south gate of the capital.

When he learned of the arrival of Zhang Guifang, Jiang Ziya summoned his generals. "General Huang, how do you appraise Zhang Guifang as a commander?" he asked.

"Now that you ask me, I can only tell you the truth," Huang Feihu answered.

"What do you mean, General?" Jiang Ziya asked further.

"Because Zhang Guifang is a sorcerer, and he overcomes his adversaries with witchcraft," Huang Feihu explained. "Before combat, opponents usually exchange their names, but once he learns your name, he'll cry it out during combat, and then say, 'Why don't you get down from your horse?' At his cry, you fall from your horse at once and are taken alive. This makes him very difficult to beat. We must remember that we can't tell him our names. Otherwise, not one of us will escape capture."

Jiang Ziya was worried, but many of the generals were unconvinced.

"It's preposterous," one of them said. "How can we fall just because our names are called? If that's the case he only has to call a hundred-odd names and we'll all be his prisoners."

Zhang Guifang, meanwhile, ordered General Feng Lin to give the first challenge. When it was reported, Jiang Ziya asked, "Who would like to fight the first battle?"

Ji Shuqian, one of Prince Wen's sons, was hot-tempered, and he scorned Huang Feihu's warning. He rushed onto the battlefield to meet the general under a blue banner. Dressed in red robes covered with gold armor, the general had an indigo face, red hair, and sharp tusks protruding from his mouth.

"Are you General Zhang Guifang?" Ji Shuqian asked.

"No, I'm not. I'm Feng Lin, commander of the vanguard. By order of His Majesty, we've come here to suppress the rebels. As your master has not only assumed the title of king without authorization but also accepted Huang Feihu, he should offer his neck for us to chop off his head. How is it that he has the gall to resist the punitive army? Tell me your name at once. I'll knock your block off with my wolf-tooth clubs."

Shuqian answered with great fury. "Every duke in the kingdom is delighted to join us, and Heaven's on our side too. How dare you invade our land! You're simply bringing about your own end. But I'll let you off today. Just tell Zhang Guifang to come out and meet me."

"You scoundrel! How dare you insult me," Feng Lin cursed angrily.

He rushed forward whirling his wolf-tooth clubs, and Shuqian met him with his lance. After thirty rounds, neither had gained a clear advantage. Shuqian was a skilled fighter. He put up a defence so tight that nothing could get through. With only his short clubs, Feng Lin could not get near him. Seizing the first opportunity, Shuqian made a lightning attack and stabbed his opponent through the left calf, compelling him to turn and flee. Shuqian, however, did not know that Feng Lin was also versed in magic arts and set off in hot pursuit.

Feng Lin looked back and saw Shuqian close on his heels. He recited a spell, opened his mouth and spat out a cloud of black smoke that turned into a net containing a red ball as big as a rice bowl. The red ball smashed into Shuqian's face, knocking him from his horse and onto the ground. Feng Lin immediately turned his horse about and beat Shuqian to death with his wolf-tooth clubs. He hacked his head off and took it to Zhang Guifang as proof of victory. Zhang Guifang ordered that it be hung at the gate of the camp.

Jiang Ziya was very distressed at the loss, and King Wu deeply grieved. The generals gnashed their teeth in anger over the defeat.

The next day, Zhang Guifang demanded that Jiang Ziya come out to meet him.

"Without entering the tiger's den, how can I catch the tiger cub!" Jiang Ziya said resolutely. "Array the troops for battle."

With generals lined up on either side, he left the city and rode onto the battlefield. There below the pennants of the opposition, he saw a general in white robes covered with silver white armor. He wore a silver helmet and rode a white horse. From head to toe, he resembled a statue of ice.

Zhang Guifang watched as Jiang Ziya led his well-disciplined army from the city in perfect order. Surrounded by stalwart warriors, Jiang Ziya was riding a black-maned horse. Dressed as a Taoist, he had a flowing silver-white beard and carried a pair of swords. Zhang Guifang then saw Huang Feihu on his divine ox under the flying banners.

He was filled with fury and spurred his horse forward. "Jiang Shang, you once received a favor from His Majesty. How can you rebel and help Ji Fa perpetrate evil? How can you accept Huang Feihu, a traitor? How did you deceive Chao

Tian and Chao Lei? You deserve death. By order of His Majesty, I've come here to punish you. You'd better get down from your horse and give yourself up to be tried for treason. Should you dare to resist, I'll raze your land to the ground. I don't care if jade is destroyed with the stone. It'll be too late for you to regret it then."

Jiang Ziya laughed coldly. "You're wrong, Commander. Haven't you heard that 'a good minister offers his service to a virtuous master'? The whole kingdom is rising up against King Zhou; we're no exception. You may be loyal, but you shouldn't support King Zhou in his evil ways. We adhere to law and peace and order. It's you who's insulting us. It would really be a pity if you suffered defeat here and became the laughingstock of the country. You'd better take my advice and withdraw to Zhaoge."

"I've been told that you cultivated yourself on Mount Kunlun for many years, yet you don't seem to know that everything between Heaven and earth undergoes limitless change. You speak nonsense like a child," Zhang Guifang said, then ordered, "Commander of the vanguard, seize Jiang Shang for me at once."

When Feng Lin rushed at Jiang Ziya, he was met by a tall general. They fought like a pair of tigers, neither giving an inch. When he saw Huang Feihu beside Jiang Ziya, Zhang Guifang could not control his anger. As he charged in to attack, Huang urged his divine ox forward to meet him.

"You bloody scoundrel! How dare you attack our line?" Huang Feihu cried.

Their lances clashed and a desperate battle ensued. Zhang Guifang, relying on his witchcraft, made up his mind to take Huang Feihu captive. After only fifteen rounds, he shouted, "Huang Feihu, get down from your beast! What are you waiting for?"

Losing control of himself, Huang fell down from his ox. But before Zhang's men could seize him, Zhou Ji galloped out and slashed at Zhang Guifang with his axe while Huang Feibiao and Huang Feibao snatched Huang Feihu back.

Zhang Guifang deliberately abandoned the fight and retreated. Zhou Ji pursued him. Zhang Guifang also knew his name. "Zhou Ji, why don't you get down? What are you waiting for?" he cried.

Zhou Ji fell from his horse, was seized and bound before his men could rescue him.

Feng Lin also gave up the combat with Nangong Kuo, but Nangong was unwilling to let him go. Feng Lin once more spat out the black smoke and red ball and knocked his pursuer from his horse, taking Nangong Kuo alive. Zhang Guifang returned to his camp in triumph while Jiang Ziya went back to the city, greatly upset.

When Zhou Ji and Nangong Kuo were brought before Zhang Guifang, he demanded, "Why don't you kneel and beg for your lives?"

"We're ready to sacrifice our lives. We're not afraid of death. Just do what you please with us," Nangong Kuo replied.

"Put them in the prison carts. We'll take them to Zhaoge as soon as West Qi's defeated," Zhang Guifang ordered.

Zhang Guifang challenged again the following morning, but Jiang Ziya dared not reply. There was nothing he could do but hang up the board declaring a truce. Zhang Guifang smiled when he saw the board. "Only one encounter, and Jiang Ziya's been forced to seek a truce. We can enjoy a short rest," he decided.

At this, Fairy Primordial was sitting in meditation on his Green Touring Bed when he felt a stir in his heart. He made a divination and ordered Golden Haze Lad to bring Nezha over.

The lad found him in the peach garden and told him, "Brother, Master wants you now."

When Nezha came in, knelt on a cat's-tail mat and kowtowed, the immortal said, "This isn't the place for you to stay long. Hurry on to West Qi to assist your uncle Jiang Ziya. West Qi will face thirty-six invasions. Offer your service there to the new ruler in response to the celestial phenomenon."

Nezha was filled with delight, and after bidding farewell to the immortal, he mounted his Wind-Fire Wheels, took his Fire-Tip Lance, slung his leopard-skin bag over his shoulder and sped off. Reaching West Qi moments later, he got down from his wheels and went to the Prime Minister's mansion at the Lesser Golden Bridge.

When his presence was announced, Jiang Ziya recalled his own Taoist origins and ordered that he be admitted. Nezha entered, knelt down and kowtowed, greeting him respectfully as his uncle.

"Where do you come from?" Jiang Ziya asked.

"I'm a disciple of Fairy Primordial. My name is Li Nezha. By order of my master, I've come to serve you."

Jiang Ziya was delighted, but before he could say anything, Prince Huang Feihu rushed forward. He expressed his gratitude to Nezha as well.

"Who's attacking us?" Nezha asked.

"Commander Zhang Guifang of the Green Dragon Pass. He's a great sorcerer and has taken two of our generals. The Prime Minister had to proclaim a truce." Huang Feihu answered despondently.

"Since I left Mount Qianyuan to aid my uncle, how can I stand by and watch like an idle spectator!" Nezha thought, and spoke before Jiang Ziya again. "Uncle! The board of truce cannot stop this war for long. I'll meet him and take him captive."

Jiang Ziya gave his consent and ordered that the board of truce be removed. When Zhang Guifang learned of it, he summoned Feng Lin. "Jiang Ziya hasn't fought with us for several days. He must have gotten reinforcements from somewhere. Go out and challenge him."

Feng Lin left the camp immediately, rode to the city wall, and gave the challenge. In the Prime Minister's office, Nezha asked for permission to meet Feng Lin.

"Be very careful," Jiang Ziya warned him. "Zhang Guifang can make you fall just by calling your name."

"Don't worry, Uncle. I'll see what I can do."

He mounted his Wind-Fire Wheels and went out of the city. There he saw a hideous general with a savage blue face and red hair, fiercely brandishing a pair of short wolf-tooth clubs.

When he saw Nezha approaching, Feng Lin asked, "Who

are you?"

"I'm Li Nezha, nephew of Prime Minister Jiang Ziya. Are you Zhang Guifang, who downs an opponent by calling his name?"

"No. I'm Feng Lin, commander of the vanguard."

"I'll spare your life. Just tell Zhang Guifang to come out and see me," Nezha demanded.

Feng Lin was very angry at the insult and spurred his horse forward, brandishing his short clubs. Nezha fought back with his lance. The two battled back and forth beneath the city wall for twenty rounds.

"Nezha's of uncommon appearance. If I don't make the first move, I'm likely to fall victim," Feng Lin thought.

He made a feint, then sped off with Nezha in hot pursuit. He turned his head, and when Nezha got close enough behind him, he opened his mouth and spat out his magic black smoke. The red ball within it flew straight at Nezha's face.

"This is sorcery, not proper Taoist magic," Nezha commented.

He pointed at the smoke, and it immediately disappeared. When he saw that his sorcery was rendered powerless, Feng Lin howled in a fury. He turned back to engage Nezha. But Nezha quickly took the Universal Ring from his leopard-skin bag and hurled it at Feng Lin. It hit him on the left shoulder and broke the bone. Feng Lin almost fell from his horse and hastily withdrew inside the Shang camp. Nezha stood outside the camp gate, demanding that Zhang Guifang come and meet him.

Zhang Guifang heard what had happened, and when he was informed of Nezha's challenge, he burned with rage. He mounted his horse, took his lance, and left the camp. When he saw Nezha swaggering about before him, he demanded, "Is that Nezha riding on the Wind-Fire Wheels?"

"Yes, that's right."

"Is it you that wounded the commander of my vanguard?"

Nezha yelled at him, "Oh, you fool! I hear that you say a man's name and he will fall. I've come here especially to deal with you."

He lunged with his lance, and Zhang Guifang parried the blow with his. The battle continued fiercely for forty rounds. Nezha had been taught by Fairy Primordial and plied his lance like lightning. Though Zhang was skillful and experienced, his strength was quickly exhausted, and he had to resort to sorcery.

"Nezha, get down from your wheels at once! What are you waiting for?" he cried loudly.

Nezha was nervous for a moment, but he kept his feet firmly planted on the wheels.

Zhang Guifang was astonished. "This trick has always worked. Why does it fail today? I must try again until Nezha drops from his wheels!"

He called again and again, but Nezha stood firm and then grew impatient. "What a crazy fool you are, Zhang Guifang! As I'm unwilling to get down from my wheels, what's the use of your howling and barking?"

Zhang Guifang went livid with fury and lunged at Nezha, determined to fight him to the death. But Nezha's strength never slackened, and Zhang was soon exhausted. His whole body was bathed in a sweat. Nezha pulled out his Universal Ring and sent it flying through the air straight at the Shang general.

What became of Zhang Guifang? If you want to know, you must read the next chapter.

JIANG ZIYA VISITS MOUNT KUNLUN

The Universal Ring flew through the air and smashed into Zhang Guifang, breaking his left arm. He swayed perilously in the saddle but managed to keep his seat and fled. Nezha returned to the city.

"How did it go?" Jiang Ziya asked.

"His left arm was wounded by my Universal Ring."

"Did he call your name?"

"Yes, he did a few times, but I simply ignored him," Nezha replied.

All the generals were puzzled as to why Nezha did not fall from his wheels. Mortal beings all possess souls. Zhang Guifang's art was to disperse the soul, so naturally, people fell when he called their names. Nezha, however, had been reincarnated from lotus flowers and had no soul. That was why Zhang Guifang had no power over him.

As both Zhang Guifang and Feng Lin had been seriously wounded, they sent an urgent report to Grand Tutor Wen for reinforcements.

Jiang Ziya had also been pondering over the situation. "Though Nezha scored a victory, what can West Qi do if Zhaoge sends a larger army? We're still in danger," he thought. He took a bath, changed his robes, and went to see King Wu. "I've come to take my leave, Your Highness. I'm going to Mount Kunlun to see my master."

"The army beyond the city poses a grave threat to us, and no one can take your place. Prime Minister, don't be too long," King Wu urged.

"I'll be only two or three days," Jiang Ziya promised

and then summoned Nezha. "You and Wu Ji should do everything possible to guard the city during my absence. There's no
need to engage Zhang Guifang. I'll make further plans after
my return."

He left West Qi and rode invisibly on a dust cloud to the
Unicorn Cliff, where he found the scenery there as enchanting
as ever.

"It's been ten years, but the scenery is still fresh and
new," he sighed.

Looking around, he saw that the clouds and haze in a riot
of colors with the sun shining brilliantly behind. Cypress trees
covered the mountains in a green cloak, and slender bamboos
lay half-hidden in a light mist. Outside the Jade Emptiness Palace, exotic flowers bloomed and delicate grass exuded a sweet
fragrance. Upon the peaks, peaches were just ripe, and before
the caves, green herbs waved gracefully in the breeze. Fairy
cranes could be heard calling high in the sky and phoenixes
danced, displaying their colorful feathers. White deer and black
monkeys could be seen now and then among the trees while
black lions and white elephants roamed over the hillsides. A
blessed land. A paradise.

He passed Unicorn Cliff and walked to the Jade Emptiness
Palace. He dared not enter but waited there patiently until
White Crane Lad chanced to come out.

"White Crane Lad, would you please report my arrival to
my master. I would like to see him," he addressed the lad.

White Crane Lad entered the palace and knelt down before
Heavenly Primogenitor. "Jiang Shang's waiting outside for
your order."

The immortal nodded his head. "I've just been wanting to
see him."

When Jiang Ziya entered, he knelt down and greeted his
master, "May my master live forever!"

"I'm delighted that you've come. I was telling the Immortal of the South Pole to give you the 'List of Creations'. You
must build a Terrace of Creation on Mount Qi and hang the
list in it. Your life's mission is to be accomplished there."

But Jiang Ziya remained on his knees. "Zhang Guifang's

using his powerful sorcery to lay siege to West Qi. As my learning is negligible, I'm powerless against him. I beg you to show
some compassion and help me out of this predicament."

"You're a prime minister now, enjoying wealth and power. How can I concern myself with every aspect of your work!
As West Qi's guarded by a virtuous ruler, you needn't fear sorcerers at all. In times of emergency, men of great talent will appear of their own accord. There's no need to ask me for help.
You may go now," his master replied.

Jiang Ziya dared not make any further request and so left
the Jade Emptiness Palace. But he had barely passed the gate
when White Crane Lad hurried up from behind, calling,
"Uncle, Grand Master asks you to see him again."

Jiang Ziya reentered and knelt down.

"Keep my words in mind. After leaving here, don't answer anybody calling you from behind. If you do, West Qi will
suffer from thirty-six invasions. There'll be a man waiting for
you in the East Sea district. Be careful. You may go
now," the immortal told him.

As he left the palace, the Immortal of the South Pole came
to see him off.

"I came here to beg him for help," Jiang Ziya complained. "But he's unwilling to help me. What shall I do
now?"

"This is all destined by Heaven. The only thing now is
not to answer anyone calling your name. I'm sorry that I
can't escort you any further."

Jiang Ziya walked to the Unicorn Cliff holding the "List
of Creations" in both hands. He was just about to get onto
his dust cloud and ride off when he heard someone calling him
from behind.

"Jiang Ziya, Jiang Ziya."

"So someone is calling me from behind. I mustn't answer
him," he warned himself.

The man behind called him again, but he still refused to
reply.

"Prime Minister Jiang!" the man shouted angrily. "Jiang
Shang! So unfeeling as to forget your old friends. Though

you're prime minister, how can you ignore me, when we have been together for forty years in the Jade Emptiness Palace! Why don't you answer when I've called so many times?"

Jiang Ziya could not help turning to look. He saw a man wearing a green scarf, a robe with long sleeves, and a pair of hemp sandals. He was carrying a glittering sword in his hand and a dried gourd on his back. It was Shen Gongbao, his fellow disciple at the Jade Emptiness palace.

"Brother, I didn't know that it was you. Master told me not to answer any call from behind. I'm sorry if I've offended you," he explained.

"What's that in your hands?" Shen Gongbao asked.

"It's the List of Creations."

"Where're you going now?"

"To West Qi to build a terrace to put this in."

"Which side are you on, Brother?"

Jiang Ziya smiled. "How can you be so absurd! I'm the prime minister of West Qi. Prince Wen entrusted me with the care of King Wu. Two-thirds of the kingdom belongs to us already, and the 800 marquises are glad to make obeisance to us. I am helping King Wu in his effort to dethrone King Zhou and fulfil the wishes of Heaven. Don't you know that the phoenix singing on Mount Qi is an omen of welcome for the new sagely ruler? King Wu is as virtuous as Yao and Shun, and the kingly aura of the Shang Dynasty is fading and will disappear in this generation. But why do you ask me such a peculiar question?"

"In spite of your prediction, I'm going to leave this place right now and do my utmost to protect the Shang Dynasty and King Zhou. Jiang Ziya! I'll do all I can to hinder you if you help West Qi," Shen Gongbao said angrily.

"How can you say that, Brother! We must strictly obey Grand Master's orders. How dare you go against him?"

"Jiang Ziya! Listen to me. You'd better come over and help me destroy West Qi. That way we can remain friends, and there'll be no bad feelings between us. It's the best for both of us, don't you think?"

Jiang Ziya was serious now. "You're wrong, Brother.

What you suggest runs contrary to Grand Master's orders and to the will of Heaven. It's absolutely out of the question!"

"Jiang Ziya!" Shen Gongbao grew even angrier. "What powers do you have? You spent a mere forty years here. But listen to what I can do: I can move mountains, stir up the oceans, subdue dragons and tigers, fly on a crane to the Ninth Heaven, plant lotus flowers in fire, and ride on auspicious light for thousands of years."

"There are your achievements, but I've got my own as well. One's success doesn't depend merely on the number of years one's spent," Jiang Ziya objected.

"Jiang Ziya! Your magic doesn't go beyond the five elements. You know only how to move mountains and stir up seas, and that's all. Don't you know that when my head is cut off and thrown up into the air, it can wander for thousands of miles on a piece of red cloud. When it returns to my neck, I become a perfect whole as before. Is that not wonderful? What can you do? You just brag about helping King Wu. You'd better burn that list and come with me to Zhaoge. You can be prime minister there too."

Jiang Ziya was quite befuddled by Shen's words. "The head is the most vital organ of the body, but he can cut it off, throw it into the air, let it tour for thousands of miles and then have it return to his neck as before!" he thought, and then said to Shen, "Brother, if you cut your head off, and it does return to your neck, I'll burn the list and go with you to Zhaoge."

"You must keep your promise," Shen Gongbao demanded.

"A hero's promise is as weighty as Mount Tai. I won't break my word."

Shen Gongbao took off his scarf. Raising his sword in his right hand, he grasped his hair with his left, and cut his head off. His body remained erect. In a twinkling, he threw his head high up into the air. It whirled round and round and soared higher and higher. Jiang Ziya was naive. He watched in admiration as it disappeared.

The Immortal of the South Pole hadn't returned to the Jade Emptiness Palace straightway. He saw Shen Gongbao chasing Jiang Ziya to the Unicorn Cliff and then talking with him, gesticulating and stamping. Then he saw Shen's head fly high into the sky.

"Jiang Ziya's honest. He's being deceived by that wicked bastard," he thought, and instantly called, "Where's White Crane Lad?"

"Here I am, Master."

"Hurry! Transform yourself into a white crane at once, seize Shen's head, and carry it to the South Sea."

White Crane Lad immediately did as he was instructed.

Watching the sky attentively, Jiang Ziya stamped his feet when he saw what was happening. "What shall we do? A white crane's carried the head away," he cried.

Unexpectedly, the Immortal of the South Pole came up from behind him and slapped him vigorously on the back. He turned and saw the immortal. "Why have you come back again?"

The Immortal of the South Pole pointed at him and scolded, "You really are a fool. He's a sorcerer, but you're so easily taken in. If his head doesn't come back, he'll start bleeding and fall dead in three hours. Grand Master told you not to answer if anyone called you from behind. Why did you answer him? Don't you realize that now you will suffer thirty-six invasions? What would we do if you had burned the list! White Crane Lad has transformed himself into a white crane and carried the head to the South Sea. When Shen Gongbao dies, you'll be out of trouble."

"Brother, forgive him. The most important precept of Taoism is compassion and mercy. Take pity on him, for he's spent so much effort to achieve all this. It's cruel to see him die," Jiang Ziya protested.

"If you forgive him, he won't forgive you! Don't regret it when you suffer from thirty-six invasions," the Immortal of the South Pole warned.

"Even if I suffer at the hands of so many enemies, how can I forget the virtue of mercy?" Jiang Ziya persisted

All the while Shen Gongbao was anxious to find his head. He knew that he would bleed to death if his head did not return within three hours.

Yielding to Jiang's earnest pleading, the Immortal of the South Pole waved his hand in the air, and the white crane opened its beak. In its haste, the head joined the neck with the face to the back. Shen quickly pulled his ears and turned it around. When he opened his eyes, he was astonished to see the immortal. The immortal rebuked him, "You beast! How dare you fool Jiang Ziya with your sorcery! You should be taken to the Jade Emptiness Palace for trial. Be off with you!" Then he turned to Jiang Ziya. "You may leave now. Be careful on your way."

Shen Gongbao was so humiliated that he dared not say a word to the immortal, but he turned to Jiang Ziya and said, "Go then! I'll turn West Qi into a sea of blood and a mountain of bones. I promise you that!"

He stormed off, filling the place with hatred.

Jiang Ziya held the list in both hands and rode his dust cloud to the East Sea. He came to a mountain with exquisite rocks, high peaks, and steep cliffs. Clouds and mist merged together over tiny islands carpeted with exotic flowers and fragrant grass. Pine trees and bamboos covered the slopes. It was just like the Penglai Fairyland.

Jiang Ziya was enchanted by the delightful scenery. "I wish I could give up the vulgar world to come here to meditate on a straw mat and recite the Taoist classics!" he thought.

As he stood there lost in thought, huge waves suddenly began to lash the shore, and a great wind arose. In an instant, black clouds filled the sky, completely enveloping the mountain. "How strange!" he cried out in alarm.

As he gazed at the churning sea, a huge wave split open and a completely naked man appeared.

"Great immortal! I've been a wandering soul for 1,000 years, never achieving reincarnation. A few days ago Virtue of the Pure Void told me that a great master would come this way today at this time, and he ordered me to attend on you. I beg you to release me from my suffering in this bitter sea. I will never forget your kindness," the man cried.

"Who are you?" Jiang Ziya asked. "Why do you remain

here for so long? Tell me honestly."

"I'm none other than the soul of Bai Jian, a general under Xuanyuan. In a battle against Chi You, I was killed by a burning missile and fell into the sea. My soul's been confined here ever since. I beg that you let me enjoy a happy end. I will always be grateful for your kindness."

"So you're Bai Jian. By order of the Jade Emptiness Palace, you must come with me and offer your service to West Qi."

Jiang Ziya flung out his fingers and five peals of thunder roared, releasing Bai Jian's soul from the sea. Bai Jian immediately fell on his knees and kowtowed in gratitude.

With great delight, Jiang Ziya took him along and continued on his way to West Qi. Moments later, they reached their destination only to find a great wind raging through the trees, filling the air with dust. Jiang Ziya found to his surprise that the gods of the five routes had come to welcome him.

They cried in unison, "When we were at Zhaoge, you told us to come to Mount Qi and make ourselves ready to serve you. We knew that you would come this way today and came to meet you."

"I'll choose an auspicious date on which you'll start the construction of a Terrace of Creation. Bai Jian shall supervise the work. As soon as the terrace is completed, I'll come here to conduct the opening ceremony."

Bai Jian and the gods of the five routes acknowledged their orders and began the construction on Mount Qi. When Jiang Ziya returned to his mansion in West Qi City, he met Wu Ji and Nezha and asked them to be seated.

"Did Zhang Guifang challenge us?"

"No, he didn't," Wu Ji replied.

Jiang Ziya then went to the palace to see King Wu. "What did you achieve on your trip to Mount Kunlun, Prime Minister?"

Jiang Ziya dared not tell him all the details, as the will of Heaven must be kept a secret. He also said nothing relating to Zhang Guifang.

"You've spared no pains in your service. I feel most uneasy, Prime Minister," King Wu said with concern.

"That's the way I should always serve the nation. Why should I be afraid of hard work!"

The following day, Jiang Ziya had the drums beaten to summon his generals. He issued orders to Huang Feihu, Nezha, Xin Jia, Xin Mian for that night.

Meanwhile Zhang Guifang was anxiously waiting for the reinforcements from Zhaoge. It never occurred to him that Jiang Ziya would make a night raid on his camp. Late that night, hearing the roar of cannons and the shouts of men, he hastily put on his armor, mounted his horse, and rode out of the camp with Feng Lin. In the red glow of hundreds of flaming torches, he saw that the Zhou warriors had completely vanquished his army.

Riding on his Wind-Fire Wheels and wielding his Fire-Tip Lance, Nezha fought his way towards them like a fierce tiger. At the sight of him, Zhang Guifang immediately took flight. Huang Feihu engaged Feng Lin in the left camp while Xin Jia and Xin Mian launched an attack on the right camp. They met little resistance and soon got through to the back camp, where they broke open the prison carts and set Nangong Kuo and Zhou Ji free.

The situation was hopeless. Zhang Guifang and Feng Lin had no choice but to escape while they could. Corpses lying in pools of blood littered the Shang camp, and the army was in tatters. Zhang Guifang took the remnants of his troops and retreated to Mount Qi.

"Never since I became a commander have I lost a battle. But today we've suffered a terrible defeat. I feel devastated!" Zhang Guifang told Feng Lin.

He hastily wrote an urgent report to Zhaoge requesting reinforcements. Jiang Ziya and his men, meanwhile, had returned to the city in triumph, singing and dancing.

Grand Tutor Wen was holding a conference with his generals and advisors when Zhang Guifang's report arrived. He read it and gasped in astonishment. "I gave Zhang Guifang a big army, but the outcome's pitiful. He's not only unable to win but has suffered terrible losses. We've not been successful in the east or south either. In addition, numerous bands of brigands are staging uprisings all over the kingdom. What shall I do? How can I leave here when the country's so weak? But if I don't go, West Qi cannot be defeated."

Ji Li moved forward. "How can you go to the front and leave no responsible official in the palace? Why don't you invite some of your talented friends from the mountains and ask them to reinforce Zhang Guifang? The matter can then be settled, and you needn't worry about having to go there personally."

As a result of this decision, four Taoists lost their lives, and the first names appeared on the Terrace of Creation.

If you want to know what happened thereafter, just read the next chapter.

38

FOUR HOLY MEN IN WEST QI

At Ji Li's suggestion, Grand Tutor Wen recollected his old Taoist friends. He clapped his hands in delight and laughed. "I'm so busy all day long that I've completely forgotten my old friends. If you hadn't mentioned then, I don't know when we would have been able to subdue the rebellions," he said. He then ordered, "Generals, don't come and see me for three days. Ji Li and Yu Qing must stay here to guard my headquarters. I'll return in two or three days."

He then mounted his unicorn and clapped his hands on its horn. The beast rose swiftly onto the clouds and winds, enabling the Grand Tutor to traverse the universe in a twinkling. He went to Nine Dragon Island in the West Sea and landed near a cave on a peak. He was just admiring the scenery when he saw a lad coming out of the cave.

"Is your master in?" he asked.

"Yes. He's playing chess with his friends."

"Would you please tell him that Grand Tutor Wen of the Shang Dynasty's here to call on him?"

The four holy men came out of the cave to meet him. They laughed and asked, "Brother Wen! What wind brings you here?" They then ushered him inside, and when greetings had been exchanged, they sat down on the round straw cushions.

"Where do you come from, Brother?" they asked.

"I've come especially to pay you a visit."

"We're refugees on this bleak island. What instructions do you have for us?"

"I was entrusted with the post of grand tutor by the deceased king, but Jiang Shang, a disciple from Mount Kunlun, has been helping Ji Fa rebel. I sent Zhang Guifang to attack him, but he failed. I wish to go to the front myself, but I can't leave the capital. With no other alternative, I've come to beg for your help. I'll greatly appreciate any help you can give me."

"Brother, I'll go and help Zhang Guifang," Wang Mo answered.

Li Xingba said with finality, "We four must go together. How can we let you go alone!"

Grand Tutor Wen was greatly delighted.

The four holy men were to be the four generals under the Jade Emperor, and their names were therefore on the List of Creations. The first of them was Wang Mo, the second Yang Sen, the third Gao Youqian and the fourth Li Xingba. It must be remembered that gods were chosen from inferior immortals who could not achieve the Way.

"Brother Wen, go back at once. We'll follow you to Zhaoge very soon," Wang Mo suggested.

"The matter's urgent. I beg you all to come without the least delay," Grand Tutor Wen urged.

"I'll tell my lad to send our saddle beasts to Mount Qi first, then we'll come straightway," Wang Mo promised.

Grand Tutor Wen mounted and returned to Zhaoge. The four holy men soon followed on a water cloud to Zhaoge. When they arrived, their appearance frightened the people terribly: Wang Mo wore a long scarf and a grey robe. His face was as round as the full moon. Yang Sen wore a monk's ring around his head and a purple robe. His face was as black as the bottom of a cauldron, his beard was red as cinnabar and his eyebrows were yellow. Gao Youqian wore his red hair in two coils and was dressed in a scarlet robe. His face was indigo, and tusks protruded from his upper and lower jaws. Li Xingba wore a fish-tail gold coronet and a light yellow robe. His face was as dark as a dried date and he had a long beard. They were all about sixteen feet tall, and they walked through the streets swaying from side to side.

"Where's the mansion of Grand Tutor Wen?" Wang Mo

asked some pedestrians.

"It's near the Twin Dragon Bridge, in the central south part of the city," one of the bolder citizens answered.

They soon found the place. Grand Tutor Wen came out to meet them and entertained them in his home. The next day, Grand Tutor Wen took them to the palace to see King Zhou. Grand Tutor Wen first entered the court alone.

"I have invited four sages from Nine Dragon Island to help us in West Qi," he told King Zhou.

"You're of great assistance to me, Grand Tutor. Let me see them," King Zhou answered gladly.

When Grand Tutor Wen led them into the court, King Zhou was terrified by their appearance. "How fearsome and evil they look!" he thought, and ordered that they be entertained. "Grand Tutor Wen may act as host in my place."

When he had returned to his apartments, Grand Tutor Wen and the four holy men ate and drank happily.

"Brother Wen! We must go to the front now. We'll come back here and drink with you again as soon as the rebels are subdued," Wang Mo said.

The four of them immediately left the palace and Grand Tutor Wen saw them off beyond the city of gates. They reached their destination in a minute and requested to see Zhang Guifang. Both Zhang Guifang and Feng Lin came out to meet them and usher them in. When he found that both Zhang and Feng had difficulty moving around, Wang Mo asked. "At the request of Grand Tutor Wen, we've come here to help you. I see you cannot move freely. Are you wounded?"

Feng Lin told them the whole story.

"Show me your wound."

He took a grain of elixir from his gourd, ground it between his teeth and applied it to Feng's wound. It healed instantly. He healed Zhang Guifang the same way.

"Where's Jiang Ziya now?" Wang Mo asked.

"He's in West Qi City, about seventy *li* from here. We retreated after being defeated," Zhang Guifang replied.

"Bring your troops back to the city," Wang Mo directed. Amidst the yelling of soldiers and the roaring of cannons,

CREATION OF THE GODS

Zhang Guifang's army rushed back to West Qi and camped outside the east gate.

When news got to Jiang Ziya, he said to his generals, "Zhang Guifang must have gotten reinforcements. We must be very careful."

In the Shang camp, Wang Mo was telling Zhang Guifang, "When you give the challenge, demand Jiang Ziya. We'll conceal ourselves among the banners and won't emerge until he comes out."

Yang Sen told Zhang Guifang and Feng Lin, "Stick these charms on your saddles tomorrow. Our strange beasts will fill all the other horses with terror. Without these charms, you might be thrown to the ground."

The next day, Zhang Guifang donned his armor and led his army to the city wall, where he demanded that Jiang Ziya come out and meet him. Jiang Ziya took action at once. Amidst the roar of cannons, his troops came out of the city in five square formations. Jiang Ziya rode out on his black-maned horse under the flags, carrying a sword in his hand. Zhang Guifang galloped forward alone to meet him.

"As a defeated general, aren't you ashamed to meet me again today?" Jiang Ziya greeted him sarcastically.

"Why should I feel ashamed? Don't you know that victory and defeat are commonplace events to a soldier? Things have changed now. Don't try to insult us!"

At the beating of drums, four strange animals suddenly appeared behind Zhang Guifang. Wang Mo rode on a monster, Yang Sen on a lion, Gao Youqian on a spotted leopard, and Li Xingba also on a monster with a single horn and several tails. As soon as they appeared, all the horses on the West Qi side leapt and reared in fright, throwing Jiang Ziya and all his generals to the ground. Nezha alone remained on his Wind-Fire Wheels and Huang Feihu on his divine ox.

When they saw Jiang Ziya on the ground, hat crooked and robes awry, the four men burst into loud laughter.

"Don't panic! Get up nice and easy now!" they said to him sarcastically.

Jiang Ziya straightened his hat and robes and looked at

the four evil-looking Taoists confronting him. He addressed them politely with a bow. "How do you do, Brothers. Where do you come from? What can I do for you?"

"We're from Nine Dragon Island. We're Wang Mo, Yang Sen, Gao Youqian and Li Xingba, all Taoists, like yourself. We've come here at Grand Tutor Wen's bidding to help you out of trouble. All you have to do is accept our three proposals," Wang Mo said.

"What are they, Brother? Tell me frankly. If they're good, I'll accept even thirty proposals," Jiang Ziya replied promptly.

"First of all, King Wu should know his place as a subject of the Shang Dynasty," Wang Mo said.

"You're mistaken, Brother. King Wu's always been a loyal subject of the Shang Dynasty. He behaves himself strictly according to the law and justice and has never insulted his superiors. He's already fulfilled your requirement."

"The second is that you open all your treasurehouses and distribute everything in them among the Shang soldiers. The third is that you hand over Huang Feihu to Zhang Guifang. What do you say?"

"Your proposals are reasonable. I'll return to the city and write a memorial. I'll trouble you to take it back and thank His Majesty for the favor he's bestowed on us. We've no other considerations," Jiang Ziya answered without hesitation.

The two sides then exchanged courtesies and returned to their own camps, waiting for an armistice. Jiang Ziya returned to the city and sat down in the main hall. Huang Feihu came forward and knelt before him.

"Prime Minister, please bind up my family and send us to Zhang Guifang, lest King Wu suffer because of us," he begged.

Jiang Ziya hurriedly helped him to his feet and explained, "General Huang, I accepted the three demands just now as a matter of expediency. In the face of those strange beasts, all our generals had fallen from their horses before the combat had even begun. How could we fight a battle in such an awkward situation! I had to follow a policy of appeasement so as to return to the city and consider how to deal with the matter."

Huang Feihu thanked Jiang Ziya, and the generals gathered there soon dispersed. Jiang Ziya burned incense, took a bath and then ordered that Wu Ji and Nezha guard his mansion. He set out on his second trip to Mount Kunlun. When he arrived, he dared not enter unauthorized and waited patiently until White Crane Lad appeared. He asked him to report his arrival to Heavenly Primogenitor.

Granted admittance, Jiang Ziya kowtowed before his master respectfully.

"I already know that the four Taoists from Nine Dragon Island are making trouble in West Qi. The four beasts they ride were born in ancient times when all wild beasts made their obeisance to Heaven. Though they were all born of the same dragon, they're different in appearance and nature. White Crane Lad, go to the stable in the peach garden and bring my nondescript to Jiang Shang," the Grand Master ordered.

The immortal's saddle beast had the head of a unicorn, the tail of a wolf and the body of a dragon; hence the name. It was soon brought before them.

"As you achieved great merit in your forty years of study here, I've chosen you to create gods on my behalf. I'm giving you my own saddle beast so that you'll be able to meet all the strange creatures on earth without fear."

The Grand Master then asked the Immortal of the South Pole to fetch a wooden staff. It was three feet and six and a half inches long, had twenty-one joints, and four charms on each joint. It was the Staff for Beating Gods. Jiang Ziya knelt down to receive it from Heavenly Primogenitor and begged for his compassion.

"There'll be a man waiting for you at the North Sea," his master told him. "Use this magic flag to protect yourself. There's a note hidden inside. When you're facing an emergency, take it out and read it, and you'll learn how to cope with the situation."

Jiang Ziya kowtowed, bade his master farewell, and left the mountain. The Immortal of the South Pole escorted him to the Unicorn Cliff, where Jiang Ziya mounted his nondescript. At a light tap on the horn, the beast shot through the air on a ray of red light to the sound of resonant bells. A short while later, it dropped down onto a mountain near an island in the sea. The mountain had a thousand peaks like folding screens that reflected sunlight after the rain. Creepers wrapped around ancient trees, and little birds made their nests on high cliffs. The mountainsides were dotted with rare and fragrant flowers, long bamboos and stout pine trees. Birds chirped their sweet songs, and waves roared below. It would have been an ideal hermitage for a highly cultured man.

Jiang Ziya was admiring the scenery when strange clouds suddenly appeared at the foot of the mountain. As the clouds dispersed a great wind arose, and in its midst a strange creature appeared. It had the head of a snake, the neck of a goose, the body of a fish, a beard like a lobster, hands like the talons of a hawk, and a single foot like that of a tiger. The creature had absorbed the ethers of Heaven and earth and had been refined by the essence of the sun and moon. It could throw boulders and rocks with extraordinary speed and accuracy and speak like a man. It had been born of a dragon and a leopard and was destined to support the illustrious ruler in founding a new dynasty.

When he saw this fearsome creature, Jiang Ziya was frightened out of his wits and broke out in a cold sweat. "Jiang Ziya! A piece of your flesh, and I'll live thousands of years," the creature cried.

"Me, for food?!" Jiang Ziya said to himself.

The creature jumped nearer. "Jiang Shang, let me take a bite of your flesh."

"But why? No enmity exists between us!"

"Jiang Ziya, don't imagine that you can escape today," the creature answered harshly.

Jiang Ziya gently opened his Apricot Yellow Flag, took out the note and read it over. He knew now what he had to do. "Beast!" he shouted. "If I'm destined to be your food, I won't be able to escape. Just pull up this flag and I'll let you eat me."

He stuck the flag in the ground, and it grew at once to about twenty feet high. The creature came up and tried to pull it out. First he tried with one hand and then with both hands, but the flag did not move. His hands slipped down to the bottom end of the pole near the ground, and he pulled with his neck stretched straight out. Yet again he failed.

Jiang Ziya then opened his palm towards the sky, invoking lightning and five peals of thunder. The noise so frightened the creature that he tried to let go of the flag pole, but his hands were stuck.

"You fool! It's your end now," Jiang Ziya said sternly.

"Mercy, great immortal! I'm so sorry that I failed to recognize you as a celestial being. Please forgive me. I'm innocent. It's all Shen Gongbao's fault," the creature pleaded.

"You intended to harm me! What's it got to do with Shen Gongbao?"

"Great immortal! I'm Dragon Beard Tiger. I was born during the time of Emperor Shao Hao. Since then I've lived on the essence from the sun and moon. The day before yesterday, Shen Gongbao passed here and told me that you would come this way at this hour today. He said that a piece of your flesh would give me over ten thousand years of life. He fooled me, but I was stupid to believe him. I didn't know that you had such great magic powers. Please show mercy on me, as I've so painstakingly cultivated and refined myself for several thousand years. If you spare my life, I would be eternally grateful."

"I'll only spare your life on the condition that you be my disciple."

"I will, sir."

"Then close your eyes," Jiang Ziya ordered.

As soon as Dragon Beard Tiger closed his eyes, a huge thunderbolt roared through the air. Finding his hands free, he knelt down before Jiang Ziya.

"Do you know any Taoist magic arts?"

"I can produce rocks as big as millstones out of thin air with a flick of my hand and throw them out like a plague of locusts or a thunderstorm. When I practise my art, the dust rises all over the mountain and covers the whole sky."

"If we use this man, we'll succeed everywhere," Jiang

Ziya thought to himself.

He picked up his flag and took Dragon Beard Tiger with him to West Qi, where he met the generals outside his residence. They were alarmed by Dragon Beard Tiger's appearance. The prime minister's brought an ugly spectre back with him, they thought.

Jiang Ziya smiled. "This is Dragon Beard Tiger from the North Sea. He's my new disciple."

He then entered the mansion and asked about the situation outside the city.

"Everything's been quiet," Wu Ji answered.

As five days had passed, and Huang Feihu had not yet been brought to him, Zhang Guifang said to the four Taoists, "Masters, don't you think that Jiang Shang's playing some trick on us? We've heard nothing from him in five days."

"Since he's promised us, he can't possibly break his word. Doesn't he fear that we would turn West Qi into a 'lake of blood and mountain of bones'?" Wang Mo said confidently.

Another three days passed. Yang Sen said to Wang Mo, "Brother, this is the eighth day, but Jiang Ziya still hasn't appeared. Let's go out and ask him the reason."

"Jiang Shang may look honest, but he's treacherous at heart. He may have played a trick to fool us when he realized that the situation was unfavorable to him that day," Zhang Guifang put in.

"If that be so, let's go now. If he has deceived us, we'll help you win in a single battle," Yang Sen promised angrily.

Feng Lin then took his army to the city wall amidst the roar of cannons and the savage shouts of his men. A demand was made for Jiang Ziya to come out and meet them.

Jiang Ziya mounted his beast and rode out of the city with Nezha, Dragon Beard Tiger and Huang Feihu. The moment he saw them, Wang Mo flew into a rage. "Damn you, Jiang Shang! You sneaked off to Mount Kunlun for the nondescript!"

He whipped his monster into a gallop and charged at Jiang Ziya with a drawn sword. Nezha intercepted him on his Wind-

Fire Wheels, crying, "Wang Mo, you just dare try to hurt my uncle!"

As Wang Mo and Nezha fought fiercely, sword against lance, Yang Sen could see that with his short sword, Wang Mo could get nowhere near his opponent. Nezha was gaining the upper hand. He quickly took a Sky Breaking Pearl from his leopard-skin bag and flung it at Nezha. Nezha was struck a heavy blow and tumbled from his wheels. But as Wang Mo rushed forward to cut his head off, he was intercepted by Huang Feihu. Nezha was saved, and the battle continued between Wang Mo and Huang Feihu.

At the first opportunity, Yang Sen took a second Sky Breaking Pearl from his bag and hurled it at Huang Feihu, knocking him from his ox. But Dragon Beard Tiger came to his rescue, crying, "Don't hurt him! I'm coming!"

Wang Mo was shocked at the sight of Dragon Beard Tiger, and gasped. The creature looked so queer: a huge head, a long neck, one foot, golden lights from his round eyes, a body covered with scales and fingers as strong as steel claws.

On his spotted leopard, Gao Youqian saw Dragon Beard Tiger leap savagely at Wang Mo and hurriedly took his Universe Muddling Pearl from his bag. He hurled it at Dragon Beard Tiger and hit him right on the neck. Dragon Beard Tiger hopped wildly with pain, thrashing his head from side to side.

Wang Mo and Yang Sen immediately rushed at Jiang Ziya, attempting to seize him. His three generals wounded, Jiang Ziya was left all alone to face the enemy. He fought valiantly, but was soon caught off guard by Li Xingba, who hit him in the heart with an Earth Spitting Pearl. He uttered a loud cry and almost fell from his saddle. He fled in the direction of the North Sea.

"I'll capture him!" Wang Mo shouted and set off in pursuit like a whirlwind.

Though Jiang Ziya was badly wounded, he could still hear someone chasing him close behind. He patted the horn of the nondescript and it immediately soared into the air.

Wang Mo laughed. "That's commonplace for a Taoist!

You think that I'm unable to fly with the clouds?"

He patted his monster, and it leapt into the air after Jiang Ziya. Jiang Ziya was destined to die seven times and meet three calamities. This was to be his first death at the hands of the four men.

Wang Mo was left far behind, so he cast his Sky Breaking Pearl at Jiang's back. The pearl hit him with such force that he was knocked from his nondescript. He fell down and rolled onto his back, dying with his face to the sky. The nondescript stood close beside him.

Wang Mo was about to dismount and cut off Jiang Ziya's head when he heard someone approach, singing:

> *Breezes stir the willows on a pool,*
> *And petals fall and float on the water.*
> *Should anyone ask me where I reside,*
> *My home's in the depths of clouds so white.*

Wang Mo looked around and found that the singer was none other than the Heavenly Master of Outstanding Culture.

"What brings you here, Brother?" he asked politely.

"Dear friend, don't hurt him. On orders from the Jade Emptiness Palace, I have been waiting here for you a long time. Jiang Ziya is to accomplish his missions and Heaven has determined the following: 1) The Shang Dynasty is destined to end; 2) A sage ruler born in West Qi will rule; 3) Chan Taoism is fated to break the commandment on killing; 4) Jiang Ziya is destined to enjoy wealth and power in the vulgar world; and 5) he is to create gods on behalf of the Jade Emptiness Palace.

"Friend, as a member of Jie Taoism, you're most carefree. Why do you involve yourself in other people's affairs? Don't you remember what your master wrote on the wall of his Green Touring Palace? 'Close your cave door and read the sutras; set foot on western soil and you're on the List of Creations!' You may kill him, but I can still revive him. Friend, take my advice and return to your cave while your moon's still full. If you don't, it'll be too late for regrets," the Heavenly

Master said earnestly.

"You brag too much," Wang Mo said. "We're all disciples of Taoism. How can you insult me with warnings about the full moon? Though you've got a powerful master, I've got mine too."

He raised his sword and rushed angrily at the Heavenly Master. But a young Taoist in a yellow robe with coiled hair stepped out from behind the great immortal. "Wang Mo! Enough of your violence. Here I come! I'm Jinzha, disciple of the Heavenly Master."

He raised his sword to meet the assault from Wang Mo and they fought desperately sword against sword at the foot of the mountain.

As the combat raged on, the Heavenly Master took out his Invisible Dragon Stake. It was to be known as the Seven Treasure Golden Lotus among Buddhists. He had used it to subdue Nezha and save Li Jing.

The Heavenly Master tossed it into the air, and it came down on Wang Mo, binding him to the stake. One ring tightly bound his neck, the second his waist, and the third his feet. He was unable to move an inch. Jinzha rushed forward and aimed a blow at his neck.

What became of Wang Mo? If you want to know, read the next chapter.

JIANG ZIYA FREEZES MOUNT QI

Jinzha slashed at Wang Mo's neck, severing head from body. Bai Jian, the God of Pure Happiness, collected Wang Mo's soul with his Hundred Soul Pennant into the Terrace of Creation. The Heavenly Master of Outstanding Culture put away the stake and bowed towards Mount Kunlun.

"Excuse your disciple for violating the commandment on killing," he prayed.

He then told Jinzha to carry Jiang Ziya up the mountain, and he poured a solution of elixir into his mouth. Jiang Ziya soon revived, and seeing Heavenly Master, asked, "Brother, is it that I meet you here?"

The Heavenly Master just smiled. "It's the will of Heaven and has not been for us to decide." He then ordered Jinzha, "Leave here with your uncle and help him in West Qi. I'll be there too before long."

As Jinzha helped Jiang Ziya on to his nondescript and the two departed, Heavenly Master buried Wang Mo's corpse and returned to his own residence.

Meanwhile, the generals of West Qi were deeply worried about Jiang Ziya. King Wu had gone to the prime minister's residence and sent patrols out to look for him. When Jiang Ziya finally returned with Jinzha, he was heartily welcomed by King Wu and all the generals.

"Where did you go? I've been terribly worried about you," King Wu asked anxiously.

"If it had not been for Jinzha and his master, I wouldn't have returned alive," Jiang Ziya told him.

He introduced Jinzha to King Wu and Nezha, and then returned to his own mansion.

In the Shang camp, Yang Sen had seen Wang Mo defeat and chase Jiang Ziya, but was puzzled that he still had not returned by dusk. He made a divination on his fingers inside his sleeves and let out a cry of horror. Gao Youqian and Li Xingba immediately asked him what had happened.

"What a pity it is! His thousand years of cultivation has all gone to waste. Brother Wang died on Five Dragon Mountain."

The three holy men could not sleep that night. Early the next morning, they mounted their beasts and rode to the city demanding that Jiang Ziya come out and meet them.

When the report reached Jiang Ziya, he hesitated, as his wounds were not yet completely healed.

"Uncle! Go out and meet them. With us by your side we're sure to win," Nezha urged him on.

Encouraged, Jiang Ziya mounted and rode out with Jinzha and Nezha.

"Damn you, Jiang Shang! How can we allow you to live now that you've put our brother to death!"

The three holy men urged their beasts forward to attack Jiang Ziya. But Jinzha and Nezha intercepted them. The five fought desperately.

"I should use the Staff for Beating Gods," Jiang Ziya thought as he watched the battle.

He tossed the staff into the air. There was a flash of lightning and a roar of thunder and the staff struck Gao Youqian on the head, knocking out his brains. He died at once, and his soul flew instantly to the Terrace of Creation.

When he saw that Gao Youqian was dead, Yang Sen let out a cry of fury and charged at Jiang Ziya. But Nezha quickly hurled his Universal Ring at him. As Yang Sen tried to catch it, Jinzha cast up the Invisible Dragon Stake, caught him with the gold rings, and then slashed him in two with his sword. His soul also entered the Terrace of Creation.

Seeing that two were lost, Zhang Guifang, Feng Lin and Li Xingba rushed out to join the combat. As they fought with Jinzha and Nezha, the roar of cannons was suddenly heard from the city, and a smart young general, still a child, galloped onto the battlefield. He wore a silver coronet and silver armor, rode on a white horse and carried a long lance. It was Huang Tianxiang, the fourth son of Huang Feihu. The young general galloped onto the battlefield and threw himself into the fray. His blows fell like rain, and before long he caught Feng Lin unawares and struck him a mortal blow, toppling him from his horse. Feng Lin's soul was also conducted to the Terrace of Creation.

Zhang Guifang realized that he could not possibly win the day and withdrew to the Shang camp.

Li Xingba told him, "Four of us came here to help you, but now three have died. You'd better write to Grand Tutor Wen, asking him for reinforcements. We'll get revenge for today's humiliation."

Zhang Guifang did as he suggested and sent an urgent report to Zhaoge. Jiang Ziya returned to the city in triumph and recorded the merits his generals had achieved. He was praising Huang Tianxiang for felling Feng Lin when Jinzha cut in, "Uncle, we shouldn't stop at this victory. We'd better engage Zhang Guifang again tomorrow."

"You're right, General Jinzha," Jiang Ziya said in full agreement.

The following day, Jiang Ziya took his army out of the city and demanded Zhang Guifang.

"I've never been defeated so badly. I cannot bear the insults any longer! I'll meet them myself," Zhang Guifang said angrily on hearing the shouting outside his camp.

He mounted his horse and led his men out. "You rogue! How dare you insult a commander appointed by His Majesty! I'm prepared to fight you to the end."

As he urged his horse forward, Huang Tianxiang sprang out from behind Jiang Ziya and engaged him in fierce combat. After thirty rounds neither side had gained an advantage. Jiang Ziya ordered that the drums be beaten to signal a general offensive. More than twenty brave generals rushed out to join the battle. They encircled Zhang Guifang, who fought like a wild tiger.

"Go and engage Li Xingba so that I'll have the opportunity to get him with my Staff for Beating Gods," Jiang Ziya ordered Jinzha.

Jinzha, who always did battle on foot, ran towards Li Xingba with his sword raised. Li met the attack with his iron staves. After several rounds, Nezha raced over on his Wind-Fire Wheels to help his brother.

Seizing this opportunity, Jiang Ziya drew out his staff, but Li Xingba realized the danger he was in and immediately slapped his beast. It shot into the air and took flight at once. Seeing that Lin Xingba had fled, Nezha rushed over to Zhang Guifang.

"Zhang Guifang! Get down from your horse, and be quick about it. We'll let you live if you surrender. Why not enjoy a happy and peaceful life with us?" Chao Tian and his brother cried.

"You wretches! I'll give up my life to prove my loyalty. I'll never degrade my honor. I'm not afraid of death the way you are," Zhang shouted back.

Zhang Guifang had been fighting since morning, and it was now noon. He realized that he had no hope of getting out alive. "King Zhou, I can serve you no longer, but I've been a loyal minister to the end," he cried.

He turned his lance about and stabbed himself through the throat. He fell from his saddle, and his soul flew to the Terrace of Creation. Their commander dead, most of his soldiers surrendered, and the rest fled back to the passes. Jiang Ziya and his men returned to the city in triumph.

Li Xingba had escaped in a panic, but as one of the four holy men, he was destined to follow his brothers. His beast landed on a mountain, and he dismounted and sat on the ground, leaning on a pine tree. "I didn't expect such a terrible defeat. I'm too ashamed to return to the island and meet my companions. I must go to Zhaoge and see Brother Wen to discuss how to avenge this humiliation," he decided.

He was about to get up when he heard someone singing. He looked round and found a young Taoist coming towards him. The young Taoist bowed and greeted him. "How do you do, Brother." When Li Xingba returned the salutation, he asked further, "Where do you live, Venerable Brother?"

"I'm Li Xingba, a holy man from Nine Dragon Island. I assisted Zhang Guifang against West Qi but was defeated. I'm just taking a rest here. Where do you come from?"

The Taoist was delighted. "I could've worn out iron shoes in my search for you! What luck to meet you here. I'm none other than Muzha, disciple of the Sage of Universal Virtue on Nine Palace Mountain. On my master's orders, I'm going to West Qi to help Uncle Jiang Ziya. Before I left, my master told me, 'If you come across Li Xingba on the way, capture him and take him to Jiang Ziya as a present to mark your first meeting'."

Li Xingba burst into laughter. "Accursed beast! How dare you insult me like this!"

He struck at Muzha with his staves, but Muzha blocked and returned the blow with his sword. They fought back and forth across the mountainside. Muzha carried a pair of magic swords on his back named "the Hooks of Wu," one male and the other female. Muzha shook his left shoulder gently. The male sword immediately flew up into the sky, circled a few times then dropped and sliced off Li Xingba's head.

Muzha buried the corpse and rode on a dust cloud to West Qi. When he was admitted to the Prime Minister's mansion, he bowed and greeted Jiang Ziya.

"Where do you come from, young fellow?"

Jinzha, who was standing to one side, answered for him, "He's my brother Muzha, Uncle. He's a disciple of Immortal Universal Virtue."

"What a wonder it is to have all three brothers in the same court. Your names will be recorded in history forever," Jiang Ziya said with approval.

During this whole time, Grand Tutor Wen had remained in Zhaoge keeping state affairs in good order. One day, a report arrived from Han Rong of Sishui Pass. As he read, he pounded his desk in anger. "Oh, my dear brothers! What a pity that you should lose your innocent lives. It's only because I hold the highest rank that I dared not leave here at this time of crisis. This report cuts me deeply."

He ordered that the drums be beaten, and soon all the generals arrived. "Several days ago I asked four of my friends from the Nine Dragon Island to help Zhang Guifang," he began. "Unfortunately, three of them have lost their lives, and General Feng Lin has also been killed. I would like to have your opinion as to who should go and reinforce Zhang Guifang."

He had barely finished speaking when Lu Xiong came forward and volunteered, "I would like to go, Grand Tutor."

As General Lu was a white-haired old man, Grand Tutor Wen said, "You're of venerable years, General. It may be difficult for you to achieve success."

"Grand Tutor, though Zhang Guifang's young, he acknowledges only his own talent. Feng Lin was vulgar, and the loss of his life was therefore unavoidable. A good general must be able to take advantage of an opportune time, to seize on a favorable situation, and to know how to unite the people. He must take defensive measures calmly but attack with vigor. He must be able to survive destruction, make a weak army strong and a frail one tough. He must turn danger into safety and disaster into good fortune. He must be able to adopt limitless changes of strategy and win a war that takes place a thousand *li* away. He must give full play to every warrior. Those are the requirements of a good commander. With the help of one or two advisors, I'll be sure to achieve success."

Listening to him, Grand Tutor Wen thought, "He may be old, but he's a good commander. Besides, he's loyal. I'll find him one or two capable advisors that are quick to adapt to new situations as they arise. Maybe Fei Zhong and You Hun?" When they had been summoned, he told them, "Zhang Guifang's suffered a defeat and Feng Lin's lost his life. General Lu Xiong will reinforce the front, and you two will go with him as advisors. You'll have served the kingdom well when the army returns to Zhaoge."

Frightened, they hastily made excuses. "Grand Tutor, as civil officials, we know nothing about war. We'll make disastrous mistakes."

"Both of you are good at adapting to changing conditions. That is just what the army needs now. You can take care of whatever General Lu Xiong is unable to do. We all must do our best to serve His Majesty. Make no more excuses."

Fei Zhong and You Hun could do nothing but take the seals of appointment. After a farewell feast, Lu Xiong, Fei Zhong and You Hun took 50,000 soldiers, sacrificing an ox and a horse before the great army banner, and marched off to the firing of cannons.

The summer weather was so hot that, in their armor, the soldiers found it difficult to move. Both men and horses perspired and panted under the burning sun. The sky was cloudless, and there was not a breath of wind to refresh them.

As they left the five passes, a patrolman brought Lu Xiong the news that "Commander Zhang's been killed and his head's hanging on the east gate of West Qi City."

This greatly alarmed Lu Xiong. "As Zhang Guifang's already dead, we'd better halt here," he decided, and ordered, "Camp right here." He asked, "What lies in front of us?"

"That's Mount Qi, sir."

To escape the heat, he ordered that the army camp in the depths of the forest. He wrote a report to Grand Tutor Wen requesting further instructions.

After they had defeated Zhang Guifang, Jiang Ziya withdrew to the city to await further developments. One day, a report came in that a big army had camped at Mount Qi. The report was simple, but Jiang Ziya understood the situation immediately.

A few days before, Bai Jian reported to him that the Terrace of Creation had been completed. A sacrificial ceremony was required to honor the arrival of the List of Creations. Jiang Ziya ordered, "Nangong Kuo and Wu Ji! Take 5,000 soldiers and camp at Mount Qi. Block all communications and allow no troops to pass through."

Nangong Kuo and Wu Ji carried out the order at once. At Mount Qi, they came upon the Shang army and camped directly opposite. But the weather was extremely hot, and they soon found it unbearable.

"Prime Minister ordered us to camp here, but there's no drinking water and there are no trees to provide shade. The men are bound to grumble," Wu Ji said to Nangong Kuo.

The next day, General Xin Jia arrived with an order from Jiang Ziya, "The camp must be moved to the summit of Mount Qi immediately."

Both Nangong and Wu Ji were astonished. "In such unbearable heat, we'll only die more quickly if we follow this order."

"You've got no choice. You cannot disobey an order," Xin Jia warned.

Marching up the mountain, the Zhou soldiers gasped painfully in the heat. There was no water on the mountain for either cooking or drinking. Everyone began to complain.

The Shang soldiers laughed heartily when they saw them camp on top of the mountain. "In this heat, they'll be dead in three days without even a fight!"

Lu Xiong did nothing but wait. The following day Jiang Ziya took 3,000 soldiers to Mount Qi. He was met by Nangong Kuo and Wu Ji at the foot of the mountain and climbed to the summit with them. It was so hot that the leaves of the willows and pines had withered and died, and thirsty birds and beasts had perished. Nevertheless, Jiang Ziya ordered Wu Ji to build a three-foot high terrace with all speed.

Meanwhile, Xin Mian had arrived from the capital with cartloads of supplies. When Jiang Ziya ordered that they be distributed among the soldiers, everyone was puzzled. Each man received a padded cotton jacket and a warm cap. "We'll die if we put them on!"

At dusk Wu Ji reported that the terrace had been completed. Jiang Ziya mounted the terrace with his long hair spread over his back and shoulders. He took his sword, bowed towards Mount Kunlun, then recited incantations and sprinkled magic water over the ground. As he muttered his spells, a violent wind swept through the forest, and dust filled the sky, making it difficult for the soldiers to open their eyes. Jiang Ziya was summoning the wind for his own purposes.

Lu Xiong was greatly pleased when the wind drove the

heat away. "When Grand Tutor Wen's army arrives, it'll be fine weather to do battle."

"His Majesty is blessed by Heaven, which has given us a cool wind," Fei Zhong and You Hun commented.

But the wind blew more and more violently. It blew yellow sand into the air and uprooted big trees. Everyone felt as cold as if it were winter. Jiang Ziya summoned the wind for three continuous days, and on the fourth day, heavy snow began to fall. The weather became colder and colder.

"How can we stand such cold weather in our thin clothes and iron armor," the Shang soldiers groaned.

The snow became steadily heavier, now falling in flakes as big as swan feathers. It soon covered the whole land and lay piled in deep drifts on the ground, turning the earth into a silvery white world.

"It's the seventh month of the year, the hottest season! Where does this heavy snow come from? Never before has this happened!" Lu Xiong complained to Fei Zhong and You Hun.

Lu Xiong was an old man, unable to endure the cold, and even Fei Zhong and You Hun found this an unexpected hardship. The whole army was nearly frozen to death, but in the Zhou camp, the soldiers donned their padded jackets and caps and gratefully thanked their prime minister.

"What's the depth of the snow now?" Jiang Ziya asked a few days later.

"On the summit here, it's about two feet, but down there, it must be four or five feet deep," Wu Ji answered.

Jiang Ziya mounted the terrace again. He loosened his hair, took his sword, and began to recite new charms. Soon the snow clouds above them dispersed, and the burning sun reappeared. All the snow on the summit melted and rushed down into the valley in roaring torrents.

Then he burned spells written on paper summoning another great wind. The temperature plummeted once more, and before long the whole area around Mount Qi was frozen into a solid ocean of ice.

Jiang Ziya walked out from his camp with some of his generals and stood on a high place overlooking the enemy camp below. The Shang flags and banners were scattered at random on the ground. Neither guards nor patrols could be seen around the camp. There was no sign of smoke from the kitchens. Jiang Ziya ordered Nangong Kuo and Wu Ji to take twenty armed men, enter the Shang camp and seize the officers.

The two generals charged into the Shang camp without meeting any resistance. All about them officers and men were frozen in the ice. They found Lu Xiong, Fei Zhong and You Hun and took them captive as easily as taking money from a purse. The three prisoners were then carried up the mountain to face Jiang Ziya.

What became of them? If you want to know, you must read the next chapter.

40

WEST QI CITY UNDER SIEGE

When Nangong Kuo and Wu Ji took them into the Zhou camp, Lu Xiong staunchly remained on his feet, but Fei Zhong and You Hun knelt before Jiang Ziya, begging for mercy.

"Lu Xiong, you should understand the times, obey the will of Heaven, and distinguish right from wrong. Now all people, high and low, know the wickedness of King Zhou. They've forsaken him and make their obeisance to us. We already possesses two-thirds of the country. Why are you so dull as to act against Heaven and bring about your own end?" Jiang Ziya demanded.

"Jiang Shang, you once served King Zhou, but now you're rebelling in search of honor and glory. I'm your captive, but I'm fed and paid by the king, and I'll die for him. There's no need for a lot of talk," Lu Xiong answered defiantly.

"Put them in prison," Jiang Ziya ordered.

Jiang Ziya mounted the earth terrace and recited incantations to disperse the clouds. The sun reappeared, and the ice at the foot of Mount Qi quickly melted. Of the 50,000 Shang soldiers, about 5,000 had been frozen to death. The survivors fled back through the five passes.

Jiang Ziya sent General Nangong Kuo back to the city to fetch King Wu. When he entered the palace, Nangong was admitted at once.

"The prime minister and his soldiers have been fighting at Mount Qi in blistering heat. There's no shade in the open wilderness, and they must be exhausted. What do you come to see me about?" King Wu asked.

第卅四回　哭年遇丙靈谷

"On the orders of the prime minister, I've come to invite you to Mount Qi."

Accompanied by civil and military officials, King Wu left the city and set off for Mount Qi. When they had traveled about twenty *li*, King Wu noticed lumps of ice floating in ditches and streams along the road. He asked Nangong Kuo the reason, and Nangong told him how Jiang Ziya had frozen the mountain. Seventy *li* from the city, they arrived at Mount Qi. Jiang Ziya came up to meet the king.

"What do you want to discuss with me?"

"I've asked you here to offer sacrifices to Mount Qi, Your Highness," Jiang Ziya answered.

He did not tell King Wu that the sacrifices were in fact to be offered to the Terrace of Creation.

He wrote an elegy in memory of those who had lost their lives and laid the altar with candles and incense burners. When King Wu burned the incense, he ordered that the three prisoners be brought in. When they arrived, he immediately ordered their execution. The three heads were then presented at the altar.

"Prime Minister! Why cut their heads off while we're worshiping Mount Qi?" King Wu asked in surprise.

"Those two heads belong to Fei Zhong and You Hun," Jiang Ziya answered.

"They were minions and deserve death," King Wu agreed.

When the ceremony was over, Jiang Ziya and King Wu led the army back to West Qi City.

Meanwhile, the remnants of Lu Xiong's army had fled into the five passes. Han Rong sent an urgent report to Zhaoge. Grand Tutor Wen was reading a report from Sanshan Pass that "Deng Jiugong has won a major victory over the South Grand Duke." When the report reached his hands, he opened it and read it, then stamped his foot in a rage.

"I never imagined that Jiang Shang would be so difficult. He's killed both Zhang Guifang and Lu Xiong. I wish that I could go to the front personally! But how can I, when the rebels in the east and south are still running amuck!" he said to himself. He asked Ji Li and Yu Qing, "Who do you think I should send to the front next?"

"Grand Tutor! West Qi has intelligent strategists, audacious generals and well-trained soldiers. Not only was Zhang Guifang defeated, but even the four holy men from Nine Dragon Island failed. In such a serious situation, we cannot but send the Mo brothers. They are certain to succeed," Ji Li replied.

The Grand Tutor was delighted. "If anyone can defeat West Qi, it's these four men!"

He immediately issued orders appointing the four Mo generals as commanders on the West Qi front, and Generals Hu Sheng and Hu Lei to replace them at the Good Dream Pass. When the order came, the Mo brothers burst into laughter.

"Grand Tutor Wen's fought numerous battles. Why is he so upset about Jiang Shang and Huang Feihu! Why use a knife for slaughtering oxen to kill a chicken!"

They took 100,000 soldiers and set off to the roar of cannons and the war cries of their men. Their pennants fluttered boldly, and their weapons gleamed in the sun. They marched over mountains until they passed Peach Blossom Peak and arrived at the north gate of West Qi City. There the Mo generals ordered the army to halt.

After the victory at Mount Qi, West Qi's military forces were stronger than ever, and many more areas pledged their allegiance to King Wu. One day, a patrolman came in to report. "The four Mo brothers have arrived at the north gate."

When Jiang Ziya turned to his generals for measures to repulse them, Huang Feihu anxiously moved forward.

"Prime Minister, the Mo brothers have all learned one kind of magic or another. I'm afraid they'll be very difficult to deal with. The eldest one is Mo Liqing. He's twenty feet tall, and he's got a magic Green Cloud Sword, stamped with an 'earth, water, metal, fire and wind' charm. The wind that it invokes is dark and conceals thousands of swords and spears. Anyone caught in it is instantly cut to pieces. It simultaneously produces innumerable flames and a black smoke that covers the sky. Whoever it touches is turned to ashes. The second brother is Mo Lihong. He's got a magic Universe Muddling Umbrella, decorated with jade and pearls. The charm 'wrap up Heaven and earth' on it is written with pearls. When it's opened, the sky and earth are plunged into complete darkness. If it is twirled, Heaven and earth tremble. The third one's Mo Lihai, who carries a lute with four strings that represent earth, water, wind and fire. When they're plucked, fire and wind appear much like with the Green Cloud Sword. The youngest of the four is Mo Lishou. He has a magic spotted ermine in his bag. When the animal's released, it immediately transforms itself into a white winged elephant and devours anybody in its path. It won't be easy for us to defeat them."

"How do you know them so well, General Huang?" Jiang Ziya asked.

"Because they were under my command when I fought in the East Sea district. I am telling you the truth."

Jiang Ziya became deeply worried.

A few days later, Mo Liqing said to his three brothers, "By order of His Majesty, we've come here to attack the rebels. It's been three days already, and we must take action now. As Grand Tutor Wen has honored us, we can't let him down."

"Let's meet Jiang Shang tomorrow and destroy him in a single battle," Mo Lihong said assuredly.

They drank happily that day, and the following morning, took their men to the city, demanding that Jiang Ziya come out to meet them.

In view of what Huang Feihu had said, Jiang Ziya hesitated. But Muzha, Jinzha and Nezha said, "Uncle! We can't give up the fight just because of what General Huang said! Heaven is on our side. We must adapt to every change of circumstance and not be cowards!"

Jiang Ziya came to his senses at once and ordered that they march out of the city. He bowed politely. "Are you the four Mo brothers?"

"Jiang Shang," replied Mo Liqing rudely. "You don't keep to your dukedom but take pleasure in creating chaos. You place traitors under your protection and disobey the orders of the government. You beheaded our commanders and hung their heads on your city gates. Now that we've arrived, why don't you lay down your weapons and declare unconditional surrender? It'll be too late for you to regret it when we've leveled your city and destroyed everything!"

"You're wrong, Commander. We're ministers appointed by the Shang Dynasty. We obey the law and observe the rites. We aren't rebels at all, but we've been invaded more than once by His Majesty. He's humiliated himself through the defeats suffered here. We're not aggressors. We haven't sent a single soldier to the five passes. We won't accept the accusations you've made," Jiang Ziya answered calmly.

"How dare you speak such nonsense! Don't you realize that you're facing immediate destruction?" Mo Liqing said furiously.

He strode forward to attack Jiang Ziya but was intercepted by Nangong Kuo. Mo Lihong then rushed forward but was met by Xin Jia. When Mo Lihai plunged in, Nezha flew at him on his Wind-Fire Wheels. Mo Lishou also rushed in wielding his staves, but Wu Ji galloped up and intercepted him. The battle raged fiercely from early morning till noon.

Nezha took out his Universal Ring and threw it at Mo Lihai. When Mo Lihong saw it, he immediately leapt away from Xin Jia, opened his Universe Muddling Umbrella, and shook it slightly. In a twinkling the Universal Ring dropped straight into the umbrella. Jinzha saw what had happened and took out his Invisible Dragon Stake, but it was taken away by the umbrella too. Jiang Ziya then cast his Staff for Beating Gods in the air, but he did not know that it was effective only against gods and not against immortals nor ordinary human beings. As the Mo brothers were to become Buddhist immortals and serve as the four Heavenly Kings one thousand years later, the staff was powerless. It was also taken by the umbrella. Jiang Ziya was deeply alarmed.

Mo Liqing dodged away from Nangong Kuo and seized the chance to shake the Green Cloud Sword on his back three times. It instantly poured forth a heavy black smoke that rang with the noise of thousands of swords, axes and lances. In moments, thousands of Jiang Ziya's men lay dead or wounded.

Seeing that his eldest brother had used the Green Cloud Sword, Mo Lihong opened his Universe Muddling Umbrella again and twirled it three times. Immediately, the sky darkened and fierce flames soared high in the air. A violent fire raged over the battlefield. Mo Lihai plucked the strings of his lute to intensify the attack. When Mo Lishou released his ermine, it transformed into a white elephant, devouring the Zhou soldiers left and right. Jiang Ziya was completely defeated. His men fled, leaving numerous wounded and dead behind.

In this first battle, the Zhou army lost 10,000 soldiers and nine generals while eight out of every ten survivors was injured. Jiang Ziya fled on his nondescript. Jinzha and Muzha escaped riding dust clouds, and Nezha raced away on his Wind-Fire Wheels. Dragon Beard Tiger fled through water.

Back in the city, Jiang Ziya counted the losses and found that most of his generals were wounded and nine had been killed. Six of them were princes, sons of Prince Wen. He was stricken with grief. At the same time, the Shang army returned to their camp dancing and singing. The four generals immediately held a military conference.

"Surround the city and attack with all our strength until we get hold of Jiang Ziya and King Wu," Mo Lihong said optimistically.

"You're absolutely right, Brother," Mo Liqing said.

The following day they surrounded West Qi City. Jiang Ziya dared not encounter them again. He ordered that the boards of truce be hung on the watch towers and refused to answer any challenge. But Mo Liqing disregarded the boards.

"Put up scaling ladders all round the city walls and use the cannons," he ordered.

The situation in the city became critical.

Jiang Ziya put up a strong resistance. He mounted the wall with Jinzha, Muzha, Nezha, Huang Feihu, Dragon Beard Tiger and the other unwounded generals. They defended the city with lime bottles, stone balls, burning arrows, and long spears day and night. After three days, the Shang army had suffered heavy losses but had still failed to break through the city defences.

"Withdraw the army," Mo Lihong ordered.

That night, the four brothers discussed the situation again.

"As a disciple on Mount Kunlun, Jiang Shang's well-trained in war tactics. We can't take the city by force, so we'd better besiege them until they run out of supplies. We'll prevent them from getting any reinforcements from outside, and the city will fall of its own accord," Mo Lihong suggested.

"You're right, Brother," said Mo Liqing.

But after two months, and the besieged city was still holding out. They became worried.

"It's been nearly three months, but we still haven't captured the city. What shall we do? We've got 100,000 soldiers, and our expenses are high. We'd be ashamed if Grand Tutor Wen should reprimand us. How about this: We all send our magic weapons into the air tonight and destroy West Qi City in one blow. It seems the only sensible way to go now," Mo Liqing proposed.

"Excellent idea. Let's take action tonight, Brother," Mo Lishou agreed.

Jiang Ziya was discussing with Huang Feihu and the other generals about how to repulse the Shang army when a sudden wind whipped through the hall, snapping the pole of a big banner in two. This strange phenomenon alarmed him. He quickly burned incense and made a divination with gold coins. He read the results, and his face turned pale with fright. He immediately bathed, changed his robes, burned more incense, and kowtowed towards Mount Kunlun. Hair loosened and sword in hand, he moved the whole North Sea over to cover West Qi City.

At the very same time, the Mo brothers' plan had also been discovered by Heavenly Primogenitor. He sprinkled a few drops of Divine Water of the Three Lights from his glazed vase over West Qi City where it floated on the surface of the sea.

Early that night, Mo Liqing waved his Green Cloud Sword, Mo Lihong twirled his umbrella, Mo Lihai plucked the strings of his lute, and Mo Lishou released his ermine. Dark clouds rapidly covered the sky, and a cold fog enveloped the earth. Thunderclaps rang out as if Heaven itself was about to collapse. The four brothers played their magic weapons, expecting to achieve great success and return to the capital in triumph the next day. They did not return satisfied to their camp until dawn.

Jiang Ziya sent the water back to the sea at sunrise, and the city reappeared as usual. The Shang soldiers rushed to the camp and reported the news to the four brothers. They were astonished and went to see for themselves. Sure enough, they found the report to be true. They were at a loss what to do next and had no choice but to continue the siege of the city.

Though he had saved the city from disaster that once, Jiang Ziya could not put down his defenses. Time passed swiftly, and another two months elapsed. He still had no way of repulsing the four generals. Then one day the officer in charge of the grain stores reported, "We're running short of food. Our supplies will only last about ten more days."

"What shall we do? This is more serious than if they attacked us," Jiang Ziya murmured, greatly worried.

"Prime Minister, you may demand that the rich open their private granaries and each lend us 50,000 pecks of grain. We'll return it with interest when we've defeated the enemy. That's the only solution now," Huang Feihu suggested.

"That will never do, General. It would create panic among the people and army. Let's consider it more carefully. We still have ten days."

Eight days passed. Jiang Ziya was extremely worried. But then a guard reported, "Two young Taoist lads request to see you."

When they were ushered in, they bowed and greeted Jiang Ziya, "How do you do, Uncle."

"Where do you come from? What instructions do you have for me?" Jiang Ziya asked as he returned their salutations.

"We are disciples of the Heavenly Master of Divine Virtue. My name's Han Dulong, the Poisonous Dragon and he's named Xue Ehu, the Wicked Tiger. By order of our master, we've come here to offer you food supplies."

"Where are they?"

"We're carrying them on us, but I'll show you a short letter from our master first," Han Dulong said.

He took the letter from a silk purse and handed it to Jiang Ziya, who read it carefully.

"My master told me that highly talented men would come to my aid in time of crisis, and your arrival today has proven his word," Jiang Ziya said, delighted.

When he asked them for the promised food supply, one of them took a container from his leopard-skin bag. It was full of rice, but could contain no more than a peck at most. The generals held back their laughter with difficulty. But Jiang Ziya asked Han Dulong to take the rice to the city's three granaries. About three hours later, the officer in charge came in. "All the barns are now overflowing with rice."

At this, Jiang Ziya said happily, "A blessing from Heaven on King Wu!"

They now had sufficient food to maintain resistance but were still unable to beat the Mo generals. Jiang Ziya strengthened the city defenses but dared not take any other action.

Another two months passed. As nearly a whole year had gone by, and they had still failed to take the city, the four brothers wrote a report to Grand Tutor Wen, saying that Jiang Ziya was not only good at offense but also skillful at defense, and that was why they had not won ever after so many months.

One day, Jiang Ziya was talking with his generals when a guard came in. "A Taoist at the gate wishes to see you."

When the visitor was ushered in, those present saw that he wore a cloud-fanning hat, a robe with a silk belt and a pair of hemp shoes. He bowed at the door and offered his greetings, addressing Jiang as "uncle."

"Where do you come from?"

"I'm a disciple of Jade Tripod. By order of my master, I've come to place myself at your service. My name's Yang Jian." Jiang Ziya was very pleased. He introduced Yang Jian to his generals and then took him to meet King Wu. On their return, Yang Jian asked, "Who are the generals besieging the city?"

Jiang Ziya told him.

"Since I'm here, you can remove the board of truce. I'd

like to meet them and try them out. If I don't do battle with them, how can I find out how to cope with them?"

Jiang Ziya agreed and ordered his men to remove the board of truce from the city wall. A scout immediately reported to the Mo brothers that "West Qi's just removed their board of truce from the city wall."

They were delighted and left their camp straightway to give a challenge. Jiang Ziya ordered Yang Jian to meet the challenge with Nezha.

The Mo brothers saw a general emerge from the city. He wore a cloud-fanning hat and a robe with a silk belt, rode a white horse, and carried a long lance. It was difficult to tell whether he was a Taoist or a layman.

"Who are you?" Mo Liqing asked.

"I'm Yang Jian, nephew of Prime Minister Jiang. How dare you come here hounding the people with your witchcraft! I'll teach you a lesson, and you'll die without a place to bury your corpses!"

He galloped forward and stabbed at them with his lance. The brothers had had no chance to fight for half a year and ran out on foot to engage him. They surrounded him and fought fiercely under the city wall.

As they battled, General Ma Chenglong arrived with food supplies from Chuzhou. He found that his path was blocked and spurred his chestnut horse forward.

"Here I come!" he cried.

Whirling his twin cutlasses, he fought into the circle against the Mo generals. When he saw that another Zhou general had joined the battle, Mo Lishou hurriedly released his ermine into the air. It transformed into a huge white elephant and, swooping down, swallowed half of General Ma Chenglong in a single gulp.

Seeing this, Yang Jian was secretly delighted. "So that's the devil and the cause of all the trouble. I'll deal with him!"

The Mo generals did not know that Yang Jian had great magic powers. When the spotted ermine flew up into the air again, it swallowed half of Yang Jian. Nezha saw it all, and retreated into the city, rushing to the prime minister's mansion.

"Yang Jian's been devoured by the spotted ermine," he told Jiang Ziya, who became extremely worried.

Returning in triumph, the Mo brothers drank together joyfully. Early that night, Mo Lishou suggested, "Brothers, I'll send the ermine into the city tonight to devour Jiang Ziya and King Wu. Once that's done, we can return home victoriously, and we won't need to waste our time continuing the siege."

As the four generals were already drunk, they all talked wildly. "You're right, Brother! Do it at once," Mo Liqing agreed readily.

Mo Lishou took the ermine from his bag. "Darling! You can do no greater service then to eat both Jiang Ziya and King Wu."

Released into the sky, the ermine flew off and disappeared. But the ermine was a wild animal. How could it realize that by swallowing Yang Jian it had brought disaster on itself? Yang Jian had great magic powers. He could transform into seventy-two different forms and was to become the Divine Immortal of Purity and Decency.

In the belly of the ermine, he heard everything the four generals had said. As the ermine flew towards West Qi, he grabbed its heart and squeezed. The beast fell from the sky with a shrill cry. Yang Jian swelled his body until the ermine split in two; he then jumped out. He returned to Jiang Ziya's mansion later that night and asked to be admitted. Jiang Ziya was still discussing with Nezha how to deal with the Mo brothers when a guard announced his arrival.

Jiang Ziya gasped in astonishment, "How can a dead man return to life!"

He sent Nezha to investigate. Nezha met Yang Jian at the gate. "Brother Yang! You were killed, but how can you come back here?"

"Though we both have magic powers, we're able to do different things, that's why. Hurry! Let me in. I've got something important to tell our uncle."

When Yang Jian entered the hall, Jiang Ziya asked in surprise, "You were killed on the battlefield early this morning. How can you return again? You must possess the art of restoring yourself to life!"

"I was in the belly of the ermine. I heard Mo Lishou telling it to come to the city and devour you and King Wu. But I killed the beast on the way, and I've returned here to report the matter," Yang Jian answered.

"With highly talented men like you, what have we to fear?" Jiang Ziya said happily.

"I must return to the Shang camp," Yang Jian said.

"But how will you get back, Brother?" Nezha asked.

"Don't worry! I've mastered the art of transforming myself into anything I please: a hill, a stream, gold, silver, copper or iron. I can transform myself into any living creature: bird, phoenix, dragon, lion or tiger. I can effect the transformation in the twinkling of an eye," Yang Jian answered.

"Show us one or two of your transformations," Jiang Ziya requested.

Yang Jian gave his body a shake and turned into the spotted ermine. He pranced around the floor, filling Nezha with delight. Yang Jian was about to leave when Jiang Ziya stopped him.

"Wait a minute, Yang Jian. Don't be in such a hurry. As you've got the skill, why don't you steal the weapons from the Mo brothers?"

Yang Jian immediately flew out of the city, entered the Shang camp, and landed on the canopy of the Mo brothers' tent. Mo Lishou saw it and took it in his hands. He looked at it closely but was disappointed to find no sign of its having devoured anybody.

Late that night, the Mo generals drunkenly entered their tent and collapsed into bed. They were soon asleep and snoring like thunder. Yang Jian saw his opportunity. He jumped out of the bag and tried to get hold of the weapons hanging on the tent frame. As he grabbed the Universe Muddling Umbrella, he knocked the other two weapons onto the floor. The noise roused the four generals, but in their drunken stupor, they assumed the weapons had fallen because their hooks were loose. They carelessly picked them up and hooked them back onto the tent frame then fell back into sleep.

Yang Jian flew to West Qi City and gave the umbrella to

Jiang Ziya. Nezha and his brothers came forward to inspect it as Yang Jian returned to the Shang camp. He crawled back into Mo Lishou's leopard-skin bag.

Early the next morning, the Mo brothers rose at the drum signal, and each went to collect his weapon. When Mo Lihong found his umbrella missing, he cried out in fright and called in his generals to question them.

"How could a spy have got in? The camps are so strictly guarded that even a speck of dust could not get in unnoticed," the generals replied.

"That is the weapon I have relied on to achieve great victories," Mo Lihong shouted. "What can I do now without it?"

The four brothers were greatly disheartened by the loss and were in no mood to give any challenges that day.

Meanwhile in the Purple Sun Cave on Mount Green Peak, Virtue of the Pure Void felt a rush of blood to the heart. He ordered Golden Haze Lad, "Tell your fellow disciple to come and see me at once."

Obeying his orders, Golden Haze Lad brought in Huang Tianhua. When he entered the cave, Huang Tianhua knelt down before the Green Touring Bed on which the immortal was sitting. "Master, what are your orders?"

"You'd better get ready to leave. Go to West Qi and serve King Wu with your father and brothers. But first come with me."

Following his master to the peach garden, Huang Tianhua was given two hammers as his weapons. Under the immortal's guidance, he soon learned to wield them with amazing skill and dexterity.

"I'll give you my jade unicorn and my Fire Dragon Javelin. However, don't ever forget your Taoist origins and what I've taught you," his master warned him solemnly.

"How could I dare!" Huang Tianhua answered unhesitatingly.

He bade farewell to his master and left the cave on the jade unicorn. At a gentle pat on the horn, the unicorn immediately rose and traveled swiftly on the clouds and wind. He arrived in West Qi in a moment. Huang Tianhua dismounted, asked the gateman to report his arrival to Jiang Ziya, and was ushered in.

He bowed to Jiang Ziya. "Uncle, on my master's orders, I'm here to place myself at your service."

Jiang Ziya was about to ask where he came from when Huang Feihu said, "He is a disciple of Virtue of the Pure Void and my eldest son, Huang Tianhua."

Jiang Ziya was greatly pleased. "General, how lucky you are to have a son that studies the Way with an immortal," he congratulated Huang Feihu.

When he got to his father's home, Tianhua drank happily with his family. He ate only vegetables when he was on Mount Green Peak, but now he feasted on meat. He fixed his hair in two coils, put on a hat, and wore golden armor over a scarlet robe and a jade belt.

The next morning he went to see Jiang Ziya. Jiang Ziya was surprised to see him dressed as a prince. "Huang Tianhua, you're a Taoist. Why do you ignore this and change your clothing? Though I'm prime minister, I never forget Mount Kunlun and still dress as a Taoist. At least tie this silk cord around your waist."

Huang Tianhua obediently took the silk cord and tied it up as a belt. "As I came for the Mo brothers, I have to dress as a general. I could never forget my Taoist background."

"You must be very careful. They're highly skilled in witchcraft," Jiang Ziya warned him.

"My master gave me clear instructions about how to take care of them. I don't fear them at all."

With Jiang Ziya's approval, Huang Tianhua mounted his jade unicorn and rode out of the city, hammers in hand. Galloping to the gates of the Shang camp, he gave a challenge.

If you want to learn the outcome of that encounter, please read the next chapter.

第四十回 闻太师并伐西岐

41

GRAND TUTOR WEN
ATTACKS WEST QI

When they heard that a general from West Qi was challenging them, the brothers hurried out. They saw a young general riding a jade unicorn. He was about sixteen years old and wore a gold helmet and a scarlet robe covered with gold chain mail. He held two silver hammers in his hands.

Mo Liqing moved up. "Who are you?"

"I'm none other than Huang Tianhua, the eldest son of Prince Huang Feihu. By order of Prime Minister Jiang, I've come to take you alive."

Greatly infuriated, Mo Liqing strode up to attack Huang Tianhua. Huang Tianhua fought back with his hammers. After twenty rounds, Mo Liqing hurled his White Jade Ring at Huang Tianhua, striking him heavily on the back, and knocking him from his jade unicorn. As Mo Liqing rushed forward to cut his head off, Nezha flew forward on his Wind-Fire Wheels to intercept him.

"Don't hurt my brother!" he shouted, and engaged Mo Liqing.

As they fought lance against lance, Mo Liqing hurled his White Jade Ring at Nezha. Without the least hesitation, Nezha tossed up his Universal Ring to meet it. As the Universal Ring was made of gold and the White Jade Ring jade, the gold shattered the jade into pieces.

"Damn you, Nezha! How can I let you live!" Mo Liqing cried.

He and Mo Lihong rushed forward in a joined attack, but Nezha was aware of the danger. He withdrew into the city before Mo Lihai could play his lute.

Huang Feihu was overcome with grief when he saw Huang Tianhua dead. "How could I imagine that you would be killed so soon!"

He lay Huang Tianhua's corpse in front of Jiang Ziya's mansion to await burial.

Jiang Ziya was stricken with grief too. He was alone in his mansion when a Taoist lad came to the gate and requested to see him. When the lad was ushered in, he bowed. "I've been sent here by Virtue of the Pure Void to carry Huang Tianhua back to the mountain."

Jiang Ziya was delighted at the news.

The White Cloud Lad carried Huang Tianhua's corpse to Mount Green Peak and laid it before the Purple Sun Cave. When his master walked out and saw him lying still, he directed the White Cloud Lad to fetch some water. He then dissolve an elixir pill, pried Huang's mouth open with a sword, and poured the solution down his throat. An hour or two later, Huang Tianhua returned to life. He opened his eyes and saw his master.

"How do I meet you here, Master?" Huang Tianhua asked.

"Brute! It's a sin to eat meat. It's a sin to take off your Taoist dress and forget your origins. It's only for Jiang Ziya's sake that I brought you back to life!"

Huang Tianhua felt ashamed and kowtowed before his master. The immortal then took something out and handed it to him. "Hurry back to West Qi and meet the brothers again. You'll score great success with this magic weapon. I'll be there soon, too."

Huang Tianhua bade farewell to his master, mounted his dust cloud, and got back to West Qi a few moments later. He was admitted to the Prime Minister's mansion and repeated what his master had told him. Huang Feihu was overjoyed to see his son restored to life.

The following day, Huang Tianhua mounted his unicorn, rode out of the city, and once again challenged the Mo generals.

"Today I'll fight you all to the death to determine once

and for all who is the best man!" Huang Tianhua cried when they had arrayed themselves before him.

Mo Liqing rushed in to attack with his lance, and Huang met him with his two hammers. After several rounds, Huang Tianhua gave up ground and began to flee on his unicorn. Mo Liqing set off in hot pursuit.

Seeing him close behind, Huang Tianhua quickly hung his hammers on the saddle and took out the silk bag his master had given him. From inside the bag he drew out a shining nail, about seven and a half inches long. It was the Heart Penetrating Nail. He hurled it back at Mo Liqing. With a flash of golden light, the nail struck Mo Liqing in the breast and went right through his heart. With a scream of agony, Mo Liqing fell to the ground.

When he saw his brother dead, Mo Lihong rushed out with his halberd. Huang Tianhua recovered the nail and threw it straight at him. Mo Lihong had no time to dodge, and it went right through him.

"You little brute! What do you use to hit my brothers?" Mo Lihai shouted.

Br 'efore he could make a move, his life was also ended by the nail. It was destined by fate that the four Heavenly Kings should lose their lives at the hands of Huang Tianhua, who was later to be created Bing Ling Gong, the Spiritual God.

His three brothers all dead, Mo Lishou put his hand into his bag to release the ermine, but he did not know that the ermine was really Yang Jian in an assumed form. As he reached into the bag, Yang Jian snapped at his hand, biting his fingers off. Mo Lishou screamed in pain, and Huang Tianhua's nail flew through the air for the fourth time, piercing him through the heart.

While Huang Tianhua was busy beheading the four Mo generals, the spotted ermine ran out of the bag and, in a gust of wind, returned to human form. Huang Tianhua did not know him. "Who are you?"

"I'm Yang Jian. On Uncle Jiang's orders I stayed inside

the bag as an ermine to help from within the Shang camp. You did a wonderful job, finishing them all off!"

As they talked, Nezha came over on his Wind-Fire Wheels. "I'm overjoyed, Brothers. You've won a great victory today."

They congratulated one another and returned to the city together. They then entered the prime minister's mansion and reported the victory. Jiang Ziya was delighted and ordered that the heads of the four Mo generals be hung on the city wall as a warning to invaders.

The soldiers that the Mo brothers had brought with them fled back to Sishui Pass. Han Rong was greatly alarmed. "Who would have thought that Jiang Shang would prove such a formidable opponent!"

He hurriedly wrote a report to Zhaoge. Grand Tutor Wen was quite happily reading documents in his office. One report said that "General Dou Rong of Youhun Pass has won several victories over the East Grand Duke." Another report read "General Deng Chanyu, daughter of Commander Deng Jiugong at Sanshan Pass, has repulsed the South Grand Duke." But he froze at the report from Han Rong.

"How dare Jiang Shang insult His Majesty like this! How could I have guessed that the four generals would all lose their lives! Oh, what a haughty devil you are, Jiang Shang!" The eye in the middle of his forehead opened wide, shooting forth a white beam of light about two feet long. He fumed with anger. "Right! The east and south are now gradually being brought under control. Tomorrow I'll see His Majesty and seek permission to go personally to West Qi. Only then can I be assured of defeating the enemy."

The following day, when he presented his report, King Zhou gave his immediate approval. "I appreciate it very much that the Grand Tutor is to punish the rebels on my behalf."

He ordered that Grand Tutor Wen be presented with the yellow scepter and white axes that represented royal authority. On an auspicious date, Grand Tutor Wen sacrificed to the grand banners and started off to West Qi. ‑

Before his departure, King Zhou filled a cup and handed it to him. He received it with a bow. "Your old minister has to exert all his efforts to subdue the rebels and restore peace. During my absence, I earnestly hope that Your Majesty will listen to the loyal, be diligent, and live in harmony with the ministers. I'll be able to return in about half a year."

"I've got no worries about you. I'll be expecting your victorious return, Grand Tutor."

King Zhou saw him to his mount. But the unicorn had been idle for months. It screamed and reared when the Grand Tutor mounted, sending him tumbling to the ground. His attendants helped him up. Grand Tutor Wen was straightening his hat and robe when Wang Bian, a junior minister, came over.

"Grand Tutor, it's not a good omen. It might be better to send someone else."

"Not at all, sir! A subject should work for the king without a thought of his home, and fight on the battlefield without a thought of his own life. To be wounded or even killed is nothing for a general, a quite ordinary experience. The unicorn's long been idle. That's why it threw me. Please don't say anything more about it."

He remounted and set off, taking his 300,000 soldiers across the Yellow River to Mianchi County where he was welcomed by Zhang Kui. Grand Tutor Wen asked, "Which is the shortest route to West Qi, General?"

"You can cut 200 *li* off the march if you go via the Green Dragon Pass."

The big army set off once more, marching through the Green Dragon Pass to the sound of drums and gongs. Beyond the pass, the rugged mountain paths narrowed, permitting only one horse and rider through at a time. The marching was difficult and risky. He realized it would have been faster to take the route directly through the five passes, but it was already too late for him to regret his decision.

After several days, they got to the Yellow Flower Mountain. It was green and lush with pine trees that covered the peaks and cliffs, bordered the streams and shaded the caves. In spring, flowers turned the mountain a fiery red. In summer, the lush vegetation, moistened by the rain and illuminated by bright moonlight, made the mountain look as if it was made of blue jade and emerald. In autumn, yellow flowers and red leaves turned the mountain into a blaze of colors. In winter, when snow drifts lay deep and water froze into crystals, the mountain seemed to be covered with silver and white jade. Winding streams crisscrossed across the hillsides, and beautiful birds sang sweetly in the trees.

As it was steep and perilous, Grand Tutor Wen ordered his army to halt at the foot of the mountain and climbed to the summit by himself. There he found an immense area of flat ground which seemed to have been used as a battlefield.

"How wonderful! Should Zhaoge be blessed with peace, how happy I would be to enjoy my remaining years in this tranquility."

He was admiring the green bamboos and ancient pine trees when he heard the beating of gongs. He looked back and found that troops were marching up the mountain. There was a general on horseback with an indigo face, cinnabar hair, and a mouth full of long tusks. He wore a red robe and gold armor and carried a huge battle-axe.

As Grand Tutor Wen watched them attentively, his scarlet robe, black unicorn and two gold staves were noticed by a patrolman, "Your Honor, there's a man on the hillside above spying on us."

Looking up, the general saw Grand Tutor Wen watching their movements. He angrily spurred his horse up the slope. Grand Tutor Wen felt pleased with his bold ferocity. "We could do with this man at West Qi," he thought.

As he pondered, the general galloped up before him. "Who are you? How dare you spy on our mountain hideout?"

"I like this quiet place. I wish that I could build a hut here and recite the Taoist scriptures day and night. Would you consent, General?"

The man became angry. "You damned Taoist devil," he cursed and charged at him with his axe.

The Grand Tutor met the assault with his two gold staffs, and the two fought back and forth vigorously.

Grand Tutor Wen was a great warrior. He had experi-

enced hundreds of battles and thousands of warriors, and naturally thought nothing of this opponent. Yet the man could
wield his axe quite skillfully. "I really should take this man
with me to West Qi. Though not outstanding, he may be useful to me."

He seized the first chance to pull out of the fight and galloped off towards the east. As soon as he heard the man close
behind him, he pointed at the ground with a gold staff, and a
high gold wall instantly sprung up around the general, trapping
him within. Grand Tutor Wen returned to his original place,
dismounted, and sat on a rock with his back against a pine
tree, watching for further developments.

Now this mountain was occupied by a large band of outlaws under four chiefs. When the first was taken, an outlaw
hurried back. "The great chief's been drawn inside a yellow
vapor by a Taoist and has completely disappeared."

"Where's the Taoist now?" the third and the fourth
asked.

"He's sitting on the mountaintop."

In a great rage, the two mounted and rushed up the mountain with a battle cry. As they approached, Grand Tutor Wen
mounted, pointed at them with his gold staff and shouted,
"Don't be in such a hurry, Generals."

The two chiefs were astonished to find that their opponent
had three eyes, but they boldly moved closer. "Who are you?
How dare you act so barbarously here? What have you done
to our eldest brother? Send him back, and we'll spare your
life!"

"The fool with an indigo face? He offended me, and I
killed him with my staff. What do you two come here for? All
I want is this mountain. Would you consent?"

The two chiefs gave a roar of fury and charged at Grand
Tutor Wen, one wielding a lance, the other two ridged staves.

As before, Grand Tutor Wen gave up ground after a few
rounds and galloped off towards the south. As the two pursued
him, he pointed at them with his gold staffs. In an instant,
Zhang, the third chief, was surrounded by water and Tao, the
fourth, was surrounded by a forest.

Grand Tutor Wen once more returned to the tree and sat down.

The second chief was collecting grain at the back of the mountain when some outlaws hurried to him. "Chief! Disaster! The three chiefs have all been killed by a Taoist."

Roaring like thunder, Xin, the second chief, flapped his wings and soared into the air. He hovered over Grand Tutor Wen. "You damned specter! How can I let you live after you've killed all my brothers!"

Grand Tutor Wen looked at him with his middle eye and found him fearsome and evil in appearance: He wore a tiger-head hat and had a face like a jujube with long fangs protruding from his upper jaw. He swooped down to attack Grand Tutor Wen with a pair of hammers.

The Grand Tutor thought with delight, "This is just the heroic man I want!"

As Xin struck at his head with the hammers, the Grand Tutor blocked with his gold staves. After a few rounds, Grand Tutor Wen ran away to the east. Xin pursued him, crying, "Where are you off to, devil? I won't let you get off!"

"It'll be impossible to capture this man with metal, wood, water, fire or earth," Grand Tutor Wen reasoned quickly. He pointed at a rock beside the path with his staff and ordered a yellow-scarved genie, "Lift this rock and trap that man beneath it."

The genie did as he was told, and in a moment Xin was lying beneath the rock. Grand Tutor Wen raised his staff as if to beat him on the head.

"Mercy! I failed to recognize your talent and offended you. I would be deeply grateful if you would kindly spare my life."

Grand Tutor Wen placed his staff on Xin's head. "Of course, you don't know me. I'm not a Taoist, but Grand Tutor Wen of Zhaoge. I've been sent by His Majesty to subdue West Qi and am just passing through. I punished the fellow with the indigo face because he attempted to hurt me without any reason. Now tell me which do you want: to live or to die?"

"Grand Tutor! I didn't know you were passing by this mountain. Otherwise I would have come out to welcome you. I apologize, and beg you to pardon us."

"If you would like to live, you must take me as your teacher. Follow me and place yourself at my disposal when we reach West Qi. If you achieve great merit, you'll be rewarded with a high official position and a jade belt to wear round your waist," Grand Tutor Wen promised.

"If Your Honor's willing to bestow such a favor on me, I'm certainly willing to follow you," Xin Huan replied.

Grand Tutor Wen pointed at the rock with his staff and ordered the genie to remove it. Xin Huan was so exhausted that he could not get up at once, but after a long rest, he staggered to his feet and kowtowed before his conqueror. Grand Tutor Wen helped him up and then sat down on a stone, leaning against a pine tree. Xin Huan stood beside him.

"How many men do you have on the Yellow Flower Mountain, Xin Huan?" the Grand Tutor asked.

"This mountain has an area of about sixty square *li*, and we've got more than 10,000 outlaws here with plentiful food and equipment supplies."

Grand Tutor Wen was greatly pleased. Xin Huan knelt down and pleaded, "I beg you to have mercy on the other three chiefs and spare their lives. They'll certainly do their best to return your kindness."

"Why do you beg for mercy on their behalf so earnestly?"

"Though we're from different families with different surnames, we're just like real brothers."

"Since you're so loyal to your friends, I promise to let all of them live. Now just move a short distance away," Grand Tutor Wen directed.

The Grand Tutor opened his palm, and there was a clap of thunder that shook the mountain. The three chiefs rubbed their eyes as if waking from a deep sleep. In the twinkling of an eye, the golden wall that enclosed Deng, the water that surrounded Zhang, and the trees that imprisoned Tao had all disappeared. As they returned on their horses, they caught sight of Xin Huan standing beside Grand Tutor Wen.

"Brother! Seize that accursed Taoist at once," Deng Zhong cried.

"Catch that Taoist devil, don't let him get away," Zhang and Tao echoed him.

What became of Grand Tutor Wen? If you want to know, please read the next chapter.

SURRENDER OF THE BANDIT CHIEFS

As they charged angrily at Grand Tutor Wen, Xin Huan hurriedly intercepted them. "Brothers, don't be so rude. Get down from your horses and greet Grand Tutor Wen from Zhaoge."

When they learned that it was Grand Tutor Wen, Deng, Zhang and Tao scrambled down from their saddles and knelt on the ground. "Grand Tutor! We've always admired you, but never had the opportunity to meet you. Heaven has willed that you pass by this mountain! But we've offended you and begged your pardon."

Grand Tutor Wen was led to the outlaws' camp, and then he took a seat. "Please tell me your names. I'm honored to have you all with me."

"We're sworn brothers. I'm Deng Zhong, the eldest. This is Xin Huan, the second. The third is Zhang Jie and the youngest Tao Rong. There's been so much unrest in the kingdom that we came here to seek peace. It's not our wish to remain outlaws."

"Come to the front under my command. Once you've achieved success, you'll all be ministers in the government. Why bury your talents here in the greenwood?"

"If you're willing to take us with you, we're most willing to go," Xin Huan answered.

"The state would indeed be fortunate to have your service. How many men do you have?"

"We've got more than 10,000 men here," Xin Huan answered.

"Tell everyone what we're going to do. We'll take all

第四十一回　黄花山文聘辛张陶

those who're willing, but give money and food to those who wish to go home," Grand Tutor Wen instructed.

Xin Huan did as he was told. Everyone was pleased to receive a share of the accumulated wealth. In the end, there were about 7,000 men and 30,000 piculs of grain and fodder to go with the Grand Tutor.

Grand Tutor Wen, delighted to have obtained four new generals, set off once more with his combined troops. One day he happened to look up to see a stone monument on the roadside inscribed with "Dragon Extinction Peak." He immediately halted, and then sat there in complete silence with fear and alarm on his face.

Not understanding the reason for his fear, Deng Zhong asked, "What's the matter, Grand Tutor?"

"I studied with Mother Golden Spirit at the Green Touring Palace for fifty years. When she sent me down to help the Shang Dynasty, I asked her about my future. She told me that disaster will befall you should you see the character 'extinction.' To come across this character now makes me a little worried."

Deng and other three generals laughed. "You're wrong, Grand Tutor. How can the fate of a hero be determined by one character? Heaven favors the good. With your virtue and talent, you're sure to win the day in West Qi. Remember the old proverb: 'When there's no doubt, there's no need for divination'."

Grand Tutor Wen neither smiled nor spoke. The army resumed its rapid march, and a few days later, a scout reported, "Grand Tutor, we've reached the south gate of West Qi City."

On the Grand Tutor's orders, the army halted and camped just beyond the city wall. Jiang Ziya immediately received news of their arrival.

"I didn't get the chance to meet Grand Tutor Wen when I was at Zhaoge. Now that he's here, I must go and see how he manages his army," he told his generals.

He mounted the city wall to observe the enemy camp and could not help but admiring its awe-inspiring display of weapons and pennants and its ingenious layout. He looked for a long time. "I've often heard that Grand Tutor Wen's a highly talented general, but what I see today exceeds even his reputation!"

He returned to his mansion and summoned all his generals.

"Don't worry, Prime Minister. Even the Mo generals were powerless against us. King Wu's blessed by Heaven, and any evil will disappear of its own accord," Huang Feihu tried to encourage him.

"That may be so, but the people cannot live in peace, and many generals and soldiers will suffer in battle. Peace would be the greatest blessing now," Jiang Ziya mused aloud.

In the midst of discussion, a letter arrived from Grand Tutor Wen. Jiang Ziya broke it open and read:

> Wen Zhong, Grand Tutor of the Shang Dynasty and Commander the expeditionary forces, addresses His Excellency Prime Minister Jiang Ziya:
>
> The rebellion of a minister is a major crime against Heaven. How can West Qi treacherously enthrone a king? It is unlawful. Even though His Majesty has more than once sent his forces to call you to account, you still refuse to lay down your arms and surrender. On the contrary, you have dared to resist His Majesty's army, inflicting heavy casualties, beheading its generals and insulting them, hanging their heads on the city wall. According to the law, you shall be severely punished for these crimes.
>
> By decree of His Majesty, I have come to this land to subdue your rebellion. I have powerful forces under my command. If you have compassion for the people of your city, come to my camp gate and receive the capital punishment that you deserve. Any resistance will mean your immediate destruction. I await your careful consideration.

Jiang Ziya asked, "What's the name of the general who delivered the letter here?"

"My name's Deng Zhong."

"General Deng, please return to your camp and convey

my best regards to Grand Tutor Wen. Here's my reply: We'll meet on the battlefield in three days' time."

Deng Zhong returned to the Shang camp and reported all that Jiang Ziya had said. Three days later, the roar of cannons and war cries burst out from the Shang camp. Jiang Ziya ordered his men to march out of the city in five square formations.

Standing at his camp gate, Grand Tutor Wen saw that at the first firing of cannons, a formation of soldiers, flying four green pennants, marched out under the command of four generals. All were dressed in green and carried swords and spears.

At the second firing of cannons, a formation flying four red pennants, marched out under four generals dressed in red. They carried bows and arrows and cannons.

At the third firing of cannons, a formation marched out with white pennants and four more generals. All were dressed in white and carried ridged staves and cutlasses. The fourth formation marched out at the fourth firing of cannons, flying four purple pennants and led by another four generals dressed in black. They carried axes, lances and cutlasses.

At the fifth firing of cannons a cavalry formation dressed in yellow and flying yellow pennants rode out behind four generals. Grand Tutor Wen saw Jiang Ziya emerge with Nezha, Yang Jian, Jinzha, Muzha, Han Dulong, Xue Ehu, Huang Tianhua, Wu Ji and others on either side of him. Jiang Ziya himself rode on his nondescript beneath a huge banner. Huang Feihu rode beside him.

Under the dragon and phoenix banners, Grand Tutor Wen was flanked on either side by Deng, Xin, Zhang and Tao. Grand Tutor Wen had a pale golden face and a long five-tufted beard. He rode on his pure black unicorn, holding two glistening gold staves.

Jiang Ziya spurred his nondescript forward, bowed and greeted Grand Tutor Wen courteously. "Grand Tutor! Pardon me for not being able to offer you a full salutation."

"Prime Minister Jiang! You're from Mount Kunlun. How can you be so dull as to not understand the situation," Grand Tutor Wen asked as he returned the greetings.

"As a disciple of Mount Kunlun, I do everything with justice and virtue and have never transgressed the will of Heaven. I obey my king's orders, I comply with the will of the people, and handle all things according to law. I respect Heaven and distinguish the good from the bad. Under my administration people are happy and prosperous. How can you say that I am dull?" Jiang Ziya replied.

"You know only how to argue, but don't recognize that you've committed grave errors. You insulted His Majesty by enthroning King Wu without authorization. That's an unpardonable crime. When the punitive army arrived, you didn't plead guilty but beheaded our generals! Huang Feihu is a traitor, yet you gave him shelter. Now I've come. How dare you attempt to resist me instead of yielding in unconditional surrender! That's also unpardonable," Grand Tutor Wen said angrily.

Jiang Ziya smiled. "You're wrong, Grand Tutor. Though we didn't obtain permission from Zhaoge, a son's naturally entitled to inherit from his father. What could be wrong with that? Nearly all the nobles have declared rebellion. Are they all guilty of opposition to His Majesty? The fault lies with the monarch! He's no longer fit to be ruler of the people.

"As to giving shelter to General Huang Feihu, that is also right and just. A minister has the right to leave if the ruler's cruel and improper. We've never sent a single soldier to your passes or helped any marquis in his uprising. Those generals lost their lives only because they came here to attack us. They brought humiliation on themselves. You're admired by all, Grand Tutor. It's hard to understand how you could have come here without giving the matter careful consideration. I only hope that you'll withdraw to your own side of the border. Let each side guard his own land. If you attack us, you will violate the will of Heaven. Whether you'll win or lose is uncertain. Think it over carefully. Your dignity and glory may be damaged as a result of hasty action."

Grand Tutor Wen blushed red with shame at Jiang's words, but he grew angry when he saw Huang Feihu standing under a big banner. "You rebel, Huang! Come out here at once!"

Unable to withdraw from the scene, Huang Feihu had no choice but to move forward. He greeted Grand Tutor Wen with a bow. "I haven't seen you for years, Grand Tutor. I hope I can tell you about the injustices I've suffered."

"The power and riches of the kingdom were all in the hands of the Huang family," Grand Tutor Wen cursed. "How could you have rebelled and slayed the officers appointed by the throne! Your wickedness is notorious throughout the land. How dare you defend yourself with sophistry!" He cried, "Who'll seize that rebel for me?"

"I will!" Deng Zhong shouted.

Brandishing his lance, he charged at Huang Feihu, who met him with his own lance. When Zhang Jie raced to join in, he was intercepted by Nangong Kuo. Tao Rong was then met by Wu Ji as he rushed into the fight with his staves. The six generals fought desperately.

Xin Huan saw that the three generals on his side were unable to get the upper hand. He soared into the air and swooped down at Jiang Ziya with his hammers. Huang Tianhua spurred his jade unicorn forward and intercepted him. The generals of the Zhou army were greatly alarmed to see such an evil-looking man, with a red face, a wide mouth and sharp tusks. Huang Tianhua was the only general that could resist him.

When he saw that Huang Tianhua was riding a jade unicorn, Grand Tutor Wen realized that he must be a Taoist. He hurriedly urged his pure black unicorn forward to attack Jiang Ziya with his two gold staves. Jiang Ziya spurred forward his nondescript to meet him, and they battled fiercely. That was the first battle the Grand Tutor fought in West Qi, and he handled his staffs with deadly skill. They roared like the wind when he waved them through the air. Besides, he was a great warrior with years of experience in the border areas. This made it difficult for Jiang Ziya to withstand him.

Before long, Grand Tutor Wen sent his male staff flying through the air. His two staffs were transformed from two dragons, and they could fly with lethal accuracy. The staff descended directly on Jiang Ziya's shoulder, knocking him from his nondescript. As the Grand Tutor moved forward to behead him, Nezha sped up on his Wind-Fire Wheels.

"Don't touch my uncle, you damned wretch!" Nezha cried, and thrust at Grand Tutor Wen with his lance.

The Grand Tutor had to defend himself with his staffs, and as they fought, Xin Jia helped Jiang Ziya to safety. After four or five rounds, Grand Tutor Wen cast up his staff again and knocked Nezha from his wheels. Jinzha quickly jumped forward to rescue his brother and engaged the Grand Tutor with his sword. The Grand Tutor flew into a rage and threw both of his staffs into the air, wounding first Jinzha, then Muzha and Han Dulong.

Observing his wonderful skill, Yang Jian fought his way out of the fray and engaged the Grand Tutor. The Grand Tutor noticed his uncommon appearance. "With these remarkable people in its service, how could West Qi fail to revolt!" he thought.

He raised his staffs to fight Yang Jian. After several rounds, the Grand Tutor threw his gold staffs into the air again and struck Yang Jian repeatedly on the head. Sparks shot forth but Yang Jian was not affected in the least. The Grand Tutor was astonished. "This man's extraordinary. He must have great magic powers!"

Meanwhile Tao Rong was still fighting Wu Ji. When he realized that he and his brothers were gaining no advantage over their opponents, he hurriedly took out his "Wind Collecting Pennant" and waved it several times. A great whirlwind immediately howled over the battlefield, tossing sand into the sky and scattering stones and rocks across the ground. It blew off the soldiers' helmets and tore at their uniforms, darkening the sky and making it impossible to distinguish east from west.

As Tao Rong waved his magic pennant, Grand Tutor Wen played his staffs like lashing dragon tails; Deng Zhong whirled his axe like a cart wheel; Zhang Jie swung his long lance, and Xin Huan soared through the sky, raining down blows with his hammers. In the chaos that resulted, the soldiers and generals

of West Qi abandoned their drums and gongs and fled, leaving
the corpses of men and horses all over the battlefield. Grand
Tutor Wen won a great victory.

As soon as he returned to the camp, his generals came up to
offer congratulations. "You've won the first battle, Grand Tutor, and have greatly disheartened the enemy. It'll only be a
matter of days before we take the city."

Jiang Ziya had meanwhile withdrawn into the city.
"Jinzha, Muzha, Nezha, Han Dulong and many others were
wounded by Grand Tutor Wen's staffs," he said sadly to his
generals.

"Rest for a day or two and then fight another battle with
Wen Zhong. With the experience gathered today, I'm sure
we'll win. Then we'll launch a surprise night raid," Yang
Jian suggested.

"That's a very good idea, General," Jiang Ziya said
approvingly.

On the third day, they marched out of the city to the roar
of cannons. Howling war cries, they gave a challenge to the
Shang camp. Grand Tutor Wen immediately appeared with his
generals.

When he saw Grand Tutor Wen, Jiang Ziya cried,
"Today we'll see which of us is the better man!"

He urged forward his nondescript, and Grand Tutor Wen
charged on his black unicorn. They fought fiercely, sword
against staffs. When he saw that Jiang Ziya was protected by
Yang Jian on his left and Nezha on his right, Deng Zhong galloped out to help the Grand Tutor but was intercepted by
Huang Feihu. As Zhang and Tao raced up, they were met by
Wu Ji and Nangong Kuo. Xin Huan swooped down from the
sky but was stopped by Huang Tianhua.

In the midst of combat, Grand Tutor Wen seized an opportunity to toss his staffs high in the air in an attempt to beat
Jiang Ziya again. But Jiang Ziya snatched out his Staff for Beating Gods and hurled it at the Grand Tutor's weapon. Jiang
Ziya's staff was from Mount Kunlun. It had twenty-one
joints, each inscribed with four charms for punishing gods. As
the two collided, the Grand Tutor's female staff broke in two

and fell to the ground.

"Jiang Shang, you damned wretch! How dare you break my magic weapon! I cannot tolerate your existence any longer!" Grand Tutor Wen shouted furiously.

Jiang Ziya, however, tossed up his staff again and sent it crashing down on the Grand Tutor, knocking him from his black unicorn. Ji Li and Yu Qing rushed to his rescue, and he fled away on a dust cloud.

Jiang Ziya and his generals followed with a massacre of the remaining troops before they returned to the city. At the military conference that followed, Yang Jian said again, "We'll win another victory if we make a surprise raid tonight."

"An excellent idea," Jiang Ziya approved. "Everyone may rest now and come back in the afternoon."

In the Shang camp, Grand Tutor Wen was also holding a military conference. He sighed deeply, "Never since I started my military career have I suffered defeat, but today Jiang Shang broke the female staff that my master had transformed from a dragon. How can I have the courage to face her again!"

"Don't worry too much, Grand Tutor," his generals comforted him. "Victory and defeat are commonplace to a warrior."

That afternoon all the generals gathered at the prime minister's mansion. Jiang Ziya ordered, "Huang Feihu, Huang Feibiao and Huang Ming attack the Shang camp from the left; Nangong Kuo, Xin Jia and Xin Mian from the right. Nezha and Huang Tianhua make the frontal attack; Jinzha, Muzha, Han Dulong and Xue Ehu, you follow them up. Dragon Beard Tiger and Wu Ji, stay with me. Yang Jian, burn the Grand Tutor's grain supplies, and General Huang Gun, you guard the city."

Grand Tutor Wen had been sitting alone in his tent, brooding over his defeat, when he noticed an air of violent death hanging over the camp. Puzzled, he instantly burned incense and made a divination. He read the results and smiled.

"Oh, you wretch, Jiang Shang! So you're going to raid

my camp tonight! Don't imagine you'll succeed!" He immediately ordered, "Generals Deng Zhong and Zhang Jie, meet the assault from the left; Xin Huan and Tao Rong, meet the assault from the right; Ji Li and Yu Qing, guard the food stores. I'll protect the central headquarters."

He thus made thorough preparations.

Jiang Ziya's men made ready to move into action at the signal of cannon fire. They crept out of the city in total silence and took up their positions. Early in the night, cannons suddenly roared and cries arose. The attack began. Nezha and Huang Tianhua stormed the main gate of the Shang camp, Huang Feihu and his brothers attacked on the left while Nangong Kuo, Xin Jia and Xin Mian attacked on the right.

Did they meet with victory or defeat? If you want to know, please read the next chapter.

43

GRAND TUTOR WEN SUFFERS DEFEAT

Jiang Ziya's night raid proceeded with speed and violence. Riding on his Wind-Fire Wheels, Nezha rapidly fought his way into the Shang camp. Grand Tutor Wen mounted his unicorn and rushed out to meet the enemy. When Huang Tianhua saw him, he raced over on his jade unicorn and kept him busy with his two silver hammers until Jinzha and Muzha arrived to join the combat. Han Dulong and Xue Ehu fought furiously on the left and right. The Zhou army soon broke into the Shang barracks, and a terrible massacre ensued.

While Nezha and the four other generals encircled Grand Tutor Wen, Huang Feihu and his sons stormed the left camp guarded by Deng Zhong and Zhang Jie, and Nangong Kuo and Xin Jia attacked the right camp where they met in fearsome battle with Xin Huan and Tao Rong. At the height of the battle, Yang Jian fought his way into the rear camp and set fire to the Shang army's store of grain and fodder. It was no ordinary fire that Yang Jian spat out from his breast. Flames from the magic fire soared high into the sky, illuminating the earth like the sun.

Grand Tutor Wen was fighting desperately when he saw the flames. "With the food and fodder destroyed, the whole camp's finished!" he thought. Though he continued to parry lances and swords, he no longer had his heart in the fight. When Jiang Ziya rode up and struck him a heavy blow with the Staff for Beating Gods, he leapt out of the encirclement and urged his unicorn into flight. Huang Feihu and his sons set off in hot pursuit.

As the central camp was already lost, Deng Zhong and

Zhang Jie abandoned the fight and raced off with Grand Tutor Wen to safety. Nangong Kuo had also put Xin Huan and Tao Rong to flight. When they saw that the situation was hopeless, Ji Li and Yu Qing abandoned the grain supplies and withdrew as well. Xin Huan circled in the air above Grand Tutor Wen's party, protecting them as they retreated to Mount Qi.

Just then, Master of the Clouds thought that as Grand Tutor Wen was now at West Qi, it must be time to send Thunderbolt down from the mountain. He hurriedly ordered Golden Haze Lad to bring him into the cave. Thunderbolt entered and kowtowed before his master. "My disciple, go to West Qi now and see your elder brother King Wu and your uncle Jiang Ziya. Help them deal with King Zhou. If you meet the one that has wings, you can achieve great merit."

Leaving the cave, Thunderbolt stretched out his wind-and-thunder wings and sped through the sky, covering thousands of *li* in a matter of seconds. When he approached Mount Qi, he caught sight of Grand Tutor Wen in retreat. He was delighted. "What luck to meet the defeated troops! I can give them a good thrashing," he thought.

Grand Tutor Wen looked up into the sky, and to his surprise, he saw a man with an indigo face, cinnabar hair, and tusks on his upper and lower jaws flying towards them.

"Look! Xin Huan," he called. "There's an evil-looking man approaching up there. Take care."

Before he had finished speaking, Thunderbolt gave a cry and swooped down on him with his cudgel raised. Xin Huan met the blow with his twin hammers. They fought vigorously, their weapons clashing resoundingly, but as Thunderbolt was trained by the immortal Master of the Clouds, Xin Huan was no match for him. He was soon forced to take flight.

"I shouldn't chase him now. I'll see my uncle and royal brother first. I'm sure to have the chance to meet him again," Thunderbolt decided.

After his victorious return to the city, Jiang Ziya held a conference. "Today's victory is completely due to your efforts, the virtue of our sagely ruler, and Heaven's blessing on the people," he said to his generals.

"Wen Zhong's suffered defeat because he's ignorant of the fact that Heaven favors the virtuous King Wu and our talented prime minister," the generals remarked.

As they talked, a messenger reported, "A Taoist lad is at the gate asking to see the prime minister."

When Thunderbolt was ushered in, he bowed before Jiang Ziya. "Greetings, Uncle."

"Where do you come from?" Jiang Ziya asked.

"My name's Thunderbolt. I'm a disciple of Master of the Clouds. I've come here to offer my services and meet my royal brother."

"Do you know him?" Jiang Ziya asked the princes at his side.

"No, we don't," they all answered.

"When I was seven years old, I helped my father Prince Wen escape from the five passes. I'm Thunderbolt from Mount Yan."

Jiang Ziya immediately realized who he was and told his generals, "The late Prince Wen told me more than once how this young man rescued him when he was trapped inside the five passes. It must be Heaven's blessing on our king to have such a remarkable man come to us now."

He took Thunderbolt to see King Wu straightway. As they entered the palace gate, a guard rushed inside. "The prime minister wishes to see you, Your Highness."

When Jiang Ziya was admitted, he told the king, "Your younger brother is here to see you."

"Who's my younger brother?"

"It's Thunderbolt that our late master adopted on Mount Yan. He has spent all his time studying on Mount Zhongnan."

Thunderbolt was invited to enter the court. He knelt and greeted King Wu. "How do you do, royal elder brother?"

"Dear Brother! The late king often told me how you rescued him from the five passes and then returned to Mount Zhongnan. How happy I am that we can meet today," King Wu replied warmly. But when he observed Thunderbolt's fearsome appearance, King Wu dared not send him to his mother, Lady Tai Ji, lest she be frightened. "May I trouble you,

Prime Minister, to entertain my brother on my behalf?"

"Thunderbolt's a vegetarian. Let him live with me. I'll provide him with everything."

King Wu agreed with delight.

After the major defeat, Grand Tutor Wen withdraw seventy *li* to Mount Qi. There he gathered the remnants of his troops and set up camp. He found that he had lost 20,000 men.

"Never since I began my military career have I lost a battle and so many men! I don't know what to do," he sighed to his generals.

He realized that he could not expect reinforcements from other generals because all of them had been assigned to guard their local districts. He hated himself not only for being unable to quell West Qi, but also for suffering such heavy losses. In his agitation, he opened his divine middle eye, groaning and sighing in despair.

Seeing his distress, Ji Li came forward. "Don't worry, Grand Tutor. In the sacred mountains there are many holy men living in hermitages. They have great magic powers, and many of them are your friends. If you turn to them for help, you'll certainly be assured of success."

"My mind's been so disturbed that I've quite forgotten about them. I'll go straightway to see what I can do." He instructed generals Deng Zhong and Xin Huan, "I'll be away for several days. Guard the camp closely while I'm gone."

He mounted his unicorn, and at a gentle pat on the horn, it soared into the air. Before long Grand Tutor Wen arrived at the East Sea and stopped on the Golden Turtle Island. He contemplated the immense stretch of sea and the quiet green mountain and sighed deeply to himself, "I'm burdened with state affairs. When can I cast them off and retire to a hermitage, not caring how time slips away?"

The scenery was truly magnificent. Waves as high as hills crashed into precipitous cliffs of red, strangely shaped rocks. Beautiful phoenixes danced gracefully on the mountaintop, and beside a sheer rockface a unicorn slept alone. One could hear peacocks singing and frequently see dragons crawling in and out of their caves. Deer and fairy foxes and birds and rare fowls lived in the forest. Green pine trees and blue cypresses towered over a carpet of fragrant grass and flowers. Fairy peach trees were heavy with their sweet fruit. Above the tall bamboos hung a permanent veil of misty clouds.

He wandered about the island for a long time but found that all the doors were locked. He was disappointed; all his Taoist friends had disappeared from the place. He mounted his unicorn and was ready to leave the island when he heard someone calling him from behind.

"Brother Wen, where are you going?"

He looked around and found Celestial Lotus coming towards him. He moved forward and bowed. "Where're you going, friend?"

"I came here to meet you. All our friends are on White Deer Island finishing work on the Ten Death Traps. We're to aid you in West Qi. Shen Gongbao came here a few days ago and asked all of us to help you. Go to White Deer Island first, and I'll be there as soon as I've finished refining my weapon in the eight-diagram furnace."

Delighted by the news, Grand Tutor Wen bade her farewell and went directly to White Deer Island. There he saw his friends gossiping together on the hillside.

"How carefree you are, dear friends," Grand Tutor Wen shouted.

"We heard that you were attacking West Qi. Then Shen Gongbao came and asked us to help you, so we came here to prepare the Ten Death Traps. We've just finished them. We're delighted to have you here today," Heavenly Master Qin greeted him.

"What are these traps?" Grand Tutor Wen asked.

"Each of them has its own power and purpose. We'll set them up in West Qi tomorrow. They embody unlimited internal changes."

"Why are there only nine of you here? Who's missing?"

"Mother Golden Light is preparing her Golden Light Trap on the White Cloud Island."

"Are you all ready?" Heavenly Master Dong asked.

"Yes, we're fully prepared," they answered in one voice.

"Then we'll go to West Qi first. Brother Wen, you stay here and wait for Mother Golden Light. What do you think?" Heavenly Master Dong suggested.

"That's wonderful. I feel honored by your kindness," Grand Tutor Wen replied.

The nine Taoists bade him farewell and made their way to West Qi on a watery cloud. Grand Tutor Wen sat down on a slope and leaned against a pine tree. Before long, he saw a woman, in a gold fish-tail coronet, a red robe and a silk belt, approach swiftly from the south on the back of a leopard. She carried a bundle on her back and two swords at her waist.

Mother Golden Light was surprised to find nobody there except for an old Taoist with three eyes. She looked closely and recognized Grand Tutor Wen. She dismounted and asked, "Where did you come from, Brother? Where are the other nine friends?"

"They've gone ahead to West Qi and left me here waiting for you."

They happily mounted their beasts and soared through the clouds, reaching Mount Qi in the twinkling of an eye. At the Shang camp, they were welcomed by Ji Li and other generals and in the headquarters, they met the nine others.

"Where's West Qi?" Heavenly Master Qin asked.

"This is Mount Qi. I suffered defeat in a night raid and retreated here. It's seventy *li* from West Qi City," Grand Tutor Wen replied.

"Let's go back to the city," all the Taoists proposed.

Grand Tutor Wen ordered that Deng Zhong lead the vanguard. They marched quickly back to West Qi City and set up camp. Jiang Ziya heard war cries and cannon shots outside the city. "Grand Tutor Wen must have returned with reinforcements."

"He's been away for over two weeks. As a member of Jie Taoism, he must have enlisted some friends to aid him with sorcery. We should be on the alert," Yang Jian warned.

Jiang Ziya ascended the city wall with Nezha and Yang Jian. They found to their astonishment that things were very different from before. The enemy camp was enveloped in clouds and fog. Above the central camp more than a dozen columns of black smoke hovered in the air. Jiang Ziya was shocked and the others remained silent. They descended the wall and entered the prime minister's mansion, but no one knew how to deal with the new situation.

In the Shang camp, Grand Tutor Wen was discussing with the ten Heavenly masters how to destroy West Qi.

"I'm told that Jiang Ziya's a disciple from Mount Kunlun," Heavenly Master Yuan said. "As we're all Taoists, let's first have a battle of wits and display what mysteries we know. We shouldn't merely match bravery and strength."

"You're right, Brother," Grand Tutor Wen agreed.

The Shang army marched out the following day. Grand Tutor Wen demanded that Jiang Ziya come to meet him.

Jiang Ziya rode out on his nondescript with his generals, soldiers, banners, and flags. Looking over the Shang army, he saw ten evil-looking Taoists behind the Grand Tutor, all mounted on deer. They had green, yellow, red, white and pink faces.

Heavenly Master Qin moved to the fore and bowed. "Greetings, Jiang Ziya!"

Jiang Ziya returned the bow. "Greetings, Brother! But where do you come from?"

"I'm from Golden Turtle Island. My name's Qin Wan. you're a member of Chan Taoism, and we are of Jie Taoism, but why do you insult us with your witchcraft? That isn't right," Heavenly Master Qin answered.

"Brother, how can you say that?"

"Isn't it an insult to put all the Mo brothers to death? We've come here to decide which of us is the more powerful." Qin Wan then added, "Let's not compete in a test of strength, but rather pit our magic powers against each other. As immortals, we should avoid physical combat."

"Brother, you've achieved much as an immortal. King Zhou's a wicked tyrant and has been forsaken by Heaven. A sagely ruler has made his appearance in West Qi. You ought to respect the will of Heaven which has been marked by the singing of a phoenix on Mount Qi. Since ancient times, the kind have always subdued the cruel, those blessed by Heaven have been victorious over the cursed, and the principled have won over the unprincipled. As a disciple of a famous master since your childhood, how can you fail to recognize the truth?" Jiang Ziya replied.

"According to what you say, King Wu is destined by Heaven to be the ruler while King Zhou is an unprincipled overlord. But don't you think that our arrival is also in accordance with Heaven's will? Jiang Ziya, I'll tell you what. We've created the Ten Death Traps. I would like you to see them right now with your own eyes. Let's not do physical combat, as that would violate the compassionate will of Heaven. What do you think?" Qin Wan asked.

"If that's your wish, I dare not oppose it."

The ten Taoists immediately left the battleline and returned to their camp. Within two hours they had prepared the traps, and Qin Wan came out again. "We're ready. Jiang Ziya, would you like to inspect them now?"

"I'll do as you instruct," Jiang Ziya answered politely.

He moved forward. Nezha, Huang Tianhua, Thunderbolt and Yang Jian followed closely to protect him.

"It would be most cowardly if you try to hurt us with hidden weapons during our inspection," Yang Jian warned Qin Wan.

"We certainly wouldn't do that, we won't, as you'll all meet your doom soon enough anyway," Qin Wan smiled.

"You'd better keep your promise," Nezha put in.

During the inspection, Jiang Ziya read the name of each trap as it was written to one side. The names were: "Heavenly Destruction," "Earthly Fury," "Roaring Typhoon," "Frigid Ice," "Golden Light," "Bleeding Blood," "Vehement Flame," "Soul Snatching," "Red Water" and "Red Sand." After his inspection, Jiang Ziya emerged from the enemy camp.

"Do you know all of them, Jiang Ziya?" Heavenly Master Qin asked.

"Yes, I do."

"Can you break them all?" Heavenly Master Yuan asked.

"Since I know them, of course I can break all of them," Jiang Ziya answered proudly.

"When will you begin then?"

"They are not yet fully prepared. Give me a date as soon as you've completed them."

Grand Tutor Wen returned to camp with his Taoist friends and Jiang Ziya to the city with all his generals. He entered the prime minister's mansion, eyebrows knitted. He was clearly worried.

"You just said that you could break them all. You can, can't you?" Yang Jian asked.

"How can I? They were created by Jie Taoist witchcraft, full of mysteries even I can't comprehend. Their names alone are strange to me," Jiang Ziya said gloomily.

Back in his camp, Grand Tutor Wen entertained his friends. As they drank, Grand Tutor Wen asked, "What's so special about these ten traps?"

Heavenly Master Qin then told him about them in detail. If you want to learn about their mysteries, please read the next chapter.

44

JIANG ZIYA'S SOULS
FLOAT OVER MOUNT KUNLUN

"The Heavenly Destruction," Qin Wan said, "was invented by my master using pre-creation energies. It has three pennants, representing Heaven, earth, and humanity. In the trap, humans are reduced to ashes while immortals are shaken loose and fall into pieces."

Grand Tutor Wen was delighted. "How about the Earthly Fury?"

"My Earthly Fury contains energies of the earth concentrated in a solid mass," Heavenly Master Zhao answered. "It undergoes endless changes, now appearing, now disappearing. It has a red pennant, and when it waves, thunder roars above and flames spring up from below. Neither humans nor immortals can survive in it."

"What about the Roaring Typhoon?"

"My Roaring Typhoon produces wind and fire," Heavenly Master Dong explained. "But they are not ordinary wind and fire: they existed before genesis. Millions of swords are concealed therein which emerge as the wind and fire arise. Men and immortals alike will be cut into small pieces when they enter. Nobody can come out alive."

"How about the Frigid Ice?"

"I invented it after years of assiduous effort. Though it's called 'Frigid Ice,' it's really a mountain of swords. In the center, there is wind and thunder, above is a mountain of ice cutlasses, and below there are solid ice blocks. Even those with the most extraordinary magic powers will find it difficult to escape fate when the upper and lower sections crash together," Heavenly Master Yuan explained.

"What about the Golden Light? What wonders does it possess?"

"My Golden Light is made from essence derived from the sun, moon, Heaven, and earth. There are twenty-one magic mirrors, each hung on a high pole by a ring. Any intruder, either man or immortal, is turned into a stream of blood by one touch of the golden light that shoots from the mirrors. No one can escape destruction," Mother Golden Light replied.

"How about the Bleeding Blood?"

"My trap is full of the forces which existed before genesis. Besides wind and thunder, it contains a vast quantity of black sand. If men or immortals intrude, thunder and wind arise and blow the black sand into the air. Any part of the body that comes into contact with the sand immediately turns to blood and bleeds until the whole body disappears," Heavenly Master Sun explained.

"What are the wonders of the Vehement Flame?"

"My trap contains three kinds of fire— the divine fire that immortals produce in their stomachs, the fire of air, and the fire of rock. There are three red pennants in the trap. At any intrusion, the three pennants begin to wave and the fires instantly burn the intruder to ashes. Even charms are no help," Heavenly Master Bai answered.

"And what about your Soul Snatching Trap?"

"In my wonderful trap, I block all the doors of life and open wide all the windows of death," Heavenly Master Yao answered. "It's full of the most deadly essence from Heaven and earth. I'll hold a white paper pennant inscribed with charms, and when the pennant waves, the soul of any intruder is snatched away. Death is immediate."

"What about the Red Water?" Grand Tutor Wen asked Heavenly Master Wang.

"My Red Water contains the essence of liquid. In the center, there is a platform in the shape of the eight diagrams, and on the platform, there are three dried gourds. At the intrusion of man or immortal, I cast down the gourds and they pour forth red water like a great flood. One drop and the intruder is turned into blood. Death is instant."

"The Red Sand must be a wonder too. Tell me about it," Grand Tutor Wen requested Heavenly Master Zhang.

"Yes, it's indeed a wonder. It's composed of three different parts, with a peck of sand each, representing Heaven, earth and man. Each grain of sand is a sharp sword that will reduce any intruder to powder. Not even an immortal or a Buddha can escape."

Grand Tutor Wen was extremely pleased. "Now that you're here to help me, I'll destroy West Qi in a matter of days. Even if they have millions of soldiers and thousands of generals, they can do nothing to save themselves. The Shang Dynasty must be favored by fortune!"

Heavenly Master Yao, of the Soul Snatching Trap, however, held a different opinion. "Brothers! As I see it, Jiang Ziya's magic powers are weak, and West Qi City is insignificant. They aren't worthy of the ten traps. Let me use a much simpler device to put Jiang Ziya to death. West Qi will collapse at the loss of its leader. As the proverb goes, 'A snake cannot crawl without its head; an army without a commander is reduced to chaos.' Why fight a battle when it isn't necessary?"

"Brother," said the Grand Tutor, "if you can finish him off with your ingenious art, we needn't even shoot an arrow, and the lives of our soldiers can be saved. But please tell me what device you'll use."

"Jiang Ziya will die in just twenty-one days. He'll find it difficult to escape, even if he were an immortal or Buddha," Heavenly Master Yao promised.

When Grand Tutor Wen asked him for details, Heavenly Master Yao whispered in his ear. Grand Tutor Wen was overjoyed. "Once he's dead, his whole army will certainly collapse, and we can subdue West Qi over drink and gossip. It must be Heaven's blessing on His Majesty!"

"Let Brother Yao render you this service. We're here with only one purpose: to help Brother Wen," the Taoists replied in one voice.

Heavenly Master Yao left the others and walked into his Soul Snatching Trap. There he had a platform of earth built on which he set a desk and a straw effigy. On the body of the effigy he wrote the characters "Jiang Shang," and on its head he hung three lamps to draw out Jiang Ziya's souls. At the foot of the effigy he put another seven lamps to receive Jiang Ziya's sub-souls. When everything was ready, he let down his hair, took a sword, and walked in a square before the platform, reciting charms and burning written spells. He did this three times a day.

Three days later, Jiang Ziya began to feel dizzy and restless and could neither sit nor sleep in peace. When he met his generals, he remained silent, as if at his wit's end. Sometimes he appeared dazed, and at other times irritated, never once offering any suggestions. His complexion had also changed greatly in the last few days.

Yang Jian felt puzzled. "Why does he behave like this? He's a disciple from the Jade Emptiness Palace and bears a great responsibility as prime minister and commander. Moreover, his timely appearance in West Qi was portended by celestial phenomena. Could it be that he's possibly be reduced to this state just because he can't cope with the ten traps? I really don't understand it."

He felt extremely worried.

Seven more days passed. Heavenly Master Yao had already got one soul and three sub-souls from Jiang Ziya. This meant that one-third of his spirit had already left his body. Jiang Ziya became even more irritable. He felt drowsy all the time and frequently lay in bed ignoring state and military affairs. Not one of his generals realized the true cause. Some thought that he was demoralized by his inability to cope with the enemy, while others thought that he was too weary and needed a rest.

Fifteen days passed. Heavenly Master Yao had seized another soul and another three sub-souls. This made Jiang Ziya sleep all day, snoring as loud as thunder. Nezha and Yang Jian discussed the matter with the other generals.

"A huge army is just beyond the walls, waiting for us with the ten traps. Nevertheless, Uncle Jiang sleeps and cares nothing about the present crisis. There must be some reason for it."

"It seems to me that somebody is hurting him with witch-craft. Otherwise, how could one like him sleep all the time? There's something fishy about it!" Yang Jian suggested.

"Yes, there must be some reason. Let's go to his bed-room and ask him to come here. We'll see how he reacts," they echoed.

Arriving in the bed chamber, they asked the attendants, "Where's the prime minister?"

"He's still sleeping."

They told one of the attendants to rouse him. As Jiang Ziya walked out, Wu Ji moved up and said, "Master! Why do you sleep everyday and neglect state and military affairs? We're extremely worried. Won't you discuss things with us now?"

Jiang Ziya went to the conference hall very much against his will and during the discussion remained silent. He seemed to be intoxicated. A sudden gust of wind blew through the hall, and they took the opportunity to test his mental faculties.

"Uncle," Nezha said, "this wind seems to have an evil air about it. Won't you find out whether it portends good or evil?"

Jiang Ziya bent his fingers as if making a divination and answered, "There's nothing abnormal about it. It's just the or-dinary wind that ought to blow today."

Because the greater part of his spirit had gone, Jiang Ziya's senses were also dulled. But nobody dared utter a word. The conference dispersed and they left the mansion.

Twenty days passed. Heavenly Master Yao had captured two of his souls and six of his sub-souls. Only one soul and one sub-soul remained, and they, too, soon left his body through his skull. When Jiang Ziya was found dead, all his generals, together with King Wu, stood around the corpse and wept bitterly.

"Father-Prime Minister!" King Wu sobbed. "You worked laboriously for the state, never enjoying a single day of peaceful rest. How grieved I am!"

With tears in his eyes, Yang Jian moved up and touched the body with his hand. To his joy, he found that the breast was still warm. He quickly told King Wu, "Keep calm, Your Highness! His breast is still warm, so he may not yet be dead. Let him lie on the bed and we'll see what happens."

Jiang Ziya's last soul and sub-soul floated through the air and finally arrived at the Terrace of Creation. But Bai Jian recognized them and, knowing the will of Heaven, gently pushed them out of the terrace. As Jiang Ziya was a Taoist with magic powers, he could still remember Mount Kunlun. When his souls left the Terrace of Creation, they floated on the wind to Mount Kunlun.

The Immortal of the South Pole was wandering about Mount Kunlun that day collecting medicinal herbs, when he noticed the souls meandering through the air towards him. With a cry of alarm, he rushed up and stuffed them into his gourd, then quickly covered its mouth with a cork. He hurried over to the Jade Emptiness Palace to see his master, but just as he reached the entrance, he heard somebody calling his name.

He stopped when he saw that it was Master Pure Essence. "Where did you come from, friend?"

"As I've nothing to do today, I'd like you to come with me to tour the islands and mountains. We'll look for recluses and watch them play chess."

"I'm rather busy today. Please excuse me."

"We've got no lectures at the moment. How can you deceive me?" Master Pure Essence argued.

"I've something urgent to do and really have no time. I'm sorry, but I can't go with you."

"I know why you're busy. It's because Jiang Ziya's souls have left his body!"

"How did you know?"

"I was fooling you just then. Forgive me, please. I went to Mount Qi and met Bai Jian. He told me the last soul and sub-soul of Jiang Ziya arrived there a short while ago. He couldn't accept them and when he pushed them away, they floated here to Mount Kunlun. Where are they now?"

"I was touring about idly when I saw his souls floating towards me, so I put them in my gourd."

"This matter isn't important enough to be reported to the

Grand Master. Give me the gourd, and I'll go to rescue Jiang Ziya," Master Pure Essence urged him.

The Immortal of the South Pole handed over the gourd, and Master Pure Essence mounted his cloud, flying to West Qi in a moment.

When he entered the prime minister's mansion, Master Pure Essence met Yang Jian, who bowed and asked, "Uncle! have you come to see the prime minister?"

"Yes. Go quickly and report my arrival!"

King Wu came out in person to meet him and conducted him to the Silver Security Court. He treated the immortal with the courtesy shown a teacher.

"I came here to see about Jiang Ziya. Where's his body now?" Master Pure Essence asked.

King Wu led the immortal to the bed chamber, where Jiang Ziya was lying on his back.

"Your Highness! You needn't worry. He'll revive naturally as soon as his souls and sub-souls are returned to his body," Master Pure Essence assured him.

When they returned to the main hall, King Wu asked, "Sir, what medicine will you use to restore my father-prime minister?"

"There's no medicine involved whatsoever. I'll save him from death by other means."

Late that night, Master Pure Essence put on his coronet, straightened his robes, and left the city. Black smoke billowed and cold fog swirled about in the howling wind over the ten traps.

Master Pure Essence realized how perilous the situation was. He pointed at his feet, and two white lotus flowers appeared to protect his body. Treading on the flowers, he rose quietly through the air, exuding colored, auspicious light from the top of his head.

When he arrived over the Soul Snatching Trap, he saw Heavenly Master Yao, hair loosened and holding a sword, walking in a square and reciting charms. He also saw a straw effigy with three dim lamps on its head and seven under its feet. When Heavenly Master Yao knocked loudly on the desk with his stick, the lamps went out, but then rekindled when he stopped knocking. Each time he knocked, the souls inside the gourd held by Master Pure Essence struggled to get out, but they were stopped by the cork. Though Heavenly Master Yao bowed and knocked repeatedly, the lamps continued to burn. Jiang Ziya's life was not over yet.

Heavenly Master Yao grew irritated and knocked on the desk more heavily, shouting, "Two souls and six sub-souls have come already! Why do the remaining souls disobey my call?"

Fuming with anger, he bowed and chanted and knocked incessantly.

In the air above, Master Pure Essence saw him bow down and seized the opportunity to descend and snatch the straw effigy. But Yao Bin looked up by chance and saw him dropping from the sky. He recognized Master Pure Essence at once.

"Pure Essence! How dare you intrude here!" he yelled, hurling a handful of black sand at the immortal. Though Master Pure Essence took flight immediately, his two lotus flowers were hit and dropped to the ground. He returned to West Qi City, flurried and gasping for breath.

"Master! Have you brought back our prime minister's souls?" Yang Jian asked.

"This is truly a dangerous job! I almost fell into the Soul Snatching Trap myself! I fled, but my two lotus flowers were hit by the black sand and taken by Yao Bin."

King Wu burst into sobs. "Alas! There's no hope for my father-prime minister!"

"Don't worry, Your Highness. Jiang Ziya will suffer only for a few more days. I must go now."

"Where are you going, Master?" King Wu asked.

"I'll be back soon. You just stay here and take care of Jiang Ziya's body."

Master Pure Essence rode on a beam of light to Mount Kunlun where he met the Immortal of the South Pole in front of the Jade Emptiness Palace.

"Have you returned Jiang Ziya's souls yet?" the Immortal of the South Pole asked.

Telling him the whole story, Master Pure Essence said, "Brother, I'll have to see Grand Master and ask him to show us how to deal with this."

The Immortal of the South Pole did as he was requested. Entering the palace, he bowed before Heavenly Primogenitor and reported the calamity.

"Though I'm responsible here, I can't deal with the matter directly. Tell Pure Essence to go to the Eight Landscape Palace and see my elder brother. He'll help him."

The Immortal of the South Pole returned and said, "Grand Master asks you to go and see Master Lao Zi."

Master Pure Essence sped on an auspicious cloud straight to Mount Xuandu. In a few moments, he reached the Eight Landscape Palace in Xuandu Cave. It was a fairyland of landscapes. On the steep slopes grew fairy grass and longevity mushrooms. Green pines, willows, purple chrysanthemums, red plums, pink peaches, yellow apricots, brown dates and luscious pears could be seen everywhere. Immortals sat, enjoying paintings and hermits gathered, playing chess. One could hear the singing of dragons, phoenixes and peacocks. Rhinoceroses admired the moon while happy seals and hippopotami played games in the water. The sun shone over the mountains and water gurgled in the creeks. It was a fairyland unknown to the outside world.

Master Pure Essence dared not enter the cave unauthorized but soon Chief Priest Xuandu came out and saw him there. "What urgent matter brings you here, friend?"

Master Pure Essence bowed before him. "Brother, if it weren't of major importance, I wouldn't have come here to see Master Lao Zi. Jiang Ziya's lost his souls to Yao Bin. Heavenly Primogenitor sent me here to see Master Lao Zi. Could you arrange for me to see him?"

Chief Priest Xuandu went back in. "Pure Essence requests to see you."

"Let him in," Lao Zi said.

Master Pure Essence entered and knelt down. "May you live forever!"

"You've all been fated to endure this calamity. The Soul

snatching Trap, the sole cause of Jiang Ziya's suffering, was based on my magic Map of the Eight Diagrams. This has been destined by Heaven. You must all observe the Taoist prohibitions very carefully." He ordered Chief Priest Xuandu to fetch the map. "Rescue Jiang Shang with this. You may go at once."

Master Pure Essence left the Eight Landscape Palace carring the map and arrived back in West Qi City in a blink of the eye. He was warmly welcomed by King Wu and all his generals.

"Where have you been?" King Wu asked eagerly.

"I've obtained the means to save Jiang Ziya's life."

All the generals were overjoyed.

"When will you go again, Master?" Yang Jian asked.

"At the third watch tonight."

At the third watch, all the generals went to see him off. He ascended into the air and flew over the Ten Death Traps.

From up in the air, he could see Heavenly Master Yao still diligently bowing and chanting. He unrolled the magic map, and it turned into a golden bridge that shone brightly in all the colors of the rainbow. It protected him as he raced down and snatched the straw effigy. He then took flight.

"Damn you, Pure Essence! How dare you come again!" Heavenly Master Yao growled, enraged.

He cast a peck of black sand high into the air. Master Pure Essence cried out in fright and in his panic, dropped the map, which was then retrieved by Heavenly Master Yao.

Although Master Pure Essence had gotten away with the effigy, he was frightened out of his wits by the loss of the map. Pale and gasping for breath, he made his way back to West Qi City. He descended into the city, put down the straw effigy, opened the lid of his gourd, and placed the two remaining souls and six sub-souls inside it. He then continued on his way to the prime minister's mansion.

The generals were still waiting for him there and were pleased to see him return with a smile on his face. Yang Jian rushed forward. "Master, have you brought back the souls?"

"I have. Jiang Ziya can now be restored to life. But although I was lucky to escape with my life, I lost Lao Zi's map in the Soul Snatching Trap," Master Pure Essence replied.

King Wu and the generals were delighted that Jiang Ziya would be restored to life. Master Pure Essence went to Jiang Ziya's bedside, parted his hair and put the mouth of the gourd against his skull. He patted the gourd three times. As Jiang Ziya's souls entered his body, he opened his eyes.

"What a long sleep I've had!" Jiang Ziya exclaimed.

He looked round and saw King Wu, Master Pure Essence and all his generals standing before his bed.

"Prime Minister! If it hadn't been for this master, you wouldn't have been restored to life!" King Wu told him.

Jiang Ziya fully regained his senses when he heard this and asked Master Pure Essence, "Brother, how did you know that I was in danger of losing my life? How did you save me?"

Master Pure Essence related all that had happened. Jiang Ziya was filled with remorse at the paucity of his own powers and his resulting ignorance of what had taken place.

"The map is a rare thing. What shall we do now that we have lost it?" Jiang Ziya said worriedly.

"Rest well for a few days. We'll discuss how to break the ten traps when you've fully recovered," Master Pure Essence urged.

Jiang Ziya rested for several days and then convened a conference in his mansion to discuss with Master Pure Essence and his generals how to break the ten traps.

"The traps are all sorcery, and their secrets are unknown to us, but we're acting in accordance with the will of Heaven. They cannot harm us," Master Pure Essence reassured them.

During the discussion, Yang Jian announced, "The Yellow Dragon Immortal has arrived."

Jiang Ziya immediately went out to welcome the immortal. After greetings were exchanged, he asked, "Brother, what instructions do you have for me?"

"I've come to deal with the ten traps. As we're all destined to violate the commandment on killing, some to a slight degree and some to a serious extent, we'll all be gathering here in a short while. But this place is too vulgar for my fellow immortals, and I've come here first to discuss the matter with Jiang Ziya. I propose that you build a reed pavilion outside the west gate and have it decorated with lanterns and flowers. It may be inconvenient for them to come otherwise."

Jiang Ziya ordered Nangong Kuo and Wu Ji to follow the immortal's instructions, and Yang Jian to wait at the gate and report immediately the arrival of any immortal.

"Let's not waste time on strategies now. We'll discuss the matter with the immortals once the reed pavilion is ready," Master Pure Essence advised.

In less than twenty-four hours, Wu Ji reported to Jiang Ziya that the reed pavilion had been completed. When Jiang Ziya inspected it, he ordered that carpets be laid on the floor and the interior be decorated with lanterns and flowers. All the officials except King Zhou left the city and gathered in the pavilion to welcome the immortals.

As King Wu was a virtuous ruler, a great number of immortals came to discuss the problem facing West Qi. They were: Master Grand Completion from the Peach Spring Cave on Nine Immortal Mountain; Master Pure Essence from the Exalted Cloud Cave on Mount Taihua; the Yellow Dragon Immortal from the Fairy Maid Cave on Two Celestial Mountain; Krakucchanda from the Flying Cloud Cave on Dragon Squeezing Mountain (who later became a Buddha); Fairy Primordial from the Golden Light Cave on Qianyuan Mountain; Master Spiritual Treasure from the Yuanyang Cave on Mount Kongtong; Heavenly Master of Outstanding Culture from the High Cloud Cave on Five Dragon Mountain (who later became the Boddhisattva of Outstanding Culture); Immortal Universal Virtue from the White Crane Cave on Nine-Palace Mountain (who later became the Boddhisattva of Universal Virtue); the Immortal of Merciful Navigation from the Perfumed Wood Cave on Mount Putuo (who later became the Buddhist Goddess of Mercy); the Immortal Jade Tripod from the Golden Haze Cave on Mount Jade Spring; Heavenly Master of Divine Virtue from the Jade House Cave on Mount Golden Courtyard; and Master Virtue of the Pure Void from the Purple Sun Cave on Mount Green Peak.

Jiang Ziya was kept busy receiving his celestial guests and conducting them to the reed pavilion.

When all the immortals had arrived, Master Grand Completion said, "My Taoist friends! With your arrival here today, the rise of the good and just, and the downfall of the wicked and unjust will soon be known to all. Jiang Ziya, when will you take action to break the Ten Death Traps?"

Jiang Ziya got up and replied with a low bow, "Dear Brothers! I studied on Mount Kunlun for only forty years. How can I take command? Please take pity on me, as my powers are weak, and on the people and soldiers, as they are innocent. May I trouble one of you to take my place? I'd appreciate it very much."

"I'm sorry but I doubt whether we can guarantee even our own safety. Our powers aren't sufficient to deal with their witchcraft either!" Master Grand Completion answered, greatly disheartened.

They were still arguing as to who should assume command when they heard the cry of a deer in the sky and smelt an unusual perfume filling the air.

If you want to know who arrived, please read the next chapter.

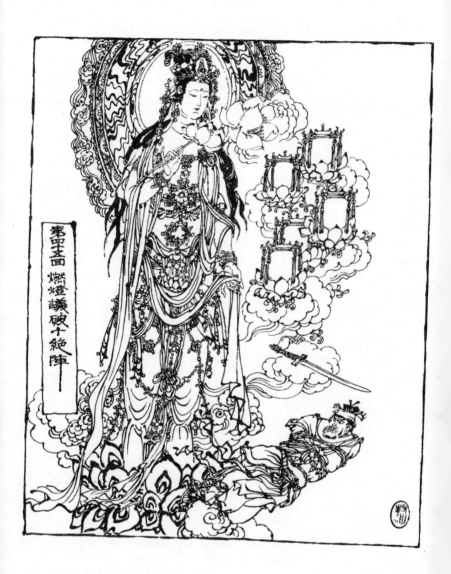

第四之面　燃燈議破十絕陣

CONFRONTING
THE DESTRUCTIVE FORCES

In the course of their discussion, an immortal riding on a deer descended through the clouds, filling the air with a sweet fragrance. It was Immortal Burning Lamp from the Prime Consciousness Cave on Mount Divine Hawk. All the immortals came out to welcome him.

After greetings had been exchanged, Burning Lamp said, "Sorry I'm so late. Please forgive me." He then asked, "As the traps are so formidable, we need a commander to direct the operations. Have you chosen one yet?"

Jiang Ziya bowed. "We're awaiting your instructions."

"I've come here first, to take over Jiang Ziya's seal of command, and second, to save some of you from doom as we fulfill the will of Heaven. You may give me the seal of office."

Jiang Ziya was delighted. He immediately handed over the seal and saluted him as commander. Burning Lamp thanked everyone and began discussing the ways and means to destroy the ten traps. As they talked, he sighed sadly to himself, realizing that he would lose at least ten men in the coming disaster.

Meanwhile, Grand Tutor Wen invited the ten Heavenly Masters to his tent. "Have you all completed your traps?"

"We finished all our arrangements some time ago. You may send a note to Jiang Ziya," they all answered.

Grand Tutor Wen immediately sent Deng Zhong to Jiang Ziya with a written challenge. After reading the note, Jiang Ziya wrote at the bottom, "We will meet you in three days time." Then he returned the note to Deng Zhong and sent him away.

When they received the reply, Grand Tutor Wen enter-

tained the ten Heavenly Masters. As they left his tent at the
third watch, they were startled to see auspicious colored clouds
over the reed pavilion of the Zhou camp: golden lanterns,
linden leaves and strings of pearls shone brilliantly in the sky.
They cried out in alarm, "A crowd of celestials from Mount
Kunlun have arrived!" Warned by the new development, each
then returned to his own trap.

The third day soon arrived. Early in the morning cannons
and war cries resounded in the Shang camp. Grand Tutor Wen
positioned himself before the camp gate, with Deng, Zhang,
Xin and Tao on either side. The ten traps were arrayed across
the battlefield.

In the reed pavilion, one could see flags fluttering amidst
auspicious vapors as the immortals began to emerge. The Zhou
forces were headed by Nezha and Huang Tianhua, and followed by Yang Jian, Thunderbolt, Han Dulong, Xue Ehu,
Jinzha and Muzha. Then came the immortals in pairs: Master
Pure Essence and Master Grand Completion, Fairy Primordial
and Master Spiritual Treasure, Master Virtue of the Pure Void
and Krakucchanda, Heavenly Master of Outstanding Culture
and Universal Virtue, Immortal of Merciful Navigation and the
Yellow Dragon Immortal, Immortal Jade Tripod and Heavenly
Master of Divine Virtue. They filed out in an orderly group
led by Burning Lamp. Master Pure Essence rang a gold bell
and Master Grand Completion struck jade chimes.

Bells suddenly rang in the Heavenly Destruction Trap, and
a Taoist with an indigo face and cinnabar hair appeared between two banners at the entrance. He raced out on a yellow
spotted deer.

As Heavenly Master Qin approached, Burning Lamp
looked around. "There's no one here destined to be sacrificed," he thought.

As he pondered, there was a rush of wind above and an
immortal dropped lightly to the ground. It was Deng Hua, the
fifth disciple of the Jade Emptiness Palace.

A halberd in his hand, Deng Hua bowed before the celestials. "By order of my master, I've come here to break the
Heavenly Destruction Trap."

Burning Lamp nodded his head, thinking sadly, "How can he escape disaster? It's been destined by fate."

Just then, Heavenly Master Qin yelled loudly, "Which of you will meet me first?"

"Don't get excited, Qin Wan. Don't begin to think that you are omnipotent!" Deng Hua shouted, rushing out to meet him.

"Who are you?"

"You devil! How come you don't know me? I'm Deng Hua, a disciple of the Jade Emptiness Palace."

"Dare you meet me in my trap?" Qin Wan challenged.

"Since I've come for that purpose, why not?"

He rushed at Qin Wan with his halberd, and Qin spurred his deer forward to meet him. They fought bravely before the Heavenly Destruction Trap. After only three rounds, Qin Wan made a feint and dodged inside the trap. Deng Hua followed on his heels. Qin Wan picked up the three pennants from the desk on the platform and whirled them in the air, finally casting them on the ground. There was a great crash of thunder, and Deng Hua fell to the ground insensible.

Qin Wan leapt down from the platform, cut his head off, and carrying it in his hand, rushed out. "You fellows from Mount Kunlun! Who dares to meet me again in my trap?"

Grieved at the loss of Deng Hua, Burning Lamp asked Heavenly Master of Outstanding Culture to enter. "Take great care," he warned.

"I will," replied the Heavenly Master and strode forward singing:

> I dare to test the blade of my sword,
> The jade dragon shrieks in fright.
> Purple vapors from my hand rise high.
> Lucky clouds emerge and cover my head.
> I grow longevity peaches in the Jade Palace,
> And discuss the Way in the golden tower.
> By order I left my celestial home,
> And came to this vulgar world, merry and gay.

"Qin Wan, Jie Taoism enjoys untrammeled liberty. Why have you created this trap to harm the world? As I am to break it, I certainly can't observe the commandment on killing. It isn't that we're unkind, but that we must enforce the law of cause and effect. Don't regret it when it's too late," he warned.

Qin Wan laughed. "You're all carefree immortals, but why are you willing to come and suffer here? You certainly know nothing about the mysteries of my trap. It isn't I that will drive you to disaster."

"We'll soon see just who will lose his life," the Heavenly Master smiled.

Flying into a rage, Qin Wan struck at him with his staves. The immortal returned the blow with his sword. After a few rounds, Qin Wan once more ran into his trap, but the Heavenly Master hesitated at the entrance, alarmed by the cold fog that hung in the air.

He heard the gold bell ringing behind him, and he mustered his courage to advance. He pointed at the ground with his fingers, and two white lotus flowers emerged from the earth on which he rode into the trap.

"Heavenly Master of Outstanding Culture! Even if you spit golden lotus flowers and produce white light from your fingers, you'll find it difficult to get out of my trap," Qin Wan bellowed.

"I don't think I'll have any problem," the Heavenly Master replied with a smile.

He opened his mouth, and a lotus flower, as large as a basin, sprang out. At the same time, five beams of white light shot from the fingers of his left hand high into the air. A lotus flower appeared on the tip of each beam of light, and upon each lotus flower were five golden lamps to light his way forward.

As Qin Wan whirled the three pennants in the air, he saw that the Heavenly Master of Outstanding Culture was protected by colored clouds hung with stringed pearls that hovered in the air around him. Though he whirled his pennants repeatedly, the immortal was not hurt in any way.

"Qin Wan, I'm sorry but I can't allow you to live any longer. I have to act against the commandment on killing."

The Heavenly Master of Outstanding Culture then cast his Invisible Dragon Stake into the air and bound up Qin Wan with the three rings. Then he bowed towards Mount Kunlun and prayed. "Your disciple is going to break the commandment on killing today." With a single flick of his sword, he decapitated Qin Wan and emerged from the now powerless trap.

When he saw Qin Wan's head, Grand Tutor Wen gave a cry of rage and urged his unicorn forward. "Don't go, Outstanding Culture! I'm coming to have it out with you."

The Heavenly Master paid no attention to him, and the Yellow Dragon Immortal flew out on his crane from behind Burning Lamp and blocked the Grand Tutor's path. "Brother Deng Hua lost his life in Qin Wan's trap. Now it's just a tooth for a tooth. We've broken only one of your traps but nine still remain. We are competing with our magic arts, not physical strength. You'd better withdraw temporarily."

Just then Heavenly Master Zhao Jiang rode out on his spotted deer to the striking of bells. "Since he's broken the Heavenly Destruction, who dares to meet me in my Earthly Fury?"

Burning Lamp ordered Han Dulong to meet the challenge. The young general leapt forward and shouted, "Don't think you can get away with this! Here I come."

"Who are you?"

"I'm a disciple of Heavenly Master of Divine Virtue. By order of Burning Lamp I've come to break your Earthly Fury."

"You dare to enter my trap, do you? You'll lose your life in vain," Heavenly Master Zhao said with a cold laugh.

He slashed at Han Dulong with his sword, and Han met the attack with his own. When they had fought vigorously for five rounds, Zhao Jiang gave up ground and fled into his Earthly Fury with Han close behind. Zhao rushed to his platform and waved his pennants, invoking strange clouds all around. Surrounded by thunder and fire, Han was turned to powder in seconds. His soul flew to the Terrace of Creation.

Heavenly Master Zhao rode out of his trap. "Friends! Why don't you send a man with magic powers? Spare the life of mortals. Who has the courage to meet me now?"

"Krakucchanda, you break the Earthly Fury," Burning Lamp ordered.

Krakucchanda strode out and met Heavenly Master Zhao. "Zhao Jiang! You're wicked to act against the will of Heaven and hurt people with your evil traps. But don't rely too much on your witchcraft. You'll find it difficult to escape today."

Heavenly Master Zhao angrily rushed at him with his sword and the two fought fiercely. After several rounds, Zhao ran into his Earthly Fury Trap while Krakucchanda hung back, not daring to follow. But at the ringing of the gold bell, he plucked up his courage and plunged inside.

As before, Zhao mounted the platform and waved his pennants. Realizing the danger he was in, Krakucchanda opened the door of his skull, and magic clouds gushed out to protect his head and body. He then threw his Celestial Binding Rope into the air and ordered his yellow-scarved genie to bind Zhao up and throw him into the reed pavilion.

Zhao Jiang landed with such force that fire burst out from his ears, eyes, nostrils, and mouth, and the Earthly Fury Trap was thus destroyed. Krakucchanda emerged and calmly made his way back to the Zhou army.

Seeing that Zhao Jiang had been taken alive, Grand Tutor Wen cried out, "Don't go away, Krakucchanda. I'm coming to finish you off!"

Jade Tripod quickly warned him, "You shouldn't behave like this, Brother Wen! By order of the Jade Emptiness Palace, we're here to break the Ten Death Traps. We've taken only two of them, but another eight remain. We're here to compete with our skill in magic, not with physical strength. Don't get so worked up. Your attitude is not worthy of a Taoist."

Grand Tutor Wen was shamed into silence. As Burning Lamp left the scene and returned to the reed pavilion, Grand Tutor Wen and his army went back to their own camp. The Grand Tutor held a military conference to discuss the situation with his eight colleagues.

"Two traps have been broken, and we've lost two of our fellow Taoists. I'm very worried by the developments," Grand Tutor Wen said.

"It's all been destined by fate. Nevertheless, we can't give up now. I'll deal with them in my Roaring Typhoon. We're sure to win with that," Heavenly Master Dong reassured him.

Back in the reed pavilion, Krakucchanda brought Zhao Jiang before Burning Lamp. Burning Lamp ordered, "Hang him up in the pavilion."

"Shall we break the Roaring Typhoon tomorrow?" all the immortals asked.

"How can we? It doesn't use ordinary wind; it's derived from the energies of earth, water and fire and conceals swords and cutlasses. How can we resist it? We'll need the Wind Stopping Pearl first," Burning Lamp replied.

"Where can we get it?" all the immortals asked.

"My friend, Woe Evading Sage, lives in Cloud Light Cave on Mount Nine Tripods and Iron Forks. He's got the pearl, so I can write to him for it. Jiang Ziya, you may send a general and a civil official to deliver the letter and bring back the pearl," Master Spiritual Treasure suggested.

Jiang Ziya sent San Yisheng and General Chao Tian on the mission. They traveled along the highway to cross the Yellow River and arrived at Mount Nine Tripods and Iron Forks several days later. Jagged peaks towered high in the sky, rocks, resembling seated tigers and ancient pines, twisted like flying dragons covered the mountain. Birds sang sweetly on the crags, and plum flowers perfumed the air.

San Yisheng and Chao Tian approached the Cloud Light Cave and asked a lad to report their arrival to the Woe Evading Sage. Offering his greetings, San Yisheng handed the letter to the immortal, who was sitting on a straw cushion. After reading the letter he said, "As Heaven has destined that all the immortals gather in West Qi to break the Ten Death Traps, I must give you my pearl. Besides, you've got a recommendation from Master Spiritual Treasure. But you must be very careful not to lose it on your return journey."

He handed the pearl to San Yisheng, who thanked him and then hurriedly left with Chao Tian. Despite the danger of the mountain path, they galloped at high speed, but when they arrived at the Yellow River, they were perplexed to find no ferries operating. They spent two whole days riding along the bank in search of one.

"There were ferry boats everywhere just a few days ago. Why are there none to be found now?" San Yisheng pondered aloud to General Chao Tian.

Just then they saw a man approaching. Chao Tian asked him, "My good man, why are there no ferryboats around?"

"You don't know it, sir, but two wicked men came here recently. They're very strong and nobody dares to oppose them. They drove all the boatmen away and closed all the ferry jetties, leaving only one open about five *li* from here. They now monopolize the river, demanding any fare that they please. No one dares argue with them."

"How could this have happened? Only a couple of days!" San Yisheng muttered in disbelief.

They continued on their way, and sure enough, they found two giants who used not boats, but rafts that they pulled across the river with ropes. General Chao Tian found that they were none other than Fang Bi and Fang Xiang.

"Where are you going, Brother?" Fang Bi asked.

"May we trouble you to ferry us over?" Chao Tian asked.

As they crossed to the other bank, Fang Bi and Fang Xiang chatted with Chao Tian about old times, and Chao Tian introduced San Yisheng as a senior minister of West Qi.

"You're a general under King Zhou. Why are you traveling with him?" Fang Bi asked.

"As King Zhou has become a tyrant, I've forsaken him for the sagely ruler in West Qi. Grand Tutor Wen is now making trouble for us, but we just got hold of the Wind Stopping Pearl to break the Roaring Typhoon," Chao Tian told them frankly.

"We've lived a miserable life. If we seize the pearl and present it to King Zhou, he'll be sure to pardon us," Fang Bi thought and asked, "Why is it called the Wind Stopping

Pearl? Do show us; it sounds fascinating."

As Fang Bi had ferried them across the Yellow River and was a friend of Chao Tian, San Yisheng took the pearl from his pocket without hesitation and handed it to Fang Bi. Fang Bi glanced at it and put it straight into his waist pocket.

"We'll keep this as your fare." he said rudely.

Without a word more, Fang Bi and Fang Xiang left them and made their way directly to the southern highway. Chao Tian dared not stop them, as both were more than thirty feet tall and extraordinarily strong. Nobody had the courage to tangle with them.

San Yisheng was frightened out of his wits and cried loudly, "We got the pearl only to lose it again! What shall we do? How can I face Prime Minister Jiang again?"

He rushed to the bank and was about to throw himself into the Yellow River, but Chao Tian pulled him back, saying, "Your Excellency! Don't be rash. We're not afraid of death, but we must remember that Prime Minister Jiang is anxious to have the pearl to break the Roaring Typhoon. If we die, he'll have no idea what happened, and as a result the country may meet with disaster. We would then be condemned by all for disloyalty and stupidity. Let's first see Prime Minister Jiang and report to him all that has happened. It's better to die under the sword than to commit suicide and be cursed by everyone."

"Who would have thought that we would meet such misfortune here?" San Yisheng said with a sigh.

They mounted their horses and whipped them to a fast gallop. They had traveled only fifteen *li* when they saw flags and banners waving before them and heard the creak of grain carts. As San Yisheng drew near, he saw that it was General Huang Feihu bringing grain supplies to West Qi.

San Yisheng dismounted, and Huang Feihu also got down from his ox. "Where are you going, Supreme Minister?"

San Yisheng knelt on the ground and began to sob.

"Why are you so grief-stricken? What has happened, Supreme Minister?" Huang Feihu inquired.

San Yisheng told him the whole story.

"How long ago was it stolen?"

"Not long ago. They can't be far away."

"Don't worry, Supreme Minister. Wait for me here and I'll get the pearl back for you," Huang Feihu said. He mounted his devine ox and sped off like the wind. Before long he caught sight of the Fang brothers swaying down the road before him. "Fang Bi and Fang Xiang! Wait a minute!"

Turning his head, Fang Bi found to his surprise that it was Huang Feihu. They hadn't seen him for many years and now hastily knelt at the roadside. "Where are you going, Your Highness?"

"Why did you steal the Wind Stopping Pearl?"

"He gave it to me as fare," Fang Bi lied.

"Give it back to me at once," Huang demanded.

Fang Bi obediently handed over the pearl with both hands.

"Where have you been these past few years?" Huang Feihu asked.

"Since we left you, we've made a living by ferrying people across the river," Fang Bi answered.

"I've forsaken the Shang Dynasty. King Wu is a sagely ruler, as virtuous as Yao and Shun. He rules two-thirds of the kingdom already. Though Grand Tutor Wen has sent armies to West Qi several times, he cannot win. As you're homeless now, you can't do any better than follow me and serve under King Wu. You'll both be given a high rank. Don't waste your talents in vain," Huang Feihu urged them.

"If you're kind enough to recommend us, we'll be grateful for the rest of our lives," said Fang Bi.

"Come with me then."

They traveled swiftly back to the other men. San Yisheng and Chao Tian were both terrified at the sight of Fang Bi and Fang Xiang, but Huang Feihu dismounted and handed the pearl to San Yisheng. "You go ahead. I'll return with Fang Bi and Fang Xiang later."

San Yisheng and Chao Tian hurried on their way and soon reached the reed pavilion beyond the city wall.

"Have you got the Wind Stopping Pearl?" Jiang Ziya asked urgently.

San Yisheng reported the whole story, but the prime minister said nothing, quickly handing the pearl over to Burning Lamp.

"Now that we've got the pearl, we can deal with the Roaring Typhoon tomorrow," the immortal said.

If you want to know what happened after that, just read the next chapter.

46

BREAKING THE GOLDEN LIGHT TRAP

Early the next morning, Burning Lamp and his fellow immortals left the pavilion to the ringing of gold bells and jade chimes. Grand Tutor Wen arrived to see how Jiang Ziya would break the Roaring Typhoon. Soon Heavenly Master Dong rode out on his eight forked antler deer, carrying a sword in either hand. He shouted a challenge to the Zhou army.

Burning Lamp looked around but was unable to find anyone destined to enter the Roaring Typhoon first. Just at that moment, Huang Feihu returned with Fang Bi and Fang Xiang.

"On my way back I persuaded Fang Bi and Fang Xiang to join us. They served in King Zhou's royal guard," Huang Feihu told Jiang Ziya.

At the sight of the Fang brothers, Burning Lamp groaned. "This is fate, and nobody can escape it!" He ordered, "Fang Bi, go break the Roaring Typhoon."

Fang Bi was a mortal without any knowledge of sorcery. He acknowledged the order and strode rapidly to the front, halberd in hand.

Heavenly Master Dong was terrified at the sight of him. Fang Bi strode up to him, crying, "Not so fast, sorcerer," and lunged at him with his halberd. How could Dong resist him? He ran away after only one round and dodged into his trap. Inspired by the war drums, Fang Bi rushed after him, ignorant of what would happen. Dong mounted the platform, picked up his black pennant and waved it vigorously. All of a sudden, a black wind, revealing thousands of swords, whirled around Fang Bi. Fang Bi was instantly cut into pieces, and his soul flew to the Terrace of Creation. His remains were thrown out of the trap.

Dong reappeared. "Shame on you, Immortals!" he cried. "How can you be so heartless as to sacrifice a mortal in my trap? Send someone with magic powers!"

Burning Lamp gave the Wind Stopping Pearl to the Immortal of Merciful Navigation and told him to break the Roaring Typhoon.

Merciful Navigation strode up and said to Heavenly Master Dong, "Friend! You're free to enjoy yourself. Why set up this trap and bring about your own destruction? You were there at the Green Touring Palace when the Taoist leaders signed the List of Creations. Your master's couplet warned you not to come here!"

"You of Chan Taoism are too conceited, thinking that you're superior in the magic arts. Friend, you're known to be happy and kind. You'd better get out of here quickly and let someone else take your place," Heavenly Master Dong retorted.

"Don't concern yourself about me when you can't even look after yourself," Merciful Navigation answered coldly.

Flying into a rage, Dong Quan stabbed at Merciful Navigation. The immortal breathed an apology to Mount Kunlun then returned the blow with his sword. After five rounds, Dong Quan gave up the fight and ran into his Roaring Typhoon Trap. The immortal pursued him to the doorway, hesitated for a moment, then followed him cautiously inside. Master Dong mounted the platform and waved his black pennant, but Merciful Navigation had already placed the pearl on top of his head, and the black wind would not come.

Merciful Navigation tossed his glazed vase into the air and ordered his genie to turn it upside down. Black vapors poured from it, and with a crash, Dong Quan was sucked inside. Merciful Navigation then ordered his genie to right the vase and carry it out of the Roaring Typhoon. He saw Grand Tutor Wen waiting outside and told him, "I've already broken the Roaring Typhoon."

He ordered the genie to overturn the vase, and Dong

Quan's robes, belt and hemp shoes fell out onto the ground. His corpse had already been reduced to a stream of blood and his soul had floated to the Terrace of Creation.

Enraged by the sight, the Grand Tutor spurred his unicorn forward brandishing his gold staves. But the Yellow Dragon Immortal stopped him. "Grand Tutor Wen! Why get so angry? We've broken only three of your traps. Seven more remain untouched."

Just then someone yelled, "Grand Tutor Wen! Leave him to me. Here I come." Heavenly Master Yuan rushed out of his Frigid Ice Trap. "Disciples of Mount Kunlun," he roared. "Which of you will meet me?"

Burning Lamp ordered Xue Ehu to answer the challenge. Xue Ehu immediately ran out with his sword ready. As he was only a youth, Heavenly Master Yuan said contemptuously, "You'd better go back, Taoist lad. Tell your master to come and meet me."

"I'm here on the orders of my commander. How can I return without your head in my hand!" Xue Ehu said furiously.

He hacked at Heavenly Master Yuan with his sword, and the two fought desperately. After several rounds, Heavenly Master Yuan gave up the combat and ran into his trap. As Xue pursued him inside, Yuan mounted his platform and waved his purple pennant. In an instant a mountain of ice with jagged edges like knives fell from the sky and simultaneously a mass of ice blocks as sharp as a wolf's teeth rose to meet it. As they crashed together, Xue Ehu's body was smashed to pieces and his soul flew to the Terrace of Creation.

As the black vapors rose into the sky, Heavenly Master of Divine Virtue sighed sorrowfully. "I've already lost two disciples here. How terrible this is!"

A moment later, Heavenly Master Yuan reappeared. "Why don't you twelve famous celestials come to meet me instead of sending an innocent mortal?" he shouted.

Burning Lamp then ordered Immortal Universal Virtue to go and meet him. The sage strode out singing:

How can I forget the root of the Way?

The fire can melt the ice and frost.
A filthy mind fails the test of a demon,
Paradise will be lost to him.

As Heavenly Master Yuan rushed over, Universal Virtue said to him, "Yuan Jue, why are you so unwise? When I break the commandment on killing, you'll lose all that you've achieved!"

Heavenly Master Yuan furiously attacked him with his sword. The sage fought back with his own. After three rounds, Heavenly Master Yuan ran into his trap, and Universal Virtue plunged inside after him.

Yuan ascended the platform and waved the pennant to summon forth the mountains of ice. But Universal Virtue quickly released a column of white light from his fingers crowned by a brilliant octagonal cloud. A gold lamp hung at each corner. This cloud not only protected the sage but also rapidly melted the terrible ice. Heavenly Master Yuan soon found that his Frigid Ice had been rendered useless. He tried to flee, but Universal Virtue instantly sent his "Hooks of Wu" flying through the air. Yuan's head was severed from his body, and he fell dead below the platform. His soul flew directly to the Terrace of Creation. Universal Virtue retracted the light from his fingers and walked out with his big sleeves swinging in the breeze.

When the Frigid Ice Trap had been broken, Grand Tutor Wen was about to take his revenge on the sage when Mother Golden Light sped over on her spotted leopard. "You Chan Taoists there, dare you come and break my Golden Light Trap?"

Looking around him, Burning Lamp could not find anyone destined to enter first. He was wondering what to do when a Taoist descended from the air. Observing his dignified bearing, snow-white face and cinnabar lips, the immortals recognized him as Xiao Zhen, a disciple of the Jade Emptiness Palace.

Xiao Zhen bowed before them. "By order of my master, I've come here to break the Golden Light Trap." As Mother Golden Light gave a second challenge, he turned and shouted, "Don't get so excited! Here I come."

Not recognizing him, she asked, "Who are you?"

"How can you fail to know me? I'm Xiao Zhen, a disciple of the Jade Emptiness Palace."

"What powers do you have that you dare to venture into my trap?" she said contemptuously.

She charged at Xiao Zhen with her sword, and he defended himself with his own. After five rounds she pulled out of the fight and sped into her trap.

Xiao Zhen yelled, "Don't run away!"

As he entered the Golden Light Trap, she dismounted from her leopard and ascended the platform. She pulled the ropes attached to the bamboo poles, shaking her magic mirrors, and a myriad of golden beams shot forth. As they hit Xiao Zhen, he gave a cry of agony and disappeared without a trace.

Mother Golden Light mounted her leopard and emerged from her trap. "I've finished him off. Who dares to meet me now?"

Burning Lamp asked Master Grand Completion to answer her challenge. When Mother Golden Light saw the confidence of Master Grand Completion, she was enraged. "So you dare to meet me!"

"There's nothing difficult about this at all. Child's play to me!"

Mother Golden Light could not contain her anger and attacked him with her sword, but after only a few rounds, she once more turned and ran into her trap. Master Grand Completion gave chase. Mother Golden Light leapt onto the platform and pulled the ropes to shake the mirrors. Master Grand Completion, however, immediately spread out his magic robe with eight diagrams and covered himself from head to toe. The golden light could not penetrate his robe, no matter how powerfully they shot through the air.

Master Grand Completion stealthily hurled his Heaven Overturning Stamp from below his magic robe and broke nineteen of the twenty-one mirrors. Mother Golden Light was startled. She hurriedly took the two remaining mirrors in her hands, intending to flash them at him. But he was too quick for her. He hurled his stamp for a second time, and as she had no time to dodge, the heavy blow instantly knocked her brains out. Her soul entered the Terrace of Creation, and Master Grand Completion left the Golden Light Trap.

Grand Tutor Wen yelled angrily, "Don't go away, Grand Completion! I must avenge Mother Golden Light."

But Heavenly Master Sun of the Bleeding Blood Trap stopped him. "Brother Wen! Don't get so angry. Let me revenge Mother Golden Light."

Sun had a date-red face and a short beard. He wore a tiger hat and rode a yellow spotted deer. Burning Lamp looked at everyone around him but could not find the one to make the first entry. Suddenly a Taoist rushed up and bowed before him.

"Please tell us your honorable name," Burning Lamp requested.

"I'm Qiao Kun, a hermit from the White Cloud Cave on Mount Wuyi. I heard that Grand Tutor Wen's forces include the Bleeding Blood Trap. I'm here to break it for Jiang Ziya."

Heavenly Master Sun shouted a second challenge.

Qiao Kun courageously answered, "I'll take you on." He strode forward and demanded of Sun, "We're all followers of the same religion. Why have you set up this evil trap?"

"Who are you? Get out of here quickly lest you lose your life," Sun said harshly.

Qiao Kun swore in great anger, "Sun Liang! Don't brag so much. I'll break your trap all right, cut your head off, and hang it on the wall of West Qi City."

Sun spurred his deer forward in a fury to attack Qiao Kun with his sword. They fought desperately for a few rounds, then Sun ran into his trap, pursued closely by Qiao Kun. Sun ascended the platform and cast his black sand at Qiao Kun. Qiao's body instantly turned into a stream of blood, and his soul flew to the Terrace of Creation.

Sun reappeared before his trap. "Burning Lamp! Don't send these mortals needlessly to death."

Burning Lamp ordered Fairy Primordial to meet him. When he saw Fairy Primordial, Heavenly Master Sun said contemptuously, "Brother, you're no match for me!"

CREATION OF THE GODS

"Don't boast so much. There's no danger in your trap for me," the immortal answered sarcastically.

Heavenly Master Sun could not control his anger. He spurred his deer forward and attacked Fairy Primordial with his sword. After only a few rounds, he ran once more into his trap. When he got to the gate of the trap, Fairy Primordial pointed at the ground with his right hand, and two green lotus flowers instantly appeared. He stepped onto the flowers and rode inside. Then he pointed towards the sky with his left hand and a column of white light topped by a colored cloud appeared in the air above him protecting his whole body.

Ascending the platform, Heavenly Master Sun grasped a handful of black sand and cast it at the immortal, but as soon as it touched the brilliant cloud, it melted like snow and disappeared. He quickly threw a whole peck of black sand at the immortal, but it disappeared too. His sand rendered powerless, Heavenly Master Sun tried to flee, but Fairy Primordial instantly threw his Nine Dragon Divine Fire Coverlet into the air, wrapping up Sun Liang. Fairy Primordial clapped his hands and nine fire dragons coiled around the coverlet. In a moment, the intense fire burned Sun to ashes, and his soul flew to join the others in the Terrace of Creation.

Grand Tutor Wen was desperate. "Don't leave, Primordial! I'm going to knock your brains out!"

The Yellow Dragon Immortal, however, intercepted him on his crane. "You're a great statesman and should not break your word. We've only broken six of your traps. You'd better wait until we meet again tomorrow. There's no need to get violent. The winner will become evident in time."

The Grand Tutor boiled with rage. A brilliant light flashed from his divine third eye and his hair stood on end. Entering his camp, he invited the four remaining Heavenly Masters to convene with him. He wept, "As one on whom the king has bestowed great favors, it should be I that sacrifices myself for the king. But it's unbearable that six of my friends have lost their lives! Return to your island and let me meet Jiang Ziya in a final showdown. I swear that I won't rest till one of us is dead."

His tears fell like rain, and the four Heavenly Masters tried to comfort him. "Set your mind at rest, Brother! This has all been destined by fate. We'll see what we can do when the time comes."

They then returned to their own quarters. Grand Tutor Wen sat alone racking his brains for a way to cope with Jiang Ziya. He then remembered Zhao Gongming, one of his best friends, who lived in Luofu Cave on Mount Emei. "If I can get him here to help me, the matter can undoubtedly be settled in our favor," he thought. He summoned Ji Li and Yu Qing and ordered, "Guard the camp. I'm going to Mount Emei and will return here as soon as possible."

He mounted his unicorn and rode on the wind and clouds directly to Luofu Cave. When he arrived, he dismounted and admired the wonderful mountain scenery. Cranes sang, deer grazed, and apes and monkeys played on the tranquil slopes. Ivy and wistaria hung over the entrance to the cave.

"Is there anybody in?" Grand Tutor Wen called, knocking at the door.

Before long, a lad came out, and finding a visitor with three eyes, asked Grand Tutor Wen, "Where do you come from?"

But the Grand Tutor asked again, "Is your master in?"

"He's in mediation, sir."

"Please tell him that Grand Tutor Wen from the capital of the Shang Dynasty has come to visit him."

Zhao Gongming hastily came out and greeted him with a smile. "Brother Wen! What wind blows you here? You enjoy riches and power in the world of men. I was sure you had forgotten me."

They entered the cave hand in hand, exchanged formal greetings, and then sat down. When Grand Tutor Wen heaved a long sigh, Zhao Gongming asked, "What's the matter, Brother?"

The Grand Tutor told him of his defeats and the deaths of the Heavenly masters. "I'm at my wit's end," he went on, "and have come here, filled with deep shame, to seek your help. Would you consider it, Brother?"

"Why didn't you come here earlier?" Zhao reproved him. "You brought defeat on yourself. But what's done is done. Go back first and I'll follow shortly."

Grand Tutor Wen delightly bade him farewell and flew back to his camp. After his departure, Zhao Gongming told his disciples Chen Jiugong and Yao Shaosi, "Come with me to West Qi." He then turned to his lad, "Take good care of the cave. We'll be back soon."

The three then set out. On the way, they descended upon a high mountain with exquisite scenery. They were admiring the landscape when a strong wind whirled up, and two tigers emerged. Zhao smiled. "I've got no horse, so let one of them be my mount." He was overjoyed when one of the pair, a black tiger, raced straight towards him. "Welcome, friend. I'm in need of your service," he muttered.

He walked up to the tiger and pressed it down with two fingers, drawing a spell on its neck. Then he mounted it and patted its head. It immediately soared into the clouds. When he reached the camp gate, the guards cried out in fear, "Look out! Here comes a tiger!"

"Have no fear, friends. It's a tame tiger," Chen Jiugong assured them. "Hurry, tell Grand Tutor Wen that Zhao Gongming has arrived."

Grand Tutor Wen came out to meet Zhao Gongming. When they returned to the tent, the four remaining Heavenly masters came up to greet him.

"You could have won, but you've lost six friends. It's very regrettable," Zhao Gongming said. He then saw Heavenly Master Zhao hanging in the reed pavilion. "Who's that man there?"

"Alas, Brother! It's Zhao Jiang of the Earthly Fury Trap," Heavenly Master Bai answered.

Zhao Gongming was furious. "That's outrageous!" he roared. "Though there are three religions, they're all equal. How can they insult us like this? I'll capture one of them and hang him here. I'll see how they feel about that!"

He immediately mounted his tiger and rode out of the camp with Grand Tutor Wen and the four Heavenly masters.

He gave a challenge to Jiang Ziya.

If you want to know what happened, please read the next chapter.

第四十七回　公明輔佐聞太師

47

ZHAO GONGMING
ASSISTS THE GRAND TUTOR

Mounted on his tiger, Zhao Gongming left the Shang camp brandishing his staff. "Come out, Jiang Shang. Come out and meet me at once!" he shouted at the Zhou soldiers.

Nezha entered the reed pavilion. "A man riding a tiger demands to meet you, Uncle Jiang."

"It's Zhao Gongming from Luofu Cave on Mount Emei. You should be careful," Burning Lamp advised him.

Jiang Ziya left the pavilion and rode out with Nezha, Thunderbolt, Huang Tianhua, Yang Jian, Jinzha and Muzha on either side. He saw a Taoist riding on a black tiger under the flying pennants. He moved forward, bowed, and greeted him. "Friend, where do you come from?"

"I'm Zhao Gongming from Luofu Cave on Mount Emei. You've broken six of the traps and killed six of my friends. In addition, you insult us by hanging Zhao Jiang over your pavilion. Jiang Shang, I know you're a disciple of the Jade Emptiness Palace. Today I'll fight it out with you to decide which of us is the better man."

He slashed at Jiang Ziya who answered with his own sword. After several rounds, Zhao tossed his staff, glaring like lightning, into the air. Having no time to dodge, Jiang Ziya was hit on the back and fell dead to the ground. Nezha took up the fight but was knocked from his Wind-Fire Wheels. Huang Tianhua rushed in on his jade unicorn, Thunderbolt flew up into the air, and Yang Jian spurred his horse forward to attack with his spear. As Zhao Gongming was busy defending himself, Yang Jian set his Sky Barking Hound on him. Taken unawares, Zhao was bitten on the neck, his robe torn to shreds.

Zhao hastily turned his tiger and fled back inside the camp gate.

Grand Tutor Wen came up to console him, but Zhao said, "Don't worry. It's nothing at all."

He took out a few pills of elixir from his gourd, mixed them with water, and applied the solution to his wound, which healed instantly.

When Jiang Ziya's corpse was carried into the prime minister's mansion, King Wu and his officials hurried over to see how he was. They saw him lying on his bed, pale and silent.

"Alas, glory and honor are both gone from him now!" King Wu said sorrowfully.

Everyone was lamenting the loss when Master Grand Completion arrived. King Wu went out to meet him and asked, "Brother, the prime minister is dead. What shall I do?"

"Don't worry, Your Highness. He's destined to suffer this calamity," the immortal said calmly.

He ordered that a cup of water be brought and then took a pill of elixir and dissolved it in the water. Prizing Jiang's mouth open, he poured the solution down his throat. In about two hours, Jiang Ziya woke up. "Oh! What agony! I'll die of the pain!"

He opened his eyes to find King Wu, Master Grand Completion, and the others standing before him, and realized that he had died and been restored to life. He tried to get up and thank them, but Master Grand Completion shook his head. "Just lie here quietly and rest. I'll go to see what Zhao Gongming's planning to do next."

Back in the pavilion, Master Grand Completion reported Jiang's recovery to Burning Lamp. Early the next morning, Zhao Gongming mounted his black tiger, took his staff, and left the Shang camp, demanding that Burning Lamp come out to meet him.

Nezha brought in the challenge. Burning Lamp and the other immortals left the camp and found Zhao Gongming, glaring fiercely, a wicked light rarely seen in a Taoist, shining in his eyes.

Burning Lamp bowed and greeted him.

"Brother," Zhao replied, "you've insulted us too often. You're familiar with our religion as well as I am with yours. Jie Taoism was founded long ago, before the genesis of the sun and the moon and Heaven and earth. Our masters both studied with the same teacher. We have a common origin, yet you hang Zhao Jiang up there, treating us like dirt. Don't you realize that by hanging him, you hang yourselves up too? Don't you know that white shoots and green stems are parts of the same bamboo, and red flowers, white roots and green leaves all belong to the same lotus! Don't you understand that Confucian scholars, Taoists, and Buddhists are really of one family?"

"Brother Zhao! Were you in the Green Touring Palace when the List of Creations was discussed and approved?" Burning Lamp asked.

"Yes, I know all about it."

"Then you must also remember your master telling you that the names of the fated are a secret, only to be known after they die? Why do you come here and make a fool of yourself by opposing the will of Heaven? You are only bringing calamity on yourself. None of us knows what fortune lies ahead. Though I've been an immortal since the beginning of time, it's still difficult for me to escape all worldly fetters. You're privileged. Why do you court disaster?"

Zhao Gongming angrily replied, "Do you imagine that I'm inferior to you in any way? I can reverse the direction of the sun and the moon! As I am older than Heaven and earth, there has never been any immortal superior to me."

The Yellow Dragon Immortal darted forward on his crane. "Zhao Gongming, now that you're here, your name must be on the list. You're destined to follow the others!"

This infuriated Zhao Gongming. He rushed at the Yellow Dragon Immortal brandishing his staff. After a few rounds, he threw his Dragon Binding Rope high in the air. It immediately bound up the Yellow Dragon Immortal and took him captive.

"Zhao Gongming! Don't get carried away!" Master Pure Essence roared.

He stabbed at Zhao Gongming with his sword, and Zhao returned the blow with his staff. After a few rounds, Zhao took a string of twenty-four pearls out of his pocket and cast these Sea Conquering Pearls up into the sky. They shone so brightly that none of the immortals could look up. Master Pure Essence was hit and fell to the ground. As Zhao raced up to kill him, Master Grand Completion strode forward, shouting, "Don't hurt my brother! Here I come."

Zhao Gongming swung around, but after only one round, he cast up the pearls again and knocked down Master Grand Completion. The combat was continued by Heavenly Master of Divine Virtue, Jade Tripod, and Master Spiritual Treasure, but they too were knocked down one after another. The five immortals withdrew into the pavilion, and Zhao Gongming returned to see Grand Tutor Wen. He ordered that the Yellow Dragon Immortal be hung high on a flag pole. He also stamped a charm on his head to prevent the immortal from escaping. Filled with delight, Grand Tutor Wen entertained Zhao Gongming and the four Heavenly masters.

When Burning Lamp returned to the pavilion, he asked, "Do you know what weapon he used?"

"I only felt a heavy blow but couldn't see clearly what hit me," said Master Spiritual Treasure.

"It shone with such a strong light that we couldn't see what it was," the other four immortals said in unison.

Burning Lamp grew worried when he heard their reports. Seeing the Yellow Dragon Immortal hanging on a flag pole made him even more uneasy.

"It's unbearable to see the Yellow Dragon Immortal suffer so. Who can help him?" he asked.

"Don't worry about it. I'll do something to help him this evening," Jade Tripod answered.

As the sun set in the west, Jade Tripod said to Yang Jian, "Go and set the Yellow Dragon Immortal free."

Yang Jian transformed himself into a flying ant and flew close to the captured immortal's ear. He whispered, "Uncle, your disciple Yang Jian's here to set you free. What should I do?"

"Just take the charm off. I can set myself free then," the Yellow Dragon Immortal answered.

Yang Jian did as he was told, and the immortal returned to the reed pavilion to the delight of his companions. When General Deng Zhong reported to Zhao Gongming that the Taoist had disappeared, Zhao made a calculation on his fingers and found that the Yellow Dragon Immortal had been released by Yang Jian. He smiled and said, "You may flee today, but you won't get away again tomorrow!"

The next day he mounted his tiger and rode to the reed pavilion, demanding to see Burning Lamp. Burning Lamp said to his companions, "You needn't go out. Let me deal with him alone."

He mounted his deer and rode out to meet Zhao.

"Yang Jian rescued the Yellow Dragon Immortal. He must be quite conceited about his skill of transformation. Let him meet me today." Zhao called out.

"Why are you so narrow-minded, friend? His talent means nothing, and all is due to Heaven's blessing on King Wu and Jiang Ziya," Burning Lamp replied.

"This is how you deceive the people!"

He lashed at Burning Lamp with his staff, and the latter defended himself with his sword. After a few rounds, Zhao once more cast the string of pearls into the air. Burning Lamp watched with his wisdom-eye, but he could not identify it. As it was about to drop on him, he spurred his deer into flight and sped off to the southwest. Zhao gave immediate chase.

Burning Lamp soon came to a slope and saw two men, one in green and the other in red, playing chess under the shade of a pine tree. They looked up as the deer approached and asked him why he was in such a hurry. Burning Lamp did not know them but related the story about Zhao Gongming's threat to West Qi and the events leading to his flight.

"Never mind, Master. We'll deal with him," they assured Burning Lamp.

When Zhao sped up on his tiger, he saw the two men, one in green with a black face and the other in red with a white face. "Who are you?" he demanded.

"How ridiculous you are, Gongming, to ask who we are!

> *We live in the beautiful haze,*
> *And we grow the golden lotus.*
> *Wine we drink in great pleasure,*
> *Kolanut we cook with its fire.*
> *We on a dragon tour the blue seas,*
> *And enjoy the quiet moon at night.*

We're Xiao Sheng and Cao Bao, hermits from Mount Wuyi, and we're greatly displeased to see Burning Lamp being so ruthlessly bullied. It's an act against the will of Heaven. You support the wicked and the ruthless but suppress the kind and virtuous. We can't tolerate it."

"How dare you insult me!" Zhao Gongming screamed furiously and charged at them with his staff.

Xiao Sheng and Cao Bao hurriedly met the assault with their swords. After a few rounds, Zhao cast up the Dragon Binding Rope. Xiao Sheng, however, smiled when he saw it.

"Ah! I was expecting this!" he cried.

He quickly took a gold coin from his leopard skin bag and threw it up into the air. The gold coin was none other than the Treasure Catching Gold Coin, which could bring down any magic weapon from the air. As it rose, Zhao Gongming's rope obediently followed it and dropped to the ground. Cao Bao quickly grabbed the rope.

Zhao Gongming roared like thunder. He cast the Sea Conquering Pearls into the air but lost them in the same manner.

Enranged, Zhao cast his powerful staff high into the air. Xiao Sheng did not know that because it was the mere weapon the gold coin was powerless against it. The staff struck him on the head, and he died in a pool of blood. His soul flew directly to the Terrace of Creation. In revenge for his brother, Cao Bao rushed up and engaged Zhao.

Burning Lamp was watching the scene from a nearby hill. "Those two were enjoying a chess game together. How could I have imagined that one of them would died innocently for me? I must help him," he decided.

He stealthily cast his Universal Ruler into the air. Zhao was caught off guard and nearly knocked him from his tiger. He uttered a loud cry and fled to the south.

Approaching Cao Bao, Burning Lamp dismounted from his deer and bowed, "I greatly appreciate your kindness in helping me out of trouble. How sorry I am that your friend in red met with disaster! Please tell me your honorable names and where you are from."

"I am Cao Bao, and my friend was Xiao Sheng. We are two hermits from Mount Wuyi. We were glad to help you out of trouble, but I never thought that Brother Xiao would lose his life at the hands of Zhao Gongming!" Cao Bao answered.

"When Zhao Gongming used his magic weapons, your friend threw a gold coin and brought them down. Would you tell me what they all are?"

"The coin is the 'Treasure Catching Gold Coin.' I don't know anything about Zhao Gongming's weapons," Cao Bao replied.

He took out the booty and showed it all to Burning Lamp. The immortal burst into laughter and clapped his hands when he saw the pearls. "Sea Conquering Pearls! Now that I've seen them, I have hopes of attaining to the ultimate in all I do. At the beginning of time, they shone on Mount Xuandu, but they've been missing ever since. I feel so relieved to see them in your hands."

"Master! Since you're sure to have a use for them, you may take them," Cao Bao said generously.

"How can I take them from you when I've done nothing of merit?"

"You ought to accept them. They're no use to me," urged Cao.

Burning Lamp bowed to express his thanks. They then went together to West Qi where they were welcomed into the reed pavilion by all the other immortals.

"Zhao Gongming hit you with the Sea Conquering Pearls," Burning Lamp informed them all.

When he took them out and showed them around, they all gasped with admiration. Disheartened, Zhao Gongming had returned to the Shang camp. When Grand Tutor Wen asked him about the outcome of his pursuit, he groaned bitterly.

"Why are you so unhappy, Brother?" Grand Tutor Wen asked.

"I've never suffered such a defeat since I became an immortal," he huffed. "I was chasing Burning Lamp when I came across Xiao Sheng and Cao Bao. They took away my Dragon Binding Rope and Sea Conquering Pearls. It's heartbreaking." He then ordered, "Chen Jiugong! Yao Shaosi! You stay here. I'm going to visit the Three Fairy Island."

"Do return as soon as possible, or else I'll worry about you all the time," Grand Tutor Wen begged.

"I'll come straight back," Zhao promised.

Riding his tiger, Zhao Gongming traveled swiftly on the clouds and reached the Three Fairy Island a short time later. At the entrance of a cave, he coughed politely and a lad came out to open the gate.

His three sisters lived on the island. The eldest was High Firmament, the second, Green Firmament and the youngest Jade Firmament. All three came out to meet him when he arrived. They conducted him inside, exchanged greetings, and then sat down.

"Where do you come from, Brother?" High Firmament asked.

Zhao Gongming explained the reason for his visit and then went on, "I've come here to ask you for either the Golden Dragon Scissors or the Golden Universe Muddling Dipper. I have to recover my own treasures."

High Firmament shook her head. "Brother, we can't do that. We were all at the conference when the List of Creations was compiled. As many of our names are on it, we've been forbidden to leave our caves. Master warned us that we should be cautious because the names on the list are a secret. Chan Taoism is destined to break the commandment on killing, but we are carefree. Besides, a phoenix sang on Mount Qi to announce that a sagely ruler was born there. Brother, go back to your cave. Wait until Jiang Ziya has created the gods. As soon as the period of creation is over, I'll go to Mount Divine

Hawk and ask Burning Lamp for the pearls. I'm very sorry, but I can't let you have either the Golden Dragon Scissors or the Golden Universe Muddling Dipper. Please forgive me."

"How can you refuse to help me!" Zhao Gongming cried disappointedly.

"It's not that I'm unwilling. I'm just worried that if we're careless, it'll be too late. I beg that you return to your mountain. The creations will take place before long. Don't be too impatient," High Firmament persisted.

"Since my family won't help me, I don't think anyone else will either," Zhao Gongming sighed.

Bidding his sisters farewell, he got up angrily to leave. Green Firmament was inclined to help him, but High Firmament stubbornly refused.

Zhao Gongming was about two *li* from the cave when he heard someone shouting behind him, "Brother Zhao, Brother Zhao!" He looked around and found it was Celestial Lotus.

"What do you want, friend?" Zhao asked.

"Where are you going?"

Zhao Gongming told her how he had lost his Sea Conquering Pearls while pursuing Burning Lamp. He then added, "I went to my younger sisters and asked them for the Golden Dragon Scissors so that I could recover my pearls, but they refused. I'm now going elsewhere for help."

"This is really ridiculous! How can your own sisters refuse to help you! Let's go back and discuss the matter with them again," she said indignantly.

They returned to the cave together and were welcomed by the sisters. Greetings were exchanged and everyone was seated. "You're from the same family. How can you disregard your brother?" Celestial Lotus began. "Do you think that only those from the Jade Emptiness Palace possess powerful magic arts, and we possess none? Now that they have the Dragon Binding Rope and the Sea Conquering Pearls, you ought to help your own brother. Should he get help from someone else, what shame you would feel! I will even let him have the magic weapon that I'm refining now."

"Sister! Give him the Golden Dragon Scissors," Green

Firmament urged.

High Firmament remained silent. She pondered for a long time, then took out the scissors. "Brother, go to see Burning Lamp and say, 'Please return the pearls to me peacefully. If you refuse, I'll cast up my Golden Dragon Scissors and create a terrible havoc.' He's sure to return your pearls at once. I tell you the truth: you must deal with this situation very carefully."

Zhao Gongming promised to follow his sister's wishes. He took the scissors and left the island with great haste.

"I'll be there as soon as my magic weapon is ready," Celestial Lotus told him.

When he arrived back at the Shang camp, Zhao Gongming was met by Grand Tutor Wen. Sitting down together inside, the Grand Tutor asked, "Where have you been, Brother?"

"I've been to the Three Fairy Island to get the Golden Dragon Scissors from my sisters. I must demand the return of my pearls tomorrow," Zhao replied.

Grand Tutor Wen received this news with great delight and entertained him that evening.

The next morning, Grand Tutor Wen mounted his pure black unicorn and with Deng, Xin, Zhang, and Tao and Zhao Gongming on his tiger, they rode out of the Shang camp and gave a challenge to Burning Lamp.

Nezha announced the challenge, but Burning Lamp was already fully aware of the situation. "Zhao Gongming has the Golden Dragon Scissors. You must all remain indoors. I'll see him alone."

He mounted his deer and rode to the front.

"Burning Lamp! You must return my pearls today! Everything can then be settled between us. If you don't, I'll show you who's the better man."

"The pearls are a Buddhist treasure and have once again found their rightful owner. You are not destined to possess them. They'll help me to attain the ultimate, so don't even dream of getting them back," Burning Lamp replied.

"Since you're so unsympathetic, the rift between us is unredeemable," Zhao shouted and urged his tiger forward.

Burning Lamp met the assault with his sword and they fought together vigorously. After several rounds, Zhao Gongming took out the Golden Dragon Scissors and tossed them into the air.

What became of Burning Lamp? If you want to know, read the next chapter.

48

THE DEATH OF ZHAO GONGMING

After several rounds, Zhao Gongming threw his Golden Dragon Scissors high into the sky. The scissors were really a pair of dragons which lived on the essence of Heaven, earth, the sun and moon. When they were high in the air, their tails locked together, and their bodies could cut man and immortal in two like a pair of scissors.

As they dropped, Burning Lamp hurriedly got down from his deer and rode away on a wooden cloud, but his deer was cut in two. As Zhao Gongming returned to his camp in annoyance, Burning Lamp fled back to the reed pavilion. The other immortals asked him about the scissors.

"They're terrible! When the scissors rose in the air, they looked like two twisting dragons, but as soon as they dropped, they became a pair of sharp scissors. I fled on a cloud of wood, but my poor deer was cut in two."

Everyone was frightened by his description. As they talked, Nezha entered. "An immortal is here asking to see you."

When the Taoist was admitted, he bowed and greeted everyone. None of the immortals knew him, so Burning Lamp asked with a smile, "Where do you come from, Brother?"

"I'm a hermit on Mount West Kunlun. My name is Lu Ya. I've come here because of Zhao Gongming. He borrowed the Golden Dragon Scissors and means harm. He knows only that he's powerful and is ignorant that there's magic more powerful than his. I'll render his scissors useless, and he'll have to die."

Burning Lamp and other immortals maintained a doubtful silence as they listened to him. Early the next morning, Zhao

Gongming rode out on his tiger. "Burning Lamp! Since your magic knows no bounds, how could you have so shamefully run away yesterday? Come out here, and we'll see who's the better man," he shouted.

When Nezha reported the challenge inside the pavilion, Lu Ya said, "I'll go to meet him."

Zhao Gongming was surprised when a short, odd but divine-looking man come out, wearing a fish-tail coronet and a red robe. He asked, "Who are you?"

"Zhao Gongming, how can you possibly know me? I'm neither a Taoist nor a sage. Listen to my song:

> My nature like clouds, my mind the wind,
> I float wherever I please.
> On the East Sea, a bright moon,
> On the South, I ride a dragon.
> I sit on a tiger in the mountains,
> And fly on a phoenix over the clouds.
> I have neither riches nor power,
> Nor am I known on Mount Kunlun.
> I care not for longevity peaches,
> Three cups of wine, I'll go my own way.
> I sit quietly on the rocks,
> Listen to the deer or play chess.
> I write poems, awing earth and Heaven,
> I play the guitar to amuse myself.
> Your years of effort will all be in vain,
> I've come here to eradicate Zhao Gongming.

I'm Lu Ya of Mount West Kunlun," he added.

In a wrath, Zhao Gongming swore, "You damned sorcerer! How dare you insult me!"

He urged his tiger forward with his staff, and Lu Ya answered with his sword. After about five rounds, Zhao Gongming threw his scissors up into the air. Lu Ya glanced up and yelled, "Just as I expected!"

He transformed himself into a rainbow and ran away. As Lu Ya got away, and Burning Lamp sat calmly in the pavilion with other immortals, Zhao Gongming became very angry. He returned to the camp grinding his teeth.

During this encounter, Lu Ya had observed Zhao Gongming and was now ready to carry out his plan. When he returned to the reed pavilion, he told Burning Lamp, "I've got a way to cope with him, but I must trouble Jiang Ziya to cooperate."

"I'll do as you instruct," Jiang Ziya answered promptly.

Lu Ya opened his flower basket and took out a sheet of paper stamped with seals and spells and charms. "Go to Mount Qi and build a platform. Make a straw effigy and write 'Zhao Gongming' on its body. Place one lamp above its head and another beneath its feet. Then worship it three times a day, recite the charms and burn the spells stamped on the paper. At noon on the twenty-first day, I'll come and help you put him to death."

Accordingly, Jiang Ziya went secretly to Mount Qi with 3,000 soldiers. He ordered Nangong Kuo to build a platform and then made a straw effigy on which he wrote Zhao's name. He did everything strictly as instructed. Finally he loosened his hair, took a sword and paced in a square, reciting charms, burning spells, and worshiping over and over again before the straw effigy.

Five days later, Zhao began to feel as if his heart was burning with fire. He walked to and fro and scratched his ears, cheeks and chin. Whatever he did, he felt uncomfortable. Grand Tutor Wen was likewise disturbed to see him in this condition and was unable to concentrate on military affairs.

Heavenly Master Bai appeared and said to the Grand Tutor, "As Brother Zhao's unwell, it would be better to let him rest. I'll meet the Chan Taoists in my Vehement Flame Trap." Grand Tutor Wen tried to stop him, but Heavenly Master Bai grew angry. "None of the ten traps has been successful yet. If we sit quietly all day long like this, when will we ever win?"

He disregarded Grand Tutor Wen's opinion, and rushed into his Vehement Flame Trap. When he completed all the arrangements, he rode out on his deer to the clanging of bells.

He approached the reed pavilion and gave a loud challenge.

Burning Lamp and other immortals strode out and heard him yelling, "You disciples of the Jade Emptiness Palace! Which of you will meet me in my trap?"

Burning Lamp looked round, but no one offered to answer the challenge.

"What's the name of his trap?" Lu Ya asked.

"It's the Vehement Flame Trap."

"I'll take him on," Lu Ya said with a smile and strode forward singing a song.

"Who are you?" Heavenly Master Bai demanded.

"Since you've gone to the trouble of laying a trap here, there must be some mystery to it. I'm Lu Ya and I've come here especially to meet you."

The enraged Heavenly Master Bai attacked Lu Ya with his sword. After they had fought several rounds, Heavenly Master Bai rushed into his trap, climbed up on the platform, and waved his three red pennants. Lu Ya pursued him inside and was instantly surrounded by fires from the sky, from the ground, and from the human world. However, Heavenly Master Bai did not know that Lu Ya had been refined by the fire of fires, so it was impossible to burn him. After four hours, he heard Lu Ya still singing within, and peering through the flames, he saw Lu Ya holding a gourd in his hand. A beam of light thirty feet high shot from the gourd, and above it appeared something with eyes and eyebrows. A white light beamed down from the eyes, and when it hit the top of Heavenly Master Bai's head, he lost consciousness at once.

Inside the fires Lu Ya bowed and said, "Please turn round, my precious." When the white light had turned a full circle, Bai's head fell to the ground, and his soul flew to the Terrace of Creation.

As Lu Ya put away his gourd and left the trap, he heard a cry behind him, "Don't run away, Lu Ya. Here I come."

It was Heavenly Master Yao of the Soul Snatching Trap. He raced up like lightning on his deer, roaring like thunder and brandishing his staves. He had a golden face, a red beard, and massive tusks extending from his huge mouth.

Burning Lamp ordered Jiang Ziya, "Tell Fang Xiang to meet him."

Jiang Ziya passed on the order, and Fang Xiang rushed into battle. Raising his halberd, he yelled, "I'm here with orders to break your Soul Snatching Trap."

He lunged at Heavenly Master Yao, who was defenceless against his overwhelming strength and quickly fled into his trap. When Fang Xiang pursued him inside, Heavenly Master Yao threw black sand down from the platform, killing Fang Xiang instantly. His soul flew to the Terrace of Creation.

Heavenly Master Yao mounted his deer and shouted, "Burning Lamp! Why are you so cruel as to send a mortal to his death? Send a highly talented man to meet me."

Burning Lamp ordered Master Pure Essence to deal with him. Master Pure Essence strode out singing, sword in hand. "Yao Bin! I entered this trap twice when you snatched Jiang Ziya's souls. Though I rescued him, today you've killed Fang Xiang."

"Even the Map of the Eight Diagrams is powerless against me! It's now in my possession. You disciples of the Jade Emptiness Palace are nothing. You may have some magic powers, but they're really not good enough." Heavenly Master Yao said contemptuously.

"This has all been destined by fate. Now you are to lose your life, but it's already too late to regret it," Master Pure Essence refuted.

Heavenly Master Yao flew into a rage and attacked Master Pure Essence with his ridged staves. The immortal muttered an apology to Mount Kunlun and met the blow with his sword. The two fought vigorously. After a few rounds, Yao Bin ran into his trap, and Master Pure Essence pursued him, entering it for the third time. He knew its power. He first emitted a brilliant cloud from his head to protect his body and then covered himself with a Divine Purple Longevity Robe patterned with the eight diagrams.

Heavenly Master Yao hurriedly mounted the platform and threw a peck of black sand at Master Pure Essence. The immortal was protected, however, by the brilliant cloud and the divine robe.

Disappointed but angry, Heavenly Master Yao was about to descend from the platform and engage his opponent when Master Pure Essence took out his *Yin Yang* Mirror and flashed it in Yao Bin's face. He fell from the platform, and Master Pure Essence bowed in the direction of Mount Kunlun, saying, "Your disciple apologizes for acting against the commandment on killing." He then strode forward and beheaded Heavenly Master Yao. He found the Map of the Eight Diagrams and returned it to Xuandu Cave.

Grand Tutor Wen was worried over Zhao Gongming's condition. When two more traps were broken and their masters killed, he fumed with rage. He kept stamping his foot. "I never imagined that so many of my friends would lose their lives." He sent for the two Heavenly Masters Zhang and Wang and wept before them. "I've been greatly favored by His Majesty and am naturally prepared to sacrifice myself, but how can I feel at ease when my friends are dying here so cruelly!"

Everyone in the Shang camp talked about the health of Zhao Gongming, who had become dull and indifferent to military affairs, sleeping and snoring day and night. An old proverb says, "Celestials never feel sleepy" for they are free from all emotions and sensations. But Zhao Gongming could sleep for seven days on end!

By chanting spells for fifteen days, Jiang Ziya had gradually expelled the primal spirit of Zhao Gongming. The primal spirit was of major importance to an immortal, enabling him to tour freely throughout the universe. But now Zhao Gongming had lost his primal spirit and became drowsy, wanting to sleep all the time.

Grand Tutor Wen's anxiety increased. "Why does Brother Zhao sleep so long and so soundly? There must be some reason!" He entered the inner camp and found Zhao snoring like thunder. He shook Zhao and called, "Brother! You're a celestial. Why do you sleep all the time?"

"I haven't been asleep; I don't feel sleepy," Zhao Gongming denied.

When the two Heavenly masters saw that Zhao Gongming's mind was deranged, they said to Grand Tutor Wen, "Brother Wen! From our observation, he's in danger. It seems he's been secretly cursed. Make a divination and find out the truth."

"You're right, Brothers," Grand Tutor Wen answered. He burnt incense and made a divination with gold coins. He exclaimed in alarm, "Lu Ya will shoot the straw effigy with charmed arrows and put him to death. What shall we do now?"

"If that's so, we must go to Mount Qi and seize the effigy. Only then can this disaster be averted," Heavenly Master Wang suggested.

"How can we do that? The place is sure to be closely guarded. It can only be done in secret," Grand Tutor Wen said cautiously. He strode into the back camp to see Zhao Gongming. "Brother Zhao! Do you have anything to say?"

"Do you have something to tell me, Brother Wen?"

"Lu Ya has placed a curse on you and is going to shoot you with his charmed arrows," Grand Tutor Wen told him frankly.

Zhao Gongming started with fright and said pitifully, "Brother, I left my mountain to help you. How will you save me from this sorcery?"

Grand Tutor Wen was deeply upset and at a complete loss what to do.

"Brother, don't worry! We'll order Chen Jiugong and Yao Shaosi to seize the effigy tonight," Heavenly Master Zhang suggested.

Grand Tutor Wen approved the idea.

As Burning Lamp and other immortals were meditating to refine their spirits, Lu Ya felt a rush of blood to his heart. Without saying a word, he made a divination on his fingers and realized what was about to happen. "Brothers, Wen Zhong has already found out what we're doing to Zhao Gongming. He's going to send two disciples to Mount Qi to steal the effigy. If it's stolen, none of us can live. Warn Jiang Ziya at once so that he'll be on the alert."

Burning Lamp immediately sent Yang Jian and Nezha to Mount Qi to see Jiang Ziya. Nezha set off on his Wind-Fire Wheels at high speed while Yang Jian rode a horse, which was comparatively much slower.

Following Grand Tutor Wen's orders, Chen Jiugong and Yao Shaosi had sped to Mount Qi on the dust early that evening. From the air they could see Jiang Ziya walking in a square, reciting charms and burning spells before the platform. As Jiang kowtowed, Chen and Yao sank quickly through the air, grabbed the effigy on the table and sped away like the wind.

Jiang Ziya heard the noise, looked up and found that the effigy was gone. He had no idea why and was anxiously puzzling it over when Nezha arrived. "According to Lu Ya's instructions, I've come to warn you that Grand Tutor Wen is sending men to steal the effigy. If it's lost, all of us will die, so you must be very careful."

Jiang Ziya was shocked. "I was kowtowing when I heard a noise. I looked up and found the effigy on the table had disappeared. Hurry, hurry! Try your best to get it back!" he ordered.

Nezha left immediately on his Wind-Fire Wheels. Yang Jian was slowly approaching on his horse. When a violent and strange wind whirled towards him he realized that the effigy must have been stolen. He hastily dismounted, grabbed a handful of earth, and threw it high into the air, shouting, "Quick, quick! There's no time for delay."

He then sat at the roadside to see what would happen. Chen Jiugong and Yao Shaosi were delighted at their success. Spotting the Shang camp not far ahead, they descended from the air and asked General Deng Zhong, who was on patrol, to announce their successful return. When they were summoned, they saw Grand Tutor Wen sitting in a chair.

"How did the raid go?" Grand Tutor Wen asked.

"When we got there we saw that Jiang Ziya was just bowing in worship. We seized the opportunity to snatch the effigy."

The Grand Tutor was delighted. "Give it to me."

Chen Jiugong and Yao Shaosi handed it to him, and the Grand Tutor looked it over, put it in his sleeves, and ordered, "You may go to see your master now and tell him of your success."

As Chen and Yao walked to the back camp, they heard a roar of thunder behind them. They turned to look, and found to their astonishment that the camp had disappeared, leaving them standing in the wilderness. They were trying to puzzle it out when a man appeared on a white horse.

"Give me back the effigy at once!" the man cried.

Chen and Yao rushed furiously at the man, each wielding a pair of swords. Yang Jian hastily defended himself with his halberd. Their weapons clashed resoundingly through the darkness of the night. Before long, Nezha arrived on his Wind-Fire Wheels, and when he saw the fierce fight, he got down and joined in.

Chen and Yao were no match for Yang Jian, and when Nezha joined in, their position was even more hopeless. Within a few minutes, Nezha stabbed Yao Shaosi to death, and Yang Jian penetrated Chen Jiugong's breast. Their souls flew together to the Terrace of Creation.

"The effigy was robbed, and I was ordered to recover it," Nezha told him.

"I've already got it back, Brother," said Yang Jian happily. "I saw them riding on the dust, raising a strange wind. I thought they might be the robbers and transformed myself into the image of Grand Tutor Wen to deceive them and retrieve the effigy. Thanks to your help, both of them are now dead."

Yang Jian and Nezha went together to see Jiang Ziya. Jiang Ziya was delighted. "Yang Jian won not only through his bravery but also his wisdom. Nezha's heroic and loyal!" he praised.

Yang Jian handed over the effigy, and the two returned to the reed pavilion. Late the next morning, Grand Tutor Wen was still waiting for the return of Chen Jiugong and Yao Shaosi. He impatiently ordered Xin Huan to investigate. Before long Xin Huan returned. "Grand Tutor Wen! I found them both dead on the way. I don't know what happened."

Grand Tutor Wen pounded his desk and roared, "Since both of them are dead, it's impossible for us to get the effigy now!"

He beat his breast, stamped his feet and wept loudly. When the two remaining Heavenly masters entered, they found him weeping bitterly. After they discovered the reason, they went with him to see Zhao Gongming. Zhao was still snoring like thunder.

Nearing his bedside, Grand Tutor Wen shouted, "Dear Brother, wake up!"

Zhao Gongming opened his eyes, and seeing the Grand Tutor, asked about the effigy. When the Grand Tutor told him the truth about what had happened, he immediately sat up. With staring eyes, he cried out, "I'm finished! Oh, why didn't I listen to my sister's advice! I'll lose my life just as she warned!" Sweat poured down his body. "I became an immortal in the epoch of the Heavenly Emperor. How could I have imagined that I would die at the hands of Lu Ya. Brother Wen, it's already too late for remorse. After my death, wrap up the Golden Dragon Scissors with my robe and give them to my three sisters. To see my robe is to see their elder brother in person." With tears pouring down his face, he gave an agonized cry, "Oh, Sister High Firmament! How sorry I am that I didn't take your advice!"

He wept bitterly and choked with sobs, was unable to speak further.

Watching the tragic scene, Grand Tutor Wen felt as if his heart was being pierced by a dagger. His hair stood on end, and he gnashed his teeth in rage. Wang Bian, the Heavenly Master of the Red Water Trap, could not hold his patience any longer. He rushed vengefully to the reed pavilion and shouted, "Which of you dare meet me in the Red Water Trap?"

Burning Lamp left the pavilion with other immortals. As Heavenly Master Wang approached on his deer, Burning Lamp said to Cao Bao, "Dear friend, would you like to meet him?"

Cao Bao rushed out, shouting, "Calm down there, Wang Bian!"

Heavenly Master Wang recognized Cao Bao. "Brother Cao! You're a free man. This place has nothing to do with you. Why are you so foolish as to come here and get yourself killed?"

"You act against the will of Heaven by supporting the tyrant against the true ruler. Don't you see that we've broken eight of your traps already. Can't you perceive the will of Heaven clearly?" Cao Bao replied.

Filled with anger, Wang Bian attacked Cao Bao with his sword, and Cao resisted with his own. After several rounds, Wang Bian ran into his trap, and Cao Bao followed closely on his heels. Wang Bian mounted the platform and splashed down a gourdful of red water. A drop touched Cao Bao's body, and he instantly dissolved into a stream of blood, his soul flying to the Terrace of Creation.

Heavenly Master Wang rushed out to the front again. "Burning Lamp! Why are you so heartless as to send an innocent man into my trap to meet his death? There are many highly talented people in the Jade Emptiness Palace. Which of you dare to meet me now?"

Burning Lamp turned to Virtue of the Pure Void, "You break the trap."

To know the outcome of the struggle, please read the next chapter.

49

KING WU IN THE RED SAND TRAP

By order of Burning Lamp, Virtue of the Pure Void rushed to the front. "Wang Bian! As you act against the will of Heaven, you are doomed. Now that eight of your traps have been broken, why don't you come to your senses!"

Heavenly Master Wang was furious. He raised his sword and struck at the immortal, who replied with his own. After several rounds, Wang Bian ran into his Red Water Trap, with the immortal close on his heels. As before, Wang Bian mounted the platform and emptied his gourd onto the ground, flooding the area with red water.

When he entered, Pure Void waved his right sleeve, and down dropped a lotus flower for the immortal to float about upon the red water. No matter how violently the red waves churned, no water touched the body of the immortal. Heavenly Master Wang then threw the gourd itself at the immortal, but he was protected by a brilliant cloud that had emerged from his skull. He floated about on the lotus for about two hours in perfect safety.

Wang Bian knew that he had lost and tried to run away. Pure Void immediately took out his Five Fire and Seven Fowl Fan. The fan could produce five kinds of fire— fire from air, stone, wood, earth, and man; and were made of the wings of seven kinds of fowls, including that of green phoenix, roc, peacock, crane, wild swan, and owl. Each wing was stamped with the seals of charms. It was powerful enough to burn rocks to ashes and boil the sea dry. Pure Void fanned Wang Bian once. Wang emitted a single cry before burning to red ash.

As the Red Water Trap was destroyed, Pure Void, Burning Lamp and all the others returned to the pavilion. Grand Tutor Wen became even more depressed. By now Jiang Ziya had already spent twenty days on Mount Qi and was ready to put Zhao Gongming to death the following day.

In the back camp, Zhao Gongming told Grand Tutor Wen mournfully, "Brother Wen, this is our last meeting. I'll be gone at noon tomorrow."

Grand Tutor Wen wept, "It tortures me that I've brought this disaster upon you."

Soon Heavenly Master Zhang came to see Zhao Gongming. He hated himself for being powerless to save him from death. They wept to see such a great celestial suffer like a mortal because of Lu Ya's curse and were grieved that his centuries of achievements would end in nothing.

At eleven o'clock the next morning, Wu Ji reported to Jiang Ziya that Lu Ya had arrived. Jiang Ziya went out to welcome him, and when they were seated, Lu Ya said, "I should congratulate you: Zhao Gongming will die at noon. What's more, the Red Water Trap has been broken."

Jiang Ziya thanked him sincerely, "Without your help, how could we end Zhao's life today!"

With a smile, Lu Ya opened his flower basket and took out a small mulberry bow and three short peach arrows, which he handed to Jiang Ziya. "Shoot the effigy with the bow and arrows," Lu Ya said. "Shoot his left eye first."

Jiang Ziya did as ordered. As the first arrow hit the left eye of the effigy, Zhao Gongming, lying in the Shang camp, roared in agony and closed his left eye. Grand Tutor Wen held him in his arms, sobbing as the tears poured down his cheeks. The second arrow hit the right eye of the effigy, and the third penetrated into its heart. Zhao Gongming died at the third arrow.

Seeing that Zhao Gongming was dead, Grand Tutor Wen wailed unrestrainedly. He ordered a grand ceremony to mark the encoffining of Zhao's body, and the bier was placed temporarily in the back camp. Zhao's death badly frightened Deng, Zhang, Xin and Tao. "With such highly talented men in the Zhou camp, how can we possibly defeat them?" they thought. This affair badly affected the morale of the Shang army.

When Jiang Ziya and Lu Ya returned to the reed pavilion from Mount Qi, all the immortals exclaimed in delight, "Without Brother Lu, how could we have put Zhao Gongming to death so easily?"

Before long, Heavenly Master Zhang gave a challenge to the immortals. "The Red Sand Trap is particularly evil. It will take a man greatly blessed by Heaven to survive it. Otherwise we'll suffer a major loss," Burning Lamp told Jiang Ziya.

"Who can we send, Master?" Jiang Ziya asked.

"It's got to be the sagely ruler. Anyone else is sure to meet with disaster."

"Though His Highness is virtuous, he's never learned how to fight. How can he break the trap?" Jiang Ziya said doubtfully.

"We cannot delay! Just ask King Wu to come here. I know how to convince him," Burning Lamp persisted.

Jiang Ziya sent Wu Ji to fetch King Wu. When the king arrived he was met by Jiang Ziya and escorted inside. King Wu bowed to the immortals, who returned the salutation.

"Master, what instructions would you give me?" King Wu asked.

"We've broken nine traps, but the Red Sand, the very last, remains. Only if Your Highness tackles it can we be assured of success. Is Your Highness willing to do it?" Burning Lamp asked.

"You've all come here out of compassion for the people. How could I refuse!" King Wu replied.

Burning Lamp was overjoyed. "Would Your Highness untie your belt and take off your robe," he requested.

When King Wu had done so, he drew some charms on the king's breast and back with his middle finger. After he had dressed again, Burning Lamp placed another charm inside the king's dragon crown. Finally, the immortal ordered that Nezha and Thunderbolt protect King Wu when he entered the Red Sand Trap.

When they came out, King Wu, Nezha and Thunderbolt

saw a Taoist emerge from the Red Sand Trap. He wore a fish-tail coronet and had a face the color of verdigris and a long red beard. Carrying a pair of swords, he rode a deer towards them singing.

"Which of you from the Jade Emptiness Palace will meet me?" Heavenly Master Zhang Shao demanded. He then saw Nezha and Thunderbolt with a man in a dragon crown, yellow robe, and dragon belt. "Who is that coming?"

"It's the sagely ruler, King Wu," Nezha answered.

King Wu trembled at the hideous countenance and ferocious manner of the Heavenly master, and almost fell from his saddle.

Heavenly Master Zhang spurred his spotted deer forward and attacked Nezha with his sword. Nezha met him with his lance. After a few rounds, Heavenly Master Zhang ran into his Red Sand Trap. Nezha, Thunderbolt and King Wu followed closely on his heels. Heavenly Master Zhang hurriedly mounted his platform, grasped a handful of red sand and threw it directly at them. King Wu was hit on the breast and tumbled into a huge pit with his horse. Though Nezha soared into the air on his Wind-Fire Wheels, he was also caught by the red sand and fell into the pit.

As the odds were against them, Thunderbolt tried to fly away, but it was too late. He was also knocked into the pit, and all three were trapped by the red sand. Burning Lamp and Jiang Ziya saw only a column of black air rising into the sky.

"King Wu will be released in 100 days. He, Nezha and Thunderbolt are all destined by fate to suffer this calamity," Burning Lamp reassured Jiang.

Jiang Ziya stamped his foot. "King Wu is virtuous but still a mortal. How can he survive 100 days? What shall we do if something goes wrong!"

"Trust in the will of Heaven. King Wu's blessed and will certainly come through. Don't worry, Jiang Ziya."

Jiang Ziya went into the city and reported the matter to the palace. Tai Ji and Tai Ren, mother and wife of the king, sent other princes to see Jiang Ziya in his mansion. Jiang Ziya told them definitely that "King Wu will come to no harm. He'll merely be trapped in there for about 100 days."

He then returned to the reed pavilion and discussed the Way with his Taoist friends. Heavenly Master Zhang returned to tell Grand Tutor Wen, "King Wu, Nezha and Thunderbolt are all caught in my trap."

Though Grand Tutor Wen expressed his delight, he was still deeply grieved at the death of Zhao Gongming. Everyday Heavenly Master Zhang threw red sand on King Wu's body to make him feel as if knives were being thrust through him. King Wu, however, was well protected by the charms on his breast and back. As he was blessed, he remained unharmed.

Meanwhile Shen Gongbao had gone to the Three Fairy Island to announce Zhao's death to High Firmament and her sisters. He dismounted when he reached the cave and asked a lass, "Would you please report to your mistress that Shen Gongbao is here?"

When Shen was escorted in, High Firmament asked, "Why are you here, Brother?"

"I've come about your brother," Shen replied.

"What's so serious that he has to trouble you?"

"Don't you know he was shot by Jiang Ziya with charmed arrows on Mount Qi?" Shen said with a smile.

Green Firmament and Jade Firmament immediately burst into tears. "Alas, we never thought that he would lose his life at the hands of Jiang Ziya!"

"Even after he got your Golden Dragon Scissors, he couldn't retrieve his pearls. Before his death, he said to Grand Tutor Wen, 'My younger sisters are sure to come here for the scissors. Tell them that I regret not following High Firmament's advice. They can see my Taoist robe and silk belt instead of me in person.' What a pity that his thousand years of cultivation was wasted."

"My master forbade us to leave the mountain. Anyone who does is certainly on the List of Creations. This was destined by Heaven. As my brother failed to adhere to these instructions, he was bound to meet with disaster," High Firmament said.

"Dear Sister! You're too heartless! You say this because you don't want to avenge him. As for the two of us, we must go to see his remains, even if it means that our names are on the List of Creations. After all, we are of the same blood," Jade Firmament said angrily.

Without another word, Jade Firmament and Green Firmament left the cave and headed for West Qi, one riding a swan and the other a bird with spotted feathers.

"They're sure to use the Universe Muddling Dipper. That'll only make things worse. What shall we do then? I must go there too to keep things in hand." High Firmament decided.

She ordered her lass to look after the cave then pursued them on her green phoenix. "Wait for me, Sisters. I'm coming too."

"Where're you going, Sister?" they asked.

"As you don't understand how to handle matters properly, I'll come with you to make sure you don't make mistakes."

As the three of them flew on, they heard someone calling from behind, "Not so fast, Sisters. I'm coming, too!" Turning her head, High Firmament found that it was Celestial Lotus. "Where are you going, Sister?"

"I'm going with you all to West Qi."

They had barely started off when someone called again, "Wait for me, Sisters." They found it was Lady Pretty Cloud. The latter bowed. "I see you are on your way to West Qi. I met Shen Gongbao, and he invited me to go there and help Brother Wen. How happy I am to meet you all here! Let's go together."

The five of them traveled on and reached their destination moments later. At the Shang camp, they asked the guards to report their arrival to Grand Tutor Wen. The Grand Tutor came out to meet them.

When all were seated inside, High Firmament said, "My brother Zhao Gongming left Luofu Cave to help you here. Unfortunately he was shot by Jiang Ziya. Now we've come to collect his corpse. Would you kindly show us where it is, Grand Tutor?"

Grand Tutor Wen wept bitterly. "Brother Zhao

Gongming was unlucky. Before he died, he told me, 'I regret not taking my sister High Firmament's advice. I've brought about my own downfall!' He asked me to put the Golden Dragon Scissors and his robe in a parcel and give it to you so that when you saw it, it would be just like seeing him in person."

As he spoke, Grand Tutor Wen broke down into loud sobs and covered his face with one of his sleeves. The five ladies wept with him. Grand Tutor Wen got up from his seat and took out the parcel. Opening it, the three sisters mourned bitterly. Their tears fell like rain. Jade Firmament gnashed her teeth, and Green Firmament flushed with anger.

"Where's my brother's coffin, sir?" Green Firmament asked.

"It's in the back camp," Grand Tutor Wen replied.

"Let me go to look at it," Jade Firmament said.

"Since he's dead, what's the use of looking at his coffin?" High Firmament asked.

"As we're here, why not go and look at it?" Green Firmament persisted.

The two sisters walked to the back camp, and High Firmament had little choice but to follow them. They took the cover off the coffin and stared at the body of their brother. Seeing that Zhao was still bleeding from the eyes and heart, they could not control their anger. Jade Firmament screamed and nearly fainted.

"Sister, don't be agitated. We'll catch the murderer and shoot him with three arrows too, to avenge our brother," Green Firmament said furiously.

"This has nothing to do with Jiang Ziya. It was Lu Ya, as fate had destined. We'll just catch him and shoot him. Then our revenge will be complete," High Firmament put in.

The next day, the five ladies left the Shang camp with Grand Tutor Wen and Deng, Xin, Zhang and Tao. High Firmament rode her green phoenix up to the reed pavilion.

"Tell Lu Ya to come out and meet me," she demanded.

When the challenge was passed on to him, Lu Ya got up and said, "I'll go straightway."

He took his sword and rushed out from the pavilion, his

long sleeves billowing in the wind. High Firmament saw that
he had the bearing and air of an immortal. She said to her two
sisters, "He's known as a hermit and is sure to possess some
ability. We'll see what he has to say and gauge the true depth
of his learning."

Lu Ya moved towards them slowly, singing a song. He
bowed before High Firmament.

"Are you Lu Ya?"

"Yes, I am."

"Why did you shoot my brother, Zhao Gongming?" Jade
Firmament asked.

"I'll tell you frankly, if you've got enough patience. Otherwise you may take action as you please."

"Go on and tell us," High Firmament said.

"To achieve enlightenment is the only proper path to follow to the Way. Immortals are those who follow the proper
way. I achieved enlightenment in the epoch of the Heavenly
Emperor at the beginning of time, and I've witnessed the enlightenment of many with my own eyes. Only those who act
with virtue progress spiritually. Who could have imagined that
Zhao Gongming would commit such an error! He sided with a
tyrant who disregards the ethical relationships and slaughters
the innocent, evoking the wrath of Heaven and the resentment
of the people. He used his magic without regard for anybody
else. Whoever acts against the will of Heaven is bound to die,
and I was sent by Heaven to put him to death. How can I be
blamed for it? My friends! Can't you see that this is not the
place for you? There are only mountains of weapons and
oceans of fire here. How can you survive? If you stay here,
I'm afraid you'll lose your chances for everlasting life. I've
taken the liberty to speak frankly. I beg your pardon if I've offended you."

High Firmament sighed deeply and said nothing, but Jade
Firmament screamed, "You damned brute! How dare you deceive us with rubbish! You shot my brother and now try to defend yourself with your slick tongue. I guess that your powers
are insignificant. What can you do to us?"

Fuming with rage, she rushed up to slash at Lu Ya with

her sword. After several rounds, Green Firmament cast her Universe Muddling Dipper high into the sky. It was such a powerful weapon that before Lu Ya had time to flee, it had caught him and threw him to the ground. Despite his great power, he was almost knocked unconscious. Green Firmament bound him tightly, stuck charms on top of his head, and hung him up on a flag pole.

"He shot my brother. I'll shoot him in return," she said.

Five hundred archers were summoned immediately, but though the arrows showered like rain, they dropped to the ground without harming him. As each arrow touched his body, it turned to ashes. Everyone was astonished.

"How can we allow him to fool us like this?" Green Firmament screamed and cast up her Golden Dragon Scissors.

"Sorry! I must be going," Lu Ya shouted.

He transformed himself into a rainbow and disappeared. When he returned to the reed pavilion, Burning Lamp asked him, "You were caught by the dipper. How did you get away?"

"They tried to shoot me, but every arrow turned to ashes as soon as it touched my body. When they cast up their Golden Dragon Scissors, I turned into a rainbow and came back here."

"We all admire your wonderful skill," Burning Lamp said happily.

"I have to leave here for a while. I'll be back soon," Lu Ya told them and took his leave.

The next day, High Firmament went out with her four companions and demanded Jiang Ziya. Jiang Ziya met them with his disciples on his left and right. He bowed down.

"Greetings, my Taoist friends!"

"Jiang Ziya!" cried High Firmament. "We're all carefree Taoists living on the Three Fairy Island. We care nothing for the rights and wrongs of this vulgar world. We've come here now only because our brother, Zhao Gongming, was cruelly murdered by your charmed arrows. Why did you put him to death so unjustly? How wicked you are! Though we know you're not the chief culprit, you nevertheless killed him. We cannot but hold you responsible! Your magic powers are too insignificant to be mentioned, and even Burning Lamp wouldn't dare offend us."

"You're wrong," Jiang Ziya replied. "We had done nothing to offend your brother, but he came here to trouble us, bringing disaster on himself. It was his destiny. He disobeyed the orders of his master."

Jade Firmament flew into a rage. "You murdered him yet make the excuse that it's all destiny! How dare you cheat us with your cunning words! I'll avenge him by giving you a taste of my sword!"

She urged her swan forward to attack Jiang Ziya and he defended himself with his sword. Huang Tianhua and Yang Jian joined in. To counter them, Green Firmament, roaring like thunder, flew in on her bird, and High Firmament also had to help her sisters. Pretty Cloud took the Eye Blinding Pearl from her gourd and knocked Huang Tianhua from his jade unicorn.

What became of him? If you want to know, read the next chapter.

50

THE YELLOW RIVER TRAP

Pretty Cloud scored a direct hit with her Eye Blinding Pearl, and Huang Tianhua fell from his unicorn. Jinzha immediately rushed forward and carried him to safety.

Jiang Ziya cast his Staff for Beating Gods up into the air. It hit High Firmament and brought her down from her green phoenix. As Green Firmament went to rescue her sister, Yang Jian set his Sky Barking Hound on her. It bit her on the shoulder, tearing off a piece of her robe.

Celestial Lotus saw it all. She opened her Wind Sack and released a fierce black wind, turning the sky dark, splitting rocks, and shaking mountains. When Jiang Ziya opened his eyes to see what weapon she had used, he was wounded by Pretty Cloud's Eye Blinding Pearl and nearly fell from his nondescript. Yang Jian fended off Jade Firmament and helped Jiang Ziya back to the pavilion. Burning Lamp knew what had hurt Jiang Ziya and Huang Tianhua. He took out two elixir pills, and both were soon cured. Huang Tianhua gnashed his teeth in hatred, swearing to take revenge.

In this first battle, High Firmament was wounded by the Staff for Beating Gods and Green Firmament was hurt by the Sky Barking Hound.

"I didn't intend to harm them, but that was obviously their purpose. Sisters, from this day on, I'll forgive neither the disciples nor the master of the Jade Emptiness Palace," High Firmament swore. She took some medicine and then told Grand Tutor Wen, "Please pick 600 sturdy warriors to put at my disposal."

When the men had been sent to her, she went to the back

第五十四回　三姑計擺黃河陣

camp and drew designs in chalk that showed all the mysteries of life and death. Based on the eight diagrams, the drawings showed windows, entrances, and exits and indicated where to advance and where to retreat. There were only 600 soldiers, but they had the strength of a million. Any intruder, mortal or immortal, would unavoidably lose his life if he ventured inside.

In half a month, the trap was ready, and the men were fully trained. High Firmament went to see Grand Tutor Wen. "My trap's now ready. Would you care to watch while I take them on, Brother?"

"Please explain the mysteries of your trap to me," Grand Tutor Wen said.

"It's based on the principles behind Heaven, earth, and man. Within it, there are pills to stun immortals and spells to confine them. It will take away their spirits, their souls, and their energy, and destroy their bodies. An immortal will degenerate into a mortal and a mortal will lose his life. It contains the secret of secrets, the miracle of miracles. Even the heads of the three religions would find it difficult to escape destruction once inside," High Firmament said proudly.

With great delight, Grand Tutor Wen ordered his army to march out of camp. He rode on his pure black unicorn, followed by his four generals and the five ladies. They approached the reed pavilion.

"Jiang Ziya! Come out and meet us in person!"

When Jiang Ziya marched out with his disciples, High Firmament said, "Jiang Ziya! Both of us are capable of manipulating the five elements and moving mountains and seas. But now I'll show you a trap that requires a far greater level of skill. We'll leave West Qi should you break it, but if you can't, we'll certainly avenge our brother."

"Ladies," said Yang Jian. "Let's make an inspection of it first, but you mustn't use the opportunity for an underhanded attack."

"Who are you?" High Firmament asked.

"I'm Yang Jian, disciple of Jade Tripod."

"I've heard that you have unique magic powers. I'd just like to see you break this trap with your wonderful transforma-

tions! We are honest; we won't do anything unless you set
your dog against us. Go quickly now and look it over. Then
see if your skills are enough to do anything," Green Firmament said sarcastically.

Controlling their anger, Jiang Ziya, Yang Jian, and others
entered the trap. On the gate they saw a small board inscribed
with the line "Nine Bends of the Yellow River Trap." There
were only about 500 to 600 soldiers in all, standing here and
there with their colored pennants. A cold wind howled, and
black fogs enveloped the earth. After their inspection, Jiang
Ziya exited it with his disciples and returned to where High
Firmament was waiting.

"Do you recognize it, Jiang Ziya?"

"You needn't ask me that. Its name is clearly written on
the board outside."

Green Firmament cried, "Yang Jian, dare you unleash
your Sky Barking Hound again?"

Relying on his magic, Yang Jian urged his horse forward,
his lance extended to attack Jade Firmament. From the back
of her swan, she met the assault with her sword. After several
rounds, High Firmament cast up her Universe Muddling Dipper. Not knowing the power of it, Yang Jian was sucked inside
in a flash of golden light and thrown into the Yellow River
Trap.

When he saw that Yang Jian had been taken, Jinzha
roared, "What devilry do you use!"

He attacked Jade Firmament with his sword, and she returned the blow with her own sword. Before long, Jinzha cast
up his Dragon Binding Stake.

"That pathetic little thing!" High Firmament smiled
scornfully. Holding her dipper in one hand, she pointed at the
stake with the other. In a twinkling, the stake fell into the dipper, and then she cast the dipper at Jinzha and threw him into
the Yellow River Trap.

Muzha was enraged. "You witch! How dare you take my
brother!"

He leapt at Jade Firmament and slashed at her with his
sword. She returned the blow with her own. After about three

rounds, Muzha shook his shoulder and sent his Hooks of Wu flying into the air.

"Those hooks aren't magic weapons. Even if they were, they couldn't hurt me at all," Jade Firmament scoffed.

High Firmament pointed at the hooks with her finger and collected them in her dipper. Then she cast up her dipper, caught Muzha, and threw him into the Yellow River Trap with the other two.

Now High Firmament angrily flew at Jiang Ziya on her green phoenix and stabbed at him with her sword. Much disheartened by the loss of his three disciples, Jiang Ziya met the challenge with his sword. After a few rounds, High Firmament cast up her dipper, but Jiang Ziya unrolled his Apricot Yellow Flag, from which golden flowers emerged to block the dipper's descent. The dipper simply turned over and over in the sky, unable to come down.

Jiang Ziya went back to the pavilion, and when he reported what happened, Burning Lamp sighed, "That's the Golden Universe Muddling Dipper. Most of us will suffer from it. It augurs ill fortune even for us immortals. Once thrown into the trap, those who don't have a good grounding in the Way will suffer the most."

High Firmament and her sisters returned to the Shang camp. Delighted that they had taken three captives in one day, the Grand Tutor asked, "What will you do with the three disciples you've taken today?"

"I'll think it over after we've met Burning Lamp," High Firmament answered.

Three men had been caught in the Red Sand Trap, and now three more in the Yellow River Trap. Grand Tutor Wen was greatly satisfied. He ordered a feast in honor of the ladies and Heavenly Master Zhang.

The following day, the five ladies rode to the reed pavilion and demanded to see Burning Lamp. Burning Lamp rode out on his deer, with all the immortals following him in rows. He greeted the sisters.

"Burning Lamp! Right and wrong will be settled today. I set up the Yellow River Trap because you've insulted us too deeply. Dare you send a man of great power to break it," High Firmament challenged.

"You're wrong to do this. You were present when the List of Creations was signed. How can you fail to understand the philosophy of cycles. Since the beginning of time, everything has operated in cycles. That was the case with Zhao Gongming. He wasn't destined to be an immortal, so he was fated to meet with disaster," Burning Lamp replied with a smile.

"Sister! No more talk about virtue and morality! Let me get hold of him and see what he can do about that!" Jade Firmament yelled.

She flew out on her swan towards Burning Lamp, but Master Pure Essence intercepted her. "Jade Firmament! Don't brag so much. As you're here, your name must be on the list."

They had only fought a few rounds when High Firmament cast up her dipper. With a flash, it caught the immortal and threw him into the Yellow River Trap. He immediately became like a drunkard. Alas, for his thousand years of cultivation! In a moment all his achievements were reduced to nothing.

Master Grand Completion could not bear to see Jade Firmament swaggering so. "High Firmament! How can you insult us and degrade your own Taoism? Don't place too much trust in the witchcraft from the Green Touring Palace!"

High Firmament flew forward to meet him, shouting, "Grand Completion! Even though you're the head disciple, you will find it difficult to escape your fate!"

"I've broken the commandment on killing already. Why should I run away from my fate? If it's destined, how could I do anything against the will of Heaven?" Master Grand Completion answered, smiling.

While he fought High Firmament, Jade Firmament cast the dipper. It scooped him up and threw him into the trap just as it had Master Pure Essence.

In the very same way, High Firmament captured the Heavenly Master of Outstanding Culture, Universal Virtue, Merciful Navigation, Virtue of the Pure Void, Heavenly Master of

Divine Virtue, Jade Tripod, Fairy Primordial, Krakucchanda and the Yellow Dragon Immortal in her trap. Once inside, the twelve immortals all lost the three divine flowers they had achieved through a thousand years of cultivation and meditation. They would only get them back after Jiang Ziya finished the creations.

Only Burning Lamp and Jiang Ziya remained untouched. Feeling her power, High Firmament cried, "Since I've already committed these crimes, why stop here?"

She used the dipper again, intending to take Burning Lamp. But Burning Lamp knew its power, and he transformed himself into a guest of wind and disappeared.

The three sisters returned in triumph. To celebrate the great victory, Grand Tutor Wen held a banquet in their honor. High Firmament, however, was silent. She worried, "What shall I do now that I've taken them? I don't know the right course to follow!"

Burning Lamp fled back to the pavilion where he met Jiang Ziya. Jiang Ziya said sadly, "I'm sorry that so many brothers have fallen into the trap. I wonder what fate awaits them."

"Though no harm will come to them, all their achievements are lost. I'll go to Mount Kunlun for help. I don't think any of them will die."

He left West Qi for Mount Kunlun, and descending from the sky, approached the palace and saw White Crane Lad beside the Nine Dragon Sandalwood Carriage.

"Where is Grand Master going?" he asked.

"He's going to West Qi. You'd better go back and prepare a quiet, clean chamber. Burn incense to receive him."

Burning Lamp returned to West Qi and entered the reed pavilion. He found Jiang Ziya sitting there alone. "Quickly order your men to decorate the pavilion and burn incense. Grand Master will be here soon."

Jiang Ziya washed himself thoroughly, and holding burning incense, waited at the roadside. Before long, Heavenly Primogenitor arrived in his Nine Dragon Sandalwood Carriage. When they heard divine music in the air, Burning Lamp and

Jiang Ziya knelt on the ground.

Heavenly Primogenitor descended from the carriage. Burning Lamp and Jiang Ziya escorted him to the reed pavilion, where they knelt and kowtowed again. Heavenly Primogenitor told them to stand up, but Jiang Ziya remained kneeling on the ground. "Nearly all your disciples have fallen into the Yellow River Trap. I beg for your compassion to rescue them from this calamity as soon as possible," he pleaded.

"This has been destined by Heaven, and nobody can change it. Don't say any more."

The master sat in silence. Burning Lamp and Jiang Ziya stood at his side. At midnight, a huge, bright, colored cloud rose from the top of the master's head, and thousands of lamps floated up and down above the pavilion.

High Firmament saw it and said, "Uncle's here. What shall we do? I didn't want to leave the island, but you two insisted. I've taken many disciples of the Jade Emptiness Palace. I can neither set them free nor send them all to death. I'm really in a quandary. Now that Uncle's come, how can I face him?"

"You're wrong, Sister! He isn't our master. We respect him only for the sake of our own master. We can do anything we please, as we aren't his disciples. There's no need to fear him," Jade Firmament reassured her.

"We'll respect him if he's polite to us, but if he's not, we'll do as we like. He's our enemy, and we can't yield before him. What's there to worry about now that we've already gone this far?" Green Firmament added.

The next day, Heavenly Primogenitor ordered the Immortal of the South Pole, "Get my carriage ready. Now that I'm here, I'll go to see the trap."

Burning Lamp led the way, and Jiang Ziya followed behind. Heavenly Primogenitor left the pavilion and rode to the front, where White Crane Lad shouted loudly, "High Firmament! Come out and receive Heavenly Primogenitor."

High Firmament and her sisters came out. They bowed at the roadside and said, "Uncle! We beg your pardon for being so negligent in the rites."

"It's fate that my disciples should suffer. Nevertheless, even your master doesn't venture against the will of Heaven. Why did you ignore his orders? You'd better go in and I'll follow right after you."

The three sisters went back in and mounted the platform to see how the Heavenly Primogenitor would move about inside. Before long, they saw the master flying about the Yellow River Trap in his sandalwood carriage held about two feet above the ground by a bright multi-colored cloud. Looking around with his wisdom eye, the master saw his twelve disciples lying on the ground, their eyes tightly closed. He sighed deeply and said, "Just because they were unable to sever themselves from all desire, they lost all the achievements they had so laboriously attained."

When he turned to leave the trap, Pretty Cloud threw an Eye Blinding Pearl at him, trying to take him by surprise. But the pearl turned to ashes before it could reach the master. High Firmament turned pale at the sight.

When Heavenly Primogenitor was seated in the pavilion again, Burning Lamp asked, "How are they now?"

"They've lost their divine flowers and their divine gates are closed. They're nothing more than mortals now."

"Why didn't you rescue them?"

"Though I am Grand Master, I must first consult my elder brother," Primogenitor said with a smile. He was speaking when they heard the cry of a deer in the air. "Here he comes now."

All of them went out to meet Lao Zi. As Lao Zi descended from the sky on his ox, Heavenly Primogenitor advanced, laughing loudly, "I've troubled you solely for the sake of the Zhou Dynasty."

"I couldn't but come, Brother," Lao Zi answered with a smile.

Burning Lamp guided him to the pavilion. Burning Lamp and Jiang Ziya then kowtowed before him.

"Have you looked at the trap yet?" Lao Zi asked.

"I've been there once. It's just as the celestial phenomena indicated. I've been waiting for you," Heavenly Primogenitor replied.

"You ought to have destroyed it. There's no need to wait for me."

The two masters then sat down and mediated in complete silence. At the sight of a pagoda floating in the air shooting forth colored beams, High Firmament said to her sisters, "The Grand Master from Mount Xuandu is here as well. What shall we do?"

"Dear sister! We've got our own master. Don't worry. If they come here again, I won't treat them as kindly as I did yesterday," Green Firmament said.

"When they enter the trap, we'll cast up both the scissors and the dipper. There's nothing to be afraid of," Jade Firmament decided.

The next day, Lao Zi told his brother, "We'll leave as soon as the trap's broken. We won't linger in the red dust of the vulgar world longer than absolutely necessary."

"You're right, Brother," Heavenly Primogenitor agreed.

Heavenly Primogenitor ordered the Immortal of the South Pole to prepare his carriage while Lao Zi mounted his blue ox. As they went out, a red haze appeared everywhere and an unusual fragrance filled the air. They soon reached the Yellow River Trap.

"You three sisters come out to meet us at once!" Lao Zi demanded.

As bells sounded inside, the three sisters emerged. They stood before the two masters, neither bowing nor offering any greetings.

"How dare you be so insolent! Even your master would bow when meeting us!" Lao Zi reprimanded them.

"We have our own master, and we don't acknowledge Mount Xuandu. As you don't show us any respect, we won't honor you. This is common custom," Green Firmament replied.

"You brazen beast! Just go in."

The three sisters turned and entered their trap, followed by Lao Zi and Heavenly Primogenitor. White Crane Lad followed behind.

What became of the three sisters? If you want to know, please read the next chapter.

图书在版编目（CIP）数据

封神演义(上):英文/(明)许仲琳编;顾执中译 .
– 北京:新世界出版社,1996.10 重印
ISBN 7 – 80005 – 134 – X

I . 封 ...
II .①许 ...②顾 ...
III . 古典小说:章回小说:长篇小说 – 中国 – 明代 – 英文
IV .I242.4

封 神 演 义

第一卷

*

顾执中　译

新世界出版社出版

（北京百万庄路 24 号）

北京外文印刷厂印刷

中国国际图书贸易总公司发行

（中国北京车公庄西路 35 号）

北京邮政信箱第 399 号　邮政编码 100044

1992 年(英文)第一版　1996 年北京第二次印刷

ISBN 7 – 80005 – 134 – X

04000

10 – E – 2656DA